TELL MUM NOT TO WORRY

A WELSH SOLDIER'S WORLD WAR ONE IN THE NEAR EAST

1915 – 1919

ISBN 978-0-9930982-0-8

Deffro

To the memory of the men of the 53rd (Welsh) Division 1914-1919

TELL MUM NOT TO WORRY
A WELSH SOLDIER'S WORLD WAR ONE IN THE NEAR EAST

rhys.david@btinternet.com

Front cover: Dewi David in Egypt 1917. (David Family Collection)
Design and Layout: WOOD&WOOD Design Consultants   wood2.com
Indexed by Angela Hall
Printed in Wales by A. McLay & Co.

Published by **Deffro**
3e Palace Court
Cyncoed Road
Cardiff
CF23 6NX
www.rhysdavid.net

ISBN 978-0-9930982-0-8

Acknowledgements

A work of this nature could not be attempted without the encouragement offered by many people. My thanks go to my wife, Susan, for urging me on and bearing patiently my many absences, to my son Dr. Huw David, to my sister, Mari Williams, and my long-time friend, Professor Donald Bailey, all of whom have read the text and made valuable suggestions. My former Financial Times colleague, Glyn Genin generously provided his expertise to bring to life the faded 100 year old pictures that appear in the published book, and in his classic designs James Wood has captured admirably the feel and spirit of the stirring times featured.

Preface

The 53rd (Welsh) Division played a prominent part in World War One but not in the theatre that most people are familiar with – the Western Front. Its members served instead in the Near East, in Gallipoli, in Egypt and Gaza, and in Palestine, where over a period of four years they helped to wrest control of the region from Turco-German forces and to bring about the collapse of the Ottoman Empire. Though they were not subject to the full horrors of the trench warfare of France, they were involved in key battles against a determined enemy in Sinai, in Gaza (where three actions spread over six months had to be fought before the town was captured), in Palestine, culminating in the capture of Jerusalem, and at Megiddo, the location from which the campaign's most famous leader, Lord Allenby, was to take his title. The campaigns are followed through the highly literate and in places very amusing letters – 110,000 words in total – sent by one Welsh soldier from Cardiff who signed up in 1915 at the age of 17 and was away until beyond his 21st birthday. As well as providing a first-hand account of the hardships endured by men of the 53rd – long marches in very difficult country, long periods with the bare minimum of food and water, extreme heat and cold, sandstorms and flooding, flies, and mosquitoes – the letters also throw extensive light on contemporary concerns, attitudes and conditions, and on family life, work and leisure in early 20th century Britain. Within this volume, which draws on a number of other published historical sources, it has been possible to use only extended extracts from the letters. The full set can be found at www.rhysdavid.net

References to the letters are contained in the footnotes included here.

CHAPTERS

Preface and Acknowledgments...iii
1 Signing On...1
2 From Splott to Gallipoli...15
3 Regrouping in Egypt..43
4 Guarding the Canal...67
5 Marching through Sinai..93
6 Setbacks at Gaza...115
7 Onwards to Jerusalem..145
8 Campaigning in Judaea..171
9 Victory at Megiddo...191
10 The Best Bunch of Lads...211
11 The Folks Back Home 233
12 Little Sister...255

Appendices
1 Log...275
2 Parcels Inventory...283
3 Selected Bibliography...291
4 Glossary..293

Index...295

CHAPTER ONE

SIGNING ON

DEWI DAVID'S WAR

1915 – 1919

Home in Splott

When their first child was born to Thomas and Hannah David in Zinc Street, Splott in Cardiff on March 1st 1898, there was little doubt which name would be chosen for him. Patriotic Welsh people from the Welsh-speaking settlement around the Garth Mountain five miles north of Cardiff – Tom, a youngest son from Pentyrch and Hannah from neighbouring Gwaelod-y-Garth at the foot of the mountain – they could hardly avoid choosing Dewi, the name of Wales's patron saint, whose day it was. Tom had moved on marriage in 1897 to a small terraced house completed two years earlier in Wilson Street in Cardiff, where he worked in the telegraph office in the recently-completed Renaissance-style, four storey headquarters of the General Post Office (GPO) in Westgate Street. Cardiff in the late Victorian era was one of Britain's boom towns, with splendid new commercial and municipal buildings rising to reflect its position as one of the principal ports of the world, exporting the coal of neighbouring south Wales valleys to all five continents. Its population had risen rapidly during the second half of the nineteenth century to reach 200,000 in the years immediately before World War One, and its boundaries had been pushed out into new suburbs such as Splott, built on the vast expanses of mudflats around the docks. In 1905, when Dewi was seven, his home town would be named as Wales's first municipal city and a new civic centre would be rising in Cathays Park on 59 acres of land that had formed part of the Bute Estate's Home Park. The Town Hall, later the City Hall was opened in 1904 and the Law Courts two years later. The National Museum, the third element in the group fronting Cathays Park, was not completed until after the war. Though not officially designated as such, the city regarded itself, and was, de facto, the capital of Wales, already important as the county town and main administrative centre of Wales's biggest county, Glamorgan.

The pre-eminence of telegraphs in the commerce and communication of the day can hardly be overstated and Tom's office job will have enjoyed a degree of status. In 1895 3.3 million telegrams were dealt with in the Cardiff District of the Post Office, stretching from Llantwit Major in the west to Usk in the east and north to Rhymney, nearly ten times the volume of letters posted and delivered. Immediately after the war in 1920 the ratio was still nearly four to one in favour of the telegram. The big growth, however, was in the number of telephone subscribers, up from 158 in 1895 to 12,073 in 1920. Cardiff itself was the site of many early experiments in telegraphy under Sir John Gavey, the Post Office Superintending Engineer for South Wales, and it was this which helped draw the Italian inventor, Guglielmo Marconi, to the area to carry out his successful experiment in sending the first wireless messages across water from Lavernock Point, near Penarth, to Flat Holm in the Bristol Channel.[1]

This was the environment in which Dewi grew up, the family having moved, after a brief interlude in Waterloo Gardens in nearby Roath, to Moorland Road, a typical, Cardiff terrace of bay-fronted houses dating from 1892. The road – just around the corner from their previous home in Wilson Street – was effectively the eastern extremity of the city, with houses on one side backing on to the natural boundary

---

1) Post Office Controlling Officers' Association Conference handbook, Cardiff, April 1921.

formed by the coal line built by the Taff Vale Railway to by-pass the city on the way to Cardiff's docks. An intelligent child, Dewi was able after Moorland Road Board School, opened in 1891 to cater for Splott's rapidly growing population, to win a place at Cardiff's first higher grade board school in Howard Gardens, near the city centre.[2] In late 1900 he was joined by a sister, Doris May, and spent his youth larking about with friends on the mudflats (or tide fields as they were known) in nearby Pengam, learning to swim in the open air pool in Splott Park, cycling to other suburbs of Cardiff, such as Roath Park and Rumney, and holidaying with his parents and sister along the south Wales coast and especially at Porthcawl, a favourite for people throughout the region, including South Wales's 250,000 miners and their families.

Splott itself, the strange name of which is probably no more than an early version of the English word "plot", would have been an exciting place to live. Its inhabitants worked in the enormous range of industries established around Cardiff Docks, a few miles to the west. These included in the late nineteenth century foundries, engine and wagon works, chemical plants, paint mills, a tar resin distillery and creosote works, metal stamping and enamelling works, timber merchants and importers, brick makers, flour mills, biscuit factories, joineries, and laundries. The jewel in the crown was one of the most modern iron and steel works in the world, built by Dowlais Iron Co. (later Guest, Keen) on East Moors to make use of imported iron ore from Spain, and intended as a replacement for its plant in Merthyr Tydfil, 23 miles to the northwest. It was not the area's first connection with Spanish raw materials. In 1873 the Tharsis Copper and Sulphur Company had also opened a plant on East Moors to refine copper pyrites from the eponymous site in Spain.[3]

To Work in Telegraphs

His career was set to follow that of his father when at 15 Dewi joined the General Post Office, or GPO as it was universally known, delivering telegrams to seamen's boarding houses in and around Bute Street, to coal and shipping offices in the neighbourhood of Mount Stuart Square and to vessels tied up in one of the city's docks, including the new Queen Alexandra Dock. This had been opened by the Queen herself on a visit to the city in 1907 with King Edward VII, the first by a reigning monarch for nearly 250 years. Covering 52 acres it was one of the biggest docks in Britain and the pride of the Bute family's Cardiff Railway Company (managing director Lord Merthyr), which operated the city's Bute Docks. In the years leading up to the World War One, Cardiff by dint of its coal exports had become one of the world's leading ports by tonnage, sending 10.5m tonnes to export markets in 1913. More than 8,000 ships visited the city in that year to pick up coal, which was loaded into the vessels by 65 coal tipping appliances serving rank upon rank of railway wagons, drawn up alongside the quays. The Cardiff Coal Trimmers' Union, representing the men who 'trimmed'" or levelled the cargoes inside ships, had a membership in excess of 2,000, many

3

2) Opened in 1885 to prepare students for entry into the city's recently opened University of Wales college, it changed its name in 1907 to Howard Gardens Municipal Secondary School and is referred to in several letters to his sister as the M.S.S. It later became Howard Gardens High School and later still Howardian High School, before closing in 1990.

3) Childs, J. *Roath, Splott and Adamsdown*. The History Press, 2012, pp50-53.

of them living in nearby Splott and including his father's eldest brother, Enoch, one of the senior deacons at the family's Calvinistic Methodist Church, Jerusalem, Walker Road. Vessels leaving Cardiff journeyed to every important port in the world, including Royal Navy bunkering stations in Aden and elsewhere, to keep the fleet supplied with its preferred best Welsh steam coal. Regular services linked Cardiff, in some cases weekly or fortnightly, with Aberdeen, Greenock and Glasgow, Bristol, Swansea and London, Hull, Middlesbrough and Newcastle, Liverpool, Birkenhead and Manchester, Plymouth, Portsmouth and Southampton, Belfast, Cork, Dublin and Waterford, Antwerp, Rotterdam and St. Malo. It was still possible, too, to transport goods by canal between Canal Wharf in the city centre and Abercynon, Cilfynydd, Pontypridd and Treforest in the Taff Valley.

The Post Office was one of the main departments of state, employing just under a quarter of a million nationwide in 1913-14 when the telephone companies – like their telegraph counterparts in 1870 – were nationalised. Messenger boy, wearing the distinctive Post Office uniform and pill box hat, was a job Dewi evidently enjoyed, as references in his letters to the good fun he and the other boys had waiting in their rest room for telegrams to deliver, makes clear. Only a few years before he joined, however, the conditions of employment of telegram boys had seriously vexed social reformers. Boys recruited from school were unestablished employees – like the many thousands of auxiliary postmen of the time, offering a cheap and convenient source of labour.[4] Boys could be released with no qualifications into the labour force on reaching adulthood and a new group brought in. In a scathing comment that would find an echo 100 years later in the debate over the use of underpaid interns by media companies, the 1905-1908 Royal Commission on the Poor Laws and the Relief of Distress said "telegraph messengers who are discharged exemplify in a very striking way the evils of a parasitic trade which lives by cheap labour partially supported by parents' wages".

Some boys did advance into the ranks of the established labour force, and, by the time Dewi joined, further training had been arranged to enable boys to obtain outside employment after two years, if they were not retained. In 1910 a standing committee on Boy Labour in the Post Office had been appointed to arrange for the complete absorption of messengers into adult grades, and by 1914 all who passed a qualifying examination at the age of 16 to show they had reached a minimum standard were being offered permanent posts. In 1911 compulsory attendance at continuation classes for four hours a week for two years had also been introduced, which Dewi received at the city's Clark's College, where his sister was later also to spend time gaining commercial skills.[5] Abler boys could advance further and become 'learners' acquiring telegraphic skills through Civil Service Commission examinations, a route his parents presumably had in mind from the start as the desired career progression for their grammar

4) Daunton, M.J., *Royal Mail*. Athlone, 1985, pp198-204.
5) Founded in London by George E. Clark in 1880, Clark's College specialized in preparing students for competitive examinations for entry into the civil service and commercial work. Branches were set up in a number of towns and cities, including Cardiff. The college was one of the early pioneers of distance learning through correspondence courses and in training women for civil service posts during World War One. It closed in the 1970s.

school-educated son. Indeed, he grasped this opportunity to the full, emerging when he was 15 from the Civil Service examination for GPO male learners with the highest marks of any of the more than 200 candidates across England, Wales, Scotland and Ireland – 1,414 out of a total of 1,900 in tests on English Composition, Handwriting, Spelling, Arithmetic and Geography. This gained him one of the two places on offer in Cardiff, against competition from 19 other local candidates.

Tensions had been rising in Europe throughout the decade as Germany under a belligerent Kaiser – son of King Edward VII's sister and hence his nephew – began to flex its muscles, threatening its neighbours to the east and west. Only two years after joining the GPO, the fun and games he evidently enjoyed with his work colleagues, teasing the female members of staff and cheeking the older and more senior employees came to an end.[6] For Dewi, several of whose older friends had joined up, including his best friend, Frank Somers, the idea of giving the Kaiser a punch on the nose was clearly very attractive. For many young men all over Britain war seemed a great adventure and a test of their manliness. On his 17th birthday in 1915 he presented himself at the Glamorgan (Fortress), Royal Engineers, Drill Hall, next to the Post Office in Park Street, where the Welsh Divisional Telegraph Service (Territorial Force) had its headquarters, claiming to be two years older – barely convincing an overly compliant recruiting officer, as he later admitted. He was still under arms in early 1919, months after the war ended, serving with the North Palestine Signals Company, in British-occupied Palestine. He eventually reached home via Alexandria where he had spent Christmas 1918, after a long train journey from Taranto at the tip of Italy, gaining his demobilisation only in April after three and a half years away from Britain. Instead of delivering telegrams Dewi would be manning signals offices, laying cables, riding camels, grooming horses, removing lice from his trouser seams, serving food, living in bivouacs or in tents, (and occasionally billets), on meagre rations supplemented by parcels from home, and enduring long marches, blistering heat, desert sandstorms, monsoon-like downpours and freezing nights.

His war took him not to France, where many of his contemporaries served, but first, with the Mediterranean Expeditionary Force (M.E.F.), to the equally horrific Gallipoli peninsula and then to Egypt, as part of the newly constituted Egyptian Expeditionary Force (E.E.F.), first to guard the vital Suez Canal, and then to help push the retreating Turks out of their Ottoman Arab provinces. Here, he had the satisfaction of seeing places that would otherwise have been merely legendary to him, including Egypt's greatest antiquities and the towns of Gaza and Palestine, familiar as names to any Sunday School-attending Welsh child of the era. The climax was being part of the forces under General Allenby that liberated Jerusalem in December 1917 from the Turks and Germans, bringing a great boost to British morale at the time.

5

6) Vd. Letter of September 23rd 1917 (www.deffro.co.uk) for life in the 'old Docks delivery-room'.

Food Parcels, Please

His adventures during the four years that he would now spend away are revealed in a sequence of fifty letters, post cards and one essay, totalling more than 110,000 words. At first they were short, simply letting his parents know how he was getting on, but with time they become much longer, going into great detail about the reception their numerous parcels had received or detailing the more humorous aspects of Army life. At other times they bemoan the sheer boredom, the hardships of enforced marches or of dragging cable wagons over steep inclines, and the occasional blockheadedness of their leaders. There is an ecstatic account of a weeklong leave in Cairo – possibly the only extended period away from camp that he enjoyed during his service abroad.

Throughout his letters there are copious references to food, or more usually the lack of it, and touchingly enthusiastic descriptions of the joy their parcels produced, especially those supplying home-made cakes. Not all of them seem to have got through. When the P & O liner, *Maloja*, sank in the Dover Straits on February 27th 1916 after striking a German mine, it may have also taken to the bottom, alongside 155 unfortunate crew and passengers, a parcel containing cake, shortbread, Keating's Powder, salmon, chocolates, Pepsin indigestion tablets, and clear gums addressed to Sapper Dewi David, R.E., in Egypt.[7] This, at any rate, is what Dewi's father, Thomas, assumed when the parcel failed to arrive, and the timing would suggest there is a good chance this was the case. The other threat was their interception by 'tin fish', a soubriquet soldiers gave to the new-fangled submarine. There was always, too, in the soldier's mind the cussedness and incompetence of the authorities in failing to ensure parcels were sent to the right place. The impression many of his letters give is that servicemen existed on a poor diet, strong in hard biscuits, much-hated marmalade, bread and skilly (a vegetable broth usually made with oatmeal and flavoured with meat). There was little prospect of living off local supplies. Much of his time was spent in desert or near-desert conditions or in the bleak Judaean hills, offering little in the way of value in food terms to the forces camped there.

The variety in the diet evidently came from parcels from home, most frequently from his parents but also from his mother's sister, his Aunt Janet, whose husband, Elias Evans, ran a grocer's shop, *The Tivy Stores*, in Carlisle Street in Splott, and on one occasion from his Sunday School. There may have been others, too, but his letters of thanks would have gone to the senders and it is only the correspondence with his immediate family that has been saved. Nor was it just food that had to be supplied from home. Socks were another commodity frequently requested, together with other items of clothing, such as shirts and handkerchiefs, and, of course, the soldier's comforter and companion, cigarettes, plus writing paper, envelopes, pen-knives, soap, toothbrushes, a mirror, a hairbrush and a host of other everyday items. Without parcels from home, containing not just luxuries but a number of essentials as well, the British soldier in the Near East in World War One would clearly have come close on occasion to starvation. In one letter in 1917 he says they would, indeed, have starved but for a gift parcel his unit fortuitously received. Napoleon

---

7) Keating's was a well-known brand of flea and insect powder.

Bonaparte declared an Army marches on its stomach; the British Army in World War One seems to have largely proceeded on the food parcels sent from home.[8]

Society in Britain

None of his own family's or his other correspondents' letters to Dewi have survived, as, no doubt, he was severely limited in the personal possessions he could transport on his three and a half year-long trek from Gallipoli and the banks of the Nile and Suez Canal to north Palestine and back. From his own writings, however, we learn much about the world he had left behind in Britain and about the changes that were already enveloping it in the first decade of the 20th century, changes intensified during the war years. The letters offer a fascinating insight, too, into the developing mind and growing maturity of someone who was a teenager during most of his service, and, just as importantly, into the life of a lower middle class family in the early years of the twentieth century. Dewi was a voracious reader, and despite his short period of formal schooling – a mere ten years – he can and does make frequent references to the Old and New Testaments, the ancient worlds of Greece, Rome and Egypt, English poetry and Welsh history and folk memories, as well as best-selling authors and popular music of the time back in Britain. His letters are full of requests to send him copies of *London Opinion* and the *Weekly Telegraph*, two periodicals of the era, and novels by Charles Dickens and Walter Scott, two of his favourites. Rob Roy is one of his requests from Serapeum on the Canal, where he seems to have had plenty of time for reading, because, as he explains, he would like something with good language in it. And, he continues, if they happen to see a Welsh book they think would be suitable, he would like them not to forget him. A year later his tastes have widened – his requested authors are Edgar Wallace, Ian Hay and Mark Twain. His reading of newspapers, including towards the end of his service, the forces paper, the *Palestine Times*, seems to have kept him remarkably well-briefed on contemporary developments at home, including the suffragist movement, and, of special interest, David Lloyd George's rise to the highest office of Prime Minister.

The language and vocabulary he uses is rich but also contains speech we now find curious – 'S'welp me', 'abso-blooming-lutely', 'By Jove', 'By Gum', 'Gosh' 'Gee Whiz' 'plumb loco', 'phisog' 'give it socks', 'in the pink', 'tophole', 'brace of shakes', 'fakamajig', 'topnotcher', 'betcher', 'kybosh', 'doolali', 'ole chulip' and many others. As his service lengthens, he slips more deeply into Army slang. The nervous and deferential youth writing on arrival in the Dardanelles is by the end of his service showing signs of being the sometimes cynical Tommy and would-be Jack-the-Lad. He constantly refers proudly to Wales and Welshness but uses the Welsh language only for occasional flavour in his letters, perhaps because his education had been through the medium of English. He has to reply to the chapel in Welsh to thank them for his gift and is anxious his father should tell him whether his Welsh is correct. A few words of Arabic – bukra, baksheesh, mungari, imshy allah – also creep into his letters, generally to impress, though he admits he has difficulty in making Arabic speakers understand him.

7

There are some remarkably good turns of phrase and compelling imagery. In apologising for his failure to find his sister a Christmas present in Jerusalem, he tells her "the miserable paltry specimens of the Birmingham jewellers' art (overseas department, remember)" that he inspected were "a gross insult to the average man's intelligence" and "would not have deceived even the dullest member of a West African missioner's flock"; or in recounting his pleasure after eating the contents of a parcel, that he "felt as contented and benevolent as the fattest old alderman who ever sat down to the weightiest table at the Lord Mayor's spread"; and "wouldn't have changed places with a diner at the Carlton"; or in thanking them for some glasses he had received, that the "goggles" were "Bond St. fit" and hung on his "nasal promontory" a treat; or that some unwelcome remarks he had heard were "enuff to make a crocodile weep champagne". For Dewi a camel is his "long-faced chum", or a "long-necked friend", being seasick is "feeding the fishes", a brush "his trusty desert sweeping instrument", conversation "chin music" and between you and me is "ongtre-noose". Despite signing up to fight for King and Country, there is not a single mention of the Royal Family or of any politician other than Lloyd George, then at the height of his popularity, especially in Wales. Nor does the word Britain appear, though the term Blighty crops up frequently in sentimental references to home. As a reflection of the times, England is sometimes used as a synonym for Britain.

There are other insights. The Victorian and Edwardian family – the George V era had only begun in 1911 – was, as we know from Dickens and other writers, very sentimental. Dewi clearly had a very easy relationship with parents and sister, and with friends and relatives, and expressed his feelings strongly. The letters are shot through with homesickness, in particular the passing of successive Christmases and holidays at home, at which he longs to have been present and which he never imagined he would still be away from when he signed up. He revels in descriptions of the family's outings in his absence and these frequently become the occasion for poignant reminiscences of happy times past in his fun-filled teenage years. His replies to their letters suggest his mother worried about him, as well she might have done. In contrast with the business as usual message of many of their advertisements, petty court cases, shipping news, and livestock prices, the Cardiff morning newspaper, the *Western Mail* contained a daily catalogue of misery for families up and down the land – columns of names and pictures showing the fallen in their peaked military caps under the label Welsh Heroes. These listed the action, the regiment and rank, and the family of the fallen, in one case in December 1917, the only two sons of a husband and wife from Lansdowne Road in Cardiff, who had died within days of each other. Other columns listed commissions won by men moving up from the ranks, and military honours, including occasionally, Victoria Crosses, some awarded posthumously. There is bitterness, too, at what he believes is a perception at home that the boys in France were the only heroes and that the M.E.F. and E.E.F. – Gallipoli notwithstanding – were on some kind of junket.

Families evidently took great interest in each other, including their personal appearance. Dewi's attempts to grow a moustache features in some letters, and his sister's passage through the rite of "putting her hair up" is also discussed. The devotion he expresses to his sister through compliments on everything from her looks and her hair to her cleverness would not come naturally from one of today's teenagers. Though we might think girls in that era were not encouraged to have careers, there is no suggestion his family did not believe Doris could achieve whatever she wanted to. He congratulates her regularly on her exam successes and backs her plans, first to train as a teacher and later, after she had changed her mind, to opt for a commercial career as an office worker. His mother is clearly idolised, though she disappoints him greatly by her failure to write regularly, a task largely left to his father and Doris. The existence of a much wider extended family than most people now enjoy is also evident. The letters are full of references to cousins, aunts, uncles, chapel members, neighbours, work colleagues and other acquaintances. He seems to have corresponded with a wide range of other family members, friends at work and colleagues. World War One was, clearly, a family affair in a way that perhaps no other war before or since have been. Though far away in Gallipoli, Egypt and Palestine, Dewi spent much of the time with friends from school or work or both, and meeting up with cousins and other relatives. Late in the war he comes across someone he barely recognises, "young Taylor from next door". He knows many of the casualties whose deaths are reported to him by his parents. He may have played on the streets with them a few years earlier.

A Revolution in Technology

As the letters illustrate, society was living through a period of rapid technological change, which, like the digital revolution of the last decade of the 20th century and beyond, must have proved both exciting to the young and active and threatening to those who felt left behind. While new inventions, further developed and exploited during the war – such as the motor car – were beyond the reach of all but the richest, the bicycle had brought ordinary citizens a big increase in personal mobility, extending the area over which they could range by many miles. Electricity was bringing to ordinary homes a range of consumer products and labour-saving devices from lighting, kettles and irons, to bar fires and vacuum cleaners. Life in rural areas might still be the same as in previous generations but cities such as Cardiff had in Victorian times developed their own reservoirs, electricity power stations and gas works, and public transport networks served by electrically-powered tramcars. Dewi's uncle Elias, the grocer shop-owner, was an early adopter of another innovation, the motor-cycle and sidecar, in which, no doubt, he and his wife Janet, took trips into the countryside. Flight – both biplanes and balloons – was also being developed, including in his own native city by Ernest Willows. His first rigid balloon – Willows 1 – flew from East Moors, not far from Splott, in 1905, and later flights were to Cheltenham and London, over the open sea of the Bristol Channel, and in 1910, after the development of new models, France. Dewi is concerned with the German Zeppelins used to bomb Britain, contrasting the risks they were facing at home with his own situation. Zeppelin raids did indeed cause significant casualties but never penetrated as far as south Wales. Before the end of the war fixed wing aircraft were being used for aerial combat, reconnaissance and bombing. Several squadrons of aircraft supported British operations in the Middle East, eventually gaining mastery of the skies, with machines superior to those available to the Germans and Turks. The Middle East campaigns also saw the use of tear gas on both sides, and of bombing missions from the air. Dewi mentions his own gas mask in one of his letters –

9

jocularly, however, as needed to deal with the vapours from a parcel whose contents had gone off. Yet, while these changes in the way warfare would be carried out in the 20th century were coming into play, the Middle East campaigns were in some ways reminiscent of battles of old. The Australian and New Zealand cavalry, who played a big part in the campaigns against the Turks, rode over the enemy's trenches wielding sabres, as their predecessors on horseback 100 years or even centuries earlier might have done.

Consumer Products, Holidays and Hobbies

It was an age, too, which had over the previous generation seen the widespread introduction of branded products. Industrialisation had made it possible to mass produce foodstuffs and domestic products, such as soap, introducing new items to an acquisitive and inquisitive market. A known name on a nationally or regionally produced biscuit or a bar of soap also gave the customer for the first time an assurance of quality and reliability – and, if necessary, recompense, something that small-scale and domestic producers operating over a much smaller area were less able to offer. Although his mother's cooking remained the product he chiefly wanted to receive, Dewi was able to nominate a whole raft of goods he needed to make life more bearable in the Gallipoli cold and wet, the desert heat or the bleak Judaean hills, most of which would have had their origins in the late 19th century and not a few of which remain available today or have only recently disappeared. He requests Crawford's biscuits, (not Huntley & Palmer's, which he disliked), St. Ivel cheese, Sunlight soap, Bournville cocoa, Ideal Milk, Rowntree's Gums, and Oxo, among other products. There are mentions, too, of Cherry Blossom shoe polish, Brasso metal polish, Pear's soap, Raleigh bicycles, Cadbury's chocolate, Remington typewriters, Allenbury's Food, England's Glory matches and Johnny Walker (as the officers' tipple). Other products have completed their life cycle and are no longer with us – for example Keating's anti-vermin powder, Nestlé's Café au Lait, (an early instant coffee), Batcher's jams and marmalade, Thos. Tickler jams, Pepsin indigestion tablets, Everlasting Strips, Maconochie stewed meat and Globe polish. Cigarettes, which he refers to variously as his Lady Nicotine, or on one occasion his ol' sleeping pardner, have changed names, their manufacturers no long feeling comfortable about promoting their nautical or manly qualities. The cigarettes and tobacco he mentions were Player's (long the British best-seller with its bearded seaman packet), Waverley, Gold Flake, Woodbines, Westward Ho!, Abdullas, State Express, Dickins, and Franklin's Shag. (On one occasion he writes home to say he has been enjoying a Romeo y Julietta cigar.)

For those who had the money to do so, including lower middle class citizens like the Davids, holidays were now an accepted part of modern life. Some traditions such as the Whitsun Treat, the Bank Holiday commemorating Pentecost, were still important, and remembered in Dewi's letters as a great source of fun, when chapel elders could be subjected to indignities on visits to places such as St. Mellons, now a suburb of Cardiff, for picnics in what were then country fields. With growing prosperity, his family, however, now regarded a week here and there at a seaside location as a vital break for recuperating after the long weeks of work or study at school or college. Weekend trips to country or seaside locations in south Wales, such as Chepstow, Tintern, Gower, Rhossili, Fontygary, Lavernock, Sully,

Swanbridge, Rhoose, Cowbridge, Peterston, and St. Fagans, were also, clearly, an important part of family life, too, all of which they would have reached by the comprehensive network of railway lines that then linked towns and villages across south Wales. For the longer holiday Porthcawl was clearly the favourite, attaining in Dewi's mind almost paradisiacal status. Many of his letters look back to the fun that he and his father had had on the beach or forward to future holidays with his family in Porthcawl.[9] There is no mention of trips into England, though he does refer to London in one of the letters to his sister, which suggests a degree of familiarity, whether from pictures or actual experience is not clear.

We learn, too, from his letters much about the hobbies and pastimes of the era, such as post card collecting, and in particular the new craze for photography that had been ushered in by the 1900 introduction of the $1 Brownie camera by the American firm, Eastman Kodak. Basically a box with a simple lens that could capture images on roll film, the Brownie meant that instead of taking mementoes of loved ones abroad, such as locks of hair, servicemen could request the latest family photos be sent out and could send back images of their own unfamiliar surroundings. Dewi's letters, particularly in the earliest years after he is sent overseas, are full of what can only be termed pleas for photos of his family, coupled with ecstatic reports of the joy they brought on receipt. A camera had been one of his possessions at home and was duly sent out but only after he had persuaded his father to take some family snaps with it first. During his stay on the Canal he evidently had time to take photos of his encampment and work base, as well as their leisure activities, diving and swimming in the Canal. There are photos, too, from his visits to Cairo (where the zoo was a particular attraction), to Heliopolis, and to Ismailia and studio shots from Cairo – a ritual many soldiers indulged in so as to be able to send photos home in desert kit. After the scramble through the Judaean hills he also manages to find time for photos of newly captured Jerusalem. Some photos were taken to photographic firms in Cairo or Alexandria to develop but some of the men also created their own developing facilities in the desert.[10] In these more innocent times the men serving overseas gained great pleasure from merely looking at the photos sent out from home of eligible young ladies.

We also gain an insight into the rapid technological changes that were taking place at that time in the dissemination of news and entertainment, as at the end of another century, 100 years later. There are references to the cinema, a fast-developing phenomenon at the time. Cardiff at this time boasted no fewer than 17, in one of which his parents were able to see General Allenby's triumphal entry into Jerusalem in 1917. Radio broadcasting to the public would not be established until the 1920s and television would not arrive for more than a decade later. Recording, however, meant popular songs – and operatic arias – were now available on demand at home as well as in the music hall or theatre. Troops were able to keep up with some of the latest songs through concert parties, sometimes organised by the military to keep the men entertained but more often the inspiration of the men themselves. The piano in this era was still going strong, as the middle class family's main way of entertaining each other. They also found their way to the various

11

---

9) July 13th; August 3rd 1916.
10) July 31st 1916.

theatres of war, offering men another way of relaxing during periods of rest. Although a good pianist himself, in Dewi's mind it is sister Doris who is the star. Most large towns and cities at the time boasted numerous piano suppliers and in some cases piano makers – the David family's piano bore the name of Marion Street, Splott, musical instrument dealer, R. Rhedynog Price, a well-known Cardiff composer and conductor. The other popular entertainment of the day, for men at any rate, was sport. The football clubs we have today had mostly formed in the late 19th century and had coalesced into well-established leagues by the start of the war. Cardiff City had been founded in 1899, a year after Dewi's birth, and quickly joined the then Southern League. The family's team, however, was the older Cardiff Rugby Club, which gains several mentions. This was a time when Wales could claim to be perhaps the leading rugby nation, beating New Zealand in 1905, though narrowly falling in 1906 to South Africa, a team the Cardiff side managed to conquer 17-0 on the same tour.

The Break with the Past

There is a view that the pre-war period inherited from Victorian times was a golden age, certainly for the richer sections of society, shattered fatally by the shots that killed the Archduke Ferdinand, heir to the Austro-Hungarian throne, on June 28th 1914. Outside the poorer working classes individuals and families were, indeed, perhaps rich in a way that they are perhaps not even today, and they were experiencing many exciting changes to the world they lived in. This was a Britain where middle class women wore fur coats, chains such as the National Fur Company promoting their wares in all the main regional and national newspapers, and where gold and silver jewellery was within the reach of families giving gifts to each other at Christmas, a situation that prevailed even after more than three years of war. Even as late as December 1917, the all-advertisement front pages of the *Western Mail* were carrying display ads from the leading Cardiff department store, James Howell & Co advertising its Christmas gift suggestions, and its Christmas bazaar. Cross Bros in nearby Working Street, could offer silver, electroplate, fancy leather goods, fancy brass goods, glass and china, and clocks. (The solitary hint that conditions were not normal was a sentence advising that this year there would be no Christmas bazaar "owing to depletion of staff", and inability to obtain toys.) For many among the rich, life carried on in a way not markedly differently from before the war, even if many of their servants – and their sons – had been conscripted. In 1916 liners were still passing through the Suez Canal, potentially under threat from both the west and the east, the longed-for women at the rails sometimes throwing parcels overboard for the men guarding the Canal to swim to recover.

These outward signs of prosperity were deceptive, however. The pre-war years had not been trouble-free. 1913 was a peak year for strikes – as well as for exports of Welsh coal. In the years immediately before the outbreak of war unrest had led to the dispatch of Metropolitan Police and Hussars to Tonypandy in 1910 to confront striking miners. There were riots the following year in Llanelli, where two people were shot dead by the military during a railway strike. Stoppages took place in the south Wales collieries over pay throughout the war, as well as in other key industries around the country, such as ship-building. By the time Lloyd

George came to power in 1916, the truce that labour leaders had offered at the start of the war, promising not to resort to strikes to settle disputes, was proving increasingly difficult to sustain. The first two years of the war had seen relative harmony, but the demands of the war economy – rising prices, harsh working conditions and overtime pressures – were by 1917 causing mounting unrest.[11] The restiveness of the industrial working classes was being matched by militancy among women demanding rights of representation through the vote, and increasing Irish demands for Home Rule had led to what would now be termed terrorist outrages on the streets of London. These events – even Ireland, where the discontent leading up to the Easter Rising in 1916 had been bubbling away for some time – are not mentioned, perhaps because they did not feature much in soldiers' conversations. There were, after all, Irish divisions, loyal to the British Empire, fighting in France and in the Middle East. Always short of food himself and delighted with every parcel he receives, Dewi also seems unaware of the food supply difficulties at home, where rationing had to be introduced in February 1918 as the German U-Boat attacks took their toll on food imports. The problem had first become acute during 1916, when coal also became scarce, but efforts to persuade the public to ration themselves were not successful.

There were other indications that society was going through one of those moments of change, though it would have come to the attention of only a very few. New music from Bartok, Prokofiev, Stravinsky, Scriabin and Debussy, was paving the way for the atonality of some 20th century composers, representing a break with the classical tradition in music. The birth across the Atlantic of jazz was a similar portent. In art, too, the Impressionists of the late 19th century had been followed by the Expressionists – among them Munch, Klee, and Kandinsky – and the Cubists, led by Picasso and Braque. Peace at home and the old ways had, therefore, begun to be threatened, even before the march to war against the Kaiser began. The position of women in society changed, too, during the course of the war, and not just as a result of the suffrage movement. Staff shortages – like those experienced by Cross Bros – had brought many women into the labour force for the first time, notably into the munitions industry, but also in other previously all-male occupations. By 1917 with 350 out of its 750 employees away the Cardiff Corporation Transport Department was employing 25 women tram drivers.

Dewi was trained in the use of arms during four months of preparation in Britain before sailing from Devonport for the Mediterranean, and he mentions Army rifle duties, too, in several of his letters. He spent time up the line, with groups that did engage with the enemy in Gaza and Palestine, as well as in Brigade and Company headquarters further back. His war, however, is largely that of a non-combatant, one of the host of support troops needed to get a single fighting man to grips with the enemy. As a record of service, it remains, nevertheless, of great significance, detailing life from the viewpoint of the ordinary solider enduring the hardships, the excitements, the dangers and sometimes the sheer tedium and desperate homesickness of military life in distant climes.

13

11) Bourne, J., Liddle P., Whitehead, I., (Eds), *The Great World War*. 1914-45. Harper Collins, 2000. 'Political Leaders in War Time: Lloyd George and Churchill'. George H. Cassar. Chap 21, p388.

(right) Dewi David, taken in Cambridge in 1915 before leaving Britain to serve as a Sapper with the 53rd (Welsh) Division, Mediterranean Expeditionary Force.

(below) Hannah, Doris and Tom David, the picture of his family that his letters urged them to send.

(bottom left) Municipal Secondary School, Howard Gardens, Cardiff, where Dewi received his secondary education.

(bottom right) Moorland Road, in the recently built suburb of Splott, where Dewi lived before enlisting.

CHAPTER TWO

FROM SPLOTT TO GALLIPOLI

MARCH 1915 – JANUARY 1916

The Welsh and the War

After a happy and comfortable life at home in Cardiff with his parents and younger sister Doris (always referred to by the family and in the letters as Doll or Dollie), life in the Army must have seemed very different for 17 year-old Dewi. On Sunday February 28th, the day before signing on, he had been accepted as a member of the family's Welsh Calvinistic Methodist church, Jerusalem, Walker Road, a precaution he and his family must have thought worth taking, given the unknown dangers he would be facing and uncertainty over when he would return. Just over two and a half weeks later, on Wednesday, March 17th 1915, he was sworn into the Royal Engineers after medical examination and given his uniform. He was off to join the Welsh Divisional Signals Company at Aberystwyth, attached to the 53rd (Welsh) Division, a Territorial Division that was to go on to have an excellent combat record in both world wars.

Dewi volunteered like a lot of other young men because his friends from school and work were joining up. A Territorial Force of 14 Home Defence Divisions had been one of the outcomes of the various commissions set up after the South African Wars, with the possibility in mind that they could be used abroad in a national emergency.[1] There were many other volunteers like him.[2] South Wales sent proportionately more men into arms on a voluntary basis than any other part of the country, their enthusiasm in large measure generated by a fellow-feeling for small nations, which David Lloyd George, Chancellor of the Exchequer and a hero for Non-Conformist Wales, skilfully nurtured. The sympathy in Wales for the Boers, which Lloyd George had helped to bring about a decade earlier, as the historian Kenneth O. Morgan points out, was now enlisted in support of "gallant little Belgium", Serbia and Montenegro – small places (like Wales), and territories that had become pawns in Big Power rivalries.[3] Nearly 280,000 Welshmen eventually served in the armed forces during World War One, of whom 123,000 were volunteers; 40,000 Welsh soldiers did not return home. At the express wish of Lloyd George, a new division, the 38th, was created in November 1914, despite initial opposition from Secretary for War, Field Marshal Lord Kitchener of Khartoum.[4] He had told the Prime Minister, Herbert Asquith, that the Welsh were "wild and insubordinate", and in need of "stiffening with a strong infusion of English and Scottish soldiers". A new regiment, the Welsh Guards, was formed, too, in 1915, by drafting in Welshmen from the other Guards' regiments. Strong interest in the idea of such a regiment had come from King George V. Nonconformist chaplains in the Army were, however, a step too far in Kitchener's view.

Some historians have recently questioned the Morgan thesis that a higher proportion of the Welsh population was engaged in the war than that of England or Scotland. Robin Barlow goes so far as to suggest the Morgan claim is based

---

1) The 53rd, to which Dewi's unit was attached, was one of 14 divisions in the peacetime army, created under reforms introduced by Richard Burton Haldane, Secretary for War, in 1908.
2) Men who were later conscripted entered into the Regular Army.
3) Morgan, K. O., *Wales: Rebirth of a Nation*. Oxford University Press, 1982, pp159-161.
4) Horatio Herbert Kitchener (1850-1916), victor at the Battle of Omdurman, which secured control of Sudan, also served in the Boer Wars, and in India and Egypt, becoming Secretary for War in 1914.

on misleading figures given by Sir Auckland Geddes, director of recruiting from 1916, in January 1918, and subsequently quoted in a book entitled *Wales: Its Part in the War*. The figures, Barlow says, were estimates and did not cover the whole period of the war. Moreover, many of the individuals who joined up from Wales were comparatively recent English immigrants and so not wholly representative of more traditional Welsh attitudes. In fact, he argues, out of a total estimated male population of 1.268 million in 1914, 272,924 had enlisted by November 11th 1918, or 21.52 per cent. Comparable figures for England were 24.02 per cent and for Scotland 23.71 per cent.[5] John Davies argues that at the time there was in any case a higher proportion of young men in the population of Wales than in England.[6]

Whichever view is taken, in Britain and Ireland as a whole, almost 2.5m volunteers had signed up by the end of 1915 for what most people expected would be a short sharp defence of the Empire and its values. In spring 1915, when enthusiasm for the war was still high and before the horrors of the trenches had begun to impact on public opinion, enlistments averaged 100,000 men per month. This joining rate could not be sustained, however, and the upper age limit was raised from 38 to 40 in May 1915. In July the National Registration Act 1915 passed into law with the aim of stimulating recruitment and discovering how many men between the ages of 15 and 65 were engaged in each trade. All those in this age range who were not already in the military were obliged to register, giving employment details. The results in mid-September 1915 showed there were almost 5 million males of military age who were not in the forces, of whom 1.6m were in the starred (protected, high skill) jobs. In October 1915 the then Director-General of Recruiting, Lord Derby, brought forward a programme, the Derby Scheme, for raising the numbers. Men aged 18 to 40 were told that they could continue to enlist voluntarily, or attest, with an obligation to come, if called up. The men who registered under the Derby Scheme were classified into married and single, and into 23 groups according to their age. Group 1 was for single 18 year-olds, then by year up to Group 23 for single 40s; Group 24 was for married 18 year-olds up to Group 46 for married 40s.[7]

The heavy losses sustained in the battles in France and the limited success of the Derby Scheme, however, made conscription inevitable, if the much bigger German Army were to be countered. The War Office notified the public that voluntary enlistment would cease, the last day of registration being set for December 15th 1915. The Military Service Act requiring men to join up was passed in the following January. Single men between the ages of 18 and 41 were liable to be called-up, unless they were widowed, with children, or ministers of religion. Conscription started on March 2nd 1916 and was extended to married men on May 25th 1916. The law went through several changes before the war's end, the age limit eventually being raised to 51. By the end of the war no fewer than 5.7 million men had passed through the Army, split roughly equally between volunteers and conscripts – the largest force ever raised by Britain.[8]

5) *Statistics of the Military Effort of the British Empire during the Great War.* HMSO, 1922. Barlow, R., *Western Mail,* October 5th 2010.
6) Davies, J., *A History of Wales.* Penguin. 1993, p513.
7) Derby initiated the idea of "Pals" battalions, groups of men who had been school friends, work colleagues or neighbours.
8) Sheffield, G., *Forgotten Victory.* Review, 2002, p53.

The eagerness with which young men signed up to join the war, even though it was expected to be over quickly, is hard to understand from this distance, but, as some historians have pointed out, the public mood was at the time subject to very different influences from today. Seeing oneself as part of a nation rather than a clan or religion was new in European history. In the 19th century national movements had coalesced across the continent around shared histories, languages and cultures and religions. This had helped to create nations but had also stirred up old rivalries. Social Darwinists in the wake of evolutionary theory were arguing, too, that nations were species, much as flora and fauna, and locked in a relentless struggle for survival. This was an age in which the military was admired, for values such as discipline and self-control, often being seen as the best and most noble part of the nation. That rivalry could be seen in fierce competition.[9] This, nevertheless, underestimates the extent to which the British people and their leaders also believed an existential threat was posed by German aggression, and the outrage felt at German actions in Europe, and in particular Belgium. Testimony to this is the stoicism with which families for the most part accepted the sacrifice of their sons, sometimes only sons and sometimes several brothers from the same household.

Germany was, indeed, seeking to achieve hegemony over Europe through its invasions of Belgium and northern France, and to extend its influence in Africa, the Atlantic and Indian Oceans to match other European nations already holding overseas possessions. Russia's borders, too, were to be pushed back further east. "As [German Chancellor] Bethmann-Hollweg's September programme of 1914 demonstrates, even at this early stage Germany was not thinking in terms of a moderate peace.[10] Rather, Belgium would become a vassal state and French power would be crushed, although France would be allowed to exist as a third-class power which posed no threat to Germany. *Mitteleuropa*, a central European customs union, would, it was planned, stabilise Germany's economic dominance over Central Europe."[11] The German authorities undoubtedly behaved badly in World War One, too, though not on the scale of the atrocities of World War Two. Around 120,000 Belgians and 100,000 Frenchmen were sent to forced labour in Germany, when local people resisted the work demands of the invader, and a similarly harsh occupation was imposed on Poland to the east. Belgium's industrial stock, plus much domestic property, was requisitioned and shipped to Germany. The stories of hardship and brutality brought over by the many Belgian refugees who fled their country played a significant part in hardening the British population's determination to beat "the Hun".

Welsh forces overseas in France and elsewhere enjoyed strong support at home, where even such unlikely figures as preachers and miners' agents addressed recruiting meetings. Connections were made with Wales's martial past and its heroes. Typical of this was the publication *Gwlad fy Nhadau, Rhodd Cymru i'w Byddin*, [Land of My Fathers, Wales's Gift to its Army], a volume of patriotic Welsh language stories about Wales published by Hodder & Stoughton on behalf of the National Fund for Welsh Troops. The selection was made by two eminent Welsh academics, Sir John Morris Jones and Professor Lewis Jones, and profits from the

18

9) Macmillan, M., *Wolfson Review*, No. 37, pp28-9.

10) Theobald Bethmann-Hollweg, (1856-1921) German Chancellor from 1909 to 1917.

11) Sheffield, p. 59.

2/6d sale were donated to the fund for its work providing additional comforts for Welsh regiments at home and abroad.[12] Mrs Lloyd George was chair of the committee and her fellow-members were a roll-call of landed gentry wives – Lady Ninian Crichton-Stuart (of the Bute family that had developed modern Cardiff), Lady Glanusk, Lady Edwards, Lady Beatrice Ormsby-Gore, Lady Herbert, and the Hon. Violet Douglas-Pennant, ably assisted no doubt by Mrs Ellis Griffiths, Mrs Pryce-Jones, and Mrs Reginald McKenna.[13] Sir John, a largely apolitical literary figure, might have seemed a strange supporter, but in 1915, writing in the journal *Beirniad*, he had attacked in bellicose terms "Germany's new religion, the nationalistic creed of Nietzsche".[14]

He seems to have had a point. While the German working man and woman were largely indifferent or passive in their acceptance of war, among German intellectuals there was a feeling that German belligerence could and should be seen in terms of an alleged spiritual antithesis between German culture and political forms – its art, music, literature and scholarship and the accompanying virtues of diligence, order and discipline – and those of its enemies. Rallying behind the war effort, a group of 93 German scholars and artists issued in October 1914 the Manifesto of the 93, which flatly refuted charges of barbarianism in Belgium, claiming the struggle against Germany's so-called militarism was a struggle against German civilisation, and that without the former there would not have been the survival of the latter. Scientist Max Planck, musician Engelbert Humperdinck and theatre director Max Reinhardt were among the signatories. Themes to emerge in the writings and speeches of intellectuals after publication of the appeal were the superiority of Germany's authoritarian constitution over the parliamentary regimes of the west, and Germany's right to world leadership. One leading historian argued that it was "subjectively recognised and objectively proven that we are capable of the highest achievements in the world and must therefore be at least considered entitled to share in world rule". Among historians there had developed since the 1890s the view that the system of old European states would soon be replaced by a small number of world states or empire in which the Germans would take their place as an equal, Britain having been forced to surrender its then pre-eminence.[15]

Welsh people could take pride in the important part Welsh leaders were playing in directing the war against this philosophy and the threat it posed to Britain and her empire. Lloyd George, Chancellor of the Exchequer since the Liberal landslide of 1906, was already a hero in Wales for his welfare reforms and the successful challenge he had mounted to the unelected House of Lords. He had exploited the not unexpected shortages of ammunition in France, given the scale of the war, to become Minister of Munitions in 1916, and had claimed credit for the improvements that had begun to come through. By the end of 1916 he was Prime

---

12) Two shillings and sixpence. Before decimalisation the currency was divided into 20 shillings, each of twelve pence. Though comparisons are hard to make, £1 in income in 1915 would be the equivalent of £50-75 100 years later.

13) The 3rd Marquess of Bute's second son, Lt.-Gen. Lord Ninian Crichton-Stuart, (after whom Ninian Park, the former Cardiff City football ground and Ninian Road in Cardiff are named), was killed in October 1915 in the Battle of Loos. Member of Parliament for Cardiff, Pontypridd and Llantrisant at the time, his statue stands in Cathays Park in Gorsedd Gardens opposite the castle his father had rebuilt and richly decorated.

14) Morgan, p159.

15) Watson, P., *The German Genius*. Simon & Schuster. London 2010. pp 531-533.

Minister, surrounded by Welsh advisers, including J.T. Davies, his private secretary, Thomas Jones, deputy secretary to the Cabinet, and Lord Rhondda (D.A. Thomas), president of the Board of Local Government. His contemporaries included the first Welsh-speaking Prime Minister – Llansantffraid-ym-Mechain born Billy Hughes, the Labour Premier of Australia from 1915 to 1923.[16] Yet, there were strong voices against war in Wales, particularly within the Independent Labour Party. Many of its activists were pacifists and hoping that by working with their fellow Socialists in Europe they could stop the drift to war. A bitter blow came with the death of Keir Hardie, Labour's first M.P., in 1915. In the by-election that followed, the anti-war candidate, James Winstone, standing for Labour, was defeated by the pro-war miners' leader, Charles B. Stanton, who won the seat with a decisive majority as an Independent. "We should have seen the danger signal when we heard that Keir Hardie had, a few weeks before he died, been shouted down when he attempted to address a meeting of miners at Aberdare." Such was the view of James Griffiths, an ILP member who was later to rise to become Colonial Secretary, in the Labour Government of 1945, deputy leader of the Labour Party and the Charter Secretary of State for Wales in 1964.[17] Dissent did grow, however, splitting Liberal and nationalist opinion, and, by 1916, when the full horrors of the Western Front – and Gallipoli – had become common knowledge, anti-war radical movements were able to attract considerable support and critics had become more willing to run the gauntlet of war fervour. Britain, unlike its Continental counterparts, had always relied on a volunteer army, and kept comparatively few men under arms, preferring instead to project power through its Navy. As a result, conscription, when it was introduced, was unpopular with many Welsh Liberal MPs – still the dominant party in Wales – and leading Non-Conformist ministers began to condemn rather than endorse the war.

The Call of the East

When Dewi joined, the war had been in progress for seven months and it had become clear that the new century and its technologies had ushered in a new pattern of warfare which would guarantee the contest would last much longer than the protagonists had expected. Early in August, after the declaration of war, the Germans had put into operation the Schlieffen Plan, which aimed to avoid a war on two fronts against France and Russia by defeating the French quickly and then redeploying resources to the east. Seven armies were launched against France in an encircling movement designed to trap the French and British forces and capture Paris but a fighting retreat from Mons by the British Army inflicted heavy casualties on the Germans and delayed their progress. The Allied retreat halted at the River Marne where British and French forces were able to turn the Germans and force the abandonment of the Schlieffen plan. Both sides now dug in for an attritional struggle that was to last a further four years but not before Allied forces had managed to hold on – just – in the face of a German attempt to secure another key objective, the key Belgian communications centre, Ypres, in a battle extending from October 8th to

16) Morgan. p277. Other advisers to Lloyd George included Sir Alfred Mond, First Commissioner for Works, a Swansea Liberal M.P, and one of the founders of Imperial Chemical Industries (ICI).

17) *James Griffiths and his Times*. Wales Labour Party, p18.

November 12th. Further actions took place around the town, the last in September 1918. Germany now chose to fight defensively in the west, trying to defeat Russia quickly in the east, at the same time stepping up its submarine blockade of Britain, including the sinking of passenger ships. The *Lusitania*, which went down with 1,198 casualties on May 7th 1915, was ultimately to play a significant part in bringing the United States, 124 of whose own citizens perished in the sinking, into the war on the Allied side.

Dewi might have been expecting, originally, to be sent to France, where the news during his training in the east of England would have been of heavy Allied casualties at the second battle of Ypres, and of German advances on the Eastern Front in Poland. He and most of his Post Office friends were destined, however, for signals duties in the Middle East, where the 53rd Division had already been dispatched in July 1915 in support of the Gallipoli operation, landing at Suvla Bay on August 9th-11th. As far back as 1832, during the Crimean War, the Royal Engineers had laid 21 miles of cable to carry telegraph messages using the recently invented Morse code system. During the rest of the century the Corps had continued to develop telegraph expertise alongside their traditional roles building roads and bridges, laying and clearing minefields and generally supporting military activities. The first telegraph troop was formed in 1870, later becoming the telegraph battalion in 1884, and wireless telegraph companies were formed in 1907.[18] In 1914, a year before he joined, the Signals Service included 31 Regular and Territorial units, but by the end of the war this had grown to 531 units, exploiting every different type of communication then available from wireless telegraphy to carrier pigeons.[19] Battlefield communications had advanced considerably by the outbreak of war, with commanders able to get in touch with units through field telephones and telegraphs and, increasingly, through radio, though this new mechanism still required the use of Morse Code for transmitting messages. The Royal Engineers itself had grown to 126,165 men by August 1915, organised into a variety of different companies with differing expertise – half as big again as the entire regular Army 100 years later.

Royal Engineers' Field Company recruits underwent a three month basic training regime, comprising five weeks' marching drill, one week firearms training, and six weeks' field engineering at R.E. headquarters in Chatham, Kent. Training for other companies, involved in different activities, such as signalling, took place at other depots. Dewi's training took place first in Aberystwyth, then in late March and April, in tents on Parker's Piece, the celebrated open space in the middle of Cambridge, where the Division had moved in December 1914.[20] The newer recruits, including Dewi, later moved to Dallington (now a suburb of Northampton) for rifle training, and then marched to Bedford, the 53rd's new base from May 1915. After returning from a last home leave and spending an overnight stay in St. Budeaux camp in Devonport, he and his fellow recruits embarked on *Megantic*, departing on October 5th 1915 to join the earlier arrivals

18) Two very appropriate mottoes were conferred on the Royal Engineers by King William IV in 1832, "Ubique", "Everywhere" and "Quo fas et gloria ducunt", Whither right and glory lead".

19) Official agreement to form a separate Signal Corps to take over the Royal Engineers' signalling responsibilities was reached in 1918 but it was another two years before the issuing of a Royal Warrant.

20) His daughter Mari b. 1940 would later attend Cambridge University to study classics.

on Gallipoli.[21] It was one of several vessels he was to sail in on his way to and then back again from the Middle East theatres he served in, and one with a famous history. The 14,878 tons liner was launched in 1908 and made her maiden voyage from Liverpool to Montréal on June 17th 1909. In 1910, after Scotland Yard's Inspector Dew had arrested the infamous Dr. Crippen and his mistress, Ethel Le Neve, in Quebec, they were escorted back to England aboard *Megantic*.

The Dardanelles Campaign

The Gallipoli (or Dardanelles) campaign will go down in history as one of the worst defeats suffered by the British Army, "brilliant in conception but lamentable in execution".[22] It was first proposed in November 1914 by French Justice Minister, Aristide Briand, as a means of relieving pressure on the Western Front, which only a few months into the war had turned into trench warfare deadlock, and enthusiastically adopted by Winston Churchill, the First Lord of the Admiralty. A principal objective was to ensure an effective supply route remained open through the Black Sea and the Dardanelles to Britain's and France's ally, Russia. That country's trade routes through western Europe were blocked by the Central Powers, Germany and the Austro-Hungarian empire, and other sea routes were either too distant or, as in the case of the Baltic Sea, blocked by the German Navy. The Dardanelles itself had been closed by the Ottoman rulers on the outbreak of war in August 1914, and a few months later in November the Sultan, Mehmet V, had declared a jihad or holy war against the Allies. Another consideration lay powerfully at the back of British minds and perhaps not the obvious one. Joining up with the Russians to march on the Central Powers[23] from the east would certainly have presented grave difficulties, the author A.N. Wilson points out. A real threat was materializing, however, in the other direction from the German-financed Berlin-Baghdad railway. This had the potential to create a new fast route extending down to the Persian Gulf, and hence India's doorstep. The Germans had been keen for some time to exert influence in the Near East, where the French and British were the dominant external powers, the Kaiser offering himself as "friend and protector" of Mohammedans on a visit to Damascus in 1898. His dream was to extend German influence throughout the Holy Land and to push on through Arabia towards India. In pursuit of these objectives a German syndicate had in 1903 secured concessions to build railways and roads for the Ottoman Empire and by the start of the war tracks had been laid from Scutari on the Black Sea through Turkey to Konya, Adana, Aleppo and Harran with plans to extend through Tikrit and Baghdad to Basra and its rich oilfields. For Britain this raised the real risk that it would lose access to the new fuel now vital to the Royal Navy and the merchant marine, following the switch from coal-firing, and enable the Germans to make their presence felt all the way to India. The Suez Canal would be effectively by-passed.[24]

21) Constructed by Harland and Wolff, Belfast, in 1908 for the White Star Line's Liverpool-Canada route, the 14,878 ton *Megantic* entered service as a troopship in 1915. Eight transport ships had previously sailed on July 19th from Devonport carrying the first 53rd Division soldiers sent out to join the British, French, Australian, New Zealand, Indian and other Empire troops already entrenched.

22) Howard, M., *The Causes of Wars*. Temple Smith, 1983, p186.

23) The Central Powers Alliance also included Bulgaria and the Ottoman Empire.

24) Wilson, A.N., *After the Victorians*. Arrow, 2005, pp134-6.

Opinion in Turkey had been divided over whether to remain neutral or, if not, which side to join in the Great War. The country's leader, Enver Pasha, favoured Germany, where, as military attaché, he had learned to admire German military training, while others within the Young Turks, the revolutionary groups seeking reform, preferred Britain and France, as did most of the public.[25] Inept British diplomacy in the end tipped the balance in favour of the Central Powers. Despite Cabinet opposition Enver Pasha had gone ahead and signed a secret treaty of alliance with the Central Powers, though this did not commit Turkey to taking part in combat. Britain, which had been asked to help rebuild Turkey's navy, chose, without knowing about the treaty, to renege on a deal to sell two battleships it had contracted to build, creating intense disappointment and anger throughout Turkey, where funding for the vessels had been raised through collection boxes in hospitals, coffee houses and railway stations, and outside mosques. Even schoolchildren had contributed, and back in Britain the vessels' Ottoman crews were waiting to take delivery. The decision by Britain to keep the two battleships for its own use made it all too easy for the German Ambassador to the Ottoman Empire, Hans Freiherr von Wangenheim, to persuade the Turks that Britain could not be trusted and to offer to make good Turkey's loss. Two German naval vessels, the *Goeben* and the *Breslau*, were renamed and transferred to the Ottoman Black Sea fleet, their German crews given fezzes and Ottoman uniforms and enlisted in the Sultan's navy.[26] These two vessels, commanded by German Admiral Wilhelm Souchon, had previously been engaged in the first naval action of World War One when they had managed to evade the light cruiser HMS *Gloucester's* guns while passing through the Mediterranean. They had been allowed to enter the Dardanelles, strictly in contravention of Turkey's supposed neutrality, but only after the imposition of steep terms on the Germans in the event they should win the war. Ironically, Turkey's decision, pushed by Enver Pasha, to fight alongside Germany came at a time when that country's influence in Constantinople had weakened. The position carefully built up by Wangenheim, ambassador to the Porte, had been undermined by the Kaiser's support for Turkey's old enemy, Greece, over the Albanian question in 1913-14 and his abandonment of the Turks during the Balkan wars.[27] They were persuaded now to join the Central Powers not least because they hoped a victorious alliance would enable them to regain control of Egypt from Britain, and the Russian Caucasus with its oilfield, and even bring Persia under their control. The Turks were able to bring to their new allies an army of 600,000 troops in 38 divisions.

On the British side military over-confidence now took over from diplomatic ineptitude. The Ottoman Empire had crumbled after defeats in the 1912-1913 Balkan Wars. Bulgaria had gained her independence. Salonika, birthplace of Turkey's future leader, Mustafa Kemal (Ataturk), Crete and the Aegean islands had gone to Greece, Italy had seized Tripoli and the Dodecanese, and Britain had proclaimed the annexation of Cyprus.[28] With the Turkish Army lacking weapons

25) Enver Pasha was a Turkish military officer and a leader of the Young Turk revolution. He was the main leader of the Ottoman Empire in the Balkan Wars and World War One.

26) In 1917 *Goeben* was attacked in an air raid from Britain while lying in harbour at Constantinople. A Handley-Page bi-plane, flew the 2,000 miles, refuelling at Pisa and Salonika. The bombing sank a submarine and damaged Turkish military headquarters in the city but *Goeben* survived.

27) The Porte, shorthand for the central Government of the Ottoman empire referring to the gate giving access to the block of buildings that housed the principal state departments in Constantinople.

28) Askin, M., *Gallipoli: A Turning Point*. p4.

and the country bankrupt, blasting a way through the Dardanelles and seizing Constantinople (now Istanbul) looked straightforward enough in London. The Royal Navy drew up plans for a concentrated attack involving a squadron of eighteen battleships (most of them too obsolete to be used against the formidably re-equipped German Navy). The Cabinet met on January 28th 1915 and authorized an action against Turkey by ships alone. On February 19th a British and French fleet, led by the British battleship, HMS *Queen Elizabeth*, bombarded Ottoman artillery along the coast. The officer in charge, Admiral Sir Sackville Hamilton Carden, cabled Churchill on March 4th advising their expected arrival in Constantinople in two weeks' time. On March 18th the main attack was launched, under Vice-Admiral Sir John de Robeck, who had taken command of the fleet from Carden after the latter had succumbed to stress and needed to be recalled. Though the Turkish defences in the straits were now almost breaking, the French battleship, *Bouvet*, sank after hitting a mine, and further losses occurred, including HMS *Ocean* and HMS *Irresistible*. Other vessels were badly damaged. The Navy had originally asked for Army support but had proceeded on its own as a result of Kitchener's reluctance to take men from the Western Front. In the face of these naval setbacks the decision was taken to scale up the operation. General Sir Ian Hamilton,[29] who was in charge of all British military operations in the Middle East, signalled to Kitchener: "The straits are not likely to be taken by battleships alone. It must be a deliberate and prepared military operation, carried out at full strength to open a passage for the Navy." Kitchener concurred but in the succeeding six weeks that it took for many of the troops that would be needed to arrive from Britain, and in the lull that ensued, the Turks, their morale restored after repelling the world's most powerful navy, were able to put in place firm plans for the defence of the peninsula.

German Colonel Otto Liman von Sanders, who had arrived in Constantinople in 1913 as head of the 40 strong German military mission, had by December that year been raised by the Sultan to the command of the Ottoman First Army Corps, his mission quickly growing to more than 2,000 military advisers. His appointment had put him in nominal charge of both Constantinople and the Straits, a move that had drawn strong protests from Russia because of the potential threat to communications through the Black Sea, if the Turks joined the war and decided on a blockade. As a compromise, von Sanders was made a General – a rank deemed too senior for command merely of an Army corps – and promoted to be the Corps' Inspector-General without operational command. In 1915, with a land attack now expected, he was put in charge of the new Fifth Army, raised for the purpose of repelling the Allies, tellingly observing of the period leading up to the Allied invasion after the failure of the naval expedition: "The British allowed us four good weeks of respite for all this work before their great disembarkation. This respite just sufficed for the most indispensable measures to be taken." Roads were constructed, small boats assembled to carry troops and equipment across the narrows, beaches were wired and makeshift mines constructed from torpedo-heads. Trenches and gun emplacements were dug along the beaches, and troops were regularly taken on long marches to avoid lethargy. German involvement with

24

---

29) Sir Ian Hamilton (1853-1947) served in the Boer War, Sudan, India and Burma, rising to chief of staff to Lord Kitchner, C-in-C South Africa in 1901. He was appointed in March 1915 to command the Mediterranean Expeditonary Force tasked to gain control of the Dardanelles.

Turkey's military efforts was to run deep during the war. The German armaments manufacturer, Krupp, set up a factory in Constantinople and sent out 4,000 skilled men to make shells.

Advance British preparations were by contrast chaotic, as the official history of the Royal Engineers, laments, describing the expedition as one for which no adequate staff preparations had been made.[30] "To the scene of operations were sent out, on the afternoon of the day following their appointment, the Commander-in-Chief and his Chief Staff Officer, together with a hastily collected General Staff but without representatives of the A. and Q. [Adjutant and Quartermaster] branches. Hamilton, as C-in-C. and Major-General Walter Braithwaite, his Chief of Staff, had been given a task for which they had been allowed no time to choose or consult their staff, general or technical, or to appreciate the military and naval position. The vanguard of generals was quickly followed by their army and its vast equipment, hastily and indiscriminately loaded without regard to any orderly plan for disembarking on a hostile coast and going into action without delay. The ships which had been hastily collected for this great force were compelled to return to Alexandria for three weeks to be unloaded and reloaded on sound military lines. Meanwhile, every foe from Berlin to Constantinople took note and made the necessary preparations for a stout defence of the Dardanelles." As the history succinctly puts it: "A secretly planned and executed combined naval and military operation could perhaps have landed unopposed on Gallipoli in the early months of the war but the Allies lacked the resources for two co-ordinated offensives in the East and West. Having delayed, however, the subsequent effort was marked by hasty improvisation and little, if any, staff preparation."[31]

Writing not much more than 10 years after the war in a history of the 53rd (Welsh) Division specially commissioned by the *Western Mail*, military author, Major C.H. Dudley Ward, presented a bleak picture of the chaos, confusion and sheer bad luck that overwhelmed the men at Gallipoli, including Hamilton.[32] Sir Ian's own reconnaissance by sea of the north western shore of the peninsula from its isthmus to Cape Helles during the naval campaign was prophetic. He came to the conclusion that the geography of the northern half of the peninsula precluded any landing at all and the southern half presented difficulties which had no parallel in military history "except possibly in the sinister legends of Xerxes". The 5th century B.C. Persian king, having bridged the Hellespont by lashing ships together, defeated the Greek Army at Thermopylae. He was then defeated at sea by the Athenians at Salamis in 480 B.C., and, following the burning of the Persian fleet, was forced to withdraw back to Persia, as he now lacked the means to maintain provisions for his large land army. Behind the beaches on Gallipoli lay Achi Baba, a 600 ft. high hill, Kalid Bahr, a 700 ft. high plateau, and a small mountain, Sari Bair, running up in a succession of almost perpendicular escarpments to 970 ft., and covered with thick jungle and a network of ravines.

25

30) Pritchard, H.L., Maj-Gen, (ed.) *History of the Corps of Royal Engineers, Vol VI*. Institution of Royal Engineers, 1952, p5.
31) ibid., p1-2.
32) Dudley Ward, Maj. C.H., *History of the 53rd (Welsh) Division 1914-1918*. Western Mail, 1927, pp44, 47-50.

Sir Ian concluded that the beaches were either so well defended by works and guns, or else so restricted by nature, that it did not seem possible even by two or three simultaneous landings to pass the troops ashore quickly enough for them to maintain themselves against a rapid counter attack, which the Turks were bound to attempt. "It became necessary, therefore, not only to land simultaneously at as many points as possible but to threaten to land at other points as well," he later wrote.

Hamilton wanted to use the main allied force landing at Cape Helles in the far south of the peninsula – the site today of the main British memorials – to break through Turkish defensive lines, seize the village of Krithia and Achi Baba hill and join up with Australian and New Zealand forces moving across from their landing site at Anzac Cove, north of Kabatepe.[33] The forces would then combine to push northwards and, by driving the Turkish forces from the heights defending the Dardanelles Straits, enable the British fleet to pass through. In the assaults that followed, however, British, French, Australian, New Zealand, Indian and Newfoundland troops were exposed to all the horrors of early 20th century warfare[34] – contested landings, desperate assaults, and digging in for trench warfare. In scenes to be repeated forty years later by Allied troops in Normandy, the Australians landed a mile off target in terrain completely different from what had been expected – at the foot of a steep hill rather than on a beach. There followed a day of heavy fighting, advances and retreats, after which the generals in charge on the ground felt evacuation was essential. Eventually, the southern hemisphere troops managed to dig in and cling to the modest ground they had gained. This was the first but not the only time Allied troops were to find themselves off course during the campaign.

British troops had even more difficulty establishing themselves at Cape Helles. They were obliged to make repeated attempts under very heavy fire to secure the beaches, on several occasions swarming back to the boats sent for the wounded. Communications between commanders were poor, failing to identify weak spots where the Turks could have been surrounded, and concentrating exhausted British troops instead in areas of the greatest Turkish strength. Repeated attempts were made by the British forces to break through to the higher ground but three battles around the village of Krithia, the first at the end of April and the last in June, failed to achieve the intended breakthrough. Hamilton decided to try a different plan to secure the same objective, using the reinforcements sent out from Britain, in the shape of the 53rd (Welsh) and 54th (East Anglian) Territorial Divisions and the 10th (Irish) Division (the last, one of the divisions in Kitchener's New Armies).[35] These troops, which were landed early in August in and around Suvla Bay, would bolster the Australians further south and would seek to "grip the waist of the peninsula" through the capture of strategic points at Maidos and Gaba Tepe.[36] A big containing attack would meanwhile be launched much further south at Helles, while the combined Anzac forces and the fresh reinforcements delivered the knock-out blow that would gain the Allies the command of the Narrows.

---

33) The Australian and New Zealand Army Corps, always known by their acronym, Anzac.

34) Newfoundland was a separate British possession and did not become a Canadian province until 1949.

35) Kitchener had foreseen a long war – unlike many others – and to bring the British Army rapidly up to strength had set about raising 'New Armies' each consisting of six divisions. Kitchener had not been a fan of the Territorial Force formed in 1908, of which the 53rd formed part.

36) Dudley Ward. p18.

Gallipoli Casualties	Dead	Wounded	Total
Total Allies	**53,000**	**96,937**	**149,937**
United Kingdom	32,000	–	–
France	9,798	17,371	27,169
Australia	8,709	19,441	28,150
New Zealand	2,721	4,752	7,473
British India	1,358	3,421	4,779
Newfoundland	49	93	142
Ottoman Empire	**56,643**	**107,007**	**174,828**

Source: Australian Department of Veterans' Affairs

Unfortunately, despite some progress, the landings of fresh troops at Suvla Bay in early August were crowned with confusion, changes of plan, and the lack of any clear idea of what the units were expected to do. Heat and lack of water made things worse, for although provision had been made for water, measures to distribute it were inadequate. Troops actually cut the hose of one water lighter 100 yards offshore to fill their water bottles, depriving the rest of the force of this supply. Speed might, nevertheless, have carried the day but the period after landing was characterised by altered orders, commands not getting through, misunderstandings and delays, all of which enabled the Turks to hold on to the initiative. The 53rd landed amid this confusion on the night of August 8th/9th 1915, lacking vehicles or horses and many of the supplies they would need. Each man had 200 rounds of ammunition but no reserves were landed. Divisional artillery had been left in England under orders for France. On arrival the different units from the 53rd and other divisions were immediately ordered off in support of other troops already engaged in fighting but lacked maps to guide their officers. Burning scrub as well as Turkish fire made the situation even more desperate in some places. "Those brigades that had landed on the night of August 6th/7th, [the main August landings] unless they were on an easily recognisable feature did not really know where they were. All are agreed that the country was most difficult. Units of the 53rd Division would, having only a few hours' acquaintanceship with the place, be in a worse case," Dudley Ward wrote.[37] Commanders were, it seems, sent off with their troops knowing nothing of the position of the enemy and practically nothing of the troops they were meant to contact.

By the middle of August the fighting had died down and the 53rd Division was taking its turn manning a line south of Lala Baba at Amzak Dere. Its casualties had amounted to 123 officers and 2,182 other ranks in just five days fighting, but now dysentery and jaundice were to take over, laying the men low. Though there were further sallies and small engagements, the failure of this latest initiative meant the battle for the peninsula was effectively over, the Turks having repelled all attempts by the Allies to seize control of the higher ground and hence control of the straits. By October debate had started in Britain over the possibility of pulling out. Hamilton, who was against such a move for fear of the damage it would do to British prestige, was recalled to London on October 16th (and effectively

27

37) Ibid, p31.

dismissed), to be replaced by Lieutenant-General Sir Charles Monro.[38] Gallipoli had demonstrated that an opposed amphibious landing is one of the most difficult acts that any force can be asked to undertake.[39] Moreover, the assault of April 1915 amounted to the first time men had ever attacked a coastline defended by the weapons of warfare of the industrial age.[40] Hamilton lacked sufficient troops and landing craft, as well as labouring under poor command and control arrangements, inadequate communications systems, and chaotic logistics. His men faced the tactical situation of the Western Front, a stalemate – but in harsher terrain and under a Mediterranean sun.

The Voyage East

Dewi arrived in Gallipoli in October after the main battles had taken place but before some of the worst weather conditions suffered by the troops on both sides. Indeed, if nothing else had convinced the military commanders that they were engaged in a fruitless exercise, the storms of November 27th did. Yet, the conditions his fellow-soldiers had been enduring in the preceding months seem from his correspondence not to have given rise to any apprehension in his mind. The journey, after leaving Devonport on October 5th, had taken them first to Malta, which they reached nearly a week later on October 11th. Four days later they were in Lemnos, landing on October 19th at Mudros, re-embarking two days later for the final leg. At Mudros they were confined to their ship at first, as a rather plaintive letter recounts. "We have been on board this vessel exactly fourteen days now and, believe me, it is very monotonous, especially as we have been in port since Friday. One gets rather bored being cooped up on a ship not moving an inch in port for four days. It's alright at sea but sticking still and not allowed to land fairly puts the kybosh on it."[41] The trip as a whole, however, despite the time it took, seems to have been uneventful. "We had a very calm voyage," he tells his parents after they had reached their final destination, "no rough weather at all and that perhaps accounts for my not 'feeding the fishes' [42] and enjoying the trip after the second day." The furthest Dewi would previously have travelled by sea might have been a trip across the Bristol Channel in one of the pleasure steamers that plied in summer between Cardiff and the Somerset and Devon coastal resorts of Weston-super-Mare and Ilfracombe.[43]

In the first of his letters on the voyage east, he is at pains not to be too specific about his location for fear of falling foul of the censors, though it would have been public knowledge that the 53rd were in the Mediterranean theatre of operations. Men were under strict instructions not to give away information that could lead the enemy to gain valuable intelligence and his letters home start almost invariably with date but no address. Censorship of letters was the responsibility

38) Sir Charles Monro (1860-1929) served in the Boer War and played an important part in the First Battle of Ypres. He replaced Hamilton as C-in-C of the B.M.E.F. in October 1915.

39) Sheffield, p95.

40) Lee, J., *A Soldier's Life: General Sir Ian Hamilton 1853-1947*, Macmillan 2000, p xxvi.

41) October 18th 1915.

42) November 14th 1915. Feeding the fishes, euphemism for being seasick.

43) The Bristol Channel was one of the main areas for paddle steamer cruises in the UK. P & A Campbell's White Funnel fleet, which began operations in the late 1880s, dominated coastal cruising and ferry operations for the next 80 years. A successor company still provided services in the first decades of the 21st century.

of unit officers throughout the Army who were attached to each base to carry out random checks. Letters had to be submitted unsealed and the officer, after reading the contents, would delete any parts he considered to be of a sensitive military nature. He would then seal the envelope, stamp it with a censor stamp and forward it to the Army Postal Service. To ease the burden brought about by the need to look at correspondence from hundreds of thousands of soldiers, "honour envelopes" were introduced in March 1915. The writer signed a declaration on the envelope that the letter inside referred to nothing but private and family matters. These envelopes were the "Green 'Uns" that Dewi mentions in several of his letters.[44] Right at the very start he was clearly alive to the possibility of a random check on one of his letters. He closes his October 18th letter with a few words in Welsh, the language he used with his parents – Yr eiddot yn gariadus – and then provides a translation in English – Yours Lovingly – for the benefit of the censors, adding a P.S. "I put 'Yours lovingly' in brackets in case the Censor deletes the Welsh translation of that phrase."[45] A military ban on the use of Welsh in letters was, in fact, a sore point with Welsh soldiers and the press and public opinion back home in Wales. It was as late as December 1917 before a Welsh censor was appointed to survey letters sent home in Welsh from the Western Front. Dewi's only other mention of censorship comes nearly three years later when he advises that he has some films ready for developing but it would be no good me "trying to post 'em, 'cos they're particular about photos and like as not destroy 'em, so I'm not taking any risks and shall keep 'em with me in the old pack until a favourable opportunity arises".[46]

At Mudros he was following earlier waves of British and French soldiers who had passed through on their way to Gallipoli. A naval force under Admiral of the Fleet Rosslyn Erskine Wemyss had occupied Lemnos in 1915 with a brief to prepare the harbour for operations against the Dardanelles. Little effort, however, had been put into creating a proper base, as the British had confidently expected that, once the initial landings had taken place and Gallipoli had been taken, the forces could be more conveniently supplied from the docksides of Alexandria – that is, at any rate, until Constantinople and its port facilities were in British hands. The expedition's senior Royal Engineer, General A.W. Roper, who carried the title Technical Adviser to the Commander-in-Chief, had requested supplies be sent to build piers but these never came. The consequences of not having a properly-supplied base became apparent in May when two battleships, HMS *Triumph* and HMS *Majestic* were torpedoed by German submarines near the Gallipoli peninsula. No ocean-going ships henceforward would proceed beyond Mudros. Cargoes would be transferred here to smaller vessels for onward despatch, a decision that had serious but unforeseen consequences. "The complete tonnage of maintenance stores and supplies was to be handled at least twice in a harbour quite inadequately developed for the purpose."[47]

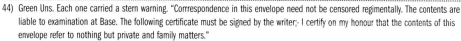

44) Green Uns. Each one carried a stern warning. "Corrrespondence in this envelope need not be censored regimentally. The contents are liable to examination at Base. The following certificate must be signed by the writer;- I certify on my honour that the contents of this envelope refer to nothing but private and family matters."
45) October 18th 1915.
46) March 23rd 1918.
47) Pritchard, (ed.), p17.

Serious congestion was the result, with some vessels having to wait six or eight weeks to enter the harbour to discharge. Steps were taken after serious problems in July to develop better facilities but these continued to be hampered by lack of a proper organisation at the top, a shortage of stores for putting in place the facilities needed, and a lack of skilled labour. The Gallipoli invasion had been planned in great haste, and there had been little time to lay in, even in Egypt, stocks of engineer stores adequate to maintain a force of the size to be employed on the peninsula. "The congestion at Mudros was such that only ships containing items vitally essential to the operations could be handled... Cargoes of engineer stores were either delayed in unloading or even returned to Egypt. Thus, a situation arose where the very materials which were required to increase the unloading facilities were those which did not arrive... The result of these difficulties was that Gallipoli suffered more acutely from shortage of engineer materials than any other campaign. Availability of stores always set a limit upon what could or could not be done."[48]

After their brief stop in Mudros, Dewi's unit transferred to *Redbreast*, which took them the rest of the journey to the Gallipoli peninsula. He wrote back with the partial details but again without disclosing the exact location to his parents.[49] "I am quite well and feeling in the pink. Our sea trip is over, and since writing last we have landed at an intermediate base where we stopped two days [Mudros] and left there last Thursday afternoon arriving at the peninsula [Gallipoli] and joining our company on Friday morning.[50] Our present abode is a dug-out on the coast, which we have just put the finishing touches to. We have made ourselves fairly comfortable by now and the six of us are in the same dug-out. For the last few days the weather has been rather cold, and wind blowing the sand about made it very uncomfortable but today has been fairly warm and sunny and I have just returned from a bathe in the bay.[51] I am able to head my letters now [that is include an Army postal address] so you will be able to answer them," he continues. In a letter to his sister, however, he regrets not being able to tell her more about where they have been and for the first time hints at the poor food he would have to endure during his four years away. "I'm sorry but you'll be disappointed when I tell you that I can't say much about Geography as we only landed once but you wait till I come back. I'll have heaps to tell you then. You are quite right, Doll, and I do find it peculiar after only being home, these flies are a nuisance. Glad you like our ship because you wouldn't have liked the grub on her."[52] There remained the hope that the great adventure would soon be over, even though it was only eight months since he had signed up and two months since he had been sent abroad. "It would be nice, as you say, to be home for Xmas with you all and I should dearly love to have that experience. I won't spend another Xmas away from home, if I can help it."[53] When

---

48) Ibid. p18.
49) October 25th 1915. *Redbreast*, a passenger cargo vessel built by A & J Inglis, Glasgow, and launched April 18th 1908. Requisitioned by the Admiralty for use as a fleet messenger in 1915 she was one of a number of Special Service Ships, or Mystery Ships, heavily armed merchantmen with concealed weaponry, designed to lure submarines into making surface attacks. The codename referred to the vessels' home port, Queenstown (Cobh), Ireland. Torpedoed on passage in the Skyros/Doro Channel in the Aegean, July 15th 1917.
50) The company arrived at Suvla Bay on October 22nd and landed on C Beach. Dewi joined 53rd Signals at Lala Baba.
51) October 25th 1915. Their abode, Lala Baba, was a hill 48 metres high, between the southern side of Suvla Bay and the Salt Lake. Now the site of a cemetery, formed after the Armistice, covering an area of 1,136 square metres and containing the graves of 200 soldiers from the United Kingdom.
52) November 14th 1915.
53) November 22nd 1915. He was away for another three Christmases.

the war had started in the autumn of 1914, the strong belief in Britain had been that it would be all over by Christmas *that* year.

Dug-outs, Flies and Iron Rations

Established in positions at Suvla Bay, Dewi was working in the Signals Office on six hours on, 12 hours off shifts. "We are still going strong out here and living underground all the time," he reports, adding that they had settled down into the run of things all right and were "getting quite used to the life out here".[54] A week later he is still there and evidently accepting of his new lot. "We come and go at the Signal Office just the same as working in the P.O. at home."[55] Much of his time would probably have been spent sending and receiving Morse Code messages between headquarters and the various positions occupied by forward troops. Life is monotonous, he tells his parents (perhaps to allay any fears they might have), the only evidence of war coming from newspaper reports sent out. "It's quite a change to take up residence at this secluded quarter of the globe, where there are no Zeppelins or startling placards to worry you."[56] The German Airship or dirigible, the Zeppelin, named after its creator, had first dropped bombs on East Anglia in January 1915, and intermittent raids on the south east of England, London, and the Midlands continued for most of the duration of the war, the last raid taking place as late as August 1918. Navigation and reliability were temperamental but they proved difficult to destroy until it became clear that a combination of explosive and incendiary bullets was needed to set fire to the craft's highly inflammable hydrogen gas bags. The German Army abandoned the use of dirigibles as bombers after one of its craft was shot down in September 1916, but the German Navy continued its raids. Of 84 Zeppelins built during the war more than 60 were lost, roughly evenly divided between accident and enemy action. A total of 51 raids had been undertaken, in which 5,806 bombs were dropped, killing 557 people and injuring 1,358 while causing damage estimated at £1.5 million. Though Zeppelins never raided Cardiff or other parts of Wales outside their range, Dewi's concern is representative of the fears they raised in a British population that had not had war – unlike their Continental counterparts – brought to their doorsteps in their island home.

Even away from the line where some fighting was still taking place, conditions were far from pleasant. On arrival the weather had been mild but in a letter three weeks later Dewi mentions rough weather "monsoons or some such nuisances", with the wind blowing like fury and rain such as he had never before seen in his life, flooding the dug-out ankle-deep in water and mud.[57] "We didn't know how to sleep but eventually solved the problem by utilising some corrugated iron as a bed. Since that storm it has been very cold here and the wind is strong, blowing practically all day. We have, however, improved our dug-out since that experience, and have put a better roof of corrugated iron, instead of frail waterproofs." Another well-documented storm affecting Gallipoli is mentioned in his next letter. The three day storm is described as very fierce, with awful rain and the

31

54) October 31st 1915.
55) November 4th 1915.
56) November 8th 1915.
57) October 31st and November 22nd 1915.

ground ankle-deep in slush.[58] "The wind also was so strong that you could hardly stand. Most of our chaps had their dug-outs swamped out and waist-deep in water, which took some bailing [sic] out, I can tell you, but fortunately we had plenty of corrugated iron on our roof, which kept us fairly dry, so we took in about a dozen "homeless" chaps whose dug-outs were untenable during the storm, so we were like sardines in a tin in our place. However, I managed to keep dry alright and got off pretty lucky. (We have had decent waterproof coats supplied to us.) We are just recovering from the effects of our experience and it has been very cold since."[59] From other accounts of the flooding in late November it would appear the heavy rains had turned the dried out river beds back into rivers. This is what happened at Amzak Dere, close to Suvla Bay, where barricades erected higher up by the Turks gave way sending water hurtling down, flooding trenches to a depth of more than 3 ft.

On Sunday November 28th troops awoke to find it snowing. Dewi, bivouacking at Lala Baba in Suvla Bay, is sympathetic with the problems of the men in the trenches. "The weather will surely get worse, as the winter gets on and I am dreading the thoughts of a few more storms like that. The poor fellows in the trenches, however, had a fearful time and we count ourselves jolly lucky in getting off so lightly."[60] The picture of the terrible storm of November 27th-30th in the Official History makes grim reading.[61] "A violent thunderstorm was followed by a torrential downpour lasting 24 hours that soaked men to their skins, giving way only to an icy hurricane blowing from the north. The rain turned to a blinding blizzard and then to heavy snow, which itself was followed by two days of exceptionally bitter frost. The severe cold following the floods proved an unbearable strain to men whose health had already been undermined by the hardships of the summer campaign. Hundreds were dying from exposure... all over the plain, streams of utterly exhausted men were struggling back to the beach, many collapsing on the roadside and freezing to death where they fell."[62] The likelihood of bad winter weather had been one of the factors leading the British to face up to the inevitable fact that the Gallipoli campaign had been a failure and that the only choice was withdrawal. The invasion of Serbia by the Central Powers in October 1915, moreover, gave them the use of a trunk railway from Vienna through Belgrade and Sofia to Constantinople, making it possible to reinforce the Turks with guns and ammunition, not to mention German military advisers, greatly increasing the threat to British positions on the beaches from the much higher positions held by the Turks.[63] It would take many months for Britain to be able to match the other side's improved armaments. Just as importantly the likely bad weather from November onwards would make operations for the Allied forces, still largely confined to the beaches, extremely difficult. Gales in the Mediterranean were likely to disrupt the small vessels now responsible for bringing supplies from Lemnos

58) December 3rd 1915.
59) Ibid.
60) Ibid.
61) *The Official History of the War: Military Operations, Egypt and Palestine. Vol. II,1*, p420, p432-3.
62) The effects of fighting, few reinforcements, and the dreadful blizzard of November reduced the Division to just 162 officers and 2,438 men (about 15 per cent of full strength), precipitating the withdrawal back to Mudros in Lemnos and then Alexandria. *www.1914-1918.net/53div.htm*.
63) Pritchard, (ed.), p69.

and to batter the 24 piers constructed on the beaches, which would need constant repair. Troops would need better protection in their trenches and huts, requiring yet more supplies to be delivered. After earlier severe gales had hit the peninsula on October 8th 9th 27th and 31st, Hamilton, who was shortly to be replaced by Monro, was asked by Kitchener, for an estimate of probable losses, if an evacuation took place. Kitchener himself began a week's tour of the positions on Gallipoli on November 9th, cabling home on November 22nd to recommend Suvla and Anzac should be evacuated but Helles retained. During the blizzard at Suvla – where the flooding was at its worst – there were 5,000 cases of frostbite and more than 200 men were drowned or frozen to death. The War Committee on receiving Kitchener's report decided complete evacuation was the only option, with Cape Helles also to be abandoned.[64]

These grand strategic issues would not have concerned Dewi, whose pre-occupations were much more mundane. One of his first letters, written after the *Megantic* had landed in Lemnos, told his parents, "For myself I am quite alright and feeling very contented, owing perhaps to the fact that I have just risen from the best meal (tea), I have made since sailing."[65] By the time they had landed at Suvla Bay in October, the realities of life soldiering had, however, begun to be felt. "The food is very good, considering the conditions," he reported, "except that we have to be sparing with the bread and every alternate day or so are obliged to manage with biscuits. Today, for instance, we had one loaf between six men to last all day. Jam is very plentiful and syrup, which goes O.K. with rice at dinner."[66] The following month brings news of canteen supplies. "Today or tomorrow should see the arrival of the canteen order we put in about a week ago. We have to wait for these things, you know, for the canteen is such a long way off. [67] So, with a lot of luck we'll have tinned salmon (just think of it) in our mess tins very soon. It makes my mouth water when I think of it. We do live extravagantly and no mistake." His parents, probably like most back in Britain with sons in France or the other theatres of war, were by now into the routine of parcel-sending, as the longing for something more than the Army could supply started to be felt. "The grub continues to be all right but please send out some decent fags and chocolates. Everybody's fed up with smoking the issue of Tabs." Parcels he tells them were gloated over, bringing everybody out of their dug-outs like so many rabbits from a warren.[68] He was still not complaining. "The grub here is very decent and we have been served out with warm underclothing and cardigans recently," he wrote on November 14th. They were able to draw money occasionally, Dewi writes home, so it would not be necessary to send any out. "Unfortunately, we can't spend it very freely. The only chance we get is the weekly canteen order and then we never get half the stuff we order," his P.S. continuing: "Please send those things which you have mentioned. They are just what I want. I should like also some malted milk tablets, cocoa, tinned fruit, lobster and a diary for '16, if you don't mind, please."[69]

64) Pritchard, (ed.), p72.

65) October 18th 1915.

66) October 31st 1915.

67) November 4th 1915. Canteen, the camp shop where liquors and provisions were sold.

68) Tabs, Army issue cigarettes.

69) November 14th 1915. The lobster would have been tinned, like much of the food sent out from home by his parents. Lobster – like oysters – was then a much commoner food and available to all classes at the time, even if only in tins.

A week or so later, the limitations of the canteen had become apparent. "I haven't seen your parcel yet and hope it hasn't been lost on the way. They say that there have been a great many mail bags washed overboard in a storm so it doesn't look very cheerful does it?"[70] He goes on:"I have plenty of warm clothes but you might send me 2 pairs of socks in your parcel, please. We are unable to buy anything here because that canteen order we put in is a proper wash-out. For instance, we put in for about 30/- worth of eatables etc. last week and in the end all we got was 2 Lemonade powders each in our dug-out. I am still going strong and quite well. Hope you are all quite fit and in the best of health and that Mum is alright after my letters come," he writes, no doubt worried about the impression his letters, combined with newspaper reports on the progress of the Dardanelles campaign, might be having.[71] During the November storms it had proved impossible to land food, he reports, "so we have had to exist on iron rations ever since. I would give much for a good square meal, believe me. The weather will surely get worse as the winter gets on and I am dreading the thoughts of a few more storms like that."[72] Iron Rations consisted of an emergency ration of preserved meat, cheese, biscuit, tea, sugar and salt carried by all British soldiers in the field for use in the event of their being cut off from regular food supplies. In 1914 it comprised 1 lb. preserved meat, 3 oz. cheese, 12 oz. biscuit, $^5/_8$ oz. tea, 2 oz. sugar, $^1/_2$ oz. salt, and 1 oz. meat extract. A few days later he describes the continuing effect of the failure to land food. "As you say, I have met all the CF [Cardiff] fellows who are here and, of course, learnt all the wrinkles as to the mode of living. We have, as you say, not much choice in the matters of eating and drinking and just at present bread is a great luxury. It does get monotonous chewing biscuits for five days out of six. However, I am glad to say that I am still able to enjoy my food and become as hungry as a hunter by every mealtime, which proves, I think, that I'm quite fit and well but, By Gum, you wait until I see a good square meal. Gee! I won't half make a hole in it."[73] The news that a pudding and cake were on the way had made him feel "potty", he tells them. Second only to the weather – and lack of food – for discomfort, however, were the pests they encountered. In a letter to his sister shortly after they arrived in Gallipoli he mentions flies as a nuisance, and a month later, when back in Salonika, he comments on remarks his cousin Beat's fiancé, Hughie, had made about the flies that were pestering him, too, in Gallipoli.[74] The flies, because of the debilitating diseases, including dysentery, they brought, were also responsible for the poor physical condition that many of the men now found themselves in.

Back to Lemnos and Salonika

The 53rd, after its long period in the line, had been considered for the honour of being last to leave the peninsula once the decision to withdraw completely had been taken but its numbers were so reduced and their physical fitness so compromised, their commanding officer recommended instead they be sent speedily to a healthy climate to recuperate, to be brought up to strength, provided with artillery and

70) November 22nd 1915.
71) November 22nd 1915.
72) December 3rd 1915.
73) December 6th 1915.
74) November 14th and December 20th 1915.

generally completed as a division. On Monday December 6th Dewi moved with other troops to A Beach, Suvla Bay, and exactly a week later he embarked from its south pier on board *Rowan* for the day-long move back to Lemnos, changing ships the next day to HMAT *Karroo*, for a further short evacuation to Mudros East on December 15th where he had landed briefly only two months previously after the voyage from Malta.[75] Three days later it was yet another vessel, HMS *Folkestone*, which took the retreating troops to Salonika where they were put up initially at Wood Square Camp before a move two days after Christmas to Lembet Camp on a hill a few miles outside the town, where he joined the 12th Corps Signals – "a different job on a more advanced scale," in his words.[76] In total 205,000 British and Empire and 47,000 French troops were evacuated from Gallipoli.

At Lembet, the men were able to rest after Gallipoli and to get back under canvas after the six-man dug-outs and trenches of the peninsula. Christmas in Salonika seems to have been a modest affair, though undoubtedly more comfortable and less hazardous than it would have been in Gallipoli. Writing home on Boxing Day 1915 his next letter hopes his parents and sister have had a happy Christmas at home and says he and his fellow-soldiers did not do very badly, considering. "A few of us together managed to have a fairly decent feed in the town but it would be an insult to compare it with a Xmas dinner at home. In the evening we had a camp concert which went very well and eventually went to bed congratulating ourselves upon the way we had made ourselves believe it was Xmas." He apologises for not writing sooner: "As I told you, our moving about made it impossible to write but you know by now what has taken place at our last address.[77] I was hoping to receive your parcel with the pudding by Xmas but I am sorry to say nothing has turned up since Aunt Janet's parcel and the cake."[78] A gift from a British newspaper's readers scarcely made up for what they were missing. "I nearly forgot to tell you we had Xmas Pudding for dinner yesterday, an Army ration, of course, and you know what that is – just enough to make you want a lot more. It was a present from some newspaper or other and I for one was very grateful for it, although it wasn't nearly enough of a share."[79] It wasn't the first Xmas Pudding he had tasted lately, he tells them. "At the base we were at last, I had a square inch of pudding allotted to me – that was another gift. But just wait until your parcel with that Xmas Pudding in it arrives for me – By Gum, I won't half give it socks.[80] I haven't had a parcel since Auntie Janet's came and the last letter was yours, dated November 22nd. I have no doubt, however, that there are parcels and letters galore on the way and hope to goodness they arrive soon. I could just do with a nice parcel now with a good pudding or one of those superb cakes Auntie sent. My Word! It makes my mouth water when I think of it now."[81]

75) The 1,493 tons *Rowan*, owned by the Laird Line and built in 1909 by D. & W. Henderson of Meadowside, Clyde, sank on October 9th on a voyage from Glasgow to Dublin after collisions off Corsewall Point with two ships, the American steamship *West Camak*, 5,721 tons, and the *Clan Malcolm*, 5,994 tons. HMAT *Karroo*, His Majesty's Australian Troopship.

76) December 29th 1915. Lembet is now a suburb of the Greek town of Evkarpia, about four miles north of modern Thessaloniki, (Salonika). The British Lembet (Road) Camp was around Karaisin – now Polihni, east of the Lembet Road and slightly further south – the area immediately east of, and perhaps including, today's Pavlou Mela barracks.

77) The evacuation from the Gallipoli peninsula.

78) December 26th 1915.

79) January 2nd 1916.

80) Socks, schoolboy slang for a treat or indulgence.

81) January 2nd 1916.

Though at first on Gallipoli he had had enough funds, he soon starts to feel short, as he is quick to report from Lembet. The Army seems to have paid its troops irregularly, leaving the men desperate when they needed to supplement meagre rations with food bought outside, or to buy other items for their pleasure or amusement. "One thing I like about this camp," he writes, "there's a few canteens here, run by Greeks, you know, therefore, you can take it from me, the prices are pretty salty. You can get quite a lot of stuff from them, if you have money, of course. Unfortunately, I have *no* money at present – in fact I am absobloominglutely stoney. Awful plight to be in isn't it, and if we don't have a pay day soon, I don't know what I shall do. By the way, Dad, that 10/- note[82] came in jolly handy, another one wouldn't go bad, I assure you." Even as he writes, however, there is a promising development "Hip! Hip! – Sorry to interrupt, but what do you think, the orderly sergeant has just been to our tent and asked how much pay we want and departed with our pay books, thus he has saved my life – bless him. Just as I was shouting about being stoney, too. 'Smarvellous, Corn in Egypt[83], what do you say?"

His main complaint is that all he is doing at present is pick and shovel work and he was soon confessing he had nearly forgotten how to handle a key.[84] Much of his time – as later on the Canal – was spent on fatigues – boring Army digging, cleaning, fetching and carrying, and other routines. He had found, too, that the quartermasters' stores and other local sources could not supply the range of comforts and necessities that would make life bearable and, for these, requests had to be sent home. His first letter after landing at Suvla Bay had asked his parents to send out chocolates, sweets, Spearmint, cigarettes, envelopes and candles, and to this list were added in one of his next letters more envelopes, chocolates and cigarettes, Pepsin indigestion tablets, malted milk tablets, tinned fruit, soap and socks. Before they headed for Egypt he has added pleas for cake and biscuits, a Balaclava helmet (at the time he wrote, to protect against Gallipoli's cold), a group photo from home, cocoa, tinned fruit (again), and lobster, a 1916 diary, two pairs of socks, Rowntree's Gums, chewing gum, Keating's Flea Powder, Zaccharine [sic] tablets, and preserved fruit. For the rest of his service many of his letters close with a similar list of products that could only be obtained from home.[85]

Hard Won Lessons

Historians remain divided on whether or not the Gallipoli campaign was a wasteful diversion or not and whether its successful prosecution would have led to a shortening of the war. In this respect it is in the same category as the Norway expedition of 1940. Gary Sheffield, who makes a strong case that, given German intentions, World War One had to be fought and won, doubts if Germany's defeat would have come sooner, even if Constantinople had been taken and the Turks knocked out of the war. It would have been difficult, he argues, to press home the advantage by a direct advance into Austria-Hungary. And, although the opening of the Black Sea would have relieved pressure on the Russians, this on its own

82) January 2nd 1916. 10/-, ten shillings.
83) Genesis 42.2. 'Behold [Jacob] said I have heard there is corn in Egypt.' Famine forced Joseph's brothers, who had sold him into slavery, to visit him in Egypt to buy corn.
84) January 2nd 1916. Key for sending Morse Code.
85) October 25th, November 4th, 8th, 14th, 22nd, 1915, January 2nd, 1916.

would not have been enough to prevent the revolutions of 1917. Other largely forgotten British campaigns of the War in Salonika, in Mesopotamia and in support of the Italians were similarly misconceived, he argues. The alternative view is that if the Dardanelles had been forced, Turkey would have had to surrender, the Ottoman Empire would have been in British hands, and the command of Mesopotamia, Syria and Palestine would have given Britain confident control of the Near East and the Mediterranean and greatly weakened both the Austro-Hungarians and the Germans. A British victory would have shortened the war and saved many lives.[86] Looked at through the long lens of history, others have argued that the Turkish decision to fight, leading ultimately, after the break-up of the Ottoman Empire to the modern Middle East with all its inter and intra state tensions, lies at the root of the most intractable geopolitical problems of the twentieth – and current – century. "In hindsight, it appears inevitable that the Porte would have in the end been drawn into the burgeoning conflict, as were other neutrals in the region, Italy, Bulgaria and Greece. And yet this is to mistake cause and effect: it was Turkey's entry into the war in 1914 which ultimately drew the other powers in, by offering up the Ottoman Empire as war booty."[87]

The failure had other consequences, just one being the decision by Churchill, as one of the chief protagonists, that he had to resign from office. Others saw an opportunity. French troops had landed at Salonika, nominally still a neutral port, in October 1915, an advance guard for an Allied force that would try to bring relief to the Serbians in their struggles against the Austrians and encourage the Greeks to enter the war in support of their Orthodox co-religionists. The German-born king of Bulgaria, "Foxy" Ferdinand, had vacillated over which side to support. Now, seeing the difficulties the British and their allies had encountered in the Dardanelles, he decided the Central Powers were likely to be the victors. An Allied force proved unable to offer effective assistance and the Serbs had to flee to the sea through the mountains where 100,000 men, the remainder of a 400,000 strong army, were rescued by Allied vessels. The retreat of the Serbian Army, encumbered by thousands of refugees, old men, women and children, became one of the most tragic and terrible episodes of the whole war. "Before the final struggle over the mountains of Montenegro to the waiting Allied ships, the refugees had to be abandoned to Bulgarian mercy and to the swifter fates of starvation, cold, typhus and dysentery."[88] If events in Gallipoli had been turning out differently, Serbia might have found itself fighting only on one front and the Allies might have had one fewer opponents." (The Salonika expedition also proved futile. British and French troops failed to make progress beyond Salonika for much of the war, as a result of strong Bulgarian resistance, and were forced to remain behind barbed wire defences – the so-called "Birdcage".)[89] The Royal Engineers Official History accepts that the Dardanelles campaign failed in its main object – the capture of the Turkish capital – but it argues the attack on the straits helped persuade the Germans to cancel their big spring offensive in the west, brought Italy into the war, kept Greece neutral and actually delayed

86) Wilson, pp136-7

87) McKeekin, S., *The Berlin-Baghdad Express*. Penguin, 2011 p100.

88) Barnett, C., *The Great War*. BBC Books. p65. Wells, H.G., *Outline of History*. Cassell, p1080.

89) Pritchard, (ed.), pp107-111. While there, Royal Engineers built piers and harbours, restored a Roman aqueduct to deliver water – half a million gallons a day – to the base, and developed and ran the railway network.

Bulgaria's entry.[90] The hard-fought battles also destroyed much of the Turkish Army. "The lessons learnt during the landing and subsequent fighting ... taught us many lessons concerning the conduct of combined operations – lessons which have proved invaluable on many subsequent occasions, particularly during World War Two."

A New Start in Egypt

The carnage at Gallipoli deeply affected both sides and remains the predominant memory of World War One in Australia and New Zealand, where Anzac Day rather than Armistice Day is the main war remembrance occasion. As in France, trench life in Gallipoli was horrendous. Because the Turks occupied higher ground, Allied forces had great difficulty securing positions safe from shellfire. And throughout the campaign they were short of guns and ammunition, the priority for which was the Western Front. As importantly, the campaign took place at the start of the British Army's learning curve. "At Gallipoli in 1915, the British troops lacked experience, artillery, ammunition, scientific gunnery, aircraft, Lewis guns, Stokes mortars, technical and tactical know-how – everything, in short, that contributed towards the success of the 1917-18 offensive [in France]. The exception was courage, which the British and Anzac troops had in abundance, but courage by itself was not enough."[91] There was heroism on both sides, and, subsequently, a remarkably gallant response on the part of Mustafa Kemal, the commander of Turkey's 19th Division on Gallipoli, whose defence of the south of the peninsula proved crucial. He later became Turkey's first president in 1923, after the abolition of the Sultanate, with the title Ataturk, (Father of the Turks). His message, inscribed on one of the Gallipoli memorials to fallen British and Commonwealth dead, reads:

> "Those heroes that shed their blood and lost their lives... You are now lying in the soil of a friendly country. Therefore rest in peace. There is no difference between the Johnnies and the Mehmets to us where they lie side by side now here in this country of ours... you, the mothers, who sent their sons from faraway countries, wipe away your tears; your sons are now lying in our bosom and are in peace. After having lost their lives on this land, They have become our sons as well."

On Saturday January 16th Dewi's unit marched to Salonika Docks to sail back once again to Lemnos where the following day they embarked on *Hororata* for the passage two days later to Alexandria in Egypt.[92] The 9,461 ton New Zealand vessel, named after a small town in New Zealand's South Island, had been part of the first convoy bringing Australian and New Zealand troops to the World War One theatres. Egypt was the destination for all the men evacuated from the Dardanelles and already contained a garrison of 100,000 troops to deter the Turks from attempting its recovery. By the end of 1915 no fewer than 800,000 men, 180,000

90) Pritchard, (ed.), p94.

91) Sheffield, pp 95-6.

92) The 9461 ton *Hororata* of the New Zealand Shipping Company, London, was used as a troopship under Commonwealth of Australia control until September 11th 1917. *Hororata* was one of the ships assembled in King George Sound, Albany, W. Australia, for the first convoy. This left on November 1st 1914, carrying Australian and New Zealand troops overseas.

animals and 50,000 wounded were to pass through the country.[93] On Thursday January 21st Dewi's unit disembarked at Alexandria, and were allocated to a new organization, the Force in Egypt. This was under the command of General Sir Archibald Murray,[94] a former Chief of the Imperial General Staff – head of the British Army – from September to December 1915 who had succeeded Sir Charles Monro, Commander-in-Chief of the Mediterranean Expeditionary Force since November 25th 1915, on the latter's appointment to the command of the First Army in France.[95] Sir Archibald was to maintain his headquarters in Egypt, to command troops assembling and refitting there and be responsible for the defence of the Suez Canal. Until the situation was later resolved, he would be one of three General Officers Commanding operating simultaneously in Egypt. Lieutenant-General Sir John Maxwell[96] until he was given command of the EEF was separately in charge of troops in the Egyptian Delta, the Western Desert and Sudan, and administered martial law over the whole country, including the Canal Zone. Major-General Edward Altham, meanwhile, was G.O.C. Levant Base, a pool of stores of all kinds for the Gallipoli, Salonika and Egyptian theatres. The Official History describes the men of the 53rd and the 54th (with whom Dewi would serve briefly later) as being at this stage very weak.[97] The divisions had left Gallipoli severely depleted by casualties and sickness after experiencing extremes of climate – burning sun followed by Arctic blizzards – and the attendant afflictions, sunstroke and frostbite. "Rest, re-organisation, training and complete re-organisation were necessary [after the rigours of Gallipoli] before any campaign that involved marching could be undertaken. For the purpose, no better situation than Egypt could have been found. Its climate from November to March is as healthy and invigorating as any in the world."[98]

Alexandria itself was but a brief stop and Dewi would hardly have dreamt when he arrived that he would be spending Christmas 1919 in the city, not having returned home in the meantime. Then a transit point for thousands of British soldiers, Alexandria had for more than two thousand years been one of the Mediterranean's most important cities. Founded around a small Pharaonic town in 331 BC by Alexander the Great, it became a centre of Hellenistic civilisation, Roman and Byzantine Egypt for almost one thousand years, until the Moslem conquest of Egypt in AD 641 and a move to a new capital in what is now Cairo. While there and on visits, British and Commonwealth soliders would have been able to wonder at some of the greatest sights of the ancient world in the city where Cleopatra and Julius Caesar began their famous love affair. Their stay in early 1916 was, however, short. The day after arriving Dewi's unit was settling into Beni Salama camp, an ancient site spread over a low terrace above the modern flood plain near Wardan, 40 miles north of Cairo on the western margin of the Nile Delta. On February 6th

93) Pritchard, (ed.), p169.
94) General Sir Archibald Murray (1860-1945), served in the Second Boer War and was appointed chief of staff to the British Expeditionary Force in Belgium and France in August 1915, stepping down in January 1915. He commanded the Egyptian Expeditionary Force from January 1916 – June 1917.
95) The First (and Second) Armies were created in December 1914 to succeed the British Expeditionary Force, badly depleted in the battles at Mons and Ypres.
96) Lieutenant General Sir John Maxwell (1851-1929) served in Sudan at the Battle of Omdurman, in the Boer War and on the Western Front before being given comand in Egypt.
97) *The Official History of the War:* Vol. I, pp94-95.
98) Mortlock, M.J., *The Egyptian Expeditionary Force in World War One*. McFarland & Co. Jefferson, 2011, p6-7.

Dewi found himself briefly attached to the London Brigade and ten days later after a day's break – the only proper leave he had had since sailing in October – he had moved to Fayoum, home to a British army headquarters 57 miles south of Cairo in the desert, and one of a number of different locations to which troops from the 53rd Division were posted over the coming months. By this stage they had become part of another new force, the Egyptian Expeditionary Force, successor to the Mediterranean Expeditionary Force that had been gathered together for the Dardanelles campaign, and were due to be joined by 6,000 fresh troops from Britain, whose despatch to replenish depleted battalions had been announced on January 1st.

Before the end of his war Dewi's personal pilgrimage was to take him to Cairo and then the Suez Canal, to Ismailia, Sinai and, after the capture of El Arish in 1917 on to the Battles of Gaza and Beersheba, on a trek through Palestine and, finally, with Allenby, to the liberation of Jerusalem at the end of 1917, an honour the 53rd shared with the 60th Division. The British Army then pushed on to Aleppo in Syria, driving the Turkish and German forces back all the way, until the signing of an Armistice in Mudros on October 31st. This was a distance approaching 500 miles from the Canal, nearly all of which Dewi had to walk. After many disappointing Christmas Days, separated from family and Christmas fare, he was able to enjoy, seven weeks after the wider cessation of hostilities on November 11th, a splendid dinner with his comrades on Christmas Day 1918 at the Grand Hotel, Alexandria. The printed menu, signed by his wartime companions from the Welsh Divisional Signal Co. R.E. (T.F.), makes appetizing reading even today and may have erased some memories of years of bully beef and hard biscuits. It started with Oxtail Soup and Filet de Poisson Lutèce, followed by Choufleur Polonaise, Roast Turkey, Potatoes, Salade Romaine, Plum Pudding, Scotch Woodcock and Dessert. A concert with piano accompaniment followed, performed by among others the Welsh Rarebits, an assorted group of privates, pioneers, sappers and doctors. Major W. Hampson, M.C., was in the chair, and two of Dewi's closest friends were on the organizing committee, Sergt. Aubrey Mills and Corpl. C.G. (Pip) Pippen.[99] In March 1919 after a sea voyage from Port Said to Taranto, the principal British Mediterranean dispersal camp, at the tip of Italy, he arrived back in Le Havre by train, taking a boat the next day for Southampton, and then travelling on to Fovant, an Army dispersal camp on Salisbury Plain. The next entry in Dewi's log for March 22nd is written in capitals HOME. His demobilisation came through in April, four years and one month after his decision as a 17 year old to sign on for what he no doubt hoped at the time would be a short and possibly even enjoyable adventure serving King and Country. Dewi returned as he left, a sapper, the equivalent to a private in the infantry, Regimental No. 452339. He was now old enough to vote, and a more mature and wiser individual. He was transferred to the reserve and instructed to rejoin in Deganwy, in north Wales in case of emergency, his year of birth on his demobilisation papers still given as 1896, two years early.

99) Lutèce (Lutetia in Latin) is the ancient name for Paris. Scotch woodcock, a savoury dish consisting of creamy, softly-scrambled eggs, served over toast spread with anchovy paste or Gentleman's Relish; Romaine, lettuce; choufleur polonaise, cauliflower cooked in lemon and coated with breadcrumbs, chopped boiled egg and parsley. The 'Welsh Rarebits' were the divisional concert party.

Megantic, the 14,878 ton White Star liner requisitioned for war service, in which troops were taken to the Mediterranean.

Gallipoli. Suvla Bay in 2008, where men of the 53rd division had landed ninety years earlier.

(left) Gallipoli. Anzac Cove in 2008, where Australian and New Zealand troops landed.

(below) Gallipoli, restored Turkish trenches 2008.

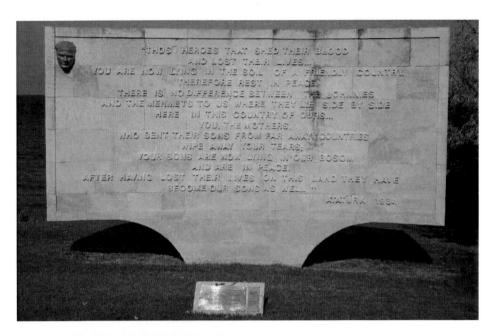

(above) Turkish leader Ataturk's tribute to the fallen British, French and Empire dead.

(left) A solemn compliments of the season, probably from Salonika, 1915. Dewi is left.

(right) *Hororata,* the troopship on which the men of the 53rd Division sailed for Alexandria in January 1916.

CHAPTER THREE

REGROUPING IN EGYPT

JANUARY – MAY 1916

Egypt's Strategic Importance

E gypt had with French agreement become a British protectorate on December 17th 1914, though it had been effectively under British control since the battle of Tel el Kebir in 1882. In that encounter an Egyptian Army revolt, led by Egyptian Colonel, Ahmed Urabi, was put down by the British military, keen to defend British interests in the country, and in particular the strategically important Suez Canal.[1] The 100 mile long Suez Canal, completed after ten years' construction in 1869 by Frenchman Vicomte Ferdinand de Lesseps, had eliminated the need to travel around Cape Good Hope to reach India and British dominion and colonial possessions in the East. Before 1914 British policy in the Middle East had been to avoid excessive entanglement in local political affairs and to prop up the decaying Ottoman Empire as the most economical method of protecting the route to India. Racked with internal divisions, the Ottoman Empire had had little option other than to allow the British to control defence and foreign policy and to occupy key posts in Egypt's internal administration. The British for their part regarded "Brother Turk" half-patronisingly and half respectfully as "good fellows". "The most powerful man in Egypt was the British representative; he was responsible to the Foreign Office, and not the Colonial Office, but his functions were more those of a Governor than a diplomatic representative."[2] The post usually went to a General and, up to the outbreak of war when he left to become War Secretary, had been filled by General Sir Douglas Haig. The liberator of Jerusalem during the successful Palestine campaign of 1917, Field Marshall Viscount Allenby, assumed the role in 1918. The High Commissioner's Turkish opposite number and nominal local ruler was the Khedive but in December 1914 the British had deposed the then holder of this title, Abbas Helmi, deeming him to be too favourable to the Turks and the Central Powers, and had installed his uncle, Prince Hussein Kamel Pasha, instead as a new Sultan of Egypt. The senior British official was also renamed High Commissioner. This post from January 1915 was held by Sir Henry M'Mahon.[3]

As tension had increased in the years leading up to the war, the British were very conscious of the threat to their lifeline posed by the Ottoman Empire, which extended across modern Syria, the Lebanon, Jordan, Israel and Palestine and down the Red Sea coast of modern Saudi Arabia. To meet this danger, units, mainly from Australia, New Zealand and India, were sent to defend the Canal in 1914. This would ensure Britain could continue to draw on an increasingly important source of troops and materiel, as the war proceeded and the demand for fresh men on the Western Front in France and in other theatres grew. It was also the training ground for the reserve of Dominion and Indian troops still waiting to be deployed. Its importance as a highly strategic asset was, of course, also obvious to the Turks and Germans, yet its defence presented some problems. Internal transport links within Egypt were poor. No metalled roads existed outside the cities, making it difficult to move men and equipment around. A single track

1) Colonel Ahmed Urabi, an Egyptian army general and nationalist, led a revolt in 1879 against Tewfik Pasha, the Khedive of Egypt and Sudan in protest at the increasing European domination of the country. It was crushed in 1882 when Britain invaded at the request of Tewfik, thereby commencing the 40 year British occupation of Egypt. Khedive was the name given to Turkish viceroys ruling Egypt from 1867 to 1914. French khedive from Turkish hidiv, lord

2) Cross, C., *The Fall of the British Empire*. Paladin, 1970, p111.

3) Sir Henry M'Mahon (1862-1949) saw service mainly in India before being posted to Egypt. He retired in 1916.

railway ran along the western side of the Canal, the 30 miles from Cairo to Ismailia, and thence north to Port Said and south to Suez. (Cairo, where there had been strong European influence for 40 years, enjoyed transport infrastructure much like that of many European cities, with good roads and electric trams running from the centre to the outskirts.) Faced with these communications difficulties, and to minimise the risk of conflicts, the British chose at the start of the war to withdraw a 30,000 strong force in the Sinai Peninsula, ceding the territory back to the Turks, and concentrate troops for the defence of the canal on the western side of the canal (where there was also a threat from Senussi tribesmen to their rear).

The Turks had begun preparations in late 1914 to use their 65,000 strong strike force in Syria to challenge the British position in Egypt and to re-establish the suzerainty lost when the Khedive had invited the British in 30 years earlier. In November the Turks had put 8,000 men in El Arish in northern Sinai (which the British would recapture in late 1916). By the end of January 1915 the Ottoman Suez Expeditionary Force under the leadership of German Colonel, Friedrich Freiherr Kress von Kressenstein, had brought sufficient men forward to launch two small columns against British positions at Kantara in the north of the Canal Zone and at Suez in the south. On the night of February 2nd/3rd they were able to bring up 5,000 men opposite Ismailia, a further 5,000 between Tussum and Serapeum, and 2,000 for a second assault on Kantara. To the amazement of the British they had managed to drag steel pontoons (for crossing the canal) and six inch guns across the desert. Many of the Turkish soldiers had travelled barefoot, marching seven hours each night through the desert to save water and avoid detection, inspired by fiery speeches from Moslem chaplains. Ottoman Christian and Jewish soldiers had been left behind at Beersheba to create a purely Islamic army engaged in a jihad.[4] Not surprisingly, the troops were exhausted. In the attack that followed only two Ottoman companies managed to cross the Canal, after encountering strong resistance from 30,000 men of the Imperial Service Cavalry Brigade and the Bikaner Camel Corps, the Egyptian Army and Indian artillery. Turkish artillery had been effectively silenced by the guns of three of the four cruisers at their stations on the Canal – HMS *Hardinge*, and the French vessels, *d'Entrecasteaux* and *Requin* – and all those who crossed were either killed or captured. With further British forces being quickly mobilised, the Turks withdrew but the difficulties the British encountered in transporting cavalry units across the Canal and the lack of water supplies for men and horses in the desert allowed the Turks to retreat in good order with guns and baggage. Forewarned against possible future attacks, the British dug a powerful defence system behind the Canal and built up the imperial garrison in Egypt to 100,000 men by the end of 1915, an increase of 30,000 on a year earlier. Further Turkish raids over the course of 1915 were on a much smaller scale, though a mine was placed in the Canal in April, and von Kressenstein personally led another charge in May.

The failure of the Gallipoli offensive heightened the threat to the Canal by relieving the pressure on Turkey and releasing forces for possible attacks. Turkish rail communications with Palestine had also improved, bringing their forces nearer, and Bulgaria's entry into the war in October 1915 meant German support could be provided more quickly. Stronger defence of the Canal would as a result be necessary.

4) McMeekin, p175.

The earlier incursion confirmed, however, that defence of the Canal along its length and from its western side was not advisable, as Kitchener had pointed out in November 1914, not just because of its length but also because of the large number of troops that it committed. In late 1915 the Cabinet authorised new positions to be established in the desert seven miles east of the Canal and agreed to provide extra troops. Port Said was the new headquarters of these defences with an advanced headquarters at Kantara.

Threats on Both Sides

The German-officered Turkish Army to the East was not the only threat facing the British and Empire troops in Egypt, however, and actions had been taking place in the west. A strongly Moslem group, and originally well-disposed to Britain, the Senussi were responding to the declaration by the Sultan of Turkey, Mehmet V, in November 1914 of a Holy War and his call for all Moslems to share in the defence of their faith. With encouragement and some support from the Turks and the Germans, who were keen to keep the British occupied after the failure of their own attempts on the Canal, the Senussi tribesmen in the Western desert were harassing British positions, forcing a tactical withdrawal in November 1915 from Sollum, the British border in Egypt with neighbouring Tripoli. A new position was taken at Mersa Matruh, a coastal town 150 miles west of Alexandria and linked to it by a railway line. Though now a largely forgotten encounter, contemporary accounts read a much wider significance into the events. The part-publication, *The Great War*, went so far as to suggest the affair was of more importance than any fighting taking place at that moment in Europe.[5] "From many points of view Egypt had become, for the time, the most important region of strategy of all theatres of war. Momentous issues were being decided by comparatively small forces, fighting on difficult waterless stretches of sand and rock. The rising of the Senussi had been long prepared to time with the great Turco-German attack against the Suez Canal. Nuri Bey, brother of Enver Pasha, led the Turkish troops supporting the Senussi." Advocates of a return to a very pure form of Islam, the Senussi made the mistake, however, of confronting the British Army, by making stands and holding positions, rather than adopting guerrilla tactics. Superior British numbers – including units from the 53rd Division – were able to counter their efforts. In late 1915 and early 1916 British forces drove the Senussi back from their positions west of Mersa Matruh and captured their leader Jafar Pasha. A few weeks later, an armoured car detachment under the Duke of Westminster made a dash across the desert and rescued the crews of two naval vessels, *Tara* and *Moorina*, who were being held captive after their ships had been torpedoed early in November 1915 in an action by an Austrian submarine off the North African coast. The men had been handed over to the Senussi and marched 180 miles into the Libyan Desert, where they were forced to endure hard labour. *Tara*, an armed merchantman commanded by Captain Gwatkin Williams with a largely Welsh crew, had before the war been a steamer operating between Holyhead and Dublin. The Senussi were to cause problems intermittently for another two years, tying up units of the 53rd Welsh Division at Fayoum and Wadi Natrun for long periods, but they were never able to fight again as an organised force and were finally defeated in 1917.

5) Wilson, H. W., (ed.), *The Great War, The Standard History of the All-Europe conflict*. Amalgamated Press, Part 97, pp473-4.

To the East the Germans spent much of 1915 making preparations for further assaults against the British position in Egypt. The Ottoman railway from Baghdad was extended 100 miles south to Beersheba from Nablus by October, under the direction of engineer Heinrich August Meissner (Meissner Pasha), the builder of the Hejaz railway from Damascus to Medina. This raised the possibility of moving men and materiel much more quickly to any new front.[6] Von Kressenstein was also promised the arrival of German Special Forces by February 1916. The British priority, however, was to reduce the number of troops required to maintain the active defence of Egypt and the Canal, so that troops could be released for the Western Front. Military planners had concluded that, if the Turks were to plan another advance on the Canal, there were three possible routes: from Aqaba in the south towards Suez; a central route from Beersheba or El Arish towards Ismailia; or along the coast in the north. The first of these would present an army with insurmountable rocky country, while the coastal route was vulnerable to shellfire from the sea. If the Turks could cross the desert by the central route, however, they could strike at Ismailia, usefully positioned on the 30 ft. wide Sweet Water Canal. This had been built by the Suez Canal Company on the western side to provide fresh water from Lake Timsah during the canal's construction and subsequently became the source of water supplies for Cairo, Port Said, and Ismailia itself. A decision was taken, therefore, to occupy the Sinai Desert's Qatiya Oasis, where, by sitting astride the most likely line of advance, a smaller number of British troops could hold back the Turks from an advance on the Canal. British occupation of the oasis area, which stretched eastwards from Romani and Qatiya to Bir el Abd, would also deprive any advancing Ottoman troops of drinking water. A forward position in the Qatiya-Romani area, as well as denying the Turks a place to assemble, would also make it possible for the British to organise a mobile column for offensive operations and prevent the enemy from bombarding the canal with long range artillery. To supply the British troops due to be pushed into the area a standard gauge railway and a pipeline of Nile water were brought out from Kantara. Camel companies consisting of 2,000 camels and donkey companies, also 2,000 strong, were organised to improve the mobility of the force, the total complement in the end reaching 35,000 camels and 8,000 donkeys. Wagon trains were also created – six divisional trains, each consisting of 72 limbered wagons[7], and two mixed horse and motor transport trains, every one capable of carrying 72 tons of supplies. As a result of this better organisation the initiative from 1916 began to pass to the British, even though they would face three stiff battles when the decision was made to advance further and take Gaza.

A number of small battles took place during the first moves into Sinai. A force of 3,650 men under von Kressenstein surprised advance posts at Qatiya, Oghratina and Hamisah on Easter Sunday, April 23rd 1916, but after some initial successes was beaten back. Earlier in the month, immediately before the raid, a combined British force had advanced into the desert to destroy wells and pumping equipment, which had made random attacks on the Canal possible. A similar sortie was carried out in June when cisterns were drained and sealed to prevent them refilling after rain. The day after the Turkish raid Australian and New

47

6) McMeekin, p270.
7) Limber, detachable front of gun or cable carriage, consisting of two wheels, axle, pole and ammunition box or cable drum.

Zealand mounted troops were deployed around Romani to patrol and reconnoitre the area and a new defensive line was drawn between Mahamdiyeh and Katib Gannet, covering Romani. Work continued, meanwhile, on extending the railway and water pipelines to support an advance across Sinai. Ottoman aircraft managed to fly over the Suez Canal a month later, dropping bombs on Port Said and inflicting 23 casualties. In reprisal the Royal Flying Corps bombed El Arish and Ottoman camps along a 45 mile front parallel with the Canal. (Further away in the region, the Turks were enjoying more success. An ill-equipped British Army, which had landed at Basra in November 1914 intending to push on to Baghdad, had reached Ctesiphon only 25 miles away but was forced by strong Turkish opposition to retreat to Kut in December. A total of 8,000 men under General Charles Townshend were surrounded and starved into surrender on April 29th 1916, despite repeated and desperate attempts to relieve them, including offers of money to the Turks. Recapture of Kut, the loss of which was seen as a humiliation for the British Army, would not come until February 1917.) In Europe, where the earlier German attempts at sweeping through to the Channel and encircling Paris had been resisted, trench warfare had now taken over. Two continuous lines of entrenchment, in some places no more than a few feet apart, now ran from Switzerland to the North Sea, behind which millions of men toiled and prepared for sallies, living in conditions of squalor, and suffering from dysentery and other new diseases, such as trench foot. In eastern France the Germans mounted a massive assault in the first half of 1916 at Verdun but were held back by French troops as good as their motto, "Ils ne passeront pas". At the same time the Germans were mounting a second offensive against the British at Ypres, fighting the Royal Navy to a draw at Jutland, and sinking by submarine large tonnages of British merchant vessels, while also engaged in a life and death struggle with the Russians to the east.[8]

Heat, Sand and Insects

By early March 1916, after the evacuation from Gallipoli, there may have been as many as 400,000 British and colonial troops (and hospital patients) in Egypt in 13 divisions of the Mediterranean Expeditionary Force and the Force in Egypt, the largest British army ever collected outside France, and the strategic reserve for the empire. During the course of the month, however, 10 divisions were sent to France. There was a change of command, too, Maxwell, previously in charge of troops in the Egyptian Delta, the Western Desert and the Sudan, handing over to Murray on March 19th. A new Egyptian Expeditionary Force was created out of the remnant of the Mediterranean Expeditionary Force and the men dispersed to various camps. The first stop after Alexandria for the brigades of the 53rd was Beni Salama, near Wardan, 40 miles north of Cairo. A report quoted by Dudley Ward described Wardan as a thoroughly uninteresting place, with a small native village on the far or east bank of the Nile, the railway line, the usual canal, "crawling with bilharzia germs", and nothing else but desert rising up to a ridge.[9] The desert, too, confounded the expectations of the newly arrived men, used to a green and verdant

---

8) Second Battle of Ypres, April 22nd to May 24th 1916; Battle of Jutland May 31st 1916. Though neither side inflicted decisive damage on the other in this latter encounter, the German Navy retired to port afterwards and Britain retained control of the surface of the sea for the rest of the war.

9) Bilharzia, a minute liver fluke present in the waters of the Nile, required the lacing of the water with chloride to make it drinkable.

homeland, by not being flat or even the same from place to place. Instead, it was a tumbled mass of sand dunes and hillocks, on a rocky limestone bed, hard enough to play football on in some places and soft as flour in others. Experience of desert was unfamiliar to British troops. "The first unpleasant shock ... was the intense heat of the day and the chill that descended as soon as the sun went down." Sandstorms were another unfamiliar hazard, like great banks of fog reducing visibility to less than a yard, making breathing difficult and cutting into faces. These could last for days and reinforced the soldiers' perception of the desert as a harsh, sterile and alien environment.[10] Beni Salama was of some strategic importance, however, to the defence of Wadi Natrun, one of the routes through which the Senussi could advance on Cairo. Royal Engineers fortified villages, built outposts, erected hutting and arranged water supplies. The Senussi emerged, however, on a different route, occupying the Baharia oasis, from which tracks led to Fayoum, only 40 miles from Cairo, precipitating another move by the 53rd on February 14th to new headquarters in this important oasis, today one of Egypt's biggest cities.[11]

Life for the 18 year old – Dewi had his birthday on March 1st, two months after arriving in Egypt – was a sometimes frustrating mixture of activities aimed at bringing the exhausted troops from Gallipoli back to full fitness and retraining. Duties, and especially fatigues, in effect military labouring jobs, could be tedious, and there were plenty of physical problems to overcome, from the flies and other insects to the heat and the sand in the desert. The obligatory regular health jabs for cholera and other diseases were another pain, not to mention continued shortages of food. As historian Niall Barr explains, soldiers adapted to the desert conditions but never learned to live with flies, which were attracted to the Army by the refuse it generated and, in particular, human waste, both very difficult to dispose of in the desert.[12] "The armies fighting in the desert found that no matter how carefully they disposed of the detritus and waste that they inevitably produced, their rubbish dumps and latrines formed perfect breeding grounds for the hordes of insects that followed the army wherever it went." Dewi found the flies even more of a problem in Egypt than they had been in the Dardanelles, increasing in numbers daily and enjoying Army jam. "When you're eating bread and jam you've got to wave it about before shoving it in your mouth," he writes from Fayoum.[13] According to another veteran quoted by Barr, "there were millions of flies, literally millions. They were in everything and on everything. They were in our food, they were in our clothing, they were in our ears, wherever we turned there were millions of flies. If you put a piece of paper down it would be black with flies in a few moments." Apart from their nuisance value, flying creatures could also cause serious illness, including dysentery, which laid many men low, as in Gallipoli. Dewi also reports being bitten by mosquitoes. "A few nights ago when I was on duty at the Signal Office I had the misfortune to get badly bitten on my hands and face by mosquitoes, as did several others. They are rotten little insects and generally attack you when asleep. You can hear their Buzz-z-z! quite distinctly. I went to our doctor and had some stuff to put on my face and I am glad to say it is nearly quite well again.

10) Bourne, J., Liddle P., Whitehead, I., (eds), *The Great World War. 1914-45*. Harper Collins, 2000. Barr, Chap. 7, The Desert Experience', p125.
11) Pritchard,(ed.), p202-3.
12) Barr, chap 7. p127.
13) March 25th 1916.

Anyhow, I don't want to experience such a thing again so have bought a mosquito net for nights."[14] The next month he has to tell his parents that he is recovering from boils on his neck and an abscess on his face, which has to be lanced. The abscess left no mark but he blames the incident – whether correct medically or not, since he may just have been in a rundown condition after the exertions of the preceding months – on the earlier mosquito bites.[15] His purchase of a net may well have been a wise precaution. The war poet, Rupert Brooke, was bitten on the lip on his way to the landing at Gallipoli, as a member of the Royal Naval Volunteer Reserve. He developed an abscess and sepsis and died on April 23rd, 1915. He was buried in an olive grove on the island of Skyros. Dewi himself describes being similarly bitten in July 1916. In a letter from Fayoum to his sister who has written a school essay on Egypt, no doubt drawing on some of his observations in the letters she had received, he warns that what the experts say is not the whole story. "I must give you one little tip about Egypt, [...] if you ever get a question on Egyptian animal life, answer it thus:- 'Egypt produced little else as regards animal life, except flies, mosquitoes, beetles, and dirty camels (with an acute accent on the "flies"). By One Who Knows.' You'll get 100% marks for that answer, if the teacher that examines your papers has a brother out here herself. These Egypteologists (?) [sic] can say what they like about that subject but what I've told you is the truth, the whole truth and nothing but the truth."[16] At Serapeum, near Ismailia, on the Canal, where the unit was based from the beginning of June until it moved north in late November, the flies were still causing annoyance and inconvenience. "You can't read, sleep or eat for them in the day time, unless you've got a net over your face, knees and arms. You'd scarcely credit what a plague they are and they can't half bite either. We have a couple of strafing stunts every day and drive 'em out with towels but, although we've nets on the door and windows, they appear again in a very short time, with plenty of reinforcements. They can't half replace casualties quickly."[17]

There is no further mention of health for several months. Indeed, virtually all his letters from the beginning to the end of his four year service are signed off with the salutation "I'm in the pink" and the hope that his parents and sister at home are similarly placed. In July, after the move to the Canal, he responds to something his father has written about his good fortune in staying fit. "Yes, Dad, thank goodness, I still continue to have the best of health all through this little trip and s'pose I must be a bit of a 'tough un', as you put it, and am sure this pleases you to know that I am quite fit and a philosopher through it all."[18] Indeed, his main encounter with the Royal Army Medical Corps during his service seems to have come when he had a bout of saddle-soreness in 1918 after riding many miles through Palestine bare-back. His own doctor from home, Dr Samuel, who had similarly signed up, attended him, though there is some doubt whether he recognised his patient or let on that he did.[19]

14) February 29th 1916. The Army did not supply nets.
15) March 25th 1916.
16) June 15th 1916.
17) July 14th 1916.
18) July 13th 1916.
19) Physician and surgeon, Dr Henry (Harry) Samuel, MRCS, LRCP, practised from 264 Newport Road, at the junction with Beresford Road, less than half a mile from the David family home.

For their part, the RAMC seem to have been the butt of pointed humour from their fellow-soldiers, being known variously as Linseed Lancers, poultice wallopers, pox doctors, scab lifters, Run Away Matron's Coming, Rather a Mediocre Crowd, Rob All My Comrades, and – in an ingenious backwards acronym – Can't Manage A Rifle. Dewi for his part seems to have had a dread of the medics, judging by his reaction to admonishments from his sister over the saddle-soreness episode. Whether jokingly or not, he tells her: "The experience will be more than sufficient, you may be sure, to guarantee my doing everything in my power to give both hospitals and surgeons a very wide berth indeed. They are co-operated in crime and work hand in glove in their nefarious designs upon their poor helpless victims with the aid of zinc and paraffin and anti-septic. The former are bad enough, every tent, marquee, bivouac, even the grub smells and tastes of chloroform, but the latter, clothes stained with chemicals and reeking of socotrine aloes, and valerianate [sic] of ammonia[20] – individually, and, as a species, I love 'em like the devil loves holy water. Never did like these poultice wallopers and medicine fiends myself. [...] Some people say that they never even kiss anybody, being in mortal terror of the germs supposed to be exchanged. Of course, it may be all rot – I'm speaking from hearsay. Why ever didn't I make myself known to Dr. Sam, did you say? – my dear young lady, I never encourage these fellows who dabble in medicine."[21]

Broke in Beni Salama

The meagre rations the 53rd Division were receiving were, no doubt, partly responsible for the somewhat jaundiced views Dewi was by now sending home. In Egypt, as in Gallipoli, the supplies needed to keep the forces going were in short supply and the surroundings were not very inspiring either. In language we would now find outdated, to say the least, but typical of contemporary attitudes, he tells his sister shortly after arriving and in response to her inquiry as to his whereabouts: "We have been dumped in the desert among the camels and Arabs and get bread and dates for dinner. [...] So, you see how very important it is that chaps spending a 'holiday' on the desert have plenty of food sent out. One thing we are thankful for and that is we are able to buy stuff at the canteens, if you've got the cash. We were in a desperate condition a few days ago, no brass, no parcels, only bare army rations (bread and dates for dinner, you know). If the fags hadn't lasted out, I don't think many would have survived but at last the welcome day arrived and when they shouted 'Fall in' for pay, not one of us was 'choked off' for not 'doubling up'. Of course, by this time some of the fellows had a terrible thirst, well, in fact, that pay parade saved the situation."[22]

He had taken the decision when he joined up to allot part of his Army pay to his mother for her to save for him, an arrangement that put him in some difficulties and which he eventually cancelled so that he could buy more of the necessities and delicacies he wanted locally. In the meantime, he relied on money they sent him in the form of postal orders. "Thanks very much for the P.O. for £1 which I received quite safely. I assure you that it was quite a godsend but it is expired [spent] by now. You see, I can't resist buying butter and such delicacies and having a few feeds

---

20) Socotrine Aloes, an extract from the leaves of A. Perryi (Baker) prepared on the island of Socotra, and on the African and Arabian mainland.
21) July 29th 1918.
22) February 6th 1916.

up town because, when you've got cash on you, Army rations aren't very tempting. But I mustn't grumble, we get bread every day."[23] Postal orders are mentioned in another letter to his parents, making it clear how important such subventions were. "I have received your 20/- order. Thanks very much for it. A few more would be very appreciable, as it comes in handy for buying grub. We don't get extra special rations and it's alright to have money to buy tinned fruit, etc. in this climate. At present, I'm broke to the wide. Of course, I don't draw much, as I send you that allotment. By the way, I hope you get it alright. I may say also that things aren't very cheap out here."[24] Home-made delicacies in such circumstances were much appreciated. "Auntie's [cake] is reposing behind me as I write (or rather part of it). I'm keeping that parch [pristine] until tomorrow, chewing every morsel about fifty times to have the taste as long as possible. I tell you, we go daft out here when we get home made cake." In a letter the same day to his sister he comments on some remarks his cousin Beat's fiancé, Hughie, also on service on Egypt had made, that Dewi had grown. "Well, I suppose I have sprung up a little but as for getting fat, Oh dear, no, Dolly, you don't get fat on bread and jam and skilly."

A day's leave in Cairo, the ancient sites, bazaars, restaurants, pleasure parks and fleshpots of which would, however, become familiar to thousands of British troops during the two world wars, had raised spirits in February while he was at Beni Salama camp. Service in the Near East for all its hardships did bring the possibility of seeing distant places that an ordinary British 17 year old could only visualise from film shows in the rapidly developing cinema industry back home. The visit seems to have been his first day's leave away from camp since setting sail in October the previous year. "We left the camp by train in the morning and had until 5 pm in that town.[25] In that time we managed to take a trip to the Pyramids and the Sphinx. [...] The Pyramids are about an hour's ride by tram from Cairo and after seeing all the tombs etc. of the old Egyptian kings we returned to Cairo again, not before, however, we had had our photographs taken on camels in front of the Sphinx. After returning to Cairo we visited the old bazaars, which are very interesting and a mosque, doing the round of the city in a carriage. We got back to camp safely, and thoroughly satisfied with our day's outing." His sister later writes to ask if he had seen the Mummies but he has to disappoint her. "No, Doll, I didn't see the Mummies but later on, if I get to Cairo again, I intend visiting the museum to see them. Of course, you know the British Museum in London has collared most of 'em. When I come home again we'll go up there to have a deco [dekko]," he writes.[26]

Bivouacs in Fayoum

Fayoum, in contrast with Beni Salama, was a green oasis 60 miles south of Cairo, separated from the River Nile by a narrow stretch of desert, and skirted on its northern side by a large lake fed by the Bahr Yusef, a tributary of the Nile. Fayoum itself is "the most picturesque of the places we saw in our Levantine travels. Who will forget the great silvery palms, gently rustling, as the cool evening breeze came

23) March 2nd 1916.
24) March 25th 1916.
25) February 16th 1916. Train carriages were basic and open, to allow air to circulate.
26) April 7th 1916.

softly breathing over the hot fields and sweltering villages – a sigh of relief after the grilling heat of the day," an officer is quoted as saying in the Divisional history. "Who will forget the lazy, querulous creaking of the water wheel, the sweet fragrance of the flowering bean fields, and the glorious sunsets."[27] For the ordinary soldier, arriving after a journey through the surrounding desert, it will have been a pleasant enough spot, unaware it was a place of considerable historical importance in its own right, and scene of a number of ancient discoveries. Its treasures include Mummy drawings, said to be the world's first true life portraits, possibly the first paved road in the world, dating back more than 4,500 years, ancient Ptolemaic waterwheels used to irrigate fields, and what was probably the world's first dam, built to control the Nile's floods.[28] Successive occupants, including the British, were there because of its location in a fertile valley where roads, and, later, the local canals and the rail networks, converged.[29] By co-incidence, the modern region that has grown around the small town of 100 years ago agreed to a memorandum of understanding in 2010 with the University of Wales Institute of Cardiff (now Cardiff Metropolitan University) to create a new international university in Egypt.

There were, however, practical problems facing men in camp. They were not issued with tables, and had only candles to light their bivouacs, so letter writing was difficult. A month on he was having to rise at 5.30 am and be in the stables to groom the horses by 6 am. "Try and beat that Dad, but, of course, I am quite hardened now after all these months at a similar programme. On parade again at 9 am, shaved, and with clean arms. Then comes the usual fatigues, but we have a rest in the afternoon, too hot to work, and perhaps a guard duty in the evening, mounting at 6 pm."[30] Particularly when camped in desert, fatigues were needed to keep the blown sand at bay. Fatigues and marches had the secondary purpose, however, of hardening the soldiers for the marching and the campaigning that lay ahead. His duties, too, changed, and must have come as a shock to a town boy. Early in March he was assigned to work with the many horses the Army kept for use in the desert. In the absence of roads – and motor vehicles – horses and camels were by default the main forms of transport. A few days earlier he had told Doris that he has been cured of any problems of getting out of bed in the morning, facing the choice of a 6 am reveille or a field punishment. "I don't want to be strapped to a wheel for being late on parade," he writes.[31]

He was no doubt jesting but Field Punishment for more serious offences could be surprisingly harsh. Introduced in 1881 following the abolition of flogging, it was a common punishment during World War One, a conflict in which the death penalty for desertion was also imposed. A commanding officer could award field punishment for up to 28 days, while a court martial could award it for up to 90

---

27) Dudley Ward, p54.

28) The site was known to the Greeks as Crocodilopolis, because of its role as a centre for the worship in the Pharaonic era of Sobek, the crocodile-god. Named Petsuchos, and embellished with gold and gems, the crocodile lived in a special temple, with sand, a pond and food. When the Petsuchos died, it was replaced by another.

29) The first railway system connected Fayoum in 1874 with the Nile Valley and a network of light (small gauge) railways that ran throughout the province. Around the turn of the 20th century the British built good roads and revised the irrigation system, reclaiming some land for agriculture.

30) March 2nd 1916.

31) March 2nd, February 29th 1916.

days, either as Field Punishment Number One or Field Punishment Number Two. F.P. No. 1 consisted of the convicted man being placed in fetters and handcuffs or similar restraints and attached to a fixed object, such as a gun wheel, for up to two hours per day. During the early part of World War One, the punishment was often applied with the arms stretched out and the legs tied together, giving rise to the nickname "crucifixion". This was applied for up to three days out of four, up to 21 days total. It was usually applied in field punishment camps set up for this purpose a few miles behind the front line but, when the unit was on the move, it would be carried out by the unit itself. During the war F.P. No. 1 was issued by the British Army on 60,210 occasions. F.P. No. 2 placed the prisoner placed in fetters and handcuffs but he was not attached to a fixed object and was still able to march with his unit. In both forms of field punishment, the soldier was also subjected to hard labour and loss of pay. F.P. No. 1 was eventually abolished in 1923, when an amendment to the Army Act, which specifically forbade attachment to a fixed object, was passed by the House of Lords. However, physical restraint remained a theoretical (though rarely imposed) possibility.

Fayoum did have some sympathies with the Senussis. But, as a small town, it also had the advantage, of being "civilisation", with its own restaurants, and Dewi's mood becomes correspondingly cheery. "The only drawback here is the water, which has to be filtered and boiled before use, and is, of course, scarce, otherwise we like the place very much." They were also allowed in the town and thus able to make necessary purchases, and also get a few decent meals in the principal restaurant, he reports. The troops were evidently welcomed by local expatriates. "A few nights ago a few of us went to an American resident's house who had invited us to tea, and we had a very decent time, finishing up with a bit of a concert. We all thought it was very decent of them and also appreciated their kindness very much. They were evidently not 'too proud' to entertain us."[32] His next letter comments on some mocking remarks that must have come back to him "I haven't been out visiting since I wrote you last and by the tone or your last letter about my giving a song, I venture to think that you're making fun of my bass voice. The three of you have been having a fine laugh at my expense, I expect, with Dad as ringleader. What would you say if I told you that I had given renderings of *Rocked in the Cradle of the Deep* and Tosti's *Farewell* at that house?"[33] I learnt the latter while listening to Gorwel's gramophone when I was home last. You know how it goes, 'Goodbye Summer, Goodbye, Goodbye'. My word, I created a fine impression on the company. The hostess wept but some rude chaps who were there said she did so through laughing so much. However, be that as it may, I reckon I paid dearly for that tea. It was a deuce of a struggle to get down to the final 'Beware' in the first song." The British and American residents of Fayoum later opened a reading and writing room that British troops could use, where, according to Dewi, they were able to see all the recent magazines and periodicals and pass away a few hours in the evening very

---

32) February 20th 1916.

33) April 7th 1916. *Rocked in the Cradle,* a popular Victorian hymn, written by Emma C. Willard 1787-1870 during an ocean voyage, music by Joseph Knight 1812-1887. 'Rocked in the cradle of the deep, I lay me down in peace to sleep; Secure I rest upon the wave, For Thou, O Lord, hast power to save. I know Thou wilt not slight my call, For Thou dost mark the sparrow's fall.' *Farewell* was the most famous work by Italian song composer, Francesco Paolo Tosti (1846-1916). Gorwel was their next door neighbour in Splott.

enjoyably. The use of the writing room made it possible, he remarks, to send a letter written in ink and not pencil for the first time since he had been on active service. "Though I'd forgotten the way with a pen. A shovel's more my line now," he adds.[34]

At least the weather was improving as Spring arrived. In January the weather in Greece had been cold under canvas in the mornings, and at night, but a month later in Beni Salama he was re-assuring his mother that he was OK for underclothes, which were regularly issued, but with the weather warm not much needed.[35] The weather is ideal two weeks later and the issue shortly of helmets and khaki drill hints at much warmer weather to come. In his next letter he says most of the men had bought khaki cotton shirts – the only article of underclothing that was bearable in the heat. By March the weather, in contrast with the snowfall in Britain, is "melting", even though it was still only Spring.[36] By now he had received the Balaclava helmet and socks he had requested, while on Gallipoli, for the very different weather conditions there. The former was too hot to wear but the latter, he writes, are "jolly useful".

Huts and Showers in Helio

The next move brought a change to very different and even warmer surroundings and the chance to enjoy the delights of being closer to the Egyptian capital, where divisional headquarters, and 53rd Signals had moved by mid-April. "We have left Fayoum and are now at Abbassia near Heliopolis and within a tram-ride of Cairo. It's great, I can tell you.[37] We can drink water here without being afraid of getting poisoned. Plenty of it, pure, good and clean, doesn't want filtering, boiling etc., like at Fayoum. Plenty of wash stands, and, listen! – shower baths. Couldn't believe it at first, 'sglorious and further, we've given up tents, living in cool huts of rushes. Lovely, we have a separate one for a mess, too. Well, it's absolutely A1. Then we get up at 4.30 am, on parade at 5, and work till brekker, rifle inspection at 9 am and we've finished for the day except feeding the nags dinner and teatime. You see, it's too hot to work during the day and we appreciate the arrangements. Above all, I must tell you the bread is glorious, not sour at all like before, and we revel in it. Funny how you talk about good bread and water after seeing 'life' on active service, ain't it? But I haven't finished, Oh No, we only got to walk into Helio' and there's open air 'baksheesh'[38] cinemas, and cafes and ices and pop – Oh Lummy, I could go on for hours like this. Feel like a kid after being to St. Mellons, S'help me, I do."[39] There were still discomforts to bear, however. In May he describes a heat wave, suggesting the weather had become even hotter than was normally expected. Other reports mention temperatures at the time as high as 123 degrees Fahrenheit in the shade, uncomfortably hot at any time but particularly for men living in tents in the open countryside. "The perspiration has been rolling off us. You sweat just as much sitting down doing nothing as you would if working hard, and Oh! what thirsts

34) April 5th 1916.
35) January 13th 1916. February 6th, 20th, 23rd 1916.
36) March 25th 1916.
37) Polygon Camp, Abbassia. He moved from Fayoum April 16th.
38) Baksheesh, usually a tip or gratuity, but here and elsewhere in the sense 'free'.
39) April 28th 1916. St. Mellons, a village east of Cardiff and one of the family's favourite places for a walk and a picnic.

we've all got. It's been just like an oven. I thought I was acclimatized by now but this beats everything."[40]

Heliopolis made a big impression after the rigours of the peninsula and the desert. The town (Sun City in Greek) had been planned as a place of luxury and pleasure by the Belgian industrialist, Baron Edouard Louis Joseph, whose Heliopolis Oases Company had created wide avenues, complete with water, drainage, and electricity from 1906 onwards. Visitor accommodation was provided by the luxurious Heliopolis House Palace Hotel, using furniture from the famous British furnishers, Maples.[41] Built in the open desert between 1908 and 1910, it had 400 lavishly furnished rooms, including 55 private apartments and was intended as the supreme expression of the new town's architectural style. Other facilities included a racetrack, golf course and park, and houses for rent in a variety of designs for different social classes, as well as apartments, tenement houses with balconies, and bungalows for the workers of the company. Cairo's attractions also proved very welcome after the desert. "Saw the zoo and had a feed at Anzac Hotel. Spiffing place, opened for us blighters in the King's Armee. You can eat apples till you're sick of 'em there for nixes,[42] and the waitresses – Oh my! waited on 'and an' foot by the ladies of the land, actresses and millionairesses and 'Eaven knows who. We're in clover here, no getting away from it. Concerts in the Y.M. [YMCA] and all the rest of it. Tomato sandwiches, 1 piastre. Tell you straight, we're treated like kids, gettin' petted too much and gettin' soft again but somehow or other the C.S.M is always here to pull you up with a jerk on parade, an' remind you you're his for a bob, body and soul.[43] That's the only thing that spoils the harmony or else you'd think you were home, 'aving such a reel [sic] good time." Other soldiers' letters describe the pedlars thronging the streets, selling carpets, oranges, cigarettes, roses, rabbits, cakes, beds and all manner of goods. The zoo and the bazaar were among the wonders of Cairo that troops found most appealing, one particular attraction being Saïd, the hippo, who answered to his keeper's call. The Anzac Hostel was another magnet, through which thousands of troops passed. It could accommodate 300-400 men a night but sometimes took in as many as 700.[44] Formerly the building of the Cairo Bourse, it was open day and night for three and a half years. The YMCA, its funds supplemented by the Government and by the British and Australian Red Cross, was to play an important part in keeping British forces in Egypt entertained and away from the all too available temptations of a less salubrious kind. In addition to building a soldiers' club on the quay at Alexandria, the YMCA took a lease on the Ezbekiah Gardens in Cairo. These boasted an open air theatre, a restaurant and an outdoor swimming pool – a gift from the US – as well as a cinema, concerts, plays, billiards, roller skating and

40) May 16th 1916.

41) The Heliopolis Palace Hotel opened as Africa's most luxurious hotel on December 1st 1910, and became a travel destination for foreign royals and international business tycoons. In the two world wars the hotel was transformed into a military hospital for British and Dominion soldiers. Closed in the 1960s, it housed the offices of various government departments. In January 1972 the building became the headquarters of the Federation of Arab Republics – the short-lived political union between Egypt, Libya and Syria. In the 1980s, after renovation it became an Egyptian presidential palace, and headquarters of President Hosni Mubarak's administration. In February 2011 it became the focus for demonstrations that overthrew the Egyptian president later that year.

42) Nixes, nothing.

43) April 28th 1916. C.S.M., Company Sergeant Major. Bob, slang for one shilling, equivalent at the time of UK decimalisation in 1971 to 5 new pence. A reference to the King's Shilling, the 'earnest', or inducement, pressed on soldiers to bind them to the Army.

44) Mortlock, p37.

various games. The aim of the YMCA was to offer fighting men a means of satisfying their "homing instinct". "The camp sing-songs, the entertainments, the canteens, the writing-rooms, the religious services, were all directed definitely to draw men's thoughts away from the hard business of fighting and to remind them of home."[45] There was always a threat to the good times, however, and not just in the burly form of the C.S.M. "I expect they'll shift us soon, that's their way when they sees swoddies[46] livin' like staff officers. I expect they'll politely ask the Turks to start scrappin' again for our benefit to make us hard and then we'll have to start the old game, making rissoles out of bully and biscuits like iron. Shove it in a mess-tin, it'll make something, as we used to say. Anyhow, you needn't entertain the slightest worry on my behalf, as you can see we can complain of nothing and are having the best time we've ever had yet."[47] His fears were, indeed, realised. They were obliged "after five weeks of bliss" to leave what he describes as the "the best and finest camp in all Egypt", where he could, he says, have stayed till the end of the war, when the posting to the Canal – and a return to tents and the end of showers – came through. On May 27th the bulk of the Division was ordered to take over No. 2 Section Canal Defences from the 2nd Anzac Division and headquarters was transferred to Moascar on the Canal. This left only the 159th Brigade to the west dealing with the remaining threat from the Senussi.

Yearning for Action

From their first arrival in Egypt after the disappointment of Gallipoli, and as they settled down into the drudgery of training, fatigues, and garrison duty in the desert, he and his fellow-soldiers were clearly feeling some (misguided, as we can now see) envy at the lot of men sent to France, which appeared at that stage a much more glamorous adventure. After describing his travels to date as a Cook's World Tour, he wrote from Fayoum that he was tired of his surroundings, somewhere he would remain for a further three years. "You say in your letter that you hope I stop in Egypt. Well, I don't know – I wouldn't mind a change now. I've seen enough of the Near East. You see the wandering habit has taken such a hold on us that we like a change now and again. It would be alright if we got to France, wouldn't' it? More honours. You see, here we are in Egypt on garrison duty and other units are making a name for themselves."[48] A few months later, he was still wishing he was somewhere else. With the confidence of one who was unfamiliar with the full horrors of the Western Front, he wishes he was where his wounded cousin, Tom Jenkins, had been in France.[49] In a letter from Serapeum he again regrets not being nearer the action, despite more news of injuries to his cousin, who was shot and gassed in France and spent much of his life an invalid sitting in a chair coughing. Indeed, Dewi seems to have begun by this stage to have relished the image of himself as a hardened soldier, and the polite timidity of his early letters home has, after a year's service, disappeared. His language, too, has changed – his letters now increasingly full of soldier slang and abbreviations. Letters to his sister were written in a joking way, clearly intended to amuse. "You were saying in your letter about

45) *Service with Fighting Men.* YMCA. Quoted by Mortlock. p.37.
46) Swaddies, swoddies, ordinary soliders.
47) April 28th 1916.
48) February 29th 1916.
49) April 7th 1916.

not knowing me when I return home and Dad even hinted at my keeping a Charlie Chaplin moustache. What if you find me a rough looking bullet-headed scoundrel? By the way, I've just had all my hair off and look like a Hun or Convict 99. It's alright Mum, don't scold, it'll grow again alright, don't you worry, and when I come home I shall plaster it with Brilliantine and part it down the middle, wear loud socks and pegtop trousers – be a proper Knut.[50] By the way, I've got an awful pair of pants at present, as baggy as anything, my breeches are being mended, you see."

The subject of his personal appearance comes up again in April. "You are very much relieved, it seems, that I haven't grown a 'hirsute decoration on my upper lip' (think that's the phrase). Well, Doll, I did once make a bet with a chap on Gallipoli, I'd grow one before him. So, we started, I trained mine with bacon fat and Batcher's apricot jam, anything to wax it. Of course, we didn't have many conveniences out there, like tubes of pomade like Dad buys, so had to use the first thing to hand. Well, the time allowed was one month, if I remember rightly, and mine was coming on A1, but woe is me, a few days before the month was up I was outside my dug out and all of a sudden a shell came along, took my Charlie Chaplin moustache clean off. I was awfully cut up about it and, of course, had to hand over the stakes, a packet of 'Tabs' and a cap badge to the other chap. That's why I've never tried to grow one since but I wormed the secret out of the other chap, how he'd grown his. It seems he had trained it in all his spare moments with a pot of chicken and ham paste sent out by his adoring Aunt Priscilla. Some day I'll try that dodge. (I guess Mum won't send me any paste *now*.)"[51] A month later he is begging his father not to tell "those girls in the P.O. about my hirsutal appendage and what I used to force the upper lip adornment. That is for your private consumption. They may think me a bit of an ass, p'raps, you never know, sarcastic creatures these young ladies. Why, I've already been offered a bottle of pomade or some such luxury for cultivating the growth. Serious, this, you know, when I got the letter offering it, I had the breeze up, I can tell you, and shaved the whole blooming lot off straightaway."[52]

A Bright Lot of 'Erbs

The rather world-weary view he developed of Egypt seems to have stemmed mainly from the sheer monotony of army life that he had complained about consistently since his long passage by sea to the Near East. He particularly disliked telephone work, one of his duties while at Fayoum, possibly because of the demanding nature of the officers he was trying to put into contact with each other. With not much happening he also found there was little news to report. "We do duty here in the Signal Office, which is on the railway station, and do not have a very strenuous

50) March 25th 1916 to Doris. Brilliantine was created around the turn of the 20th century by French perfumer, Edouard Pinaud, to soften and shine men's hair. The head shaving might have been to avoid head lice, a known problem among troops.
   A great fashion shift in 1908 brought important changes to both men's and women's silhouettes, including the introduction of a tapered look from the hips to the ankles. Pegging, creating width in the hips and closeness at the hem, was popular up to the beginning of World War One. www.fashionencyclopedia.com Knut, Victorian slang for a fashionable young man about town. Derived from a popular song about a subaltern who took undue care over his appearance by Arthur Wimperis (1874-1953). 'I'm Gilbert, the filbert, the Colonel of the Knuts.'
51) April 13th 1916.
52) May 31st 1916.

time," he had written from Fayoum.[54] A general dislike of Egypt – by May "a rotten old place" – extended to its people, Egyptian and Arab, and the extensive network of Greek traders alike. Before leaving for the Near East, 17 year-old Dewi's contacts with people from outside Britain would have been confined to the seamen from the Gulf and from the Indian sub-Continent living in Cardiff Docks – Lascars as they were then popularly known. His job had involved delivering telegrams to the boarding houses where many of them lodged, perhaps recalling them to a ship due to leave Cardiff with a cargo of coal or sending them to a different port elsewhere in Britain. Before the telephone had become widespread, a message sent down telegraph wires and pasted on to a form for delivery in an envelope by a uniformed telegraph boy on a bicycle was the speediest way of communicating messages. His conversations would most probably have been pleasant, or even jocular, but perfunctory. Away from Butetown, the streets of Cardiff were almost entirely white, even though the 1911 census had shown the city to be exceeded only by London in the size of its overseas-born population. British people at the time, however humble their status in life, were, however, imbued with attitudes of superiority towards all other races, including most other Europeans, it has to be said, and the views Dewi expresses about the people he encountered in foreign parts will have been representative of his times and the society he inhabited. They vary from the dismissive to the patronising and, not to put too fine a point on it, what would nowadays be branded racist. The language used includes words which were common then but unacceptable now, and he has no compunction in one of his letters, when thanking his Mum for a parcel containing his favourite iced cakes, to write he would like to do the clinging ivy stunt (presumably hug her), if she didn't object to his "lip being à la Sambo owing to a mosquito bite".[55]

Apart from the general quaintness – to European eyes at any rate – of some of the peoples he met, one of the main characteristics, as Dewi saw it, was a desire to fleece the poor British soldier. Whether this was the case or not, traders throughout history have seen an opportunity to make money out of armies on the move: the other side of the coin was that the British solider, if Dewi was typical, was usually broke. Throughout his letters there are repeated references to his own lack of cash. His letters are peppered with complaints about the price of goods, requests for Postal Orders, thanks for receipt of the same, and references to lack of funds.[56] He had a lucky break in March, however, when he seems to have received a 20th birthday pay increment. The year 1916 in truth only marked his 18th but he had put his date of birth two years back in order to join up. Money was needed not for luxuries but for many necessities, including food and other supplies that the Army seems not to have had the capacity to deliver, given the large number of divisions refitting in Egypt after Gallipoli and joining from Australia and India. The Army experienced considerable difficulties maintaining an adequate supply of food to soldiers across the Channel on the Western Front: the problems of getting sufficient calories out to Egypt, more than 2,000 miles away, were even more severe.

59

---

53) February 20th 1916. The Signal Office seems to have been a low hut built of sandbags, not much bigger than a detached garage, in which a unit of six worked.
54) July 27th 1918.
55) January 2nd, February 6th, 20th, 23rd, 29th; March 25th, April 5th 1916.

Egypt was, naturally, a source of fascination to his parents and especially his sister. Writing from Fayoum not long after arriving in Egypt, he tells his sister, "So Hughie has been writing you about the bazaars and natives. He is quite right and, as Dad says, they are practically only half civilised. Worse than that, in fact, and they don't half do you down, if they get the chance with these rotten old piastres. We call 'em 'disasters' and they are, too, no kid. A quid here lasts about as long as five bob in England. Very 'disastrous' for us, I can assure you. You see, a piastre is worth tuppence ha'penny [roughly one decimal penny] and we can't help looking on 'em as pennies. If you have a bottle of lemonade, one piaster, $2^1/_2$d gone west, bang straight off the reel. And, that's why we're so abso-blooming-utter-lutely stoney always.[56] Most of those he met were what he describes as "Mohammedans" but others who had been converted would, he writes, "proudly show you a cross tattooed on their wrists and say, 'Me Christian, Johnny'. Yes, they always call us Johnnies, shouting out in the 'shahrias' (streets) as you pass, 'Sae-eda Johnnie'. (Good-day). And they come up and pester you to let them clean your boots, saying 'Butts cleen'. I s'pose they mean 'Clean your boots?'. Then we either say 'Imshy-yallah', which means 'Buzz off, vamoose, skiddadle', or 'Bukra' (tomorrow), sarcastic, like. Oh! we are seeing life, I can tell you."

Their attachment to religion also fails to impress. "The Moslems are very pious, though, if taking a praying carpet out in the street and kneeling down bumping your forehead against the pavement has anything to do with it, but I doubt whether they're always so devoted. They seem to like English fags because they always pester us for 'Cigaretta baksheesh Engleezi,' which translated from the Ancient Greek means, 'Give us a fag, gratis'. Well-educated, we're getting, believe me." Sometimes when they went for rations, horse's fodder etc. locals could be persuaded to carry the lot in return for a 'Cigaretta baksheesh'. "By the way, it's a deuce of a heavy job, sacks of bran etc.," he adds. Another sight surprises him. "The inhabitants of the outlying villages pass along the road by our camp going to market in the town and it's always the donkey or the woman who carries the load. The man, her husband, rides on another donk, doing and carrying nothing. Lazy blighters, what? Anyhow, 'nuff said about the Arabs, we'll pass on to more pleasant topics, they're a bright lot of 'erbs, I must say." His advice to anybody coming to Egypt is, bring plenty of 'tin', go to Shepheard's Hotel, Cairo, and stick there.[57] "You'll only spoil a holiday coming up the line as far as we are, to study the peculiar customs and manners of 'John Cherry Blossom'. My next holiday I think will be amidst the mountains and valleys 'o'r Gogledd yn Gwalia wen' [of the North in fair Wales]. You'll come, won't you Doll, and help me forget 'the call of the East'? You've heard these traveller Johnnies say that, haven't you, in books. Blessed if I know where the 'call' comes in. They must mean the 'Far East'."

56) April 13th 1916.

57) Tin, slang for money. Shepheard's Hotel, established in 1841 by Englishman Samuel Shepheard, became Cairo's leading hotel and one of the most celebrated in the world between the middle of the 19th century and 1952, famed for its grandeur and opulence and as the place where international aristocracy and celebrity elites sipped tea on the terrace. After service as the British headquarters in World War One, and as the rendez-vous place for allied officers, politicians and spies during World War Two, the hotel was destroyed in the Cairo fire of 1952 but rebuilt in 1957 on its present location in classic style.

Cosmopolitan Cairo

The women he met during his time in the Near East were as different as could be imagined from the women office workers he knew in Cardiff, or his sister and her friends. In an earlier letter from Fayoum he explains the social distinctions he had observed. "Well, Dolly, you can see and form a slight opinion of Egypt + Egyptians now you have seen Kismet.[58] How did you like it? It's quite true about the veils, yashmaks they call them out here, the ladies of the well-to-do class wear them but the poorer classes don't, instead they wear bangles round their ankles and their feet bare, also they have rings through their noses and are invariably tattooed on the lower lip and chin. (Silly fatheads.) It's all very funny at first but you soon get to take no notice of them, instead you stare at any European ladies who happen to pass, which isn't often. As for my taking a liking to any of those young ladies, as you suggested, not me. Wait till I get back to Cardiff. They're the best, can't beat 'em, Doll. By the way, you must be getting quite a young lady yourself by now. When I went to Cairo I visited the bazaar, just as you saw at Kismet. It's a very famous bazaar and awfully quaint, as you can imagine. They have bazaars in all Egyptian towns, they even have one here in this outlandish place."

Doris clearly had a view of Cairo as a primitive place. "You seemed surprised to hear of tramcars in Cairo, why, Dolly, it's a deuce of a big place, when you come in by tram, it's almost like entering Paddington." In fact, European influence had been strong for more than 30 years and Cairo physically resembled many of the great Continental cities. Indeed, after his first visit he had written of the Egyptian capital: "The population consists solely of Egyptians and Arabs but there are some decent buildings here."[59] An American missionary had noted about this time that a modern European Christian city was arising in Moslem, Arab Cairo, its broad boulevards, ornate private homes, cool green parks, palm-girt avenues and elegant administrative buildings suggesting Paris, Lisbon and other handsome capitals.[60] The programme for the concert given in Alexandria by the 53rd Division Welsh Male Voice Choir in January 1919 tells the same story, its pages containing advertisements for very British – and, indeed, some Welsh-sounding businesses then operating in Alexandria and in Cairo. Opposite the list of popular Welsh airs, piano and violin solos to be performed by the servicemen we find 'Davies, Bryan' "the old established British firm," offering everything for kit renewal," "uniforms cut to order or ready to wear in Gabardine, whipcord, drill etc." plus camp beds, Wolsley valises, sleeping bags, shirts, caps, ties and other men's clothing requirements – with branches in Cairo, Alexandria, Port Said and Khartoum. Overleaf, the very obviously Welsh retailer, 'Roberts, Hughes', established 1903, catered for all requirements in the sporting line for tennis, cricket, football and boxing. The latter were still there at the time of World War Two, announcing themselves in the Services Guide to Alexandria as sole agents for Mappin & Webb, the London silverware merchants. Even 'Francois Frigieri', operating from one of the main shopping thoroughfares, Boulevard Saad Zaghlouol, describes itself as a "British firm", selling Dunlop garden hose and Yale locks, among other ironmongery and garden implements.

58) March 25th 1916. *Kismet* (Fate or Destiny in Turkish and Urdu), a three-act play written in 1911 by Edward Knoblauch (later Knoblock), ran for two years on the London stage. The story was made into the 1953 musical of the same name.
59) February 16th 1916.
60) Mortlock, p31.

In the early years of the 20th century Egypt had a domestic population of 12m people, living in teeming cities close to the banks of the Nile. Among them, however, was a large expatriate population that had been responsible for bringing modern commercial developments to a huge country four times the size of Britain. In Cairo and Alexandria lived 57,000 Greeks, 40,000 Italians, 24,000 British, 21,000 French, 4,000 Russian and 25,000 others. They led lives largely separate from the native population: expatriates accused of crimes went before a separate consular system outside the Egyptian legal system.[61] The Greeks, in whose hands much of trade rested, Dewi regarded no more highly than the local Egyptians and Arabs, having a similar reputation for driving a very hard bargain. He puts the failure to receive a photo he had had taken in Cairo down to the photographer being Greek. "As regards my own photo on a camel it hasn't come from Cairo yet. I have written to the photographer but am afraid they are lost, he was a Greek, you see, so that puts the matter in a nutshell. So, I shall have to have it taken again, when I get some cash."[62] Reflecting later on his purchase of a scarf for his sister he prides himself on "making the Gippo pull down all the boxes", so that he could view the widest possible selection.[63]

An inability to converse with ordinary Egyptians cannot have helped and it is not clear what, if any, training British soldiers had in dealing or conversing with the people they encountered. Dewi tells his sister in another letter – whether ironically or not is not clear – that "we are all making great strides in the Arabic and Egyptian lingo". Just after St. David's Day he mentions his Arabic again. In such an outlandish hole as this I don't s'pose they know of a St David. Anyway, two old Arabs were awfully anxious to know what I wore in my cap and what for.[64] Of course, I told 'em the tale by signs and my fluent knowledge of Arabic. Personally, I have no trouble at all with my Arabic but the Arabs have." He probably made a few initial attempts to learn some words but not much more than was needed to ask for basic essentials or to understand the calls shouted out to visiting troops in Cairo and on other visits to centres of population. Relations between the British and the Egyptians were the worst in the whole Empire, observers have noted, the two sides disliking and finding difficulty detecting virtues in each other. Indeed, serious unrest occurred in Egypt during 1917-18. "The Egyptians regarded the British as invaders who had moved in by force. The best revenge was to plunder the soldiers as much as possible. The British on their side regarded the Egyptians as lazy and corrupt, ungrateful for schemes for their benefit," argues historian Colin Cross. The Egyptians became actual objects of hatred among many British soldiers in a manner that happened nowhere else in the British Empire.[65] Britain, of course, had made many promises to leave Egypt but departed only after the overthrow of the last king, Farouk, by Colonel Abdul Gamel Nasser, in 1954, an event that precipitated the Suez crisis of 1956, the last time Britain involved itself directly in Egyptian affairs.[66] The alternative view is that after 1882 Britain had at least brought stability to a country previously bankrupt and racked by civil war under

61) Cross, p111.
62) March 25th 1916. To Doris.
63) May 14th 1916.
64) April 5th 1916. Probably a leek, worn by Welsh soldiers on March 1st for St. David's Day.
65) Cross, p111.
66) Wilson, p51.

weak Turkish leadership, putting its finances on a sound basis and bringing in an era of law, order and prosperity unknown for centuries, all with a pre-war garrison of only 5,000 men, backed by the largely British-trained and officered Egyptian army and police. Britain, too, had restored and improved irrigation and provided ports, railways and other public utilities.[67]

By the middle of May Dewi's time in Camp Abbassia was drawing to a close but not before he had had a change of job and an opportunity to mix more closely with native Egyptians and, for once, get a better supply of food. For a short while – probably never having had the need to cook for himself at home – he finds himself in the mess and assigned two Egyptian helpers: "I have been initiated into the most noble brotherhood of mess orderlies, my --- I've got it --- escutcheon now being stew dixies rampant, crest – cross soup ladles.[68] It's a very important job, I can tell you, and my – haw! – staff, consists of another sapper and two Egyptians, namely Ahmed and Mahaman, whose job is to clean up and wash tables while we dish out the chuck.[69] My word, you ought to see me at mealtimes, a ladle in one hand and a mug in the other shouting, 'Any more for any more'. 'Roll up, roll up'. They come from stables like hungry wolves when they see the grub and it's a deuce of a job keeping 'em in a queue. But I'm aisy [sic], there's one advantage, mess orderly gets plenty of grub, you know – Ah! Not a word. DED is there every time." It was a job which he quickly realised enabled him to feed himself better than might otherwise be the case. His letter includes a newspaper cutting of a poem about the cook looking after Harry Smith – who turns out to be himself. "All you've got to do is substitute DED for Harry Smith and you'll comprunny," he writes.

Writing to his sister shortly afterwards he adopts the more familiar, and perhaps even boastful, approach one would expect from an older brother. Replying to remarks she has made, he responds: "So you don't think you'll want tuition in 'graft' pick and shovel? Well I don't mind teaching you how to drink iced lemonades to try and keep cool. I'd be a jolly good instructor, I can tell you." He is still enjoying the break that his job in the kitchens offers. "Well, thank heavens, I haven't got to work hard here." You wouldn't know your bad old brother amongst the pots and pans in his shirtsleeves and cook's pants on." Home, however, is still very much in his thoughts."So Mary is spliced [married] now then? Good luck to 'em, says I, but don't forget, old girl, if there's any marzipan knocking about, don't give it to Gorwel's dog next door, send it out here. It'll go down alright with bully beef. Shove it in a dixie and boil it all up."[70] Mess Orderly was just one job a lowly sapper could be called upon to perform during his service and in the course of four years Dewi's occupations went well beyond those for which he had been recruited. By the end of May his mess duties were over and his unit was on its way to Serapeum for Canal garrison duties. He would stay there for the next five months until the British went on the offensive against the Turks, re-occupying Sinai and advancing on Gaza.

63

67) Pritchard, (ed.), p161.
68) Dixie, cooking pot for field kitchen use.
69) Chuck, food.
70) May 16th 1916.

(left) Dewi, in tropical kit, probably taken in a Cairo studio during 1916.

(below) Dewi (centre) on Cairo leave March 1916 - an opportunity to visit the zoo, the Pyramids, ancient mosques and the bazaars.

(below) Anzac Hostel, Cairo, previously the Cairo Bourse, where men from Britain, Australia and New Zealand could get a meal, a bed or a relaxing drink and a read while on leave.

(bottom) Cairo, the mosques of Sultan Hassan and El-Rifai, one of a selection of contemporary postcards soldiers could buy to send home.

CAIRO. - General view with the mosques of Sultan Hassan and El-Rifai.

(above) Dewi on his "refractory steed". When not signalling and cable-laying, he was regularly employed looking after horses and camels.

More Postcards – (right) Cairo, Tomb of the Khalifs.

(below) Cairo, The Sphinx and the Pyramid of Cheops.

EGYPT. – The Sphinx and the Pyramid of Cheops.

CHAPTER FOUR

GUARDING THE CANAL

MAY – DECEMBER 1916

The Pendulum Swings

Dewi's stay in "the best and finest camp in all Egypt", at Abbassia near Heliopolis, came to an end on May 26th with the order to move to Spinney Wood, Ismailia, a then recently developed town roughly half way along the Suez Canal. A transfer came a few days later to a more permanent camp at Serapeum, a few miles to the south between Ismailia and the Great Bitter Lake. Several months of relative inactivity followed, leading to boredom and disillusion on the part of the troops stationed there, enlivened only by the opportunities to indulge in swimming and other sports. They would have to wait for most of 1916 for the decision to join the gathering offensive against the Turks in Sinai, and for some real soldiering again. In the meantime, the British presence at newly fortified points along the Canal was intended to deter Turco-German assaults.

After being pushed back from Qatiya in April, the main Turkish force in summer 1916 had lain behind a line of hills 60 miles from the Canal, with the British occupying a new defensive line around Romani, 23 miles east of the Canal, which the railway line from the canal had reached by August. Regular reconnaissance by mounted brigades in early summer found the desert largely empty apart from Bedouins. In July, however, the Royal Flying Corps reported that 8,000 Turkish troops had been moved up from El Arish and were gathering near Bir el Abd, Bir Jemeil and Bir Bayud, east of Romani, and had been joined by other forces in neighbouring locations. Under von Kressenstein's leadership a combined force of Turks, Austrians and Germans launched a series of raids on British positions around Romani in early August. Their aim was to envelop the southern flank of the British forces and to gain a position on the railway between Kantara and Romani. This would give them rail access all the way to the Canal and the opportunity to shell it. The intended British re-occupation of the Sinai Peninsula would, moreover, be prevented. The Turkish lines, however, after some initial successes, became overstretched, and, with no reserves being deployed, they fell back in disorder. Difficulties supplying water and intense heat, which made marching in soft sand difficult, prevented an effective British follow up so the Turks were able to effect a withdrawal, though with the loss of 5,000 casualties and 4,000 prisoners. The Turks beat off a follow-up attack by Anzac mounted troops near Bir el Abd, their previous forward position, on August 9th but then undertook no further offensive operations, withdrawing towards El Arish.

The Battle of Romani, as it became known, having been won by the British forces, Murray decided to clear the Sinai peninsula altogether and to occupy El Arish, as a preliminary to moving forward through Gaza and Palestine to Jerusalem and beyond. The Battle of Romani was the first British success of the World War One against the Ottoman Empire and the last serious effort by the Turks to oppose a British advance across the desert. The climax of the battle is described in the official history of the 53rd. "As the morning light rapidly drove away the darkness, and disclosed the desert once more to the Turks on Wellington Ridge, this was the spectacle... Immediately before them across the ridge lay lines of the 8th Cameronians with bayonets fixed, prepared to assault. Behind the Cameronians a company of Royal Welch Fusiliers was being brought up in support to the right of the firing-line. To the right flank of the Turks was a company of the 7th Cameronians, already working round either to enfilade or attack them in the flank.[1] Below, on the desert, to the west and south, were innumerable parties of mounted troops commencing to move eastward…The Cameronians commenced to advance with the bayonet and this decided the matter. The Turks put up the white flag."[2]

The Turks were also being challenged further south by a revolt among their Arab subjects, who seized control of Jeddah and Mecca in June, and Taif in September. The maverick British colonel, T. E. Lawrence, joined Arab forces besieging Medina and persuaded the Arab commander, Feisal, to adopt a strategy of menacing the Hejaz railway, built with German assistance to link Constantinople with the holiest shrines of Islam and to improve the political and economic integration of the distant Arab provinces with the Ottoman state.[3] Crucially, because it linked back to the main Turkish Army in Syria, it was also the main source of supplies for the Turkish garrison, as well as offering solid stone-built stations that could form defensive positions. Lawrence saw that a guerrilla threat along the length the railway would oblige the Turks to defend all the way back to Damascus, a distance of 800 miles. The Turks were, indeed, forced to deploy large numbers of troops to guard, not always successfully, against a prolonged campaign of sabotage. In a separate manoeuvre, a force of Arabs, led by Lawrence, captured the Red Sea port of Aqaba early in July. "For the rest of the war the Turks stood on the defensive and the Arabs won advantage over advantage until, when the peace came, they had taken 35,000 prisoners, killed and wounded about as many, and occupied 100,000 square miles of the enemy's territory at little loss to themselves," he later wrote.[4] Once Romani had been occupied, the Royal Engineers pushed the railway and pipeline forward, with local Egyptian labour working under the direction of sappers and mounted troops patrolling ahead in a fan shape. Over a period of several months hundreds of miles of roads and railway were built and pipelines laid. Filters to deal with 1.5m gallons of water a day also had to be installed and large quantities of stone brought in from distant quarries. "Kantara, which had been a small and insignificant canal village, was now an important railway and water terminus. And laps across the desert were marked by standing camps of huts, by tanks, reservoirs, railway stations, aerodromes and signal stations."[5]

The Rise of Lloyd George

In France the most catastrophic encounter of the war – from the British point of view – was taking place, the 140 day long Battle of the Somme. Haig, the British Commander-in-Chief on the Western Front, (by now a Field Marshal) has taken much of the blame for the British losses – 19,000 killed on the first day – July 1st 1916 – and 415,000 dead or wounded by the time the struggle ended in November. The position is, now recognised, however, to have been much more complicated. His defenders point out that the French, on whose land the Germans were being

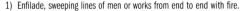

1) Enfilade, sweeping lines of men or works from end to end with fire.
2) Dudley Ward, pp62-63.
3) Feisal bin Hussein bin Ali Hashimi (1885-1933) organised the Arab revolt against Ottoman rule with the help of British colonel, T.E. Lawrence. He was later king of Iraq (1921-1933).
4) Lawrence, T.E., *Guerrilla*, Entry in the fourteenth edition of *Encyclopaedia Britannica* 1939.
5) Dudley Ward, p65.

fought, were the senior military partner. Against his better judgment that the attack should take place in Flanders, Haig deferred to the wishes of the French General Joseph Joffre that it should be at the point where the French and British armies met in northern France. The need, pressed by Joffre, for urgent action to relieve pressure on the French at Verdun – an even longer and more brutal 10 month attritional battle – also led Haig to agree to act before his Army, many of them only recently-conscripted, was ready. Other mistakes, including the War Office's initial opposition to the development and use of tanks – which the Royal Navy had ended up trialling with the enthusiastic support of Churchill, as First Lord of the Admiralty – magnified these errors.[6] When the two great contests of 1916 – Verdun and Ypres – closed towards the end of the year, more than a million lives had been lost or blighted by injury, yet the stalemate continued.

Lloyd George had by this stage emerged as a key figure in a divided British Cabinet, a fount of ever bolder ideas for winning the war. He had left the Exchequer, where he had been since 1908, to become the first Minister of Munitions in May 1915. On July 7th 1916 Lloyd George moved from the Ministry to succeed his old "enemy", Kitchener, as Secretary of State for War. Kitchener, a national hero, the "Constable of Britain" in Churchill's phrase, had been made War Secretary at the very outbreak of hostilities but drowned on June 5th 1916 with nearly 600 others when HMS *Hampshire*, the ship taking him to Archangel for talks on providing greater British military support for Russia, struck a mine near the Orkneys. Lloyd George, like Churchill and unlike most of the rest of the Cabinet, was reluctant to leave the war planning to the military. Both politicians were firmly in the "Easterners" camp supporting the idea that interventions in the east, as at Gallipoli could provide the required knock-out blow – a short-cut to victory. Kitchener, shy and cautious by nature, Asquith and Foreign Secretary, Sir Edward Grey, were "Westerners" who wanted resources concentrated on the war in France. Lloyd George argued strongly for the sending of British troops to Salonika to support the Serbs, though this had not happened on the scale he wanted, and for the sending of machine guns to Romania, suggestions that were the beginning, too, of Lloyd George's poor relations with the man responsible for presenting strategic advice to the Cabinet, General Sir William Robertson, chief of the Imperial General Staff, (CIGS), a post he had inherited in December 1915 from Murray.[7] Much of the press still argued that the professional leadership of Haig and Robertson was preferable to civilian interference, which, it believed had led to disasters at Gallipoli and Kut. Robertson, who has been described as "brusque to the point of rudeness", barely concealed his contempt for Lloyd George's military opinions, to which he was famed for retorting "I've 'eard different". The Lloyd George camp's view is patent in the deferential prose of a hagiographical early biographer, whose judgments would now be regarded as highly partisan.[8]

6) Barnett, p83. Leonardo da Vinci had proposed the idea and produced illustrations of armoured vehicles. H.G. Wells and Jules Verne also envisaged their use in their science fiction novels.

7) Sir William Robertson (1860-1933) was the only British soldier to rise from the rank of private to Field Marshal. A "Westerner" like Haig, he had supported the concentration of British efforts on the Western Front in opposition to Lloyd George who wanted a war on all fronts until U.S. forces could be persuaded to join the main effort in France.

8) Edwards, J.H., *Life of Lloyd George*. Waverley Vol. 4, p226.

"Early in 1915, even though he was burdened with the weight of his responsibilities as the custodian of the nation's finances, he took so keen and intelligent an interest in the military situation that he sent a communication to Kitchener in which he pointed out the probability that Germany would seek to crush Serbia in order to secure a through route to Constantinople. For that reason he urged the desirability of an Allied expedition to Salonika in order to protect Serbia and to keep Bulgaria out of the war... Months later he was among the first to foresee the peril of Roumania [sic], and he strongly urged that steps should be taken to make her invincible against the concerted action of the German and Bulgarians, which he divined in the German retirement on the Somme. But once more procrastination prevailed in the councils of the Allies."

Events had tragically moved in Lloyd George's favour but intriguing continued after Kitchener's death. Lloyd George has subsequently taken much of the blame for bringing Asquith down later in 1916, plotting against him with his friends in the press (principally Max Aitken, later Lord Beaverbrook), and disingenuously posing as a patriotic critic of the policies of the government he served in. Whether he, almost alone, could see the way to cut through the inefficiencies and stubbornness that was causing the war to drag on and bring nearer the prospect of British defeat (as his admirers claimed), or whether he was using every means, deceitful or not, to seize the premiership (as his detractors argued), is not clear. Perhaps a little of both. His advocates can certainly quote examples of a decisiveness brought to Government both as the Minister of Munitions and as Secretary for War. His rather unusual transfer in 1915 from the Exchequer to the department responsible for armaments had arisen partly out of the failure of the British to secure a hoped-for breakthrough in the Battle of Neuve Chapelle in the Artois region of France as far as back as March 1915. This had been blamed by the British Commander-in-Chief, Field Marshal Sir John French[9] and by critics, such as Lloyd George, on supply shortages, characterised at the time as the "shell scandal". A more hostile critic of Lloyd George argues he unfairly denigrated Kitchener's record in ramping up munitions production – an enormous task, given the vastly greater scale and longer durations of the battles that were being fought, when measured against expectation – and that the new Munitions minister benefitted to a large extent from plans already in place.[10] The convoy system – designed to reduce losses to vital merchant shipping from submarine attack – was also an idea he picked up from his wartime aide, Colonel Maurice Hankey, who held the position of secretary of the War Cabinet formed by Lloyd George in December 1916. Yet, others, have argued that Lloyd George brought a change of style and tempo rather than substance, and that this in itself was important. As the minister in charge of armaments from June, following the formation of the War Coalition Government, he insisted business and labour were taken into partnership with the Government to ensure the best utilisation of engineering and metals resources. A census of all the machinery in the UK was taken, which showed a large number of lathes and tools not in use on Government work. As a result, all the main machine tool makers were taken into direct

9) Sir John French (1852-1925), commander of a cavalry division in the Second Boer War, was made Chief of the Imperial General Staff in 1912, but resigned over the Curragh Mutiny in March 1914. He served as Commander-in-Chief of the British Expeditionary Force in Belgium and France for the first two years of World War One.

10) McCormick, D., *The Mask of Merlin*. Macdonald, London, 1963 pp97-98.

Government control. Under Lloyd George's leadership the new Ministry developed into a mammoth organization that directed and controlled thousands of workshops and factories, with employees by the million and expenditure in thousands of pounds.

There were other potentially less popular measures. To ensure productivity was maintained in Britain's factories, licensing hours – three hours at lunch time and four and a half hours in the evening, with a three hour gap in the afternoon – had been introduced under the Defence of the Realm Act at the outbreak of war in August 1914.[11] Other provisions of the Act, one of the most draconian ever introduced by a British Government, affected even apparently innocent private and domestic activities. Fear of Zeppelin raids provoked a ban on the lighting of bonfires and the flying of kites, while other provisions made it a criminal offence to feed wild animals (to avoid wasting food) and restricted the sale of binoculars. Reports, verbal or written, that might cause alarm or spread disaffection among His Majesty's troops or the civilian population were central to the legislation, and prosecutions and a very small number of executions of miscreants did indeed take place. Lloyd George has also been credited with the unification of the Allied military command under the French general Ferdinand Foch. He also secured the appointment of railway entrepreneur, Sir Eric Geddes, elder brother of director of recruiting Sir Auckland Geddes, to take charge of military railways behind British lines in France, with the honorary rank of major-general. Whatever the judgment made, Lloyd George inherited office as a Prime Minister at a time when the war was still in the balance, though the dangers for Britain were perhaps not as great as those that confronted Churchill in 1940. The Somme battles had been fought to a standstill, resulting in a modest gain of ground by the Allies, but their Italian allies after two years of repeated attacks had advanced fewer than 10 miles on a narrow front on the Austrian frontier north east of Venice. The Russians had made even less progress, succumbing to heavy defeat at the hands of the Germans and severe losses of men and materiel. Britain, too, as we have learnt, was facing internal threats from strikes by workers at home protesting over working conditions, rising prices and excessive overtime, and, within a few months, serious trouble would flare up in Ireland.

Like most Welsh people, Dewi needed little convincing that Lloyd George was making a big difference. He was confident the "Welsh Wizard" was the key to British success. "I have just read Dafydd's speech at the Eisteddfod and really can't find words to express myself. He is a marvel and I think the country need have no doubts as to his ability in the capacity of Secretary for War. Why a man with that spirit – the Welsh ysprŷd – could overcome any obstacle likely to crop up. I'd back him up against any sausage eating Bethmann Earwig they like to put up. You can tell he's a Cymro alright by his speech and by Gum! I'm prouder than ever that I

11) Lloyd George went further. A huge munitions factory was constructed between Carlisle and Gretna on the borders between England and Scotland, employing 25,000 people, many of them housed in two new towns, specially built for the purpose, but also, by necessity, in digs in Carlisle. All licensed premises over an area of 320 square miles, including Carlisle city, were taken into state control, a system that prevailed until 1971 when the state breweries and pubs were sold back to the private sector by the Government of Edward Heath. Other restrictions included a ban on the sale of 'chasers' and 'treating' (the buying of rounds), fixed prices (so different pubs could not compete) and payment of commissions for salaried managers (technically civil servants) on the sale of food and non-alcoholic beverages but not on alcohol. Convictions for drunkenness plummeted, with beneficial effects on productivity.

am also a Cymro and that the same blood runs in my veins. A Welshman "in the field myself" I can only say "Cariwch ymlaen" Dafydd bach, cewch i mewn a ennill i ni" ["Carry on, little Dafydd, get in there and win for us].[12] Dewi was writing after Lloyd George had been greeted with adulation by the crowd at the Eisteddfod in Aberystwyth, coming close to being mobbed as he stepped out of his car. In Wales, where he was already a hero after his earlier successes in securing the right of Nonconformists to burial in church land, in winning the battle for disestablishment of the Anglican Church, and for his subsequent welfare reforms as Chancellor, the dynamism he brought to his new job confirmed his popularity.[13] The Welsh solicitor, unlike his predecessor, saw the importance of projecting an image as a dynamic man of action. He cultivated and fed the press, addressed the crowds and visited the front. "His vitality and buoyancy was contagious, imbuing the public with confidence, determination and belief in ultimate victory."[14] In this he foreshadowed Churchill and the role he was to play in World War Two. Dewi's "Earwig", Theobald von Bethmann Hollweg, the German Chancellor, also had to battle internal rivalries. He was replaced in July 1917, seven months after Britain's Coalition government leader, Asquith, gave way to Lloyd George.

Always Merry and Bright

Dewi spent the next six months on the canal, where units of the 53rd were on garrison duty ensuring no new threat emerged from the Turks to the east and still under some threat from the Senussi in the Libyan Desert under their leader Sayyid Ahmed. Each ten mile sector of the Canal was manned by a brigade, one battalion at the pontoon bridgehead and on the banks, maintaining patrols, one at the railhead, and two in the front line about a mile east of the road. A quieter life on the Canal encourages reflection on Dewi's part, about the Army and its peculiar ways, on the companionship he is enjoying, and the general frustrations of being far away from what he would consider civilisation and all its comforts. His morale remains generally good, though there is plenty of evidence within the letters that he is missing the home he had left a year earlier and struggling with a lack of money and a poor diet. Ismailia Spinney Wood, a holding camp where he spends a week at the end of May, is a disappointment after Heliopolis. "Oh yes" he tells his parents, "I thought it wouldn't last long, that glorious five weeks of bliss in our last camp [Abbassia]. I could have stayed there till the end of the war and there was much wailing and gnashing of teeth when we heard we had to hop it elsewhere. However, we shouldered our equipment, blankets, etc. and marched away cheering ourselves up as best we could by singing 'I've got a motter (sic) always merry and bright' just like that old chap in 'The Arcadians'.[15]

---

12) September 8th 1916. David Lloyd George, speaking at the annual Welsh cultural festival in Aberystwyth. Theobald von Bethmann Hollweg, German Chancellor.

13) Although agreed before the War, disestablishment was delayed and not enacted until 1920.

14) Bourne, J., Liddle P., Whitehead, I., (Eds.), *The Great World War. 1914-45.* 'War leaders,' Chap 21, 'Political Leaders in War Time: Lloyd George and Churchill.' Cassar, p387

15) May 31st 1916. *The Arcadians* was a popular musical of the time, lyrics by Arthur Wimperis and music by Lionel Moncton and Howard Talbot. One of its characters, Doody, sang: 'I've gotter motter [motto] — Always merry and bright! Look around and you will find Every cloud is silver lined; The sun will shine Although the sky's a gray one. I've often said to meself, I've said, "Cheer up, Cully, you'll soon be dead! A short life and a gay one!'

Moving, presumably without much in the way of transport, was strenuous. "My word it's hard shifting while it lasts. I should imagine our company has about as much stuff as a couple of armies put together. If you ever think of moving, I'll get leave to help you. I'm a dab hand at it. And carrying grand pianos, sideboards, and dressing tables up and down stairs would be absolutely child's play. I laugh at the thought of such light stuff after my experiences of carrying cable wagons under my arm etc. But it's not only shifting stores that counts because when you've finished that, there's your own personal kit and when you've got that on, you can take it from me, you feel like a pack-mule." His father had clearly sympathised, though by this time he had moved again down the canal. "You're quite right, Dad, about shifting. It's not bad to have one now and again. It not only affords you new surroundings and faces but in its way it is a gentle reminder that you must pull yourself together and get a move on." Discipline is getting tougher. "It's a bit thick when after you've worked hard lugging heavy stuff all day, as we did last move, and then get pulled up by the officer, 'all the bloomin' lot of you' for 'dodging it' and 'being unworthy of the name of a British solder' all through a couple of Tired Tims who took advantage of nightfall and vanished for a time."[16]

Their short stay at Spinney Wood en route to Serapeum brought a return to tents. "It's a rotten change after those huts which we all liked so much. Then, there's no shower baths here and we've got to resort to buckets again. The township is about half an hour's walk from our camp and isn't much of a place, not a patch on Heliopolis, so, you see, we've backed a deuce so to speak. However, there are some lovely avenues of trees and parks here to shade from the sun when walking into town." There would, of course, have been no electricity – food would have had to be cooked over open fires and at night in their tents they had to use candles. Writing to Doris in August he describes pulling the candle nearer to look at a photo of her.[17] At first he is encouraged by new tasks, his previous cooking duties at Abbassia, which he had enjoyed, having come to an end. "Our Sig. Office is pretty busy, as you will guess when I tell you it's an Army Corps. Just like a P.O. [...] I thought when I went on duty first that I had forgotten sounders and keys and was wondering how I would manage. (I hadn't touched a key since Salonica but I went in and sat down and as soon as I took hold of the key I was slashing away an X message feeling a very pleasing thrill as the dots and dashes were registered to a nicety. Any non-telegraphist reading that last phrase, Dad, would think I was rather dramatical but *you* understand. There's an art in it, Eh! What! And you can take a pride in it, too. The instruments are just like the old P.O.T.S. sets and that's a lot towards comfort."[18]

Serapeum, where he reports on June 1st to 163rd Brigade Signals, is little more, it seems, than a railway siding and tents, and a few canteens, a few miles further south.[19] Having just told his parents about his previous move he talks resignedly about having to shift again, this time to what is evidently a much less busy operation. "Am now doing duties with McKinnon and another chap in a Brigade

16) June 30th 1916.

17) August 27th 1916.

18) May 31st 1916. A telegraph sounder produced an audible sound when connected to an electrical telegraph. When the current was switched off, the armature dropped to its resting position, resulting in a 'click'. When the current returned, the armature was raised back to the upper arm, resulting in a 'clack'. Thus, as the remote telegraph key makes and breaks a contact, the sounder echoes the up and down state of the key. P.O.T.S., Post Office Telegraph Service.

19) June 10th 1916.

HQ office on the banks of Suez Canal.[20] We're not having a bad time at all here. Only three of us operators and two motor cyclists from our company in our tent. We are with a lot of East Anglian chaps, very decent fellows indeed."[21] The surroundings do not amount to much, however. "No cinema or iced lemonade here, Dolly, and we've only managed to exist during the last fortnight, which has seemed an eternity without money or fags, and I do believe we'd have gone absolutely plumb loco through monotony, if this old Canal wasn't here to swim about in half the day."[22] This was not his first experience of swimming as a break from his duties. Based at C Beach, Lala Baba, he had been able to have a bathe in Suvla Bay the previous October.

Money continued to be a problem, with repeated requests home for funds, and delight when his mail brought him some relief from his penury, or the paymaster paid a visit. Thanking those at home for a food parcel, he writes: "The former has done much to replenish the larder of our private mess I mentioned in my last, and now the P.O. – well, you know what it is to have money in your pocket or rather you can't imagine what it's like to have absolutely nixes, especially out here. It will come in jolly handy for such luxuries as are obtainable from the canteen, although it goes against the grain, you bet, to fork out to Greek proprietors. Besides this is such an out of the way place that naturally or purposely they don't forget to shove on the prices. I strongly suspect the latter is the cause [sic]."[23] Greek canteen tea, needless to say, is not to be compared with tea sent in parcels from home. He does enjoy the occasional victory over the traders, however. "I was out of paper until about two hours ago, when I luckily contrived to 'do' a Greek for a writing pad. Takes a bit of doing I can tell you, so congratulate me, they all did in our hut, shook hands and called me a marvel."[24] His permanently sorry financial state crops up again later the same month when he describes ten difficult days. "Our position was most pitiful and I never was so badly off before. Worst time I've had for ages. No money, no fags, sans everything, in fact, and I really don't know how we pulled through. I was as miserable as sin and making journeys to and fro to the office all day at intervals of about two hours to see if there was any parcels, although I knew it was hopeless, – no luck, not even a L.O. or W.T.[25] Things were pretty desperate and there was an ugly glint in our eyes. Came a day, however, and we were told, 'Pay today boys'. Gee! I nearly went plumb loco. That especial paymaster has my eternal blessing upon his devoted head, and I felt just the same as I used to when off to Porthcawl for holidays." In the same letter he announces he was cancelling his allotment of 10/6 in favour of his mother so that he could draw the full pay he was entitled to, a move made when he joined up, presumably under the impression that virtually all his needs would be catered for while in the Army. "Thought you wouldn't mind, please tell me. The fact of the matter is I've overdrawn on my pay book to start with, not a lot, of course, about 30/-, then again half the time I've got nixes to rattle in my pocket, things are dear here, too. Besides, when I get my camera I should never be able to get films etc. on what I draw now and it'll be worth

---

20) A.A. McKinnnon. A colleague from the GPO in Cardiff.
21) The 54th (East Anglian) Division, part of 21st Corps. The 53rd (Welsh) Division was part of 20th Corps.
22) June 15th 1916. Plumb, sheer, downright; loco, crazy, originally from U.S. plant of the same name, causing brain disease in cattle.
23) June 30th 1916
24) July 13th 1916.
25) August 27th 1916. *London Opinion* and *Weekly Telegraph*.

it to send photos home. Also, I shall be able to send a collection of P.C.s and that, if I get a chance, as you asked me. Don't get the breeze up will you? I shall have to wait a month or so, however, before I can draw my new pay, if it is cancelled." It came through sooner than he expected. "I have received a notification from the O.C.," he writes a month later, "that my allotment has been cancelled on and from the 1st of next month.[26] By then I shall have paid off my debt in my pay book. It's been pretty rotten mouching [sic][27] around with no money and things are so dear. However, now I shall be able to rub along O.K. and send you some more postcards and views into the bargain. I shall want the cash, too, now that my camera will be out very shortly. Besides I was forgetting I must certainly buy that mosaic brooch when the first opportunity offers itself."[28] This, it seems, was a present he had promised his sister.

Marmalade for Dinner

Shortly after arriving in Serapeum Dewi describes a typical work shift, now made more agreeable by the delights of their own camp food, garnered from parcels from home.[29] "I am writing this in the Sig. Office and have just come on for the all night duty after having sampled some camp-made oatmeal, blancmange, peaches, tea, + biscuits. Oh! Yes, we're going strong, I can tell you. We make tea every night about 9 pm and bread pudding occasionally. Mac's a dab hand at cooking and we've all got our little jobs – fetching water, chopping sticks, and washing dishes, and run a little mess on our own. Our stove consists of a few old biscuit tins and it's more like a civvy camp, like the one we had down Sully with Bill + Bon.[30] There's only five in our tent so we can do a lot to make us comfortable in the way of grub." This private supply seems to have been vital to the health and sustenance of the troops, as Army food remained in seriously short supply and would only get scarcer when the march through Sinai began later in the year. Reflecting on the meals they received from the canteen, he looks forward to joining his father on trips into the south Wales countryside and calling into the Unicorn in St. Mellons for bread and cheese and hop-bitters. "It'll be some change for me after bread and marmalade and tea full of flies every day for dinner," he says. Later in June he expresses his delight at receiving a note – presumably 10/- – among other essentials. "That note was soon changed into piastres, you bet, and I didn't half shift some stuff at the canteen to commemorate the event. I have been broke for a long time and you can guess how it was appreciated after the rotten Army tuck"[31].

The heat and isolation of their surroundings made dreams of a return home no doubt even more attractive. Their camp is situated in a glade of trees which is watered by flooding a series of paths around them. "They get no rain, you see. These trees shade our tents considerably from the sun but even then it's too hot to move hardly. We are completely cut off from other camps and the outer world, as it were, and it's dreadfully quiet." Being in an isolated spot does have its advantages,

26) September 9th 1916. Officer Commanding.
27) Mooch. To loaf, stroll about.
28) September 9th 1916.
29) June 21st 1916.
30) Sully, seaside village between Barry and Penarth, Glamorgan.
31) June 10th, June 21st 1916.

however. "It's a nice change to be with a small section away from the Company, you get so much more freedom. With them, of course, we daren't carry on cooking etc. in front of the tent or else it would mean orderly room." They are at the whim, however, of another inconvenience – the weather. "I have been interrupted, " he writes, "by the lights in the office going out, windows and doors blown open and sand blown in, in clouds, the message pads are fluttering all over the floor, the reason being a monsoon has suddenly sprung up and the wind is so hot and fierce, you really can't imagine what it's like.[32] It's lasted about five minutes but is now dying away again and perhaps I will be able to continue."[33] The khamseen, which is probably what he meant, is compared in the Divisional history with the opening of an oven door, bringing hot blasts of wind that filled the air with sand and darkened the sun. Blowing in from the south, it could last three days. As one officer reported, "120 degrees in a bell tent is not a desirable temperature. During our stay in Fayoum active work was impossible between the hours of 8 am and 5 pm so we have to reveille at 3 or 4 am. The normal way of spending the afternoon was to lie on one's bed, clad in a towel, with a bucket of water handy in which to dump the towel at intervals."[34] To his mother, who was always worried whether or not he was wrapped up well enough, he writes to say he did not think it was necessary to send his light vests as he was very partial to his old greybacks.[35] "They're flannel, and medical men say the best things to wear in any climate, warm or cold, so think I will act up to their advice and stick to 'em, which is easily practicable, the way we perspire just now. I had shorts issued out to me a few weeks ago so am quite in keeping with "le dernier cri", so to speak."[36]

The rotten food theme returns in subsequent letters. At the end of July he describes the ecstasy with which his unit discovered they had been lucky with parcels, the delivery of which was sporadic and the subject of much anguish for men serving in such a remote spot. "We were moping in the hut, no fags, no money, and no grub, as desperate a plight as you could ever imagine three R.E.s to be in, when, for some reason or other, I disappeared to stroll along to the Sig. Office (I think it was to cadge a Woodbine). Anyhow, arriving there I found a mail in, and my eyes bulged out like saucers, for, would you believe it, there were *six* parcels for our hut, truly a David, Mac, Smith mail. I soon collared 'em and staggered over to our caboosh with my load.[37] I opened the door and you ought to have seen those chaps' faces when they saw the manna, drew their hands across their foreheads to wipe away the beads of cold sweat and looked quite dazed, suddenly collapsing on top of me. Down we went, parcels underneath, and stayed until Mac realised it might be a cake he was sitting on. I will not attempt any description of the ensuing scene, of the furious hacking with jack knives at the knots which wouldn't come undone, the tearing of sacking and canvas and, following that, the disgraceful but, nevertheless, glorious orgy which took place." One commodity that the Army seems to have had in abundance was marmalade. Writing on receipt of a parcel, he recounts: "We felt at peace with all the world, except the cook, whom we politely informed that we didn't

77

32) Monsoon. He means Khamseen.
33) June 21st 1916.
34) Dudley Ward, p55.
35) Army shirts.
36) July 13th 1916. Dernier cri, the latest fashion or the newest thing.
37) July 31st 1916. Caboosh, a small room for cooking.

much care if he went to work in a much hotter place than Egypt. We were independent that day but he thoroughly deserved it, fancy offering us marmalade for dinner, at which we gave a hollow ironical laugh, like the villain in the Theatre Royal. We knew all about it in the afternoon, though, you bet. The after effects, O Lor', my poor tummy. Simply had to lay down and let it pass off and didn't have even the energy to get up and punch old Smithy's head for torturing us with offers of Cadbury's chocolate. And what with the Players and State Express [cigarettes] knocking about – 'Vat a game it is, Oy! Oy!'."

The effects (and memories) of the parcel have soon worn off and he tells the folks back home it was, indeed, surprising that they thought he and his colleagues looked so pleased in a photo he had sent. Early in August Army fare for dinner was bread and marmalade again, he tells his sister, but he and his companions have managed to get some supplies for their own cook-up. "Well Dolly what do you think we made for dinner today? You'd never guess. P-a-n-ca-a-k-e-s with c-u-r-r-a-n-t-s in 'em. They were scrumptious, and, no kid, but they were as good as you'd get at the Dutch Café."[38] Used eggs and all to make 'em." Later the same month he is back to praising the contents of a parcel sent from home. "By Gum! Those pears! We had 'em for supper with Ideal Milk and crowed we had never tasted anything like it for donkey's years. I am now looking forward to the one posted on the 1st inst. Until then, the throes of anxiety and A.S.C. rations for me.[39] By the way, please keep on sending those packets of tea, café au lait and lump sugar, if you don't mind, we like it better and it never struck me before to ask you.[40] I assure you we don't get tea like nectar every day and the boys and myself quite enjoyed the change from Greek canteen tea." Such reminders of home could induce poignant memories. "The label on the packet brought back vivid memories of the squabbles Dolly and I had over fetching tea from the shop, especially if I was deep in Tom Merry, and which, if you remember, always ended in Mum declaring she'd go herself."[41] He is still dreaming of home cooking, too, which he expects to be sampling soon, and waxing sarcastic again on the food they get provided. He tells his mother: "I guess you'd better get about umpteen cakes and puddings and about puftyfive [sic] hocks and sausages ready, for I'm sure we shan't be long now. My word, Mum I'd like to have as many quids as the times I've dreamt about your apple and rhubarb tarts? [...] Anyhow, you'll see, I guess this 'ere Army's worked some miracles on me in the grub line, specially."

The repeated references in the letters to food and parcels is perhaps the strongest indication that the men in Egypt were near starving on Army rations and he apologises for going on at length about this topic. "S'cuse me harping on grub but when you've had one piece of camel (I'll swear it wasn't pig) as salt as the Suez for brekker, cup of tea for dinner (could have had marmalade as well but told him to

38) August 3rd 1916. The Dutch Café, a landmark mock-Tudor building in Queen Street, Cardiff, its first storey decorated with pictures of Dutch heads. Demolished in 1987 to make way for the new Capitol Centre.

39) Army Service Corps.

40) Nestlé brand Milkmaid café au lait was sold at 6d, 11d and 1/10d a tin under the slogan, 'Leaves no Grounds for Complaint', and described as 'unequalled only by the true café au lait as served in France'. The copywriter clearly meant 'equalled only'!

41) August 15th 1916. Tom Merry, a fictional schoolboy, was the principal character in the St Jim's stories which appeared in the boy's weekly paper, The Gem, from 1907 to 1939. The stories were written using the pen-name Martin Clifford, the majority by Charles Hamilton, more widely known as Frank Richards, creator of Billy Bunter.

keep it, as I was afraid I'd be getting yellow jaundice through the blamed stuff 'fore long), and skilly for tea (when I had a row with cookie for doing me out of half my regulation issue of potatoes i.e. 2 $^{156}/_{264}$ [ths] ozs. per man), it sort of haunts one, naturally.[42] We've had peas (?) twice since we've been here (like marbles) but they only remind me of green peas I uster [used to] get. I've kept a few of the former in case I run out of ammunition in a tight corner and will risk breaking the Hague rules about dum-dums."[43] There follows a long light-hearted discourse suggesting just how much he and his fellow soldiers are craving home food. "Anyhow, we of the E.E.F. are very broad-minded and, as we are supposed by common report to be the best fed army in the world, swallow our troubles (the same as the grub, it's not much) at one gulp and pass a vote of heartfelt sympathy with the worst fed blighters, whoever they might be, and end the meeting by singing our famous anthem, 'Here we suffer grief and pain, The next blooming place'll be just the same'. 'Nevera [sic] mind', as the Gippos say, 'nuff's as good as a feast on that subject.'"[44]

The desert could supply nothing in the way of foodstuffs and all armies sent to the Middle East experienced great difficulties in bringing up enough supplies. Ammunition came second to water and this meant rations took a poor third place. Fresh food was virtually unobtainable and men had to subsist on very little for days on end. The permanent food crisis is made worse, he next reports, when their private mess goes "bankrupt" and their parcels are exhausted. "Yes! The smash so long averted has come. We're down to our last spoonful of tea and have had to do without peaches for four nights and payday is not until a week hence. Naturally, the cook has us at his mercy and we can't afford giving him any more old buck nor tell him to keep his rotten grub. Further, the cigs have run out and we're like a lot of moping Gippos – down and out. (Before the referee shouts 'ten' please send out another such packet as last time, that we may be able to chuck up a quid as well as a sponge.)[45] At present, we are forced when nearing the canteen to make a detour round the back of it, lest the sight of piled up tins of 'Gold Flake' [cigarettes] and 'Bartlett Peaches' goad us to do something rash which would result in an interview with the Provost Marshal and a closer acquaintance with field punishment enclosures.[46] You have to be careful, too, in times of trial how you speak in this hut of ours. I remember only yesterday Jack Smith was looking very serious and Mac offered him a penny (which he hadn't got) for his thoughts. 'Oh!' he said, roused from his reverie, 'I was thinking of the cakes ma mither uster make.'"

In the same letter he chides his mother for perhaps not being industrious enough in making cakes to send out to him. "We villains are hardened somewhat to such hard times, which are common occurrences in the profession of arms, but, I venture to say, never have we been so sadly reduced, no, not since the 15's as at present.[47] It causes me to gloat over the date of the next English [sic] mail and tick off with mechanical precision the days, nay, the very hours, intermediate. Consequently, much

42) August 15th 1916.
43) The expanding dum-dum bullet was outlawed under the Hague Convention of 1899.
44) The adapted words of a hymn by Thomas Bilby (1796-1872). 'Here we suffer grief and pain, Here we meet to part again, In heaven we part no more.'
45) Ten, the count in boxing. A trainer deciding to retire his fighter would 'throw in the sponge' (into the ring).
46) Provost Marshal, the officer in the Army responsible for military discipline.
47) The months of 1915 when they were in Gallipoli.

as it pains me to broach the subject of 'vittles', allow me to encroach on your generosity by giving a few tips on the next parcels, dear Mum. Please do not imagine me in any way presumptive but somehow or other I am inclined to think you are not utilising as much as I would like the wide scope of your culinary genius. Now, I suggest that you employ it to make some lap cake, jam roll and Welsh Cakes. Teisen ar y Mên (Think that's right) now and again, as I know of a chap "yn yr Aipht" [in Egypt] who'd go absobloominglutely stark, staring mad with joy to see 'em turn up.[48] Besides, there are lots of other creations in flour, currants, and baking powder prone to your art which I can't remember just now. Don't forget, Mum, if it's only as compensation for not writing. I know you'd like making cakes better so there's a trump, will you?

Bully Beef and Irish Stew

His letters give some indication of the variety of packaged food that had by the early years of the 20th century become available as a result of new technologies, such as canning. The process had originally been developed for Napoleon's armies in the early 19th century and the main demand had come from armies and navies, including those of Britain, which were as a result able to extend their campaigns and expeditions of discovery. By the latter half of the 19th century canned food had become popular as a middle class status symbol, the preservation process making it possible to eat fruits and vegetables out of season, including exotic fruits, such as pineapples, and to have meat available at all times. Demand for canned food increased rapidly during World War One, as military commanders sought cheap, high-calorie food that could be transported to the trenches of France and to desert locations in the near East without spoiling on the way. Army supplies were initially, however, low-quality – bully beef (cheap corned beef), pork and beans, and Maconochie's Irish Stew.[49] By 1916 widespread boredom with cheap canned food among soldiers resulted in the military purchasing better-quality food to improve morale, and complete meals in a can began to appear.

The canned food sent from home, such as peaches and sardines, were the luxuries and variety the soldiers felt they needed to supplement their diet. "As regards tinned stuff, any sort of fruit or meat will be OK but fish is no good in this hot weather. Send plenty of chocolate, big chunks, you know, and toffee from the market, something to chew. A box of Abdullas [cigarettes] would not go bad either, Virginias, y'know, nothing Gippo for me, thanks. Beef paté, like Aunt Janet once sent, is the goods (another tip). By the way, you can send 11lb parcels, I know it for a fact, so make inquiries, I should. Lemon cheese is another excellent commodity and I thoroughly recommend St. Ivel's Cheese, while tinned sausages are a treat, at least they were last time I had 'em. Don't be dismayed, but I rather think I've acquired an expensive taste on active service."[50] Many of these suggestions were taken up by his parents and subsequent parcels did, indeed, contain lemon cheese, beef paté and some of his other requested items. He was right, too, about the weight of permissible parcels. A Post Office circular of August 18th 1914, shortly after the outbreak of war, had listed the weights and prices of parcels that could be sent as

48) Teisen ar y Mên. Literally, cake on the stone or Welsh cakes.
49) Tinned meats supplied by the Aberdeen firm of the same name
50) August 15th 1916.

up to 3lb 1s. (one shilling), 3-7 lbs 1s.4d., and 7-11lbs 1s.7d. Letters at the time could be sent for 1d. per oz.[51]

In September another long passage praises the food received in parcels from home and excoriates the provisions available from the Army Supply Corps.[52] "We people who are guilty of that abominable habit of living mainly upon charity are as a rule in dire straits when this 'hearth relief' arrives and I can assure you I was not by any means an exception to this particular rule on this auspicious occasion. True, I know whence the next meal was coming from but that's just it, what I want to impress upon you. My position as a swoddy was infinitely more critical than the individual in the periodicals who doesn't know from where his next meal is coming. You see, I knew only too well that the A.S.C. were providing it, also – Alas! – what was of far more import, what that meal was sure to consist of. Fully aware, was I, that T. Tickler Esq.'s wonderful discovery in marmalade would adorn our festive board and thrust its objectionable presence upon us in overwhelming forces.[53] Reports to the effect that great reinforcements of this commodity had been hurried up had been received and, unless I could manoeuvre a skilful counter-attack immediately with hard cash, my sector would undoubtedly fall. Was ever a general in so precarious a situation?"

A long and lyrical account is given of the joy he experienced when a registered letter from home did eventually arrive containing funds he could buy supplies with. "Far over on the skyline the post orderly could be seen advancing, under all sail. Would he or would he not fail me, surely the god of war would have pity and spare me the humiliation of surrendering my trusty jacknife to that exultant tin pot of slithering yellow [marmalade]? Anxiously, I scanned his features through my binoculars until nearer and yet nearer he came. Into the office at last with his precious bag, and breaking the seal sent man after man into exstasies [sic] over some trifling envelope. Desperately, I scrutinised this Santa Claus' visage and strove hard to gain some sign, some glance of recognition only to be foiled time and again by raucous, never-ending calls of 1564 someone, 9451 someone else etc. etc. I turn away, a pitiful subject of hopelessness and dejection, and brace myself to face the inevitable when – when I hear a voice, as if in a dream, borne to my ears through miles of space '720 – 720, where the _____ are you 720?'. Never! it can't b-be, my ears deceive me, my poor head. O! cruel sun to work such devastation, to cause such woe, and drive a bloke plumb loco! But what is this clutched within mine right paw, an envelope, a thick 'un, with the sun – Good old Sol – causing the beautiful blue lines upon it to dance and glitter in its rays. 'O! harbinger of joy,' (this to the postman) 'ask for a pint of nut-brown ale and it is indeed thine, thou excellent man'. The explorer who first discovered these regd. envelopes, too, hath my eternal blessing upon his noble cranium. What rapturous shouts, what eulogistic cries, born only of unbounded delight. O! play the viol, sound the lute, for David's clicked for a 1 quid note.[54] Then, straightway to the Field P.O., the happy possessor of riches beyond avarice wends his way, eager to affix his signature and procure the coveted

---

51) One shilling = 12d. (pence), equivalent to 5p, post decimalisation.
52) September 8th 1916.
53) Tickler's supplied a range of savoury and dessert canned foods to the Armed Forces in World War One, including, as well as marmalade, Tickler's plum and apple jam, popularly known as Tommy Tickler's jam.
54) 'Strike the viol, touch the lute,' from 'Come Ye Sons of Art, Ode for Queen Mary's Birthday', 1694 by Henry Purcell.

filthy lucre. From thence forthwith to the canteen. 'A lemonade, thou Greek knave, and look slippy about it or, by my halberd, you shall live to rue the day.' I quaff the goblet handed to me with all speed by this Thessalonian poltroon. 'Here's a health unto those who love me well', quoth I, 'and, by St. David, I mean it'. The larder swelled by apricots and chicken paste, I depart for dejeuner. My heart bears high within this breast for is not yon Tickler fellow, forsooth, already a beaten man? 'Climb down, sirrah, climb down'."[55]

Spare Berth to Blighty Wanted

Perhaps because they were able at Serapeum to bathe twice a day in the Suez Canal, his spirits rose. "If we had money, parcels, and fags we would want for nothing else, as this place is simply composed of a railway siding and tents," he had reported shortly after arriving.[56] They were now in huts and sleeping in beds. "Haven't got a bad little crib. Beds, and all now Swank. (Home-made of course, a couple of planks and nails and what more d'ye want.) Am O.K. myself and carrying on quietly, still enjoying the bathes."[57] The improvements carry on, with the residents of his hut engaging in some D.I.Y.[58] "It's a decent change [the move into huts] and ours has gone through the same transfiguration as you suggested the old lime kiln be subjected to.[59] Beds, a table, shelves etc. were soon rigged up on turning carpenters for a time, and we've now got quite a respectable looking household. I don't suppose, however, that it will be any good when we get orders to shift, singing that song about leaving our little wooden hut[60] for them. We'll have to clear sharp as usual." The beds they had made were huge successes, and it was the first time he had slept off the ground since leaving Blighty "so you can guess how I enjoyed it", he tells Doris in a separate letter.[61]

Ennui at having the same old routine duties every day is, nevertheless, profound. He describes his day as being spent half in the Canal itself and half in the Signal Office.[62] Ogling the cruise liners still rather surprisingly able to pass up and down the Canal is another pastime. "We're sort of cut off from the outer world and civilisation and we have perforce to live the simple life. Sometimes a liner comes past and this is one of our keenest delights. You'll see us all rush up the bank to have a look at the civvy passengers, like a lot of kids looking at a puff puff. And the boys get quite delirious if there any white girls aboard. I don't know what they must think of us on board because we're like a lot of savages from the wilds, rushing to see this new device of the white man." One of his companions makes a habit of hailing every passing boat and asking if there's a spare berth back to Blighty but, never getting a satisfactory answer, "sadly wends his way back to the tent to wait for another boat". Passengers on the boats respond by throwing provisions to the soldiers on the bank. "One boat did chuck a lot of stuff to us castaways once,

55) September 8th 1916.
56) June 10th 1916.
57) June 30th 1916.
58) July 13th 1916.
59) Tintern, vd. letter June 10th 1916.
60) *Little Wooden Hut,* a popular song, 'I wouldn't leave my little wooden hut for you'.
61) July 14th 1916.
62) June 15th 1916.

cigarettes, milk and tinned stuff." Just my luck, he writes, "happened to be on duty at the time and so couldn't plunge in after the good things. Pretty exciting too, chaps from both banks racing to the middle for the prizes."[63] Letters from home perhaps expressed concern at the risks of swimming in the Canal, which he seeks to allay. "As regards the swimming business, there's no need whatever to put yourselves out about it. We're like young cruisers in the water now with such excellent practice. On the other hand, the water in this part of the globe is the most buoyant to be found, so buoyant in fact that one can almost go to sleep on the surface. Say, I've had some acquaintance with this Suez, I guess. What with having swum across, rowed across and walked across – to complete my record I should now very much like to steam along it to Blighty. You can quite understand my yearning for a sight of the beauties of "Hen Walia" [Old Wales] again."[64] It was much the same elsewhere along the Canal, as the Official History makes clear, writing about Ferdan further to the north. "Those who were on the edge of the Canal would sit on the banks in the cool of the evening and watch large steamers cautiously make their way up and down, with all lights on, orchestras playing, ladies singing. All ranks bathed daily."[65] The endless routine and monotony could make it easy for soldiers to lose track of time in the desert and while separation anxiety – the absence of familiar surroundings and people – could affect all soldiers, men in the desert were particularly prone to it due to the barren and bleak nature of the terrain, as one historian notes. "Omnipresent desert saturates consciousness making the mind as sterile as itself. The boredom known as desert weariness or nostalgia was a common reaction to garrison duty but made worse in the desert."[66] Not surprisingly, his old hankering to be nearer the action had not entirely dissipated and he is perhaps conscious they are having a quieter, if not more comfortable, time than troops serving elsewhere.[67] A few months later "still in same old hole" with "nothing exciting to record", he concludes wistfully: "We're carrying on quietly as befits a waiting game. Our men have just biffed Johnny Turk one in the eye further up the line (my rotten luck) and did it well, too. Rumour has it that their war cry was 'Owns back for Suvla, you blighters', bless 'em, the dear little rascals. Glad to say that the Welshmen there showed 'em how to handle bayonets very creditably, too, so I am given to understand."[68]

A Passion for Photography

At first he writes that that same old hole – Brigade Signals at Serapeum – does not justify more than basic photography, one of his new passions, so he encloses a packet of views of Port Said instead.[69] "Never been there myself but hope to get a chance some day. Looks a pretty decent place, doesn't it? If it had been possible to obtain some P.Cs. of the place we're at, you may depend upon it I should certainly have got some. It really wouldn't pay a photographer to waste his films on this delightful spot and would be simply a loss of time and money. You see, this is a

63) July 14th 1916. They would have had to swim.
64) July 13th 1916.
65) Dudley Ward, p63.
66) Barr, p129.
67) July 31st 1916. "Guarding the Canal, good enough for kids."
68) August 27th 1916. Probably the Battle of Romani, in which the Royal Welch Fusiliers played a prominent part.
69) The town built at the northern extremity of the Suez Canal. Now Egypt's second most populous city.

section of the 'wilds' and there's absolutely 'nixes' here." He does send one photograph he has taken of a pontoon bridge to Doris but adds: "It's a regular nuisance, too, because, ten chances to one, when you want to cross to the canteen the other side the blooming things swing open to allow liners full of globe trotters to pass through."[70] Dewi was not untypical of World War One soldiers in taking a great interest in the still relatively new public pursuit of photography, sending home post cards and later photographs of his surroundings – including photos taken by his colleagues and then developed in makeshift developing rooms. His letters are filled with requests for pictures from home, and asking their reaction to his photos. He is impatient at the delay in receiving a group photo of his parents and Doris, following a visit they had made to one of the leading studios of the day, prompting him to write: "You ought to see old Whitlock and choke him off. Tell him in a voice of reverberating thunder that the Khedive orders him to 'Get a move on', 'Pull himself together' etc. That ought to do the trick, I think."[71]

He did not have his camera with him until late in 1916, and was anxious his parents should not deprive themselves of the opportunity to take photos they could send to him. "I should like you to buy one for yourself and carry on with the good work. I long for one out here, though, because I could take such interesting photos and ought to have thought of it long before. Mac has, I think, infused some enthusiasm for photography into me."[72] Much of what he sent would have been of a fabulous nature to his parents and sister – the banks of the river where Moses was found, the pyramid of Cheops, Matarieh, where Mary rested, ordinary Egyptians, Bedouin ladies and, towards the end of the war, views of the Holy Land, and in particular the Holy City, and campaigning shots. Pictures of exotic creatures, such as a camels, would also have interested the folks back home, as would his less than flattering description of these beasts. Camels are "curious creatures...the most sulky, ridiculous, unreasonable quadruped on the face of the earth. He is always grumbling about something in a peculiarly objectionable, grunting manner which gets on one's nerves, and emitting noises something like a fog-horn out of order. They always look to me as if afflicted with some great sorrow. Utter disdain and contempt of man can be read in their eyes and they always bear the appearance of confirmed pessimists and 'Dismal Jimmies'. They have truly always got the hump and a more miserable looking object would be hard to find. 'Enough to make a camel laugh' would be the much better way of describing something really humorous, I think."[73]

By September three months into his stay at Serapeum he is sending home snapshots of their surroundings, possibly using a borrowed camera.[74] These include pictures of his Norfolk and Suffolk companions, a local Egyptian policeman, "a native" he says, "of this Elysian country, and a direct descendant of Potipher"[75], a "stately vessel" passing through the Suez Canal, and their small

70) September 9th 1916.
71) June 15th 1916. Founded by Henry Whitlock in 1864 in Birmingham, the photographic chain H.J. Whitlock, had branches in a number of leading cities, including in Duke Street Arcade, Cardiff. Clients included Queen Victoria and the Prince of Wales (later Edward VII).
72) August 27th 1916.
73) September 9th 1916.
74) September 8th 1916.
75) In the Bible Joseph, was sold to Potiphar, captain of the guard, as a household slave.

encampment stalwart "Signal Residency" or the "Elysium of Rest", as he describes it. "The first thoughts which would spring up in the minds of the uninitiated upon the contemplation of the picture, I would imagine, would be – 'Pioneers' Settlement' – 'It looked so calm and peaceful there,' as they sing about Ireland. You have no doubt heard much of the 'far-flung outposts of our Empire'. Voila! the genuine article. The only thing is, talking about the Empire, I must adhere to the truth, the sun *does* set here but it's generally very reluctant to do so, and lets us know all about it during the time it's on duty viz. 7 am – 6 pm." A final picture, he tells his sister, is of a pair of demure Egyptian belles. "I assure you they stand for all that is beautiful amongst the female sex of the Near East. In fact, they are the 'last word' in fascination, just as Mr Bourneville informs you on the posters that he is the 'last word in cocoa'. They are of a very retiring, modest nature, as you can imagine when I tell you that the young lady on the right actually drew the crinoline across her face to hide her adorable dimples. The photographer in this instance experienced great difficulty in getting miladies to pose and to allay their fears, assuring them as best he could in Arabic that his camera was not a new pattern Lee-Enfield, as they had supposed. These are the type of fair sex which disclaim any acquaintance with rouge, while the latest hats, fashions, and coiffures from Paris do not interest them in the least. They are never accompanied by Poms or Pekingese and the mere existence of theatre, automobiles, and tennis racquets are quite unknown to them.[76] Quite content, these ladies are, to live and die in the village of their birth, tending cows and carrying water pitchers. Frequently they are to be seen accompanying their husband and master when he is abroad, trotting unwearyingly on foot behind the ass upon which the latter comfortably rides, yet one never hears of an Egyptian branch of the Women's Social and Political Union."[77]

A complex reference follows to the playwright and political activist, George Bernard Shaw's satire on contemporary attitudes to women's rights and advancement, *Mrs Warren's Profession*. "It wouldn't do, I'm sure, for Miss Warren to preach the new belief of the 'women's rights' creed out here, for instance. The men wouldn't take it so calmly as in England. These people, you see, are totally devoid of such foolish customs of civilisation."[78] In the play Mrs Warren is a brothel owner with premises across Europe, who has chosen that occupation as means of supporting her daughter, Vivie, – the Miss Warren referred to – to study mathematics at Cambridge University. Cardiff had itself been something of a hotbed of suffragism and he will have expected his remarks to have amused his independently-minded sister. In 1913 Mrs Pankhurst was charged with incitement to cause damage and imprisoned after addressing a suffragette rally in the city, home at the time to the biggest branch of the Women's Suffrage Society outside London. Several years earlier in 1908 there had been serious disturbances following a suffragette meeting in the city's Cory Hall, and two meetings had had to be abandoned a year earlier because of "rowdyism".[79]

---

76) September 8th 1916. Poms, Pomeranian, popular breed of dog.

77) The Women's Social and Political Union (WSPU), founded by Emmeline Pankhurst, was the leading militant organisation campaigning for women's suffrage.

78) September 8th 1916.

79) May, J., *Millennium Cardiff*. Castle Publications. 1999, p36.

His enthusiasm for the gentle art [of photography] was, he wrote in August, at fever pitch so that the arrival of any camera would be a red letter day. "You will shortly have such a collection as will put the National Art Gallery in the shade completely. However, I am not under any circumstances to be neglected even then. You will have no difficulty whether [probably 'either' is meant] in procuring another V.P. Kodak (sold of all chemists) which will enable you to 'carry on quietly' for an indefinite period." A few months later, photography is still popular, as is another sport. "At present we are cricket and photography mad. Spent all day yesterday, very near, at the wickets. It's a fine game. Old Mac stumped me twice."[80]

Canal Races and a Fine Day Out

As generations of soldiers have found, sports were the best antidote to boredom and fatigues. In later letters he talks about the many football and "rugger" matches they enjoyed but the main leisure pursuit while on Canal Zone duty was swimming, including on one occasion a race organised by the officers to commemorate – though he does not mention this fact – the landing of reinforcements at Suvla Bay on Gallipoli exactly one year earlier. "Well, of course, we get lovely bathing here," he tells them back home, "but it's always calm. Don't I envy you being able to indulge in surf bathing, not half. Every time a big boat comes along I take full advantage of the little waves caused by it, they're the only kind we get, you see, and when I float on my back and feel them lifting and falling underneath me, I shut my eyes and say, "'Strewth! 'Sreminds me o' Porthcawl' and expect every moment to open my eyes and find Dad coming up hand over hand to duck me. I'm terribly disappointed every time, of course." The race was against a team of black soldiers from the Caribbean. "Ten of us swam in the heat and the first four picked. The race was across the Canal about 120 yards, that is, and we went like greased fork lightning.[81] Some race. Our 'captain' came in first by about six inches and I and another chap on top of one another dead heat as second, and the fourth a foot or so behind. My word, it was a pull across, and the winning post officer declared it a very good race, 'matter of inches', those were his words (not bad, my first aquatic accomplishment eh?). The other six never came in at all, chucked it up half way. Anyhow, we few were pretty evenly contested. I s'pose it's because, being in the same section, we always bathed together and know each other's points. One for the old R.E's, what?" His comments on the contest itself, once the team had been picked, shock today but he was expressing feelings of superiority which were no doubt representative of the time and would have been shared by the overwhelming bulk of the population at home at this high point in the history of the British Empire. "We four swam a relay race the next day against a quartet from the British West Indies Regiment. The prize was 100 piastre note, the officers backing the losing team to stump up. We stripped off and when I saw those darkies with big arms and muscular chests I said to the other chaps, 'I think it's adieu to that quid. It's us for a lose [sic], and darkies can always swim'. Well, we started and what a surprise we had, I swam third and did my little bit, and we knocked the beggars into a cocked hat, beating them by about 80 yards at the finish.

---

80) August 3rd 1916

81) The canal's width varied from 400 feet in flat ground to 300 feet in shallow cuttings in three areas, with banks 40 feet high on both sides. It was originally dug to a depth of 26 ft. but has subsequently been increased to 79 feet.

You should see the officer's face. ... He had been so cock-sure that he never brought any money for the prize. But we got it alright, don't you worry, and our hut had a feed that night, not 'arf we didn't ('Dado', that's me, was in funds, d'ye see). Anyhow, we made rings round 'em and, although I was tempted before we started to sing, 'Oh! darkies, how my heart sinks really'[82], when scrutinising their biceps, I didn't forget to ask 'em to pay my best respects to 'Uncle Tom' when we finished.[83] We had our photos taken afterwards, victors and vanquished, in 'black and white'. I hope it comes out, I'll send you one then." There follows a sketch of the race and an apology for boasting.

His months on the Canal – perhaps because of long periods of enforced idleness, punctuated by mind-numbing fatigues – seems to have been when he felt most homesick, one year into his departure from home and with no notion of when it would all end. Every one of his letters during these months reflects on outings they used to have as a family and the good times he had with his father, as well as looking forward to the resumption of this fun. Heliopolis had left him feeling just like a kid after going to St. Mellons, a month later he is reflecting on a camping expedition with two friends to Sully, and the prospect of a visit to the limekilns at Tintern and a trip up the Wye Valley. He is pleased for his father who has managed a side-car trip but wishes he could have been there. "When you talk of St. Fagans, Cowbridge, etc. it makes me think of green fields and shady lanes and then I'm brought back to the stern reality of miles and miles of hot sand."[84] It is Porthcawl he yearns for, however, as he dreams of returning there. "Just fancy coming back from the beach to tea as we used to ...and then off for a stroll on the green and Lock's Common."[85] He did not move far from the Canal for his leisure but there is one mention of a day away and of an amusing incident trying to draw money from the Post Office in Ismailia, "a perfect little French township, with appropriate two storied houses, plainly but tastefully built, tree-shaded with deep verandas over which climbed innumerable plants", as another account describes it.[86] This gives him an opportunity to reflect, again in a patronising way, on "the natives". Writing in the demotic style[87] he has now adopted for conversations, he says: "Being disappointed over my Alex [Alexandria] leave, I had a day at Ismailia yesterday with another of our boys.[88] Directly I landed on the platform I bent my steps towards the Civil P.O. (you can easily guess what for). Yes, too blooming true, it was for that five quid. [...] Well, I got to the M.O. [Money Order] counter and accosted the Egyptian

---

82) Stephen Foster's song *Old Folks at Home*. 'Way down upon de Swanee ribber, Far, far away, Dere's whar my heart is turning ebber, Dere's whar the old folks stay. All up and down de whole creation, Sadly I roam, Still longing for de old plantation, And for de old folks at home. All de world am sad and dreary, Eb'rywhere I roam. Oh! darkies, how my heart grows weary, Far from de old folks at home.' The song has been recorded (with the original words) by among others, Paul Robeson. It is the state song (to updated words) of Florida, location of the Suwannee River mentioned in the first line.

83) Harriet Beecher Stowe's novel, *Uncle Tom's Cabin*, to which he is referring, has been described as the most popular, influential and controversial book written by an American. Stowe's novel gave such an impetus to the crusade for the abolition of slavery that President Lincoln half-jokingly greeted Stowe as 'the little lady who started the great Civil War'. The later connotation attached to 'Uncle Tom' – a compliant slave – had not yet been formed.

84) August 3rd 1916.

85) June 30th 1916.

86) Dudley Ward, p64.

87) Dewi makes extensive use of what linguistic experts call eye-dialect, with words written to sound as they are pronounced rather than as correctly spelt. The intention is to suggest a dialectical, or uneducated form of speech and is differentiated from spoken ear-dialect because it appears on the page, where it can only be seen, not heard.

88) November 4th 1916.

clerk, 'Hi! Matey, where's my five quid' and hands [sic] over the notification. He says, 'are you Sapper David'. Says I, 'Be'old 'im in the flesh.' 'Well, we must have a letter from an officer or the Provost Marshal to certify that you are this man.' I showed him my pay book, my identification disc, my photo and goodness knows what for proof, all to no purpose. He was adamant, so I went out, saying how sorry I was under my breath, and made a bee line to the Provost M. office.

"They sent me to another P.M. and at last I got a bloke in the office to write a paper saying 'I certify that this man is D.E. David etc.' Took it back to the Egyptian and, blow me, if he didn't want a signature then, so I had to go back again and got them to put a stamp and signature and several other official-looking characters on it for luck. Again I approached the silly blighter and asked him in a bored voice whether it was all serene now or would he prefer my photo on the paper printed in Egyptian hieroglyphics. For a wonder he said it would do now, and, if the wires hadn't been between me and him, I'd have either fallen on his neck or given him a wipe.[89] Then he says, 'Do you leeve in Cardeeff.' 'Yes' I said 'near the biscuit factory on the mud.'[90] Oh! he was an inquisitive blighter but I was one too many for the silly old cuss. After all this palaver and preliminary speechifying and at last I had the precious notes under my shirt in my belt, I heaved a sigh of relief. 'Gee!,' I said, 'Can I go now, or d'ye want to know whether I was born in Upper Zinc Street or Little Zinc Street' – Come and have a drink with me, will you.'[91], He says 'I tank you, no, I do not drink ze beera,' and all the clerks seemed to think it was a huge joke. [...] After this, naturally, I felt a bit fagged so we went and had a feed. Not bad, indeed, for Greek cooking but, as I said to my pal, 'Jim, I'll make up for this when I get home,' – he concurred. Then we decided that a drive in a 'garry' was good for the health and boarded the first one on sightseeing, not 'arf, riding about in a carriage and pair, leaning back, smoking Gold Flake and looking bored in the approved millionaire style.[92] We got sick of that, so dismissed the coachman and went to the Empire Club and had tea and bread and *butter* – Oh! but it tasted good after these months. Then we had a few games and looked through the latest illustrateds [magazines], issuing forth some time later for fresh worlds to conquer. We went round the shops then – could hardly recognise 'em at first."

Ismailia – one of three principal Canal zone cities together with Port Said at the northern extremity and Suez at the southern end – was an attractive place to visit, and no doubt popular with off-duty soldiers, particularly those, like Dewi, manning small outposts. Named after Ismail Pasha, Khedive of Egypt, it was built as a depot by the Suez Canal Company in 1861 and included a Garden City for European employees. Dewi completes his time in Ismailia with a visit to the shops to buy presents for his sister, a pursuit whenever he gets the chance to go to a substantial town on leave. He and his companions are not going to let the opportunity of another decent meal pass, however. "But I haven't finished with 'our day out' yet, have I? 'Well, Jim,'[93] he'd say to me, 'think we'd better take in more supplies now,

89) Wipe, slang for a kiss.
90) Spillers Nephews biscuit factory, erected in 1896 in Moorland Road, a redbrick Cardiff landmark alongside the main Great Western Railway line. Transferred to the Co-operative Wholesale Society in the 1920s, it was burnt down in the 1980s and replaced by housing.
91) Zinc Street, his birthplace, one of a series of streets all bearing the names of metals.
92) Garry, possibly a Persian name for a carriage.
93) Jim, Dewi uses this name for himself, sometimes signing his letters this way, and sometimes addresses colleagues likewise.

hadn't we?' every hour or so, – so you can guess we got outside some stuff that day. You see, he was just like me, hadn't seen a restaurant for ages. In the night we went to a cinema and enjoyed it top-hole – and felt like kids seeing pictures for the first time. Came from there and buzzed off to the station, catching the 9.30 train back – tired out. Arriving at the station we did the two miles to our hut on donkeys and tumbled in. I wasn't a bit sorry to get back – back to the simple life, peaceful and no worry. Strikes me, I'll be a shepherd or something like that when I get home – it sort of grows on you, the wilds."

Life on the canal eventually came to an end once the threat of further Turkish-German incursions had gone. The way had been cleared by the Battle of Romani for the British advance through Sinai into Gaza and Palestine. The order to move came in November 1916 and on the 13th of that month Dewi reported to Coy. [Company] at Ismailia. By November 21st he was settling into Moascar Camp, before moving further north a few weeks later to El Ferdan, Kantara, Romani and the long advance through Sinai. Serapeum was a base that remained in British military hands until 1954 when the RAF moved out after the election of President Nasser, organiser of the military coup that overthrew Egypt's last king, Farouk. Two years later Britain made an unsuccessful intervention in Egypt to try with the French to prevent the nationalisation of the Suez Canal that Dewi had been sent to help protect 38 years previously.

(above) The Office Dug-out, where six men worked in shifts sending telegraph messages in Morse Code to and from headquarters.

(right) Serapeum, the Signal Office, Dewi's base from June to November 1916 during the Suez Canal defence phase of operations.

The British Army employed a large force of Egyptian labourers for general duties, here seen moving a hut.

Liner passing up the Suez. Passengers on board threw supplies overboard for troops to swim out and collect.

(above) Dewi diving in. Modesty was not required in the desert and in all-male company.

(left) Dewi (far right) enjoying a dip with three fellow-soldiers in the Canal. Daily swims were a way of keeping cool in the intense desert heat.

Contestants in the Whites v Blacks swimming race, (August 1916) organised by officers to commemorate the Suvla Bay landing a year earlier. Dewi is third from right, bottom row.

Farmer with oxen, ploughing. Egyptians went about their business largely unconcerned by the troops around them.

Egyptian soldier. Local troops served mainly on internal security duties.

Camel Corps crossing the Suez Canal on a pontoon bridge. With few road vehicles available, the Army relied heavily on camels for transport.

Heavy equipment being unloaded for road-making. Steam rollers had to be brought from Britain to create durable road surfaces.

CHAPTER FIVE

MARCHING THROUGH SINAI

DECEMBER 1916 – MARCH 1917

Taking the Offensive

B‍ack in Britain significant events had been taking place. The costly stalemate on the Somme had brought a demand for change, and on December 7th 1916 the protracted struggle that had dominated politics for months came to a head when Lloyd George succeeded Asquith as Prime Minister. ushering in an administration in which the Welsh politicians who had strongly supported him in his rise to power played a prominent part.[1]

In the Near East, following the Turks' failure in August at Romani, a Turkish attack on the Canal was no longer a serious threat. An advance on the Mediterranean coastal town of El Arish was now planned, and with this in mind Murray re-organised his forces, creating a new Eastern Force under the command of General Sir Charles Dobell, made up of all the troops east of Suez and based at a new corps headquarters in Ismailia.[2] Another general, Sir Philip Chetwode,[3] was put in charge of a strike force, the Desert Column, consisting mainly of Australian and New Zealand mounted divisions, which would spearhead the assault on the Turkish positions. Infrastructure development continued, the railway – and, in consequence, the front – being extended at the rate of around 20 miles a month from Kantara, which had been transformed from a small junction on the Canal to a major transport hub. (Egyptian railway lines that were not vital for the transport of cotton, sugar, cereals and forages, were lifted for use by the military railway.) Lack of water, however, was a problem that bedevilled desert operations in both world wars, in contrast with the campaigns on the European mainland, and now represented the main obstacle to a complete re-occupation of the Sinai Peninsula. Troops found they could manage without food – or at any rate survive on an endless diet of biscuit and bully beef – but not without water. During November, before the pipeline reached Romani, water had to be brought up by rail in tank trucks for the large number of men and animals – not to mention steam locomotives – now being deployed in Sinai. Beyond this point water had to be carried on the backs of camels. There were shallow wells on the coastal route but the water they yielded was brackish.

Murray, the overall commander of the EEF, had moved his own headquarters from Ismailia to Cairo in October, a switch made necessary by his continuing responsibility for the defence of Egypt, and by the need to keep an eye on the Senussi in the west and the Sultan of Darfur in Sudan.[4] The Arab uprising against the Turks in the Hejaz also required his attention, as, too, did the internal situation in Egypt, the administration of martial law and the oversight he retained for the administration of British forces in Salonika. It left him, nevertheless, acting as an administrator rather than as a commander in the field henceforward, and open to criticism for the bloated size of his headquarters at Cairo – 662 staff at its peak.

---

1) Morgan, *Wales in British Politics*, p277-278.
2) Canadian-born Sir Charles MacPherson Dobell, 1869-1954, a veteran of British Army campaigns in Crete, South Africa, Nigeria and the Boxer Rebellion.
3) Lieutenant General Sir Philip Chetwode, 1869-1950) saw service in the Second Boer War, on the Western Front, and in the Sinai and Palestine campaigns. He was put in charge of the XXth Corps under Allenby. After the war he became C.I.G.S. India in 1928, and was made Field Marshal in 1933.
4) Ismailia had been the headquarters of the Army in the Middle East since March 1916, when it had been reconstituted as the Egyptian Expeditionary Force.

This would be held against him when British plans were confounded by the Turks in the first two battles for Gaza in March and April the following year. The Eastern Force at this stage consisted of three divisions – 52nd, 53rd and 54th – together with the Australian and New Zealand Mounted Division, the Imperial Mounted Division (also Australian), a light car patrol and two light armoured batteries, making a total of 8,500 sabres, 92 guns and 25,000 rifles.[5] A further division was also being formed in Egypt from yeomanry units. The 53rd had moved in November to the vast Moascar Camp in Ismailia to act as general reserve to the advancing Eastern Force. The Turks opposing them in Southern Palestine could mount only 1,000 sabres and three weak divisions, providing 12,000-16,000 rifles and 74 guns, but their control of the water supply might prove crucial. They would have to be quickly overcome to avoid having to continue to use camels to bring the very large quantities of water the Eastern Force needed.

With superior British forces advancing, the 1,600 strong Turkish infantry force defending El Arish was ordered to withdraw to a defensive system they had created around Magdhaba and Abu Aweigle. On the night of December 20th and 21st Australian and New Zealand mounted troops and the Camel Corps marched on El Arish, supported by the 52nd Division, and were able to enter unopposed. Yet, unless Magdhaba, 18 miles southeast in the Sinai Desert, a source of water for the by now thirsty horses, could be taken, a withdrawal from El Arish would become necessary. The Turks were challenged in the redoubts they had retired to over the next few days, and the Turkish commander, two battalion commanders and 1,280 prisoners of their 27th Division, together with four guns, were captured. The Battle of Magdhaba had been won. More rail lines could now be laid and the first trains were able to reach El Arish on December 31st. Because of its coastal position, El Arish was also accessible by sea, enabling stores to be landed on the beach. By the end of 1916 the objective of clearing the Sinai Peninsula and of defending Egypt and the Suez Canal by holding the El Arish area had been achieved.

The ambivalence in British political and military circles as to the objectives of the large British and colonial army in the Near East had continued until late in 1916. Robertson wrote to Murray in October before the capture of El Arish to say that his primary intention was not to win in any particular quarter of the globe. "My sole object is to win the war and we shall not do that in the Hejaz nor in the Sudan. Our military policy is perfectly clear and simple. ...[It] is offensive on the Western Front and defensive everywhere else." As late as January 1917, after the victory at the Battle of Magdhaba, Murray was ordered to send one of his divisions, the 42nd, to the Western Front. At the end of February, however, and after the troops had been sent, policy changed. An Anglo-French conference at Calais decided to pursue offensives on all fronts, timed to coincide with the big Spring push planned in France. A new offensive aimed at driving the Turks out of Palestine was, therefore, now ordered by the War Department. The plan was to push on through the broad Wadi Ghuzza – a deep watercourse running from Shillal northwest to Deir el Belah and the Mediterranean – towards Rafa and Gaza. This would force the Turks to evacuate, possibly with difficulty, their forward base further south at Beersheba and quit southern Palestine altogether. The same tactics that had been successfully

95

5) Guns, in this context artillery pieces. Sabres were the curved military sword of the cavalry.

put in place at Magdhaba – converging attacks by mounted troops – would be deployed. Equipping, feeding and watering an army on the move remained, however, one of the biggest challenges. As the railway had only just reached Wadi el Arish, seven camel trains were organised, each train capable of carrying 72 tons, as first line of transport. Six divisional trains were also put in place, with 72 limbered wagons, together with two mixed horse and motor transport trains, every one capable of taking 72 tons.[6]

The British had some significant advantages over the retreating Turkish force. As well as enjoying considerable superiority in mounted troops, General Dobell's forces were protected on their left flank by vessels operating from the Mediterranean and ample water was available by early 1917 from wells refilled by the rainfall from November onwards. In the first action of the New Year Turkish defence works at El Magruntein, just over a mile south of Rafa and poorly connected with each other, were attacked by mounted troops under Chetwode and after stubborn resistance captured at a cost to the Turks of 1,600 prisoners, four guns and six machine guns. Following the loss of Rafa, only a few miles west of Gaza, the Turks concentrated forces at Shillal between Beersheba and Rafa and despatched a total of 5,000 men to defend Gaza. By the end of February British mounted forces had managed to reach Delilah's birthplace, Khan Yunus[7], six miles north of Rafa and of the Egyptian-Ottoman frontier, and one of several strong posts along the Turkish defensive line to Beersheba. Its capture prompted the German commander, von Kressenstein, to retire his forces to a new defensive line north of Wadi Ghuzza, which, it was hoped, would cover any Allied attempt to advance up the coast, or inland through Beersheba to Jerusalem. At newly-taken Khan Yunus, British Army engineers found the largest and deepest well in the area, and the settlement soon became an important forward base. British commanders were also enjoying opportunities their compatriots in France, engaged in attritional trench warfare in pursuit of small gains, were denied. The wide open spaces of the desert made it possible to mount mobile campaigns and to adapt to circumstances. Commanders on both sides could see what troops were doing and could use reserves as they wished and when necessary.

With political backing now confirmed for a move into Palestine, Gaza was to be attacked as soon as the railway reached Rafa. Supply operations were based on the assumption that the town could be captured in one day, a withdrawal back to Wadi Ghuzza for food, water and ammunition being required if that did not happen. As the account of the campaign points out: "Success before nightfall on the day of attack was thus an indispensable condition. If Gaza was captured within 24 hours of the commencement of hostilities, there was ample water there for all men and animals, and supplies could be brought to the coast in the vicinity of this town by sea."[8] In March, however, the British advance, after several months of progress, was stopped at Gaza. Only after two defeats and a delay of several months could the march on towards Jerusalem be resumed.

---

6) Limber, detachable front of a gun or cable carriage, consisting of two wheels, axle, pole and ammunition box or cable-laying equipment.

7) Khan Yunus. A vast khan (caravanserai or caravan halt) was constructed here in 1387-88 by the emir Yunis al-Nûrûzi at a key point on the main route from Africa to Asia, to protect caravans, pilgrims and travellers.

8) Kearsey, A. Lt. Col., *Egypt and Palestine Campaigns.* Naval & Military Press. pp13-14.

Onwards to Gaza

In December – the month in which El Arish was taken – Dewi had moved from Moascar, first to El Ferdan, a few miles north (at the time little more than a ferry and a swing bridge on the Canal), then to Kantara, to Gilban, and Pelusium, and, finally, Romani, where the 158th and 159th brigades spent Christmas.[9] By December 8th Dewi was at the new Divisional headquarters in Mahamadiyah, on the Mediterranean coast north of Romani, his base for the next six weeks. Dewi's unit had moved to back up the advancing front line on his sister's birthday, November 13th, when he reported to Company in Ismailia, the French-built town where he had spent a few days in May, at Spinney Wood Camp, and a pleasant day's leave at the beginning of November. Writing from Moascar, Dewi comments to Doris that once they start moving they never know when they are going to stop next. "I've only been back with the company about a fortnight and that's the third during that short time." He goes on: "Pretty busy, we're getting nowadays, are we not? Of course, it is rather boresome for me after my recent months of leisure but I'm quite used to it now, more or less. I missed most of the inevitable manual labour this last move though, as, fortunately for me, I was in the vanguard (Ahem!) sent to open the new office. We do things on a different style altogether out here, compared with civil telegraphs. None of your waiting a few years to build an office – Signal Offices – Pooh! mere trifles – they are erected and taken over, or on the other hand dismantled and evacuated – p'raps you recollect we're absolutely 'it' when it comes to evacuating or, in other words, buzzing off – within an hour's notice."[10]

As a Royal Engineers sapper, he will, of course, have taken pride in the Corps' can-do reputation. One of the Corps' proudest boasts is that there has been no campaign undertaken by the British Army in which it has not played a part. Military engineers helped to build (and undermine) medieval fortresses and castles, and a Corps of Engineers has existed within the Army since 1716 when Michael Richards, Principal Engineer of the Ordnance Train, successfully argued for the division of the artillery and engineering functions. Since then, Royal Engineers have been involved in tasks at home and abroad as varied as designing and building military defences, barracks and ports, roads, railways, canals, surveying and mapping, telegraphy, the development of electricity, ballooning and aeroplanes, sub-sea diving, and armoured vehicles. They were also responsible for the design and construction of trenches in World War One and for building the accommodation that troops in the field needed. Throwing up or pulling down a signal office was, therefore, unlikely to be much of a problem. Moascar was relatively comfortable with larger numbers of tents than was strictly required, intended in part to bluff enemy aircraft spotters into believing a considerable force had been gathered there. Army life during their fortnight-long interlude at Ismailia, nevertheless, seemed futile for the ordinary soldier, though lightened for Dewi by a few hours he was able to spend one day with Hughie Mowbray – by now an officer. "I was 'pon fatigues keeping the desert tidy, and making it look pretty by raking paths about the camp. As it happened, I wasn't exactly working just then but was leaning on my trusty desert sweeping instrument and airing my views to two other chaps on the excellent work we were

97

---

9) Gilban and Pelusium, stations along the railway line from Kantara to Romani. Pelusium, a Roman foundation, is 20 miles southeast of modern Port Said and about two and a half miles from the sea.

10) November 27th 1916.

engaged upon at that particular moment, when somebody interrupted with – 'Get a move on there, pull yourself together, and get off that rake' – Of course, I turned and stared and there was the one and only H.M." This duty might not have had much of a purpose in Moascar, where he was writing from, but sweeping was one of the regular duties soldiers found themselves engaged on in Egypt. Wire netting tracks were laid across the desert for men, animals and vehicles to move around, and this had to be kept clear of blown sand, which could quickly cover up work that had been carried out. When a Turkish assault on the Canal was feared earlier in the war, the track was also a good place to inspect each morning for footprints.[12]

By the middle of December, when his advance with the cable wagons used to lay down the communication lines had taken him north along the Canal and then east as far as Romani, Dewi is soon looking for his cousin's husband again. "It was at our first port of call that I met Hugh after searching through five battalions of infantry. I told him of this, whereupon, like the buck he is, he suggested the canteen as a 'pick me up'. I was not averse to this, consequently we supped off pineapple chunks and 'Thin Lunch', our wines consisting of the juice at the bottom of the tin."[13] Eventually, the order to pack up and leave Romani came. "It had been rumoured for some time that the date of departure 'for fresh worlds to conquer' was not far distant, and the lists published of kit to be carried, with strict injunctions to be rid of surplus kit in any shape or form, seemed to confirm this persistent rumour. Thus it came about that one particular (I can't say 'fine' morning very well, for all mornings are fine in Egypt) my section sallied forth in desert marching order array, by which you can easily imagine was by no means bulky, but, on the contrary, 'skeleton-like' in its formation, and took to the open road. To be correct and utilise my 'mounted men's jargon', I should have said 'we hooked-in', which, for your edification, can be translated as harnessing up to our many wagons and limbers, mounting and setting forth on our journey. The great change of being on trek, passing hour after hour travelling on the cable wagon in the fresh air was a very pleasing experience to me after months of drudgery indoors and I enjoyed the 'gipsy' life so much that upon reaching our destination that evening I attacked the 'stew' so thoughtfully prepared by the cook and his mates with a vigour that surprised me, and upon dusk falling rolled under my wagon and slept sounder than ever till morning."

The Desert Trek Begins

At 5 a.m. the following morning before it was light, they found themselves rolling blankets and packing the transport camels, then breakfasting and setting off again, "onwards ever onwards", he writes, with the same programme each day. "On the third morning we left the hard road and struck a course across the soft sand of the desert. We had crossed the Suez and left that behind us long ago. And, now, the animals in the shafts (mules and horses) began to feel the strain of tugging through the heavy impeding sand, and I, as one of the wagon riders, had to relinquish my perch to relieve the weight, after which things began to liven up somewhat and the excitement commenced. Don't misinterpret that word 'excitement'. We didn't meet

---

12) Dudley Ward, p64, p59.
13) December 13th 1916.

any Turks, nor did we capture any Bedouins. No! nothing so ridiculous. What really did happen concerns a party of four, and I had the honour of being one of the quartette [sic]. It happened like this. You see, after being deprived of my wagon seat, I thought the best thing to do was to retire to the rear of the column and search among the horsemen for a mount, horse, charger, anything, in fact, to carry me, as desert tramping in the midday heat did not meet with my approval. This, I did, and met with exceptional good fortune, securing a veritable battle charger in the shape of a 'lead mule', that is, without a saddle. I thereupon mounted this noble looking steed and fell in congratulating myself on my choice." His search for a mount is understandable. Though the stages of marches, which could last several weeks, were short, the sun, the weight of equipment, and shortage of water meant a day's journey was often equivalent to one three times longer.[14]

It is impossible, he says, to attempt to describe the feeling of riding a bare-back mule. "I thought of nothing the whole time, except that old joke I was in the habit of springing on folks in my schooldays, which brought in something about seeing the point and sitting on it. That mule had a spine resembling nothing in the world more than the apex of the Pyramid of Cheops, in which I was most interested on my last visit to Cairo.[15] Howso'er, a mule of that description suited my purpose much better than 'Shanks Pony' [walking] in that rough travelling, so I determined to put myself more or less at ease (?) and, as the quartermaster had presented me with a pair of new spurs and had expressed a fervent hope that I might make good as a rough-rider, my courage soared high in consequence of his blessing. Mile after mile passed pleasingly enough, until I felt as if Will Griggs and Danny Maher had been my life-long friends.[16] Suddenly, some grey body loomed in the offing, which, upon gaining ground, and a closer inspection, proved to be a dead camel. Well, there's nothing very remarkable in a deceased member of the camel species, rather are the living ones to be avoided, but evidently mules don't hold the same opinion as one with experience. So, without further thought upon so trivial a matter, we, with cherubic innocence advanced. We had almost come broadside on, when, whether it was merely coincidence or not, I can't tell, something seemed to go wrong. I really don't know to this day the details but suddenly I found myself in company with four other mule-men, galloping madly over the desert, despite my futile efforts to draw rein and force my mount to a standstill. Things were getting serious when I remembered that I was booted and spurred and promptly dug the latter instruments into the refractory steed's flanks. As I have said before, they were new and, therefore, in no need of setting or stropping, which evidently roused the ire of my mule."[17]

---

14) Mortlock, p57.

15) The Great Pyramid of Giza (the Pyramid of Cheops), first and largest of the three pyramids in the Giza Necropolis bordering what is now El Giza. Oldest of the Seven Wonders of the Ancient World, it is the only one to remain largely intact. It was built as a tomb for fourth dynasty Egyptian Pharaoh Khufu (Cheops in Greek) over a 10 to 20-year period, concluding around 2560 BC. Initially, at 481 feet, the Great Pyramid was the tallest man-made structure in the world for over 3,800 years. Dewi had seen it in February 1916 on a visit to Cairo.

16) Will Griggs, a leading English jockey. Danny Maher was America's leading jockey in 1898 but anti-gambling sentiment and restrictions on racing led him and other jockeys to leave for Europe. In England, Maher won 1,421 races with 25 percent of his mounts. He won the Epsom Derby three times (1903, 1905, 1906), and was a two-time winner of the Ascot Gold Cup (1906, 1909). He was leading jockey in 1908 and 1913, the year he obtained British citizenship.

17) Stropping, sharpening.

He describes a scene "normally portrayed on the cinematograph" – that of a cowboy breaking in a lively buckjumper, except that he did not manage to master his steed. "Down went his head, up went his hind legs, and the ground came up to meet me. Oh! Spare me from the humiliation of another such unfortunate occurrence. The drivers (unfeeling ignoramuses) rocked in their saddles, and I could swear the mules were smiling, too. On picking myself up, I saw to my surprise that I was not the only one who had dismounted hurriedly, and, seeing a prone, motionless figure face downwards on the sand, I ran towards him and, on turning him over, found his eyes, nose, mouth, ears etc. choked with sand. He was quite dazed but after bathing his battered phisog[19] with my handkerchief and the contents of his water bottle, he showed some signs of life and pitifully begged me not to let 'them' come near him, at which I was forced to smile, although I assured him 'they' were at a very safe distance away. However, after pulling him to his feet we got back to the column and, the runaways having been recaptured, we pushed on. Not to be beaten, I now mounted mine again but a kindly sergeant having witnessed my spirited dash offered me his horse, which I gladly accepted. He was saddled up with stirrups etc. which make riding an enjoyment and proved to be a beauty – just like an armchair to ride. During the day about six other riders came to earth from their mules and provided plenty of amusement to the company. I think for my part I had had quite enough adventures for that day but being unscathed, when we halted and had fed, I turned in and slept the sleep of the just that night beneath the stars."

The trek was not without its pleasures, if the all-pervading heat, coupled with an absence of shade, the dust and other annoyances could be put to one side. "We were under the impression that the trek was going to be a long one and felt quite content, as we were enjoying it no end. At night, after we had 'unhooked', a large camp fire would be built and the company talent was given a chance to shine, variated by rollicking choruses, which we entered into with all our hearts and lungs (*some* lungs). There weren't any Carusos present but that didn't worry us.[20] They all got applause, minus the thousand guineas. Two days later, after very rough 'going', we sighted white tents and half a mile away, as far as you could see, the blue Mediterranean stretched in front of us. Here, the rest of the company, who had travelled by train, awaited us and our journey, to our regret, was at an end after 5 days of the best. We composed ourselves for slumber in the tents that night, next day I was told off for Signal Office duties as telephonist and now, I suppose, we must prepare for another sojourn.[21] It may be brief and it may not, we never can tell in this walk of life, but should orders come sooner or later for a mobile column, they will find us 'ready, aye ready'." This stop was Mahamadiyah, near Romani, which had been captured in August, and his unit would stay there until the latter half of January, before moving on to El Arish, seized six days before Christmas from the retreating Turks, and then on during February to El Burge and Sheikh Zowaid, a Bedouin town named after a legendary Moslem commander from the 7th century, just over half way from El Arish to Gaza city and 210 miles from Cairo.

Parcels were there for them when they arrived, providing no doubt welcome relief from the rations they had received while on the march. "My surprise, delight and gratitude on the night we arrived on finding a parcel from Auntie awaiting me can

19) Phisog, face

20) Enrico Caruso (1873-1921), the first great tenor superstar, sang in opera houses across Europe and America.

21) Told off, meaning assigned.

be more easily imagined than described, and I was envied by many a weary traveller who gave their simple verdict of the cakes as 'the goods'. I always did hold the opinion that a good 'tuck in' is the finest thing imaginable after a trek over the sands of Egypt, and it held good right up to the hilt on this occasion." Their new location, which the Army seems to have cleaned up to make it a suitable and hygienic location for the troops passing through, is, nevertheless, bleak, or so Dewi thinks. "This place is nothing to go stark staring mad over as a spa, and no one would venture to this lonely spot to take of its waters, unless he was suffering more or less from an attack of 'simplicity', for the very good reason that it is in no wise over-abundant and is saturated (if I may use the term with regard to liquid), with chemicals, disinfectants etc. etc., which do not tend to make it any the more palatable."[22] There is inevitably a comparison with what he clearly feels is his favourite spot. "It (the place) cannot be compared favourably with Porthcawl, for instance. The latter place has sand – so has this. The water at both tastes much the same, I expect. (I haven't bathed here yet.) But there the comparison ends abruptly. Where, here, are the rest of P'Cawl's delights, the prom, the shows, the green, the rocks, the – the – grub? Alas! No, not here, no, not here, they're taking a trip in Glamorgan land (worse luck)."

There are some delights, however, which have presumably been missing since they left Ismailia early in December, and a vivid contrast with the conditions they were experiencing exactly a year earlier when they had to retreat from Suvla Bay back to Lemnos. "There's an E.F. canteen[23] here (for which the saints be praised when pay day comes) and we'll carry on as ever, if it pleases you, in a state of excitement, which is hard to curb, now that Xmas and its inevitable parcels of good things is approaching rapidly. We intend to go the pace all the way this time with your kind contributions. Also, we shall want letters and papers (both double numbers) full of fun and the season's cheer. I don't know whether you have noticed the date of this letter but, for my own part, I have vivid reflections of this date a year ago. If you remember, our company showed them how to evacuate places in good order on that date and I can recall the feeling of relief just about this time, which I experienced on marching to the beach."[24]

Cleaning Buttons on Christmas Day

The most festive day of the year, nevertheless, brought frustration – and feelings of insubordination – at being expected to polish buttons on the morning itself, replaced later by the intense enjoyment of a concert and then a party, but he opens his letter with some musings on parcels. "I have been a martyr to cruel disappointment, mail after mail, (and we've had not a few it being Xmas week), and you can't realise what a terrible trial it has been spending the season of good cheer without the accustomed puddings and cake in unfailing quantities. I am, however, satisfied to know that those good things have been despatched and I think it needless to add that the result of Mum's genius in the plum pudding line and the iced cake will both make hurried exit from human view, no matter how late they arrive. It is very thoughtful of you to consider my taste, iced cakes being, as you will remember, one of my 'extra special lines'. He continues with a line of dots across

---

22) December 13th 1915.
23) E.F. Expeditionary Force canteens supplied soldiers' needs in the main theatres of war.
24) The evacuation from Suvla Bay. On December 13th a year earlier he had embarked from South Pier on board *Rowan*.

the page and an explanation. "This space is where I shut my optics [eyes] for a moment and forget my pitiable situation to conjure up in my mind's eye flowing visions of huge plum pudding, steaming hot, brandy alight, and decorated with holly, surrounded with cakes topped with white icing, marzipan (smack!), and little silver marbles. Now I return to earth once more and continue where I left off, my great game of patience. ('Post Orderly! – when, I beseech thee, is the next mail?')."[25]

The Army make-work routines they had had to endure at the start of Christmas Day of all days makes this absence of a taste of home all the harder to bear. "Xmas Day here was a mixed affair, not only as far as drinks were concerned, but a mixture of sadness and joviality. The day commenced in a perfectly rotten manner. We were ordered to parade at 9 am, full marching order with buttons and all brass work polished up. This naturally cast a gloom over the camp, and the order, besides being ridiculous, as we are supposed to be on active (?) service and are miles from nowhere, on the desert, was anything but pleasant to comply with on Xmas morning. The boys felt pretty fed up and appreciated the marked way of wishing us a 'Merry (?) Xmas'. As we were not in possession of cleaning material, polish etc., we were expected to use sand and water for the purpose, which did not at all meet with the boys' approval, you may guess. However, we earned the reputation of being 'the most unsoldierly, filthiest lot ever inspected'. Unsoldierly 'cos our buttons were green, I presume. Clean buttons make good soldiers – p'raps. We got dismissed three times and paraded three times and then they thought it best to supply us with polish. After that we were thought clean enough to go on a Church parade. It was a very strenuous morning – nothing but parades, dumb insolence, and hard language.[26] Dear me! What a life we are having in the Boys' Brigade. It's driving us very near crazy cleaning buttons every morning. Wish I'd joined the Army. If you forget my address, just shove down on the envelope, 'The Shiners', that'll find me. Everybody knows us by that out here. (Let Tom see this bit)." The end of this same letter finds him still cursing pointless polishing exercises. He asks his sister to apologise to his cousin, who has now arrived home injured from France. "Sorry his arm is still bad but trust that will be soon O.K. again. You'll apologise to him for me, please, that I was unable to be present to grip his paw but explain that at present I am *so* busy keeping Turks away by *cleaning buttons*. Say 'The Shinies' are living up to their good old motto:- 'All shine and no do'. It's a glorious campaign, tell him, wouldn't miss it for worlds (x!!x) Those are adjectives."

The subject of the mails,[27] some of which may have been lost at sea and others unable to keep up with the division's movements, recurs. Running the Army postal service was another of the jobs carried out by the Royal Engineers, and, although it must have been difficult ensuring mail arrived at the right places for troops on the move, the system seems to have worked fairly efficiently and to have coped with the problems that arose, even though it was frequently cursed by the men waiting for news from home. In the theatres of war the main Army post offices were established in administrative compounds, perhaps 10-100 miles from the front line. Mobile field post offices were attached to corps, divisional or brigade headquarters.

25) December 29th 1916.
26) Dumb insolence is an offence against military discipline in which a subordinate displays an attitude of defiance towards a superior without open disagreement.
27) January 10th 1917.

Here, the post office, where soldiers took their mail for sending on, would be basically a box under the care of a corporal and a couple of sappers. The box held postal orders, stamps, cash, seals for mailbags, and could be lodged anywhere in an open field, a dug-out or a tent.

Early in the New Year a rather disgruntled letter implies a move has taken place followed by a return to Mahamadiyah. "I may mention that we are still in the same spot as the one to which we were sent before the place we went to before this one and am still carrying on in the Signal Office.[28] When I'm not there I revel in general fatigues. Two simple little words – but Oh! with a wealth of meaning. Believe me, I could write a volume on loading camels, stables, and ration parties but the idea is distasteful to me. I am not morose by nature but writing that book would give readers of my acquaintance false impressions. Then again, I might add that clean buttons parades are all the rage out here still. I often wish that signal company fashions would change as quickly as those of the fair sex. The vogue of dirty buttons for, let us say six months, would come as an immense relief." He goes on: "I am not short of money, thank you, for I still have $1^1/_2$ piastres in my pocket to buy a tin of 'Brasso'. It's wonderful what an effect orders to clean buttons have on some chaps but I emphatically contradict the rumour current in England at the present time that wet canteens[29] are closing down in Egypt, owing to the fact that the men are reluctant to purchase stimulants in case they are unable to polish before the next pay day. And, it is equally absurd to believe that the R.E.s here have put in a petition signed by every sapper and driver to respectfully beg the authorities to issue out brass plated rifles and cable wagons. What we do expect, though, and, that at any moment, is an order for every man to purchase a nail brush and to exercise every caution to sound his aitches when in conversation with each other."

There was the frustration, too, at not having much prospect of leave back home while hostilities were continuing. A few months earlier he had expressed his sympathies with his parents and sister over rumours about home leave for the soldiers in the Near East – he had been away from home 18 months by then and would be away for nearly another two years. "You must have been very disappointed. Never mind, it can't last for ever." He manages also to combine praise for his sister's progress in commercial studies at Clark's College (in Newport Road) in Cardiff with another dig at Army routine. "40-44 words in shorthand. Gosh! That's great. When I come home again, I'll give you a prize. How would you like me to present you with a button from my tunic, so as you could use a mirror in the mornings? I will, if you're a good girl and if those aforementioned buttons aren't rubbed out. Remind me of it, will you, my memory's affected since I started this sort of 'soldiering'. And don't forget the typewritten letter. I'm longing for that. Doesn't matter if Mr John does read it, tell him I'll polish all his typewriters when I return, if I've got enough Brasso left.[30] Expect we'll have to use it all, tho! Can't afford to waste a single drop of that precious liquid in the desert wilderness of sun and polished brass."

28) January 10th 1917. To El Arish and back.
29) Wet canteen, selling alcoholic drinks.
30) Mr John, principal of Clark's College, Cardiff, and a frequent source of comment in his letters. Vd. Chap 10. Little Sister, p266.

For all his frustrations at Army routine, the advance through the Sinai Desert and Gaza, and thence to Palestine in 1917 was a welcome first taste of real soldiering since Gallipoli. All leave since November had been cancelled, he tells his parents, even for time-expired men to go home. Henceforward, it is the rigours of the varied Gazan countryside, rather than the boredom of garrison duty in the Canal Zone, that informs his letters. And, despite his complaints, there is perhaps a hint that he is enjoying the challenges he is now facing. By this time he had become a competent horseman, though he was still mindful of the embarrassment he had experienced previously when riding a mule on the trek eastwards through Sinai. "Feeling rather languid, y'know, just returned from a ride of ten miles with two horses each. Marvel of it was, I never bit the dust this time – I trotted like a good 'un but, you bet, I gripped – nearly squeezed the horse's ribs in. Acted up to instructions [that] a chap who saw me 'dismount' last time gave to me 'fore I started. 'Mind', he says, 'now, no *swanking*'. 'Right', say I, 'no fancy strokes this time, old man'."

A Christmas Concert

After the frustration of being made to parade and polish buttons early on Christmas morning, there was at least a decent dinner and a concert later in the day. A little extra food and a limited ration of beer had been brought up from Port Said. "Menu: – Boeuf à la underdone (very much so). Pommes de terre (desiccated, Army pattern), Fleurs de cauli (imitation) avec beaucoups sand d'Egypte. Desert :- "If-it" Xmas pudding (6 ozs.) (If it went round, you had some.) Licquers [sic], Café, Té (nixes, nothing doing). We partook of this sumptuous repast out in the open air, all the company together, while our sergeant major, like a trump, waited upon us. What d'ye think of that, eh? Jolly decent of him, wasn't it? Him, mind ye, what bawls at us and cusses us for 364 days in the year, waits on us at table on the 365th. He made a speech after. 'Well, my lads,' he says, 'I am waiting on you this Xmas day but I hope I won't be the next – I sincerely hope your mothers will have that pleasure,' and we all said, 'Hear! Hear!' like one man. Best speech I ever heard, I can tell you."[31]

The celebrations did not end there. "In the evening" he reports, "we had completely recovered from the 'blues' and adjourned to a concert which was billed to start at 7.30 pm. It was held in three marquees strung together and the whole company was there, officers and all. We were out to enjoy ourselves and, By Gum! we did. There was a proper stage with decorations, refreshments in plenty and the turns were absolutely it. It was a night of nights, and the toasts we don't drink – O! my. 'The Kamelerio Sandboys' troupe, which had appeared before the Prince of Wales, Duke of York and numerous other public houses, excelled themselves all dressed up in costumes and grease paints – yes, we did the thing properly – no kid. There wasn't a rotten artist in the whole crowd. But I think the star turn was a chap who came on as a parson and had for his text 'Of the cleaning of buttons there is no end and much dazzling is wearisome to the flesh'. Gee! that didn't half go down well. A parson never had such an appreciative audience, when he asked us to sing the well-known anthem -

---

31) December 29th 1916.

'When he cometh to gaze on his children, All his bright ones, all his polished ones, Bright gems of his crown. They shall shine with their 'Brasso', All his polished and his bright ones' etc."[32]

I thought the house was coming down. He finished up his sermon with the words, 'We are now in Part 1 Volume 1 Chapter 3 of the Great War. We, *may* not see the end of it, your children and your children's children *may* see the end, but of the cleansing of buttons there is *no* end and much dazzling is wearisome to the flesh.' Gosh! It was great. We finished up about 1 am next morning and retired, hoarse but in excellent spirits. On the whole, I think we spent a blooming fine Xmas and I hope you had such a good time as we did, that's all."

This was, of course, soldiers entertaining each other, and using cynicism to relieve themselves of their war-weariness. A more professional concert party came the following month, in the form of one of the many troops of actors, musicians, singers and sometimes magicians, which toured Army camps in the main theatres of action. "We were honoured at this remote spot this week by the presence of Miss Lena Ashwell's Concert Party, four ladies and two gents who gave us two performances in a neighbouring aerodrome. I went both nights and it was 'the goods'. They were fine singers, violinists, elocutionists and pianists, and we thoroughly enjoyed the treat. The place, which was packed both nights, held hundreds and they had a rousing reception fit for – well, fit for nobody else except four English girls and two chaps in civvies, a sight we had not seen for years, it seemed. I went there to see what a linen collar, tie, navy blue suit and parted hair looked like once again, as much as anything, and the result was entirely satisfactory. I couldn't help but envy them – what a comparison. Think I should feel awfully uncomfortable in 'em again tho'. That languid very much at ease Bertie[33] air will need a lot of practice! I could have wept when I saw 'em give the knees of their trousers a hitch when they sat down – it was too much for me, seeing the genuine article. And, to hear the soprano sing up on the top notes, – Gee! she was a stunner – from Swansea, too, by the way. Talk about applause and encores. You see, it was all wonderful to us, – we could scarcely believe it. They're gone now, worse luck, and the only memories we have is when we hear the chap in the tent behind warbling away in a falsetto to his heart's delight – not to ours."[34] Actress Lena Ashwell toured army camps both in Britain and abroad with a troop of actors, convinced that theatre could do its bit to maintain morale among the troops. They were kept away from the front lines but travelling between the different camps could itself be dangerous. Haig wrote in June 1917 to express his appreciation of the concert party's efforts. "The concerts at the front organised by Miss Lena Ashwell have been a source of endless pleasure and relaxation for many thousands of soldiers."[35] The actress was in her late 40s during the war, dying in 1957 at the age of 85.

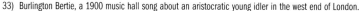

32) The words of an American gospel song, *Jewels*, words by William O. Cushing and music by George Root. 'When He cometh, when He cometh, To make up His jewels, All His jewels, precious jewels, His loved and His own. Like the stars of the morning, His brightness adorning, They shall shine in their beauty, Bright gems for His crown. He will gather, He will gather The gems for His kingdom; All the pure ones, all the bright ones, His loved and His own. Little children, little children, Who love their Redeemer, Are the jewels, precious jewels, His loved and His own.'
33) Burlington Bertie, a 1900 music hall song about an aristocratic young idler in the west end of London.
34) January 10th 1917.
35) Mortlock. p17.

The Desert Gives Way

By late February 1917 he was writing home to describe some of the rigours the advance through Sinai to El Arish had entailed, saying he had had the opportunity of testing his ability as an infantryman on the march with full kit, or, as he puts it, acting in the role of human pack mule.[36] "Now the ordeal is over (thank Heavens), I can well afford to paint this picture in vivid colours in a light-hearted, careless manner but, believe me, whilst my initiation was in progress, I saw the serious side of life, as I never saw it before. "Imagine, if you can, a cloudless sky, with the sun pouring down its pitiless rays on the rolling miles of undulating desert. You stay a moment, and listen! – "R-r-r-rub-a-dub-dub," – this inspiring sound comes faintly to your ears – without a doubt it is the drums. Then over the brow of the nearest rise they come, a file of drummers and after, in innumerable lines, the poor old rank and file. They plod wearily along, in steps, as best they can across the sand, backs bent double under the cruel weight of their packs, rifles etc. (ad finitum [sic]) and the beads of sweat upon their noble brows.[37] 'Blimey, time's nearly up for a 'alt, isn't it boys?,' says one in, a pitiful tone, and sure enough, his instinct and judgment, born of long marching has not belied him. Pheet! goes the whistle – 'Thank 'Evings – a 'alt at last' – and without more ado, down we fling ourselves with one accord and lay like logs to stretch our weary limbs. A short ten minutes, O! – such a short ten minutes and Pheet! (confound that whistle), we're off again, putting the last foot in front, until the motion is automatic, – there is no sense of feeling, we are just machines."

Though now a sizeable city with a population in 2006 of 138,000, El Arish, now designated Eastern Force headquarters and centre of operations, appears from contemporary descriptions to have been a modest place. In 1916, most of its dwellings, the fort and mosque excepted, were mud huts. The landscape, however, had changed from the desert he had had to endure for months. The village was surrounded by melon plantations, fig trees and date palms. As they advanced into the fertile plains ahead, they would encounter orange orchards, barley and wheat fields, vineyards and goats grazing. Dewi's description of the change of scenery is evocative, "And so, after 20 miles of this delightful mode of travelling, we reach our destination – dog-tired, thirsty and worn. As usual, our surroundings are most solitary and forsaken, except for a few mud-huts and their dusky inhabitants, a mile or so away. Naturally enough, you will at once ask yourselves, 'what on earth induces them to live in such an out-of-the-way hole?'. Ah! – now for some news which will explain that question, and which you have no idea how much pleasure it gives me to impart. Those villagers are occupied in *tilling the soil*. 'What on earth – tilling the – ? – You must be dreaming,' say you. Nevertheless, it is true – listen carefully in case you miss this bit – we have, actually, without the slightest ghost of a blooming doubt, left *sand* behind and have struck green fields – yes! s'welp me, if we haven't. Behold all around us, smiling fields of verdant pasture land – 'O'r glaswellt, y glaswellt hyfryd.' [Oh the green sward, the pleasant green sward]. What d'ye think of it, eh? By Gum! it's truly a grand, inspiring sight to our eyes – sons of the desert, sick unto death of the sight of the miles of horrible yellow sand."

---

36) February 25th 1917.
37) He is asking his readers to put themselves in the position of seeing drummers and rank-and-file emerging over a rise in the ground.

It was proving a delight for horses and men – the former "nearly going mad upon catching sight of it, and who now are quite content to spend all day grazing on the toothsome dainty, while the latter no longer go slouching and stumbling along, as they did on the sand, but step out, shoulders erect, proud to think and feel they have something solid underfoot, while football is played with renewed vigour, just the same as if we were playing on Splott Park. We are removed from the sea but, if the rolling breakers at the last place reminded me of P'Cawl, our new surroundings bring back trebly pleasant memories of the tide field, St. Mellons and all those other such happy meadow scenes. 'Blighty in summertime' is written on the face of it and the singing of the birds (almost forgotten but which now seems twice as sweet) add enormously to one's imagination. Indeed, our environments and our mode of dwelling has assumed an entirely new complexion altogether. [...] It is now no longer true to say 'and weekly pitch our moving tents', because we have none. Instead, it has been necessary to resort to the method adopted in the old Peninsular days.[38] "We are nothing more or less than human moles once again. Bivouacking is the order of the day and this letter is penned to you in – to use the immortal words – 'my dear old dug-out'.[39] There is, of course, nothing like having had previous experience, especially in this very fashionable way of residing nowadays. And, as you may imagine, I took to it as a baby takes to the bottle, and soon made things comfortable. A few hours hard digging soon altered the face of the globe and now, where was once a level patch of green sward, there stands a palatial, underground, 'most desirable' (to speak in auctioneer parlance) residence."

His enthusiasm for his bivouac is perhaps surprising – they consisted largely of trenches dug into the ground and then covered with whatever roofing materials could be obtained. They were perhaps cooler and more solid, however, than the tents to which he had had to become used. "Perhaps not at all suitable for most folk, owing to the fact that there is but one storey or floor, and that is merely a cellar (Irish, don't you think?). Still, it suits my 'bivvy' chum and I [sic], not only *down* to the ground but extending some feet lower than that even. At one extremity of the 'central' hall we have a most excellent mantelpiece (handmade let it be mentioned), at the other end two steps for the purpose of getting in and under (it is important to stoop when entering unless you desire to incur the wrath of the inmates by damaging the roof, which is most delicate and of which I shall have more to say). On one side there is a most interesting cavity of, I should say, 'stone-age' architecture, regarding its simplicity, which is quite unrivalled as a side-board, while an orifice directly opposite serves the excellent purpose of a candlestick. The inconveniences of this dwelling place are decidedly in the minority, that is if you give a sharp glance at it and turn away instantaneously, and, excepting for occasional landslides, which persist in precipitating themselves for the main part down the back of your neck, and the probability of one of the 'home-made' rifle racks collapsing, as you are crawling in, causing that article to descend hurriedly on your cranium or any convenient part of you anatomy, the risks are comparatively few."

107

---

38) Gallipoli.
39) February 25th 1917. They were at Sheikh Zowaid, close to El Arish.

The accommodation did have its drawbacks. He describes a deluge that overwhelmed them. "People described as not having 'a roof to shelter their heads' have invariably had my unfeigned personal sympathy. We, at last, have a roof (?) and, after last night, I am more convinced than ever that a man who has no roof at all is infinitely better off than the man who labours blissfully and under the delusion that he has a so-called 'roof', which, at the eleventh hour, fails miserably in its purpose. The latter unfortunate will always, henceforth, claim my sympathy in preference. You see, this roof is a most ridiculously simple affair, comprising merely, as it does, of – solitary blanket, Army Pattern, 1 (so described by the A.C.C.).[40] This is supported by rafters of a tinny substance, used originally for packing horse feed, very slender and pliable, I may add, strung on a piece of cable tied at each end to a minute particle of timber, known as 'pegs'. It is, as you will guess, most picturesque but, as I said before, you must look at this quickly also, and the inhabitants of the abode beneath live in momentarily [sic] dread that some idiot will accidentally touch it. (From this you may draw your own conclusions as to its stability.) Anyhow, last night (shall I ever forget it?), we two slipped into the blankets, as innocent as children of the dire calamity in store for us, and were soon dreaming of Blighty, apple-tarts etc. In the midst of these we were rudely disturbed at 4 am by a sound – it will always haunt me to the end of my days – the sound of driving rain on a roof, such as we had.

"Was there a man dismayed? – Lummy! – that's not the word – disgusted, yes! and more. Then there was the pitiful spectacle of two swoddies pulling on wet breeches and fishing for socks in the wet and gloom while at every turn particles of water came unpleasantly into contact with bare portions of our state of deshabillé. After scrambling into the nearest garments at hand, we dashed out on top to save the wretched situation and repairs to the roof (?) were effected instanter [instantly] with the aid of our waterproof sheets, and then crawling inside once more composed ourselves not for slumber but in a sitting posture for 'Fall in' for first parade, which came none too soon. Gradually the deluge subsided and, as the first rays of dawn made their appearance, the indescribable chaos of muddy blankets, tunics etc., were distinguishable and sadly surveyed by stern-faced, shivering men, who said nothing audible but, I can assure you, thought volumes. Such a catastrophe entails much additional work, as you can understand, and were you to pass along this way today, you would be struck by the array of blankets, muddy and soiled, which had obviously 'braved for several hours the deluge and the storm', spread out as plenteous as the leaves in autumn to dry. Great activity would also be noticed amongst the 'moles' busily engaged in repairing their roofs and getting things in general to look more like human habitations and less like a rag and bone stores. However, we have taken this lesson to heart and the result of our labours today shows considerable elaborate alterations to this particular establishment.

"The roof, being the main consideration, has been vastly improved upon. The sheets have been strung (more or less securely) together by several more pieces of string, (Don't smile, please, it's most serious), while a few more tin rafters have been wedged into place. The sides also have been cemented down with handfuls of sand,

---

40) Army Catering Corps.

and it certainly appears to be quite decent – in fact, you can look at it longer now without turning away – but appearances are, they say, so deceptive. Tonight we lie down in a cheerful frame of mind, convinced that, should the worst happen, our roof is, or should be, better prepared to withstand the buffeting of the elements. And, though a thousand farmers hope for rain this night, I fervently trust they'll be foiled – bad luck to 'em, say I. I voice the opinion of every man jack here when I emphasise the fact that bivouacking is O.K. when it's fine weather – but when the rain comes, blow it."

The changing environment also played to the advantage of the numerically much stronger British forces. They were now on firmer ground which made it possible to make greater use of wheeled vehicles and to bring the infantry into play. Sinai had not offered any roads suited to motor vehicles. Previously, much of the action had fallen to mounted brigades which were better able to manage travel across the desert. Horse-drawn trains of baggage and other equipment could also now replace camels, though they would be operating in more difficult and hillier country. From the desert signaller's point of view there were practical compensations. He was now linked up again with a much bigger force, too, and away from the isolated signals office he had occupied for so many previous months at Serapeum. There, the only amusement – apart from reading books and periodicals sent from home – seems to have come from diving into the Canal, developing an interest in photography and waiting patiently for parcels. They were now in the same place for two weeks, until they began their trek again, this time on towards Gaza.

Food and Fags still Needed

Food remains a pre-occupation. On December 30th he hears the post orderly shout out his name and dashes out 'breathless and hatless' to collect a parcel. "Rushed back in the tent and you never saw such a sight in your natural – talk about chaos. Button sticks, polish tins and brushes went up in the air and in $3^7/6^{\text{ths}}$ seconds (three and seventh sixths) I had 9 blokes on their hands and knees offering me jacknives to cut the cord.[41] 'Well,' I says, 'what d'ye want.' 'Pudd'n,' they says. 'Pudd'n'. 'Now or tomorrow for breakfast?' 'Now,' they says 'and tomorrow' so there was nothing for it but to obey orders. Talk about cheering when that pudd'n appeared – three times three Hip! Pip! Gosh, we were excited. And then, the cake. Oh! My, they went barmy, absolutely. Consequently, I regret to say, there was none 'left for breakfast tomorrow morning' but I think there's about 2 slices of cake there, kept 'parch' for tea today. [...] Although that one didn't arrive for Xmas, don't you worry yourselves about its reception."[42]

Although special efforts had been made to provide the men with a good Christmas feed, the Army was soon once again unable to provide adequate food supplies. Barely 10 days into the New Year Dewi writes of serious food shortages. The company has been sent a food parcel, without which, he says, they would have starved. "Fact! I'm not kidding – we had two 'fish teas' out of it, five sardines a man,

109

---

41) Button sticks, soldier's device for polishing brass buttons.
42) December 29th 1916.

and next day a 'fruit tea', one pear and one peach a man. It was great. We also are having a treat in the form of a cheese ration in place of 'Batcher's yellow mixture, guaranteed to kill', which I was beginning to fear was going to run on for ever. There's two kinds of cheese – pink cheese and white cheese. White cheese is not so bad. I stick that but my pink cheese ration gets total exemption from consumption because it's got a funny 'flavah'. Quite so, yes, – thought you'd like me to come home safe. I'm in the pink but not in with pink cheese."[43] A few weeks later, Army rations appear to have come through, and are described as very decent, with frequent rum issues.[44] They are, however, missing the canteens that usually sprang up where they settled. "I haven't blued a single half piastre since coming here, which is unusual – very unusual, indeed – and which would never have happened had there been any kind whatsoever of stores here."[45]

If food they really liked – in parcels from home – was in short supply, there was always tobacco, an almost constant request in his letters home, his tastes during the course of his service varying from Waverley, to Players to Gold Flake, all popular brands of the time. "We even have perforce to court my Lady Nicotine in Army issue cigarettes, from which you will guess the absolute direness of the situation. They are veritable 'gaspers' – at present I have one between my lips, a brand known as 'Arf a Mo' – Heavens! they're shocking.[46] Oh! for a whiff of a Gold Flake. I trust this lament will touch your heart and arouse a feeling of pity, which should materialise into an even more frequent delivery of those excellent parcels. The grub extras will be devoured with great expedition in view of our forced reliance on the A.S.C. as a means of existence and my impatience for the delivery of your parcel of the 2nd inst. surpasses all bounds."[47] As well as the comfort and stimulus they brought, cigarettes also helped to suppress appetite. Very early on in his service he had written home saying he would be waiting patiently for the arrival of that parcel with the cigs in it. "Will you please send cigs oftener, if you don't mind? You will easily understand this request by scanning the label of 'Westward Ho' baccy. 'Hungry man's food, wakeful man's sleep, old man's fire etc., etc.' "[48] Popular papers of the day were full of advertisements for leading brands such as Kenilworth, Greys, and Gold Flake, which were sold in packets of 20 for 1/2d (one shilling and two pence) 50 for 2/9d and 100 for 5/6d. They could be purchased duty-free packed in airtight tins for sending to soldiers overseas at 200 for 6/-, 500 for 14/- and 27/- for 1,000. Cigarettes then were much cheaper than today.[49]

43) January 10th 1917. Batcher's yellow mixture, the marmalade he disliked so much.

44) Introduced in winter 1914 to combat the cold of the trenches in France and Belgium, the rum ration amounted to 1/3rd of a pint a week. On the front line the ration was issued at dawn and dusk. The allocation may or may not have been different in the Near East.

45) February 25th 1917.

46) "Arf a Mo, Kaiser" was one of the most famous cartoons of the war, drawn by Bert Thomas, (1883-1966) of the Artists' Rifles to raise money for the supply of cigarettes and tobacco to the troops. It pictured a British solder having a drag, the implication being even the Kaiser could not come between the Tommy and his smokes.

47) A.S.C. Army Service Corps.

48) April 5th 1916. W.D & H.O. Wills' 'smoking mixture', Westward Ho! Tobacco. was sold in colourful tins, one design.quoting words from Charles Kingsley's novel of the same name. "When all things were made, none was made better than tobacco to be a lone man's Companion, a bachelor's Friend. a hungry man's Food, a sad man's Cordial, a wakeful man's Sleep, and a chilly man's Fire. There's no herb like it under the canopy of Heaven." It was only in the 1950s that the purportedly beneficial effects of smoking were finally discredited, the most egregious example being the advertising claim for Craven A cigarettes 'Good for your Throat'.

49) While in 1915 £1 would have bought about 350 cigarettes, the equivalent sum today, adjusted for the change in the value of sterling, would buy only around 160.

Worse was to come, as the next stage in the campaign, the assaults on Gaza and the march through Palestine, unfolded. In letters later in 1917 he recounts some instances of real hunger forcing him, he writes, to go from tent to tent in search of food. The scene was now set for the first of the three battles fought during the course of 1917 for control of Gaza, the first two of which did not go according to British plans. The first battle began on March 26th by which time Dewi had moved forward from El Arish at the start of the year to reach Deir el Belah, about 13 miles away from Gaza, the day before the battle.[50]

50) Eastern Force cavalry had entered Khan Yunus, midway between the Egyptian border and Deir el Belah on February 28th, causing the Turks to withdraw to Gaza and Beersheba. The railway was pushed forward to Deir el Belah, which became the railhead in April 1917, and an aerodrome and camps were established there.

Dewi (right) shaven-headed, with cigarette, and fellow-soldiers.

(right) Egyptian reservists taking a break from building the desert railway across the Sinai Peninsula.

(below) The tented camp at El Arish. The town was captured December 1916, on the progress across Sinai.

Minaret. The mosque was then the most prominent building in El Arish.

Dewi's friend, Hughie, and a monkey mascot, one of many such pets that men collected.

Indian Soldiers. Men from the sub-Continent served in the Egyptian Expeditionary Force and were used to replace soldiers transferred to France later in the war.

Army fatigues. Making sand walls in the desert.

CHAPTER SIX

SETBACKS AT GAZA

MARCH – OCTOBER 1917

First Battle of Gaza

As 1917 proceeded Dewi moved with his unit from Sheik Zowaiid, 20 miles east of El Arish to El Magruntein (March 8th), Rafa less than 20 miles from Gaza (March 21st), Khan Yunus (March 24th) and Deir el Belah five miles northeast of Khan Yunus (March 25th).[1] After the capture of Khan Yunus, Deir el Belah was made the site of a large British Army base and the starting point for the attacks on Gaza nine miles to the north. An aerodrome for bombing attacks and reconnaissance of Turkish positions was also built there. An ancient settlement, a mile from the coast, it was famous for the date palms that gave it its Arabic name – Monastery of the Date Palms.

After the loss of the mediaeval fortress at Khan Yunus and a failed attempt to re-occupy territory in Sinai, the Turks had withdrawn from their Shillal stronghold in the back country 14 miles south east of Gaza to a new defensive line behind Wadi Ghuzza, a deep watercourse running from Shillal north west to Deir el Belah and the Mediterranean. Fed in the rainy season by tributaries from the western slope of the Sinai range, and by springs in its bed, the wadi's floor lay some thirty or forty feet deep between rugged banks of broken, sandy clay, opening out on either side into innumerable spacious bays. In the spring of the year, with the rain diminishing, it was fordable in many places but at other times it formed an excellent basis of defence.[2] The British for their part used the months of Spring to continue to develop their training and infrastructure for the advance on Gaza. Railway and water pipelines were extended, wells and pumping plants developed, wire roads laid, and defences and hutting constructed in and around El Arish, and then in other locations further along the line of advance. The 100 miles of railway to the town had been completed at the end of 1916 and the railhead then advanced to Sheikh Zowaiid by March 1st and Rafa by March 21st. Putting down lines shipped in from Britain, India and collected elsewhere in Egypt, was, of course, only part of the task. Extensive marshalling yards and stations were also put in place at El Arish and Rafa, and at Wadi el Arish a steel girder bridge had to be built to carry trains over the watercourse. Traffic by March amounted to 16 trains a day in both directions, a limit imposed by the amount of water available for railway operations. A load of 23,000 tons was transported weekly on average. A 55,000 strong Egyptian Labour Force that had been enlisted to support British operations carried out much of the work under the supervision of Royal Engineers.[3]

The initiative now lay clearly in British hands. Since their defeat at Romani the Turks had not mounted any significant offensive operations, and their morale was reckoned to be low. By mid-March Dobell, commander of the Eastern Force, concluded preparations were complete and an attack on Gaza should go ahead. The main Turkish force was east of the city, though there was a considerable detachment holding it as well. The terrain in front of Gaza differed greatly from that experienced earlier in Sinai, offering undulating country covered with grass and young crops at this time of year, interwoven with dry water courses. Inland, the

1) El Arish had been captured on December 20th 1916.

2) Dewi provided his own description of Wadi Ghuzza in an evocative essay. Vd. Letters, July 26th 1917.

3) In total 98,000 labourers were recruited by the Army into the Egyptian Labour Force, 23,000 of whom served overseas. Most of the Egyptian Army served in Sudan, keeping order, but two battalions of Egyptian soldiers campaigned with the E.E.F.

rolling country offered few obstacles to cavalry. Gaza itself, however, was well protected by tall, thick hedges of cactus that required explosives or hand cutting for their removal. Dobell's plan was essentially a repeat of the coup-de-main successfully used against Romani and Magdhaba. Mounted forces would cross the Wadi Ghuzza in a wide sweeping movement that would cut off the Turkish line of retreat, while the 53rd Division, part of the Desert Column under Chetwode, seized the town. The 54th Division would cover the strike force against any Turkish attack from the east.[4] Numerically, British forces enjoyed a considerable advantage, being able to put into the field 8,500 sabres, 25,000 rifles and 92 guns. The Turkish deployment which was seeking to hold a line running from Gaza through Sheria to Beersheba amounted to 1,500 sabres, 16,000 rifles and 74 guns.[5] The instructions given to the division were to cross the Wadi Ghuzza between El Sire and El Breij, having first seized the south west end of the El Sire ridge as a bridgehead. As soon as the bridgehead had been achieved, troops were to take possession of the important Ali Muntar-El Sire ridge as far as El Sheluf on the north and Tel el Ahmar-Mansura on the south. The division would move off with six days' rations, with camels carrying a further three days' emergency rations.

During the week before the battle the various formations took up their positions on the line of Wadi Ghuzza. At 2.30 am on the morning of March 26th the mainly Australian and New Zealand mounted troops began their enveloping movement. The 53rd, tasked to attack strong entrenchments to the south of the town, advanced from Deir el Belah. Although the division had reached its starting points by 8.30 a.m., catching the Turks by surprise, thick fog reduced visibility to only 20 yards, delaying the attack until midday. Nevertheless, despite strong opposition from shrapnel, machine gun and rifle fire, all the objectives in this phase, including strong positions at Ali Muntar ridge, had been taken by the division, working with the 161st Brigade of the 54th Division, by 5.30 in the afternoon.[6] Dewi's itinerary puts him at key points in the advance, his log recording March 26th "158th Cable Wagon, Mansura Ridge, Capture of Ali Muntar (No. 1). Gaza entered".

The action by the 53rd Division, which suffered 3,500 casualties, would "bear comparison with the classic exploits of British infantry," according to Mortlock.[7] "The approach was over bare ground against an enemy strongly posted and entrenched, with numerous machine guns and a powerful artillery. All the advantages of observation and concealment lay with the enemy. The guns supporting the attack were few... and the narrow ridge on which lay the enemy's main position was a difficult target... The last part of the assault was blind fighting uphill through cactus hedges against unseen machine guns and riflemen. A pitiless Eastern sun beat down on men who had already marched far before deploying for attack. There was no shade and no water." With the mounted troops desperately

4) General Dobell remained in overall command, with the 52nd and 54th Divisions under his direct control. He moved his headquarters to Rafa on March 20th in preparation for the attack.

5) Beersheba in the Negev desert in Israel had grown in importance in the 19th century when the Ottoman Turks built a regional police station there.

6) Ali Muntar, 48 miles south west of Jerusalem, the high mound in the Old Testament, to the top of which Samson carried the gates of Gaza. Escaping from Gaza he 'took the doors of the gate of the city, and the two posts, and went away with them, bar and all, and put them on his shoulders and carried them to the top of a hill that is before Hebron'. *Book of Judges 16.3*

7) Mortlock, p69-70.

needing to water their horses, however, the generals had to decide whether to push on into Gaza itself. If the mounted troops were withdrawn, the infantry flank would have been left exposed to Turkish reinforcements, by now converging on Gaza. Dobell gave the order at 6.00 pm for the mounted divisions to withdraw and later in the evening, despite the protests of the commander of the 53rd, it, too, was told to pull back. In fact, the Turks had all retired in haste to Gaza town, which was now surrounded except on its south western side. Victory had been within the grasp of the attacking forces and the Turks had been on the point of abandoning their positions, with surrender likely at dawn. The mounted Anzacs had penetrated into Gaza from behind – where they met soldiers of the 53rd – and captured the General Officer Commanding and staff of the Turkish 53rd Division, who were leaving the town in cabs.[8] "The risks of continuing, however, had been considered by cautious commanders to outweigh the chances of complete success on the day."[9] The following morning, when it became evident that withdrawal had not been necessary, the 53rd was ordered to re-take Ali Muntar but, by now very tired, was driven back. Dewi reports on March 27th: "Retired 00.30 Div. Reserve Mansura Ridge. Retired El Buryabiye. Retired Wadi-El Gyhuzzu, followed on March 28th by the entry.[10] Retired Deir el Bela." All divisions had by now been ordered to move back to defensible positions behind Wadi Ghuzza.

Subsequent judgments on the two generals in charge have been highly critical. Military historian, Capt. Basil Liddell Hart, argued that a victorious position, with Gaza virtually surrounded, had been surrendered not under enemy pressure but on the orders of the executive British commanders, Dobell and Chetwode, eight miles back at In Seirat, through faulty information, misunderstandings and over-anxiety. He writes: "The harm did not end there for Murray reported the action to the Government in terms of a victory, and without a hint of the subsequent withdrawal, so that he was encouraged to attempt, without adequate reconnaissance or fire support, a further attack on April 17th-19th, which proved a costlier failure against defences now strengthened."[11] Lloyd George was equally trenchant, describing the attack as the most perfect example exhibited on either side in any theatre during the war of "that combination of muddle-headedness, misunderstanding and sheer funk which converts an assured victory into a humiliating defeat." He added: "Gaza was virtually captured when the order came to withdraw. We had in our possession, at the moment of withdrawal, intercepted wireless messages which showed the German Commander considered the position hopeless."[12] The rank and file were equally disappointed, according to Dudley Ward. "They considered they had captured Gaza, and that they had been dragged like a dog on a leash, from their prize."[13] In his report from Cairo – no doubt based on briefings from the commanders on the spot – Murray claimed the operation only fell short of a complete disaster for the enemy because of the fog and waterless nature of the country. British sources claimed total Turkish casualties were 8,000, as opposed to the official Turkish return of 2,447, including prisoners. British casualties were 397 killed, 2,900 wounded, and 200 missing.

8) Ibid p65. Confusingly, the British 53rd Division at times faced the Turkish 53rd Division.

9) Kearsey, p16.

10) Spellings for Wadi Ghuzza are not consistent in the letters. Maps use various forms.

11) Hart, Basil Liddell, *The Real War 1914-18*. Little, Brown, 1930, p208.

12) George, David Lloyd, *War Memoirs, Vol. VI*, p201-2.

13) Dudley Ward, p97.

A supposed British success was doubly welcome at a time when the campaign in France had become bogged down, the weakness of the Russians in stemming the Germans on the Eastern Front – and their vulnerability to political revolution at home – had been exposed, and British shipping was being lost at the rate of 13 vessels a day to unrestricted German U-boat warfare. After reading Murray's upbeat report, minimising the casualties incurred and maximising the successes achieved, Robertson in London cabled him on March 30th that his immediate objective now should be the defeat of the Turks south of Jerusalem and its occupation.[14] A new policy had been initiated on dubious evidence. The first battle, a dramatic attempted coup-de-main, had, in effect, been part of an offensive defence, a speculative raid into enemy territory while debate continued back in Britain on the purposes and objectives of the Eastern campaigns. The second battle was planned under War Cabinet instructions to proceed further and take Jerusalem.

The Second Battle of Gaza

The second attempt on Gaza involved a very different kind of battle and proved even more disastrous than the first, bringing heavy losses and ultimately costing both Dobell and, later, Murray their commands. There was a more immediate change, too. After the first battle the 53rd Division's commanding officer, Major-General A. G. Dallas, resigned his command and was replaced by Brigadier-General S.F. Mott.[15] The Turks, well aware of the strategic importance of Gaza – and perhaps of the lucky break they had had in March – now strengthened the town's defences in a line from the sea to Hureira, 12 miles from Gaza along the Beersheba road. Gaza became the strongest point in a line of entrenched defensive positions, with a garrison of five regiments (18 battalions), two Austrian Howitzer batteries, two German long range guns, and a Turkish battalion of artillery with reserves of troops and artillery. Beersheba, it was thought, needed only to be lightly held, given the distance from the British railhead and the absence of any water in the area.[16] The following month, by which time the railhead had reached Deir el Belah eight miles south west of Gaza, the British advanced to a line Sheikh Abbas, Mansura and Kurd Hill three miles south of Gaza. Water could be taken close to the troops in this new location by rail but storage facilities also had to be built and pipelines installed down to Wadi Ghuzza. Roads and defensive systems also had to be put in place and forward storage dumps erected. Preparations completed, a second assault was mounted on April 19th, this time using tanks and heavy artillery.[17] Because of strong Turkish reinforcement of the town, the new attack would need to differ from the previous mobile enveloping actions that had worked well in Sinai and had been tried in the first attack in March. This time artillery, bombardment by naval vessels and, for the first time in this campaign, eight Mark 1 tanks were used. Where mounted troops had been used in the first battle to try and seize the objective by

14) Robertson had supported the concentration of British efforts on the Western Front.
15) Stanley Fielder Mott, 1873-1959. After service in the South African wars with mounted infantry, he retired as Maj., King's Royal Rifle Corps 1911. He was recalled for service in World War One on the staff of the Yeomanry Mounted Division and placed in charge of 158th Bde, Gallipoli 1915; and Commander, 53rd (Welsh) Div, Egypt and Palestine 1916-1918. He retired with the honorary rank of Major General 1919.
16) Pritchard, (ed.), p263; Dudley Ward, p100.
17) The tanks, Dudley Ward reports, p101, were the subject of jest, even though their crews fought gallantly. Unbearably hot inside, and hard to manoeuvre over sand, they were part-worn machines that had been shipped 'in error'.

speed and surprise, the second battle would require infantry to make a frontal attack across open ground against well-prepared entrenchments, with the cavalry only playing a supporting role. Dewi's movements at this period brought him from Deir el Belah to Sheikh Shabasi, headquarters of XXth Corps, nearby on the cliffs of the Mediterranean, arriving on April 11th, six days before the Second Battle.

Dobell had been sent the extra infantry division – the 74th – he had insisted he needed. His plan was now a two stage assault: an initial attack by three infantry divisions would seek to secure a line from Sheikh Abbas along the Mansura Ridge, and across the El Sire Ridge, to the sea near Tell el Ujul. In the second phase, one of three methods of attacking Gaza would be implemented, depending on the Turkish response to the first assault. Phase one was completed successfully on April 17th, when Samson's Ridge was captured. The follow-up attack on Gaza itself, however, on April 19th, proved so costly, action had to be broken off and the order given to hold occupied ground and prepare for a further assault the next day. When the full toll of casualties became clear – 6,400 had been sustained and artillery ammunition was becoming short – further withdrawal was deemed necessary. Once again an outmanned and outgunned but well entrenched Turkish defence force was able to repel the British attacks. It was decided to await reinforcements from Salonika before further attempting to take Gaza. The Turks were left firmly in charge of their Gaza-Beersheba line, having secured a victory from what proved to be an impregnable position against numerically superior forces. Murray, who had by this time moved up to Khan Yunus two and a half miles inland from the Mediterranean, sent Dobell back to Britain and appointed Chetwode commander of the Eastern Force. Despite these setbacks, the first two battles had, nevertheless, demonstrated that victory could be achieved with better preparations and the Cabinet decided to press ahead – with Lloyd George particularly enthusiastic – with the advance into Palestine and on to Jerusalem. With both sides digging in, actions were largely restricted in the succeeding months to skirmishes but the Turks' railway line between Beersheba and El Auja was destroyed over a distance of 13 miles in May in an operation designed to prevent the Turks from dismantling the line and moving locomotives and rolling stock elsewhere. In June reinforcements began to arrive from other theatres.

Dewi's opportunities to sit down and write home in the early part of this period were clearly limited and no doubt his parents and sister were able to speculate on his movements from reading the newspapers back home. From the start of 1917 he wrote only on four occasions – January 10th, February 25th, March 30th, and May 17th. In the very short – by his later standards – March letter from Deir el Belah, he explains why. "I hope you have not been very anxious about me lately but it must have been pretty rotten not getting any letter from me. Anyhow, you will understand how it is when I tell you that this is the first opportunity I've had to write for a little time. You see, we have been moving about so much and have been terribly busy, having had hardly any time to wash or eat even. Also, there's been no postal arrangement from the place we're at, so I know you'll excuse me. We are roughing it a bit now on bully and biscuits and figs, so you can tell how awkward it has been all round."[18] He had received their parcels posted the month before – "the pudd'n

18) March 30th 1917.

was absolutely grand. Wish I had some here now instead of these beastly biscuits." After so many moves and such a busy time, he has, however, managed back in Deir el Belah to have a bath in a pond under some palms. "Gee! it was glorious getting the sand and dirt off after days without a decent wash." His postscript, however, says he has yet to see the land of llaeth a mêl – his way of saying they had not reached ancient Israel, the land of milk and honey,[19] and perhaps of indicating their lack of success in getting beyond Gaza. On May 8th, he moved to In Seirat, south of Wadi Ghuzza, the new headquarters of the Eastern Force, a dominating position commanding a view over the Wadi Ghuzza and the ground north of it, four miles east of the coast. They then left for Sheikh Muran on May 23rd and three days later for Shillal, on the right of the British line in Wadi Ghuzza between Gaza and Beersheba, where the 53rd had been detailed to replace the 54th. The British line at this time had been divided in two by Murray in order to establish a regular system of reliefs, the 52nd replacing the 53rd in the coastal sector. The positions occupied were now beyond the previous Turkish border with Egypt, south of Gaza city and east of Beersheba and the Hills of Moab.

Life on the Plain

With British forces resting and regrouping during the summer, and training for a third assault on Gaza, his letters become more expansive and worldly-wise again, reporting to his parents that, as he had mentioned in a letter to Doll, they had now left the "seaside". "Shame it was, too, a lovely beach, excellent bathing and Sh! – norra word – only one parade daily, talk about an idle life, except of course that horrible telephone duty, which, Praise be! I no longer endure. You voiced my sympathies to the 'Number please' girls, I see – 'pon my word, Dad, I should just like to hear some of the yarns you spin. Give 'em all the news, I s'pose, I've given you up as hopeless long ago now.[20] Writing before they departed from In Seirat on May 23rd for Sheikh Muran, he is still half-amused at the number of jobs he is being given. "Wasn't it old Wagglespeare who said, 'All the world's a stage... and in his time a man plays many parts' – something like that, I think?[21] S'welp me, if the old blighter wasn't right – goodness knows, I've been many things before this, including mess orderly, amateur muleteer, lead-swinger in chief, quarter-bloke's indispensable – drawing rations, y'know – cable-layer, and goodness knows how many more staff appointments I haven't held during my brief but brilliant, unchequered (except when that blessed donkey chucked me, of course) career, but whoever would have thought that in a few short hours I could be converted from a military telephonist, the most servile, humblest, cowed clown of all human beings to the dizzy heights of fame as a 'camel-wallah' and adapt myself to this coveted rank of office, as if all my life had been spent as trainer in Lord John Sanger's menagerie.[22] I like the job, too, it's fine being out in the open air every morning and evening after the office, and the tramping about makes one fitter than ever."

19) Land of Milk and Honey, God's word to Moses, 'Go up to the land flowing with milk and honey.' *Exodus 33.3*.
20) May 17th 1917. Probably Deir el Belah. 'Number, Please' girls, telephone operators.
21) 'All the world's a stage, And all the men and women merely players; They have their exits and their entrances; And one man in his time plays many parts, His acts being seven ages.' Jacques in Shakespeare's *As You Like It*. Act II, Scene VII.
22) John Sanger, (Lord John), 1816-1889 was with his brother George Sanger the proprietor of one of the main English circuses in the 19th century. By 1871 they had leased Astley's Amphitheatre and produced circus entertainment at Agricultural Hall in London as well as in a huge travelling tent circus.

The climate for the time being is not too unpleasant, and he sympathises with his sister on the fickle weather they are suffering back home, even if they now have the sun shining after a period of snow and sleet.[23] "Indeed, you seem so pleased to write about this new experience of summer weather that I often feel I wish I could cut a huge slice from our sunshine to send home. It's a real treat just now – not too warm, and yet every day the sun rises, blazes down all day and then sets in a blaze of riotous colour and glory. The sunsets are wonderful here, a picture no artist could paint." The Near East is far from perfect, however. From Shillal, which they reach on May 26th, he writes: "The only thing which is calculated to annoy, especially at mealtimes, are the miniature whirlwinds, which, fortunately, are not very frequent and generally occur just after midday. You'll suddenly see a small cloud a deuce of a way off, which travels at a most alarming rate towards one across the 'prairie' (or the 'veldt', if you like), and soon you can see it quite plainly – the dust rising from the ground and ascending in a clearly defined whirlwind to no mean height. Well, if you're in the line of fire – look out and not only do you get temporarily blinded but, if you're having 'chuck', then your tea and stew is going to cop it and get filled with dust and all sorts.[24] Then it's either 'jerk it back or starve, ye blighter' – fortunately, we've all got cast-iron lined insides and constitutions by now, so, barring making a few appropriate remarks on whirlwinds in general and the last one in particular, we just carry on and chaw." The better weather, the better food supplies that improved communications brought, and, for the moment, a more settled existence, together with the absence of fighting, seem to have improved morale – the spirit of the troops being, he says, "tophole". Mounted troops did make occasional contact, and the Turks, who at the time had the advantage of superior aircraft to the British, carried out some air raids. The infantry, however, were largely untroubled. The seven mile long British line consisted of a series of redoubts on broken ground on the right bank of the Wadi, covering the water and the crossings at a number of points, and was considered "rather pleasant", according to the divisional history. Battalion headquarters were camped in the crevices and crannies of the Wadi itself, where there were welcome long pools of water. "The whole line of the Wadi Ghuzza became a busy thoroughfare, which, as [Royal] Engineers constructed pipelines, assumed an air of permanency – the camps might have been a series of villages."[25]

Dewi's next letter finds him extolling the virtues of Shillal, even though he complains that because they are on a rolling plain, there is nothing worth photographing.[26] "Still I'm hoping for luck shortly – we *might* move, you know. Just fancy, we're actually now in the same place as when I last wrote. Hardly believe it, can you – in fact, I feel as if I'd been here for years and years but, nevertheless, I don't want to move – O! no, I don't like 'em [moves] so much as all that, thank you, besides between me and you and the gatepost we're having an easier time here than we've had for – Och! ever since I can remember.[27] I tell you it's an absolute jink, is this. There's plenty of water, too, thank heavens – this might be strange to you but, believe me, that's a great advantage out here and much appreciated. You see, you

23) June 10th 1917.
24) Chuck, and later chaw, are Army slang for food and chew respectively.
25) Dudley Ward, p114.
26) June 19th 1917.
27) They were in Shillal for five weeks from May 26th to July 31st.

can wash shirts like – like anything when you get a burst of energy. Anyhow, it's something to be able to keep clean – I *have* experienced quite the opposite, as you know. There is a canteen about a mile away, too, so can you wonder at me not wanting to leave this ideal spot? It's true we have to shine up for a full marching order parade once a week but we don't mind that much – we've had plenty of practice, goodness knows."

At Shillal he found time to pen his only essay – as opposed to one of his usual letters – on the new surroundings in which he found himself.[28] Dewi was showing himself to be a capable writer, able to conjure up evocative descriptions of life on the march and of the surroundings in which he found himself, and writing letters replete with historical, cultural, religious and literary references drawn from his wide reading. His campaigning had clearly left him some time for reading, and he seems to have kept well abreast of events at home through copies of newspapers and magazines sent out to him, in particular, as we have seen, the *London Opinions* and *Weekly Telegraphs* he regularly asks to receive. His parents and all those to whom they will have shown his letters will, no doubt, have been impressed to read these now very mature thoughts of a 19 year old, already more than two years away from home. The soldier's lot in this rather forgotten but nevertheless, still important corner of the war is one he had had plenty of time to philosophise on. Running to nearly 2,500 words his essay allows him to reflect on their joy at seeing the fields and hedges of southern Palestine after the arid wastes of Sinai, on scenes of peasants working in the fields as they might have done in Biblical times, and on the topography, geology and geography of the area, the climate, the flowers and other plants, and the wildlife – vultures, bee-eaters, quail, swallows, larks and sand grouse, snakes, lizards, scorpions, spiders – that they came across. He is particularly proud, however, that they are marching where from time immemorial there have been "innumerable sanguinary contests", "in the champs d'honneur where the greatest warriors of five thousand years have fought and died" – Chaldeans, Egyptians, Assyrians, Babylonians, and Crusaders led by Richard Coeur de Lion. In a later letter he expresses pleasure that his essay has been well received but admits he has painted rather too pretty a picture of what he describes as "this blighted, desolate place" and asks for Heaven's forgiveness and honourable acquittal in the eyes of his comrades "for in my saner moments I share their opinion of the locality".[29]

After just over a month at Shillal they were relieved at the end of July by the 60th Division, newly arrived from Salonika, and moved back again to the coastal sand dunes at Deir el Belah, south-west of Gaza, to take over from the 54th Division. The Turks remained on the defensive but had switched tactics, replacing daytime sniping with desultory fire throughout the night and machine gun patrols in No Man's Land. Four days later on August 3rd Dewi is back again at Corps headquarters at Sheikh Shabasi on the coast, where he reports that the sea air is boosting his appetite. "I never have suffered from loss of appetite yet, thank goodness, but, my stars, it's simply abnormal under the effects of the ozone. I could easily polish off a loaf for brekker alone but must needs restrain from such rash

123

28) Vd. letter of July 26th 1917.
29) September 18th 1917.

conduct and place the remainder of my ration book in the box with a sigh of regret, 'cos there'd be none left for the rest of the day, if I started them games – can't be did. We have our little shanty right down on the beach dug into a bit of a cliff and the water's edge is about 20 yards distant." They are feeling absolutely grand, he says, with the sea at that range, and *heaps* better for the change. "The sunsets over the sea are something ripping and we always look towards the sun when it is just on the horizon and turning the sea into silver, 'cos we like to think that somewhere, 3000 miles in that direction along that silver strip is – Blighty, our promised land. The waves sing us to sleep o'nights but sorry to say that something more forcible is required to awaken us in the morning. (5.30 am is really a ridiculous hour to go on parade, though, isn't it?) But even at that unearthly hour we rise like larks, that is, if you can possibly imagine from previous trying experience me getting up like a lark ... And, well, you understand, we're so very pleased [with] ourselves and our delightful surroundings that nothing can damp our spirits. No, not even a telephone job which, alas! has unhappily fallen to my lot, which I must needs bear patiently for a week while another chap is on leave down at Cairo. You perceive, do you not, that they know a good man to fall back upon and that the Signal Office is still under capable management – until, of course, a cook is required suddenly."[30]

A Week of Bliss in Cairo

Bliss was to follow. On August 16th Dewi and some of his fellow-soldiers were given a week's leave in Cairo, no doubt in anticipation of the forthcoming third attempt on Gaza. "Cairo leave is imminent and I am on the tip-toe of excitement and the expectation of a real jolly, tophole, gorgeous 7 days of idle luxurious holiday," he writes.[31] I sincerely hope I shan't be frightened at the cinemas, white table-cloths, a real bed etc. and return terror-stricken to my native wilds, where the waves break, the sun shines and the breezes blow and everything else is still and quiet. That would be a catastrophe but do you think that it is at all probable – just try me and see. Oh! Do, Tra-la. As I told you before, I shall take full advantage of the opportunity for taking plenty of photographs."

In the Egyptian capital the main item on the programme, he tells his parents, after the hardships of the preceding months, was food. Their journey had started with a ride to the railhead (probably at Deir el Belah), in the ration wagon with kit. This was followed by a fourteen hour journey trying to catch some sleep on the iron nuts and bars strewn on the floor of a cattle train. 'Twasn't half interesting and quite amusing and pleasant, too, to think that, there we were, riding along the very same ground that some months ago we had covered in full marching order on our pedal extremities. I quite enjoyed the situation, you bet, except for now and then when the blooming truck would give an extra jerk and all but pitch you overboard. Arriving 7 am at Kantara on the familiar blue waters of the Canal, the first stop was for refreshment. In his now customary vernacular style, he writes: "Well, we never had nothing to eat during that fourteen hours so first thing we did was to get hot on the trail of a grub shop – talk about bloodhounds, they wouldn't stand an earthly. Well, we soon run a 'Y.M.' [YMCA] to earth and steered right in for breakfast – *eggs*, bacon, bread, *butter*, tea (with *milk* and *sugar*), *cakes* and

30) August 7th 1917.
31) Ibid.

goodness knows what – Tut! thought sure I never was going to finish that tuck-in and could hardly shift when we finally chucked up the sponge and guv [sic] in. You see, we hadn't smelt that sort of tuck for years and you betcher life we made the most of it. What with our eyes nearly on our cheeks and letting in to that tommy like a lot of half-starved cannibals, we must have looked an uncivilised crew.[32] I gave that bloke behind the counter an apologetic look as much as to say, 'Sorry, old cock, you must excuse us'. He must a knowed where we come from 'cos he understood like a shot and smiled. After we'd guv that brekker a first rate towsing we got rid of that blinking kit and equipment and, to show how much I loved it, I let drive and caught the valise a deuce of a welt as a sort of farewell salute."

In their excitement they thought the doubtless slow train would never reach Cairo but at 3pm they rolled into a "real proper civilised station".[33] "Dashed outside and jumped into a cab as if we owned the whole blinkin' village. I tell you, I never experienced anything like that ride in all my natural [life]. Motors and trams and hotels and bikes – we positively held our breath – blokes walking about in civvies, togged up to the blooming nines in collars and ties, and the ladies in all their finery and silks – Gee! I guess we must have had eyes like saucers staring at everything, and all these rum-looking creatures in the streets like country yokels, or worse. And, then, we looked at ourselves, had a rude shock and felt quite ashamed of our grey boots and faded shabby-lookin' khaki and helmets. Then, we guv one great blooming big sigh – I dunno why, it sort of came natural. Well, we soon got to our *hotel*, (sound the aitch, Ahem!) – called the Anzac Hostel and run for us fellers by Y.M. people – and first thing we did was to dash downstairs and tumble into a hot bath – words fail me when I try to tell you 'bout that bath – it was just the topholest thing out, believe me. Then, we thought we'd do the heavy and went to have our boots cleaned for $^1/_2$ piastre. You should have seen that bootblack's face when he saw my boots, it didn't half drop sideways – it took him about two minutes to compose himself and settle down to the job. Poor blighter, I did feel sort of sorry for him, 'cos I just skrunk [sic] him clean out of a brand new tin of 'Nugget' besides about umpteen pounds of elbow grease.[34] He looked just about fagged out after he'd finished 'em.

"P'raps you can guess what was next on the programme – a blooming big tuck in, only they called it 'cold lunch' – coffee, brembutter, salad, meat and O! the pudd'n – By George! it felt good to be on leave just then – it made me say to myself 'Jim, old cock, you're in clover but this ain't a patch on what 76 is goin' to be like, you kin betcher life'.[35] Then we had cigars and didn't half do the 'toff' stunt – most remarkable imitation. The next stop was a French barber. Then I had a brilliant idea strike me. 'Jim', I ses, 'you don't *want* a shave terrible bad but it's some time since you experienced anything except a blinkin' 'fretwork saw' on your phisog so why not go and have a *razor* on it for a change'. So, in goes this child to a swell 'coiffeurs and shavers' establishment, where there was about umpteen pier glasses hanging round the walls.[36] Sat down and a Frenchmen worked the oracle on me in

32) Tommy, provisions.
33) August 25th 1917.
34) Nugget, boot polish.
35) His home was at 76 Moorland Road.
36) Pier glasses, large mirrors used to fill spaces between pillars in buildings.

a proper high-faluted style – Parisian style, you know. 'You want ze moustache to keep, m'sieur,' he said, serious as a judge, and, of course, not wishing to insult the poor feller, I kept as straight a face as poss and said polite like, 'Non, m'sieur, shave the blighter off, he get too much in ze way, comprenez?' So, off it came eventually. But my word! what a shave – absolutely glorious and, tho' I'm not a blessed veteran with the beard stakes by long chalks, I tell you honestly, it fair soothed me – acted just like a dummy on a nipper. Lathered and shaved me OK, with never a pull or a scratch, like my old Army pattern [razor] plays on me, and he was as dainty as a blessed girl, s'welp me Bob.[37]

"Then, the blooming ceremony started, which fair startled me – first he rubbed a block of ice over me dial [38] and then he sprayed about five scents over me and then shampooed me and sprayed some more till I didn't know if I wasn't in for an aquatic gala, for sure. I *was* some swell by the time I finished in that place, I tell you, 'cos he brushed my hair and put a blooming fine parting in it – straight as a die and looked the real goods. I don't know how the deuce he managed it, 'cos blowed if I could ever get one there before. I was so pleased that I gave him 2 piastres for himself and told him on the Q.T.[39] that he was a blooming marvel, only he couldn't comprunny simple language like that. Then, they had a bloke there who brushed your togs and chapeau when you left. When he came to me they thought a blessed sandstorm had started in the shop and I couldn't help grinning to see the clouds of sand and dust that came out of my tunic and helmet. Didn't half scare the m'sieurs who turned up their collars quick to economise in laundry bills, I reckon. Well, that little lot cost me 6 piastres but it was worth it every inch. You can judge for yourselves how swell it was – I was actually having a shave next chair to a major on the staff – absolutely – (Lummy! where's my swagger cane – Swish! Haw! Bar Jove!), and the manager bowed me out, too, and fairly beamed when I told him it was a "très bon" little shanty of his."

A soldier's pleasures after a long campaign in the desert seem to have been simple and there is no mention of alcohol. "We didn't do much that night, except drink iced lemonades in a picture show and nearly choke over Charlie Chaplin's antics and so, feeling pretty fagged, we got back to the Anzac pretty early and prepared for bed (after a feed, of course – trust us). And now came the biggest surprise of all. You'll never be able to imagine our feeling, not if you try till you're blue in the face, when we saw white sheets, white pillows, mattresses and a real bed-stead again. I was almost afraid to get into it but at last plucked up enough courage and tremblingly crept in. Crikey! I thought sure I was going to drop through at first, it was so soft. I dessay [daresay] you've heard about these fellers on leave who can't sleep the first time in a proper feather bed. Well, as far as I was concerned, it proved to be all bosh [nonsense]. I just put my head on that pillow and was just thinking it was absolutely the best thing I'd struck for years and Blow me! next thing I knew it was high time to turn out for brekker." There follows a round of visits, all evocatively described, to the Pyramids, the Sphinx and the Temple, the zoo, bazaars, and mosques, a cruise down the Nile by pleasure steamer to the Barrage, afternoon tea in an English tea garden, all with aching shins and feet from the now unfamiliar

37) So help, me God. Bob, euphemism for God.

38) Dial, face.

39) Q.T. Expression dating back to early years of 20th century meaning on the quiet.

hard pavements.[40] More "tophole feeds" were partaken, together with trips to Heliopolis, to a "White City affair" – a funfair – and a music hall, though, unfortunately, being in French and Arabic he understood little of the performance. "What I enjoyed as much as anything," he says "was seeing everyone waiting hand and foot on us. F'rinstance, we never washed our plates and mugs once the whole week we spent there." The mosques he describes as quaint old places. "All natives, of course. It was very interesting […] you've got to wear galoshes over your boots to go in and we arrived during their Sunday school time, with the Gippos sitting round with their teachers, learning the 'Koran'." As a good Sunday School pupil he was also interested to visit Matarieh outside Heliopolis to see the tree where Mary and Joseph rested with the Child on their flight to Egypt. "The tree […] is very old and they are doing their utmost to preserve it by props etc. We also saw the well where Mary drank from. It used to be brackish water until she drank it, when it became perfectly pure. We took a drink and, indeed, it was quite good, while the next well to it, one could see, was very dirty.[41] […] I also paid a visit to Rhoda Island,[42] the dead city of Cairo not far from the Pyramids, visited the mosque there and the Coptic Church and also saw the place where Moses was found in the bulrushes. It looked very ordinary you know – very much the same as the tidefield."[43]

His return journey was spent sleeping on iron nuts, and bolts and bands, in a cattle truck. "What a transformation – instead of walking about poshed up to the nines with a light belt and cane, you see us tramping 3 miles to our camp in full harness and sweating like bulls […] The first grub I had when I arrived was a plate of stew – O! Dear! the irony of it all – I almost wished I hadn't gone when I tried to stomach that […] The quicker I forget about Cairo, the better I'm thinking. Still, it did us good, if it's only the grub we've had, and, for another thing, it's given us all just a taste of what we'll get home in Blighty." He enjoyed his leave and does not brood. Indeed, his basic optimism soon leads him to convince himself he is better off *not* being in Cairo any longer at the mercy of its shopkeepers. "Well, now we've had our little outing and come back again, we feel sort of satisfied and, although we're dreadfully cut-up, the lonely, quiet desert and blue sea in front of us seems very soothing and peaceful after the hurry and bustle, the traffic, confusion and the lights of a town. I'm not sure whether I ain't a true son of the desert. But I expect these feelings are only because it was Cairo we went to for leave. You see, nobody was glad – real glad to see us down there except to bloodsuck us for our last half piastre piece. If it had been Blighty, now – well there – *if*. I reckon there'd a [sic] been a different tale to tell. It'd be no more desert for me, if I could help it."

40) The barrages are located 10 miles north of Cairo on the Nile just before it splits to form the Damietta to the east and Rosetta to the west. The first was built by Muhammad Ali, a commander in the Ottoman army, who became Khedive of Egypt in 1805. The second was built early in the 20th century as part of agricultural and irrigation reforms carried out by the British. The barrages, crossed by a set of bridges, are surrounded by parks.

41) The flight, to escape Herod's massacre of the innocents.

42) Rhoda Island, located on the Nile in Central Cairo, containing one of the oldest Islamic buildings in Egypt, the Nilometer, for measuring the Nile River's clarity and water level during the annual flood season.

43) The tidefield, near his home in Splott.

Khan Yunus for Training

Immediately on his return they are on the move, after being relieved by the 54th. Their destination from Sheikh Shabasi is Khan Yunus for training, which they reach on August 27th. A parcel from home cheers him up and, indeed, the whole tenor of his letter about Cairo suggests his spirits were high. Soldiers will, of course, always feel easier moving forward, even if there are setbacks, and there was new leadership following General Sir Edmund Allenby's appointment in place of Murray. In August its new commander put in place a major re-organisation of the now expanded E.E.F. The Desert Column became the Desert Mounted Corps under Major General Henry (Harry) Chauvel, and the infantry were organised into two corps, the XXth commanded by Chetwode, to which the 53rd Brigade belonged, and the XXIst commanded by Lieut.-General Edward Bulfin.[44] A month later the third assault on Gaza would begin and Dewi would be busy laying down communication lines to the front and carrying out a variety of other tasks. Indeed, once the onward march had begun, which was to take him in the next few months past the Turkish defensive line stretching from Gaza to Beersheba, on beyond Beersheba itself, and to Jerusalem by Christmas, his opportunities to write home were few. There would be casualties to come in the battles of the next few months – a consideration no doubt in the minds of the higher command in sending men for a break from action to enjoy, as Dewi did, the food, the comforts, the sights, and entertainments of Cairo.

Allenby had taken over the Egyptian Expeditionary Force on June 28th, after Murray had been recalled, and brought a complete change of style. While Murray has been given credit for developing the infrastructure and supply chain needed to carry the troops on towards Palestine, setting the stage for subsequent British successes, he and his headquarters staff were, nevertheless, leading too comfortable a life far from the front in Shepheard's Hotel in Cairo. This had prevented him from taking the decisions that might have led to success in the first battle, when excessive caution led to Gaza being surrendered when already in the control of British forces. The dynamism and confidence Allenby brought to the job foreshadowed the qualities of another desert warrior a generation later, General Sir Bernard Montgomery. He, too, was able to take a dispirited force and make them into victors, turning the war in North Africa in much the same way that Allenby turned the war in the Middle East. A big cavalryman, then 56 year old, and more than six feet tall, Allenby was nicknamed the Bull by reason of both his physique and personality. He knew how to get the best out of his troops and, in particular, out of the Australian mounted men, who throughout the Near East campaigns spearheaded the sweeping movements used to get behind the Turkish lines. Shortly after arriving in Egypt he visited the front for discussions with Chetwode, commander of the Eastern Force, and took the opportunity to visit all sectors and

44) Henry Chauvel (1865-1945), led dismounted Anzac troops in Gallipoli, before taking command of the Anzac Mounted Division in March 1916 in Sinai. He took part in the victories in the Battle of Romani in August and the Battle of Magdhaba in December, and in the unsuccessful First Battle of Gaza in March 1917. The following month he took over the Desert Column, later known as the Desert Mounted Corps, thereby becoming the first Australian to command a corps, and the first to reach the rank of lieutenant-general. At Beersheba in October 1917 his light horse captured the town and its vital water supply in one of history's last great cavalry charges. Dublin-born Sir Edward Bulfin (1862-1939) served in the Boer War and at Ypres and the Somme before being posted with the 60th Division to Palestine in June 1917.

to talk to a number of units. His response was to transfer most of his general headquarters to the front. The knowledge that he and his staff would henceforth share many of the troops' discomforts in the field helped to bring about a big improvement in morale, still suffering from the reverses of the Spring and made worse by the unpleasantly hot summer weather.[45]

Over the summer months both sides had continued to consolidate their positions in preparation for what seemed certain to be the final climactic encounter at Gaza. By August a well-organised trench system had been put in place on the British defensive position east of Wadi Ghuzza, and a series of strong outposts developed, defended by barbed wire. Roads were built to replace tracks unsuitable for moving large columns of men, wadi crossings engineered, sun shelters erected to protect posts from the sun, and water supply arrangements made. In places very soft sand made the use of revetments necessary to prevent trenches caving in, and dust storms required them to be frequently cleared. Railway operations also continued throughout the summer, with lines and trackside installations materialising with impressive speed, as a result of the work of Royal Engineers railway companies and the native Egyptian labour force. Over the intervening months the Kantara Military Railway, as it was known, had been substantially upgraded and two new branch lines from Rafa to El Qamle and Shillal, inland from Wadi Ghuzza, had been added to support future operations further inland. Other track and depot improvements were made. By June 1917 there were 82 locomotives at work on the railway, 75 coaches, and 1,360 wagons and trucks, operating 16 trains daily in both directions.[46] Later still the track running out from Kantara would be doubled to increase capacity to 28 trains a day. Murray had requested twin tracks be provided in April as vital to supporting any advance into Palestine and the second track to Rafa was eventually authorised on July 31st. Capacity on the railways to carry troops, supplies, ammunition and, where necessary, water in a country with very poor or no roads was, of course, the main determinant of how big an assault could take place, and how far it could extend on into Palestine and towards Jerusalem. Royal Engineers water companies matched the efforts of the railway companies, their pipelines reaching Abu Bakra on Wadi Ghuzza and Imara, 2 miles east of Shillal in June, more than 140 miles from the Sweet Water Canal at Kantara from which the water was being drawn. Rafa had also been reached by this stage and equipped with storage for 200,000 gallons in two reinforced concrete reservoirs. Two 50,000 gallon reservoirs were installed at El Rasum simply to provide the 80,000 gallons a day needed by locomotives. Action during this period was limited but there were raids on both sides and casualties.

Training back at Khan Yunus was hard and boring to judge by a typical day and the sparse rations they survived on. "The best thing I can do is to give a brief summary of our daily programme. This will [...] save much explanation whenever I have occasion in future to impart the sad news that we are down for a 'rest'. To proceed – Reveille 4.30, Gunfire (i.e. half a cup of tea) 5.0. Fall in 5.15. Physical exercises (Hear me groan) 1 hour, 10 mins. spell, rifle drill and squad drill, 1 hour. Brekker (1 ration – notice I avoid the term 'rasher' – of bacon *or* porridge (?). Rifle and ammunition inspection 8.30. Cable drill 2 or 3 hours. Dinner (1 tin of jam

129

45) Pritchard, (ed.), p284.
46) Ibid, p276.

between 6 and a peculiar mixture of sand and bread – very gritty, Ugh!), wagon inspection in the afternoon. Throw in a few fatigues, such as the cleansing of rusty harness etc., and one or two medical and kit inspections, and there you have a faint idea what an ideal restful, lieusurely [sic] time we're having.[47] Then comes tea (half a cup deducted because of the morning 'gunfire') and the sticky mysterious mess affectionately known as 'Gippo'.[48] After this our time is our own until physical jerks 4.30 ak emma [a.m.][49] Stay – I have forgotten a most vital item – inoculation (i.e. a few million germs pumped into your arm by a member of that fraternity of butchers – the Linseed Lancers) at 6 pm last evening. So, can you wonder that we are never seen without a smile on our faces and songs upon our lips – the favourites of which are 'Hi-ti-iddley-i-ti, take me back to Blighty' and 'O! my I don't want to die, I want to go home', ' sung à la fortissimo, crescendo and all the rest of the technical musical terms which mean in plain conversational English – 'a deuce of a row'."[50] Their treatment sounds harsh but the Army was seeking to toughen the men up for the hours and days they might have to spend in the field without much to eat or drink, and to familiarise them with operating at all hours, most attacks being launched in the early hours, often when the men were already worn out after long marches to get into position.

Advancing the Cable Lines

At Khan Yunus he has a new job to report – wagon-hand laying communication cables between the front lines and headquarters – and a rejoinder to the holiday that his parents and family are proposing to take at Rhoose on the Glamorgan coast:[51] "Talking about rests, let me remind you that the writer is something of an expert as far as nice, quiet lazy rest cures are concerned. P'raps I told you before that *we* happen to be in rest. But, unfortunately, there are rests and 'rests' – confound 'em. We are groaning under the injustices of the latter, the sort of rest that is distasteful, one from which, I regret to say, I have not derived the slightest enjoyment or pleasure. You understand the meaning of the verb 'i orphwys' [to rest] but your education has been sadly neglected as far as the *irregular* verb 'to rest' (Army parlance) is concerned. Again, it would seem he was being trained for the work he would spend much of the rest of the year carrying out – taking out cable wagons, sometimes physically hauling them over difficult ground with his comrades, where the land was too difficult for horses, so that telegraph lines could be laid up to the front.

Working on cable-laying, Dewi is beginning to feel far removed from his previous calling as a signaller. "Shouldn't be at all surprised if I have to take a few months course [...] when I get back, I'm afraid. I've quite forgotten the stops on those

47) Lieusurely, probably intentionally mis-spelt.
48) Army slang for soup, gravy or stew.
49) Signallers' letters pip emma (p.m.) and ack emma (a.m.).
50) September 5th 1917. Popular songs of the era. The words of the latter were written for the Western Front: 'I want to go home, I want to go home. I don't want to go in the trenches no more, Where whizzbangs and shrapnel they whistle and roar. Take me over the sea, Where the Alleyman [German] can't get at me. Oh my, I don't want to die, I want to go home. I want to go home, I want to go home. I don't want to visit la Belle France no more. For, oh, the Jack Johnsons they make such a roar. Take me over the sea, Where the snipers, they can't get at me. Oh my, I don't want to die, I want to go home.' A Jack Johnson was a 15cm German artillery shell named after the American boxer of the era.
51) September 5th 1917

Remingtons,"[52] Dewi laments, on hearing of his sister's successes in the office, insisting that he no longer has the hands of a typist or a pianist. They have been hardened by all those "honourable blisters" through reeling out cable. "I am now out of the office, you see, and hold the common or garden inferior rank of 'wagon-hand', which brings me less into contact with Dr Morse than ever." He has one consolation, however. "I have had it on good authority that the Cardiff Corporation have always posts vacant for men who are in the habit of expectorating freely upon their palms prior to delivering hefty strokes upon Macadamised roads sadly in need of repair. Failing this, I am positive that, with a few weeks of instruction, I should become a fairly efficient tar-sprayer. In fact, there are still more than a few similarly highly desirous occupations left open to me and which I feel confident I could carry out with as much dexterity as the next ex-sapper."

He describes a cable wagon hurtling across the country. "One of the familiar, inspiring sights of the plains of Palestine […] is that of an eight horse drawn cable wagon dashing along in fine style to the music of the rapidly revolving drums of wire (one of which is seen to be handled with becoming skill and ease by that scapegrace D.E.D).[53] 'Buried crossing' rings out the stentorian voice of the sergeant and the spectacle which then presents itself – that of 'yours affec' leaping from his perch, pick and shovel in hand, proceeding at 'the double' to perform the required operation, is one which would never fail to elicit your praise and admiration. But no – the lonely sand hills, the waving fig-trees, the blinding sun, and one or two solitary water camel convoys are the only inanimate and dumb spectators, unless it be the sergeant, of course, who sitting astride his palfrey watches with eagle-eye the labour of his slaves, critical and ever ready to spur laggards on with a few well-timed and appropriate phrases such as *'move*, bless you, *move'* and remarking with biting sarcasm upon our lightning-like qualities that it will of a surety 'be *dark* in a minute', tho' the sun is scarce yet overhead. Such as this is our portion, with each succeeding purple dawn – can you thus but wonder sometimes that we wish we'd not been born!"[54]

In his next letter he cheerily announces his "latest and most unexpected advancement in the profession of arms".[55] "In previous epistles I have appeared before you in many roles and have manifested my ability to tackle any and all the different jobs that have fallen to my changeable lot. Camel driver, key thumper, cable layer and excavating pick and shovel expert are but a few of the many characters I have assumed but my very latest vocation totally eclipses all previous professions and will, I trust, cause you a thrill of pride and admiration. In fine, the curtain rises and I take my call as 'Brevet-Driver-Sapper' – but this enigmatical appellation will require minute explanation to the uninitiated.[56] So here goes – to put it plainer still, I have been entrusted with the care and use of a pair of equine quadrupeds – two hefty formidable draught horses and a set of harness – just think if it. My daily round, my common task, I will set out in detail, which should be of

131

---

52) Remingtons, typewriters.

53) Scapegrace, hare-brained person, constantly in trouble.

54) September 5th 1917. Palfrey, poetic word for a saddle horse, usually ridden by ladies.

55) September 18th 1917.

56) September 18th 1917. Brevet is a term used in the military for temporary elevation to a higher rank (but without corresponding pay increase).

great interest to you. 5.30 am instead of a route march I now proceed post haste to the 'lines' and saddle up, tighten the girths and adjust the stirrups, affix the bit, mount and then with my two beloved dumb 'long faced chums' (and a mule or two on occasions) with the rest of the column ride to water, a few miles distant. We arrive back after a dusty ride and off-saddle and set to work with the curry comb and dandy brush to groom the dear things. Plenty of elbow grease needed – a most strenuous form of exercise for the biceps of the arm, I assure you. And, now, and then I smile to myself and think what you would say to see me brushing away, uttering that low 'S-s-s-s' in the approved groom style. Break off for breakfast and after an inspection at 9.30 we again return to the lines and, in less than no time, you perceive me squatting amidst the chaos of dubbing, cleaning rags, breast-pieces, saddle, stirrup-irons and straps, bits and traces – my whole harness and driving equipage (not forgetting my whips and leg iron), which I then submit to a thorough greasing, (on no account must it rust, you see), and this is another operation which requires much energy and elbow power.

"I am sure my manicurist would weep to see these hands, after that sticky duty dubbing, but I console myself by thinking that we are but cleaning harness for 'England, Home and Beauty' as they say on the Brasso advertisement, or used to. Covering up the steel and leather-work carefully with sacking and my horse blanket, I then feed away (two armfuls of tibbin, a tinful of oats and two of some other feed – dunno what they call it, but you see I've got it all weighed up).[57] Dinner and a rest till 3 o'clock. Turn out then, saddle up and off to water (same as morning) come back, grooming, another feed away and then finish. Can you possibly believe it – I can just imagine your dismay to learn that I have entirely forsaken sounders and telephones and such rough work for the more gentle and congenial occupation connected with curry combs and dandy brushes. Tut, tut, Cuthbert and Araminta, for such is the artistic manner in which I have christened my pair, are very affectionate indeed, and are awfully attached to me. They are like lambs in my hands and are as well behaved as one could wish (such is my uncanny influence over animals whether they be camels or horses). Cuthbert is my rider, while Araminta trots along in the lead. Both are of huge dimensions (naturally, as cable wagon horses must be) and are somewhat clumsy with it. Of course, they need Antipon badly before I could truthfully call them real blood chargers.[58] However, they are becoming more graceful every day under my able training. As for my horsemanship – well, I am, of course, now quite an experienced and skilful rider and bump nicely when astride dear Cuthbert's brawny back. I shall have to be photographed one of these days – I know it would please you to have one and you may be sure that Araminta shall look her real best for the occasion."

A Hint of Rebelliousness

Concern among the ranks that the censor might be reading letters seems not to have weighed very heavily, given the sardonic nature of his closing remarks on this transformation in his role. "There was, of course, a heap of trouble with the

57) Tibbin or tibn, chopped straw or chaff, a low quality feed for horses.

58) Antipon was a popular Victorian and Edwardian weight loss remedy made up of citric acid, red food colouring, water and alcohol (none of which has any effect on weight loss). It sold for more than twenty times the cost of its ingredients.

President of the Sapper's Union over my resignation (you know him well!). He is very harsh with those who turn traitors to 'the cause' (which is rather obscure) and I was given a severe reprimanding for becoming a 'driver'. The union's motto is Liberté, Egalité, Fraternité and is an institute for the promotion of an 'ideal millennium Army', the watchword being 'Down with tyranny – you needn't do it, if you don't want to' – the latter phrase referring to anything in the way of commands, fatigues etc.[59] Only the other day the previous President was deposed for 'picking his feet up when ordered to mark time and for acting generally in a soldierly like manner'. Anyhow, I am now known to all and sundry as 'Driver' and much emphasis, sarcasm and good natured stuff, which, you may be sure, is met with appropriate and telling sallies."[60] The loyal solider keen to join his friends in bashing the Hun in 1915 seems by 1917 to be waiting for it to be all over and generally keen to keep his head down, though no doubt in writing home he felt obliged to display a measure of bravado and ennui, to his younger sister in particular.

Incidents he goes on to describe perhaps set in context the feelings he was now expressing and hint for the first time at feelings of rebelliousness. Exercises aimed at preparing them for the forthcoming third attempt to take Gaza seemed pointless to the man in the camp, as a letter sent in the middle of September suggests. They had perhaps lost confidence in the higher command after the failures of the first two attempts on Gaza, they were fed up with the heat, flies and other discomforts of the desert and, in their weakened state, waiting for reinforcements. Though Allenby had arrived, his influence had perhaps not yet been fully felt. "Events move rapidly – the plot thickens – it looks suspiciously as if they mean to break our spirits or our backs and I've got so much startling news to give you that I really dunno where or how to start. I think I told you in my last letter of the recent 'rest cure' scheme they're working on us. Well, unfortunately, I have to report that we are still 'patients' and instead of being convalescent and back at work again we have been plunged deeper into the throes of this somewhat peculiar rest." The programme, he writes, had been suddenly altered about a week or so before and the outcome had been rather a shock. "Up to that time it was a common sight at 5.30 am to see us 'doubling' round the fig groves and cactus hedges, followed later by an idiotic performance of 'on the right and left foot hop' 'knees bend and stretch' and then the more racking and back-breaking ordeal of laying prone and lifting one's legs in mid-air at the pleasure of the drill-sergeant – an operation which was invariably accompanied by painful grunts and groans. 6.30 am saw us crawling off the open air gymnasium only to dash back a few minutes later with rifles and equipment and then proceed to pass a pleasant hour by sloping arms and forming platoons right and left. Very monotonous – I recollect one morning I was so bored that I actually dared to yawn right under the aforesaid sergeant's nose – Good Heavens! the next moment I was trembling most violently at the knees and expecting every minute to be the next [sic] -'Oho, yawning are you m'lad, alright we'll see etc. etc.', he bawled out – terrible sensation, I can assure you, and you may be sure that this sapper sloped and ordered his arm with the utmost vigour after that. But, I am rambling disgracefully. To proceed – well, that used to be our pre-breakfast

---

59) Possibly a reference to Cromwell's New Model Army.
60) September 18th 1917.

programme until a short time ago when, lo and behold, if they didn't change their tactics, and precisely at 5.30 am the very next morning, we were required to fall in, in full marching order, pack and all usual style, for a little morning saunter of a few miles before brekker. This has continued uninterrupted for some mornings now. Doesn't your heart bleed for us to think of us winding our way, dolorous and malcontent, over hill and dale, at such an unearthly hour when we should be enjoying our beauty sleep like other decent folk? The dirges sung in the ranks on these occasions are most weird and melancholy-sounding, two of the favourites being 'Art thou weary, art thou languid' and 'Old Soldiers never die, they only fade away'. As we are not in possession of a pibroch or two the effect is not quite so touching as it might be, though."[61]

He was at risk of being in trouble again soon after, this time for not shaving properly, as he reports when thanking his parents for a razor.[62] "As for the safety razor, well, I told you about the shaves I had in Cairo, and, after experiencing those sublime operations on my chivvy, I guess I'm fairly yearning for that Gillette. You wouldn't half have felt sorry for me yesterday morning, if you could have seen me scraping the bristles off for parade. Scraping, did I say? By Gum! that wasn't the word for it. You see this razor (?) I use wouldn't sharpen a pencil properly, leave alone clean my chivvy, and on top of that lies the fact that it's slightly rusty through hard use, so you can guess what a time I had. It was either that or risking the S.M.'s eagle eye and orderly room, so I stuck it like a good 'un.[63] Nearly tore my face off, and my eyes were watering, as if I'd copped it hot in a tear shell bombardment.[64] You can betcher life I don't use that oftener than I can possibly help – it's agony, that's what it is. I've been expecting the new one out from you, r'else I'd have bought one, you see."[65] He reports being disciplined one morning a few weeks earlier for not being clean-shaven, suggesting one of the Army's occasional purges to prevent slackness creeping in had been ordered. "One of the officers spotted me one morning on parade so it was 'Take that man's name' and me for the high jump. Right turn, quick march, halt, helmets off, and there we were s'welp me Bob, right on the blinking carpet with the records of our previous *crimes* in front of us on the desk and the O.C. behind it – s'pose you've heard 'em talk about the 'dread presence' – that's it to a T. The *desperate, villainous criminals* weren't kept waiting long and just then, when trivial incidents in my long, worthless career of crime kept passing in pageant thro' my mind (the drowning man touch, you know), as though in a dream, the S.M.'s voice came to my ears like a murmuring torrent, chanting melodiously sweet and low his evidence.[66]

61) September 18th 1917. The hymn *Art thou weary, art thou languid,*' based on Matthew 11:28 'Come to Me, all you who are weary and burdened, and I will give you rest.' Words of a Hymn by Stephen of Mar Saba (Judea), 8th Century, translated from Greek to English by John M. Neale in *Hymns for the Eastern Church*, 1862, to the tune Christus Consolator by Rev. J.B. Dykes, Hymns *Ancient and Modern*, Standard Edition. *Old soldiers never Die* was a British Army song, quoted by General Douglas MacArthur at the end of World War Two, to whom the phrase is often wrongly attributed. A pibroch is used to play Highland Gaelic piping music.

62) August 31st 1917.

63) S.M., Sergeant Major. C.S.M., Company Sergeant Major.

64) An artillery shell filled with tear gas.

65) The safety razor, enabling men to shave themselves, grew in popularity after the introduction of the disposable blade by King S.C. Gillette in 1901. The American company. Gillette, and its British rival Valet, both offered safety razor sets for 21 |- , consisting of razor and 12 blades.

66) August 31st 1917

""Sir", I accompanied So & So on a tour of inspection along the ranks this morning at 8.30 of the clock in this month of July of year of our Lord 1917 anno domini – (By Jove! I thought this is blooming interesting, he can't half spit out a good yarn – Carry on, old hass) – and he continued – 'found this man, Sapper No. so & so, name and address, age, birthplace, next of kin, occupation, and particulars of education, married or single etc. etc. etc., in a filthy condition on parade, unshaven in direct contradiction and defiance of company orders, Form K/125/A, Page 19, Para B/56/15634 dated the so & so, and' – Oh! a whole long string of it, as long as your arm. [...] He put me in such a blooming tangle I couldn't have sworn to save my life whether it was 'murder with violence' or 'drunk and resisting the guard' I was charged with. 'Golly!' thinks I, 'you ain't half going thro' it this time, David, my lad, if the judge considers all that oration for the prosecution.' Then amidst the rustling of 'King's Regulations' and scratching of APM's pens and one thing and another the bloke behind the desk cleared his throat and spake forth in stentorian tones of reverberating thunder.[67] 'Anything to say, Sapper – don't answer me back.' Well, what was a feller to do? I risked answering him back and spoke up. Dunno what I said altogether, phrased in my Sunday-best law vocabulary, but I know I was determined to give the S.M. a run for his money. However, the pith of the whole chin-music was that I wasn't aware that I was in need of a scrape. (Any port in a storm but Gee! what a crammer to tell – they were inch and a half long on my phizog – a real beard without exaggeration).

"After I finished *he* started, and fair play to him he did very well indeed, considering. As a matter of fact, if I'd have taken his little sermon to heart, he'd have wiped the floor with me. He said quite a lot of nice polite things until I was bored stiff – what he was going to do now, what he would have done before if it wasn't for such and such a thing and what he wasn't going to do in the future – Gee! 'twould have filled a book a bit easy. The main point that he was trying to get at, tho,' was the fact that I ought to consider myself swiped off the face of the earth, or something equally as drastic. Asked me if I thought I needed a nursemaid to look after me and tell me when I wanted a scrape, and that sort of very deep humour. 'You look in the glass[68] every morning, don't you,' says he 'when you brush your hair, and that, by the way, doesn't look as if it's been brushed this morning either.' Lummy! That absolutely put the kybosh on it. If he'd only known that I didn't have half an inch of glass in my kit, leave alone a hairbrush, I'd have been doing penal servitude now in all probability. Anyhow, after a sort of comic opera lasting for about 20 minutes he came to the conclusion. After a lengthy and awe-inspiring deliberation without consideration for the prisoner's feeling and suspense, the verdict was pronounced with all due ceremony and solemnity – Guilty! Oh Crumbs, yes, no doubt whatever about it, and he had a 'jolly good mind to make an example of me,' not 'arf, he didn't. By Gum. Lef' turn, quick march, helmets on – exeunt of the prisoners, out of the dread presence, into the brilliant Palestine sunshine – we breathed again, out of the valley of death – safe at last. By George! (Thus, you observe from the above, the admirable methods employed, which enable us to say proudly and with every conviction, 'We're winning this war' – and no wonder either.)"

---

67) A.P.M., Assistant Provost Marshal. Officer rank within military police.
68) Glass, mirror.

Dewi clearly did not take his dressing-down too seriously. "Well, this prisoner didn't break down into sad salt tears during the terrible ordeal of that trial nor has it preyed on his mind with dire results on his general health and constitution since. I know very well that by all the rules I should be suffering from anaemia, nervous prostration, brain-fever and a host of other complaints, but no – I still roll up with the best of 'em for my Maconochie ration – one tin between four. And, it only goes to show what a matter of fact, nerveless, phlegmatic automatum this existence develops one into that I should defy all the laws of medicine in this manner. Sometimes I think, tho', in my very sober moments, what a disgrace I have brought upon the house of David and wonder whether I shall ever again look you straight in the face again, Mum, with such a blot upon my escutcheon – I haven't quite decided upon the design of it but there's going to be a shovel, a pick, a few stew dixies and a camel rampant on it, just to begin with, you can take my word for that. [...] Ah! but what a tragedy, my friends. Let us take this lesson home and learn a lesson therefrom – all through an extra ten minutes in bed, a rusty razor and the gay demeanour of a C.S.M. Always use a safety [razor] my friends. Anyone trying to find another moral in this story and passing rude remarks upon the author's state of mind will be prosecuted."

In an earlier letter he talks about his outings with his horses, including one when he managed to pass a critical inspection and uphold the dignity of the sapper. "It will please you to know that Cuthbert and Araminta are quite well. I have been out in the wagon with them harnessed up a few times and their behaviour leaves nothing to be desired. Three days ago we had a long ride for rations with a full team in the wagon and managed exceedingly well. You see, these drivers sort of look down on us sappers condescendingly as poor dismounted men who don't know a horse's fetlock from his withers, and pity us as poor ignorant blighters who can't ride, so it was up to me to show 'em that the sappers, or at least *this* particular sapper, can beat 'em at their own game and is a proper all-round jack and master of all blooming trades. [...] D.E.D. wasn't found wanting – not he – and he walk-marched, trotted or cantered with the best of 'em. Anyhow, he was still in the saddle, cool as a cucumber, when we reached home and had never turned a hair, leave alone a somersault. A couple of days before that I turned out as wheel driver (most responsible position, believe me) in the cable wagon traces on an O.C's inspection. Parade, 'Shun – and there sat the 'Brevet Driver – Sapper' on Cuthbert's broad back, reins in one hand, whip in t'other, feet in stirrups and leg in leg-iron, all c'rect, stiff as a blooming poker, and d'you know, the feller came round and, try as he would, he couldn't find a single thing wrong with Cuthbert, Araminta or me – no fear. Got to get up early in the morning for that. I turn out at 4.45 am these times so you got to be extra smart."[69]

A month later his new-found equine pals have gone and he has had to say farewell to the stables and harness cleaning. The two cable horses have been put in the charge of some new drivers who have joined the unit. "I was fearfully cut up about it, of course, but I have one consolation, it wasn't because I proved incompetent – O! no, indeed, simply a matter of new drivers joining us. However, next day I was a sapper with a vengeance – not half – straight from stables to that adjectival[70]

----

69) September 23rd 1917. Cuthbert and Araminta, the two horses he was charged with looking after.
70) Adjectival, he is inviting them to fill in the appropriate word.

telephone switch, mind you – and you know well enough how dearly I love that job – it's just great, I don't think." He and the "durned" switchboard', will never be pals, he explains, given the way the officers treat the men at the other end. 'It's " 'Signaller, why the so & so and so & so can't I get thro' to' – and 'Signaller, d'you heah [sic] I've been ringing for 3 seconds, what the fireworks are you up to', from morn till night. You can put a match to that receiver sometimes and read a letter by the bee-utiful green light that flares up. They don't half spit blood, I can tell you. Fortunately, I'm not a nervous sort of a feller, if you can understand me." On his return from Cairo he had expressed relief that he had not been put back on telephones, a job he describes as nerve-racking. "I was on it just before I went away on leave and it fair drove me crazy – I very nearly went clean off the last day, what with rows with the 'subscribers' and one thing and another."[71]

The powers-that-be, he has decided, are using him as a stop-gap. "Any vacancy that's knocking about and urgently requires attention – 'O! detail young D' – and once again 'Jim' steps into the breach, dear friends."[72] He is quickly moved, from telephone work, however. "This week I'm on the wagons repairing cable etc. – what a game it is." Cable has to be laid, too, to match advances, and this involved night treks to get into position. "Of course, we have joy rides now and then to keep us interested. Night before last, now f'rinstance, we started out 'bout six, trekked 8 miles or so, slept under the stars till 4 am, breakfast and then kept wandering about all day till 3pm, laying lines like a lot of fools and then came home again, covered with a layer of about six inches of dust looking like a lot of millers. Quite an ideal pastime I assure you. I was suffering from ennui long before it was over."[73] Dudley Ward quotes one officer as saying Mott, now in charge of the 53rd, was "very addicted" to night operations. Men would be given an instruction by wire at about 6 p.m.to stand by to move at a moment's notice, followed by another to march out and take up a certain position and dig in after dark. They would then return to camp in the middle of the night.

Only Living for Parcels

His letters throughout this period continue to ask for food and other supplies to be sent out, declaring in June that parcels were all the troops lived for.[74] When parcels come they are received, as throughout his service, with something approaching ecstasy. "As usual, Mum has absolutely surpassed herself with those especially delicious Welsh cakes, which, without the slightest exaggeration, melt in one's mouth. They disappeared at a most alarming rate, which under ordinary circumstances would cause any witnesses grave misgivings on the probabilities of our not contracting severe attacks of indigestion but, bless you, with Mum's cakes, it's totally different. [...] The sardines, the plums, the figs, chocs etc., all up to scratch and absolutely the goods."

In August in Sheikh Shabasi it is one of his aunt's parcels that he is grateful for. "The date was undecipherable, but you will know which one it is from the contents.

137

71) August 25th 1917 Telephone customers were referred to as subscribers in the domestic market.
72) October 10th 1917
73) ibid
74) June 10th 1917.

The Welsh cakes were sublime and had kept wonderfully, and the shortbread was altogether irresistible. These two items were evacuated, as you may well imagine, with disastrous speed. Breakfast saw the sardines wiped completely off the face of the earth with relish, while luncheon was the scene of execution of that excellent paté, which, I assure you, is not at all one of the minor delicacies we have a weakness for. Chocolates – well, the least said the better about our disgusting gluttony, as far as those are concerned, and, though they arrived in a squashy, melted condition, their despatch was attended by the swiftness and gusto born of long and enforced abstinence where that particular sweetmeat is concerned. The café au lait met its doom on the beach over a roaring camp fire, having been boiled to a turn on the latter, with the aid of the Welsh cake tin, which, I may say, proved a capital billy can and has already seen considerable service. There is something homely about its blackened and shiny exterior, the result of much close acquaintance with the embers, which commands respect. It is a cherished article of furniture in our shanty and holds a position of honour."[75]
His return from leave in Cairo was eased, too, by a parcel waiting for him. "That *was* worth coming back for and I could have jumped for joy. There'd I been scoffing away right merrily down at Cairo with tablecloths and china plates and cups but, By Gum! I tell you straight, those plums and cream went down a hundred times better out of the tin. I haven't finished admiring the shirt and socks yet, either. Shan't half be a nib with those on but I'm keeping 'em 'parch' [Sunday best] for a bit till this greyback [Army shirt] gets 'done in', as you might say. The chocolates, too, were gorgeous and soon went, shortly after the paste. […] Tooth brush and paste – the very thing I wanted – do me OK – fine brush, too. I bought some tooth stuff in Cairo but the woman in the shop must have made a mistake. Never looked at it till I got back 'n I found out. It's some swank French stuff in a china fakamajig [sic] – duchess's tooth paste, I should imagine – 'tisn't fit for a bivvy anyway, a boudoir is just about its mark."[76]

Parcels were important not just as a reminder of home but as a means of keeping healthy. With lines of communication now stretching back many miles, the Army struggled to deliver sufficient food to the troops, even with the extending railways. In his September letter he describes himself as being in a sorrowful plight and apparently desperately hungry. "After a vain search and much fruitless pleading along a whole line of bivouacs for spare bread or biscuits to stay the pangs of hunger which consume me here, you see me penning this epistle and creating a diversion, as it were, by providing food for my thoughts as the only alternative to the absence of a means to satisfy the inner man. What a novel excuse to offer for this poor attempt – an empty stomach. O! that I should be reduced to such dire straits – I a respectable citizen in civilian life but now not a jot better off than the meanest, ragged, down-at-heel beggar, who never turned away from 76 empty-handed. What a humourist that food controller must be – 'Don't eat too much bread' – Ha! Ha! (hear my harsh, mirthless attempts at laughter). Surely, then, I must be one of the most strict adherents to his golden rule. However, this little tragedy is but a daily occurrence in this stricken land (which curiously enough should have been described as a land of plenty, flowing with delicacies), and serves

---

75) August 7th 1917.
76) August 25th 1917.

the admirable purpose of teaching its victims an old but well-deserved lesson, the pith of which is not to let a voracious appetite gain the upper hand with its evil designs on one's loaf at dinner-time, lest thou repent at evensong. The particular miserable victim in question is at present gazing hungrily westwards and living only for the next parcel mail, praying fervently that it may come speedily, to avert any possibilities whatever of such a dire catastrophe as that just described happening again."[77]

Letting off Steam

Young men training and working hard in difficult conditions will have wanted to let off steam and the outlet for their energies every evening was football. The summer of 1917, though filled with training, was a period when, as far as the men were concerned, there was little action, and time to be filled. "Talk about rough and tumble Gee! Whiz! – enough to gladden the heart of any man. We're not particular how many play on each side – sometimes there's about umpteen forwards and, no matter where the ball goes, there's about 20 on it all in a heap kicking, punching and shoving. 'Sappers v. Drivers', and it's war to the knife. That's the only time we can play is at night 'cos it's far too hot at any other time and getting warmer every day."[78] Swimming had become possible, too, after the August move to XXth Corps headquarters at Sheikh Shabasi, and this helped to keep morale high and to ward off boredom. Commenting on news of his parents' holiday, he writes: "I think you will be very surprised to learn that I am also now spending a most pleasant time at the seaside. In fact, the day I imagine you left for the sea – August 4th – I happened to be also bound for the briny (unfortunately however there happened to be no cab to convey *my* traps – some slight difference, you see)."[79] Their little semi dug-out bivouac has been made wonderfully comfortable with sand-bags, he tells them and, occasionally, they go for walks, though unlike their walks, it's generally for water or rations. There are other differences, too, which he highlights. "Sad to relate, however, I simply cannot draw a comparison between mine and your brekker. You see, cold boiled bacon, marmalade, and lumpy porridge twice a week is all we can boast of as a menu for that meal." The Army seems to have adopted a surprisingly cautious approach to the dangers of the sea. "We have two bathing parades a day, 6.30 and 3, and it's fine fun when we're all in together with the football, because, you must, know we're polo mad now. There are some beautiful scrimmages, too, after that leather, I can tell you, which we relish immensely. As for worrying, Mum, about me being careful – Gee whiz! Don't mention it. Why, you hardly believe it but they look after us as if we were a lot of school misses. You aren't allowed to bathe, except on parade with the crowd, you can't go out further than so far, you can't join in until the whistle blows and you *must* come out when the next whistle blows. […] I've never been mothered so much since I left home, fact, and it sort of gets a feller's back up. The water is as warm as warm all day and it's perfectly delicious – you can easily understand how much it means to us after about 3 months inland, as we have been, where the sand blows and the flies worry one to death and the air [is] stifling."

139

77) September 23rd 1917.

78) June 19th 1917. The Royal Engineers had a proud footballing record, beating the Old Etonians at The Oval in London in an invincible 1875 season to win the F.A. Cup.

79) August 7th 1917.

A few weeks later he reports on another sport they have now taken up, hinting, too, at the resentment men in the Near East were feeling at the public focus on the Western Front. This was to become a prominent feature of some of his later letters in 1918. "We chucked football when we went down to the seaside, and it was all water polo there, but now, after leaving it behind, that's knocked on the head.[80] Football hasn't started again yet. We're a stubborn obstinate lot, as you know, and now, just when it has been made known that 'the troops are to be encouraged in all sorts of sports', blow me, if the fellers don't go and chuck up a nice quiet gentle pastime like *our* football and go in bald-headed for Tiddly Winks, Snakes & Ladders, Ludo and Poker and that sort of strenuous exercise. You see, we've just had a consignment of these games from a Welfare Committee in *Egypt* (what you think o' that, Egypt don't forget us, even if Blighty does – 'course *they* think there's only one Army, only one war, only one B.E.F. [British Expeditionary Force], only one blooming Welsh Div.[81] S'pose they got a faint idea Johnny Turk is an ally? Ugh! s'pose they'd think he was a blooming tourist, if a feller turned up at No.3 Platform in helmet and shorts – or a raving maniac. Strewth! What a blessed holiday we are having."[82] He goes on to quote a letter received. "Hope you're still having *a jolly good time* in Egypt. " – Ho!, Yes, bless you, not 'arf, my blooming oath on that. Who gets all the socks, who gets all the footballs, who gets all the comforts, and gifts, and fags? O! the soldiers in France. Who else do you think? All the comforts I've ever got in well-nigh two year was two pickled onions from Lady Ian Hamilton. Since when I've used no other.[83]

Football (with or without balls sent from home), resumes its prominent part in their lives in the months ahead. A day of drills, fatigues and other Army routine, including inoculation against typhoid and a punctured gammy arm for his troubles, does not put him and his companions off. "Lo and behold, at evensong the stalwarts issue forth with confidence and determined mien to pit their strength and skill at ye ancient game of ye ball of the foot. Not the least insignificant amongst the serried ranks being one of the house of David entrusted with the responsible post of 'right half'. The feat of arms (and feet, and shoulders by the way) is contested between Headquarters and our cable detachment and I am expecting your congratulations upon reading this for the great honour that has been bestowed upon me – my section 'Cap'.[84] We enter the lists and prepare for battle – (peel your shirts, and the time is one, one-two) – to the uproarious shouts of encouragement from the spectators, much the same as the knights of old did at their 'Passages of Arms' but the shouts which welcomed their entry, 'Love of Ladies – Splintering of Lances – Death of Champions – Glory to the Brave', was on this occasion rendered with the modern and scarcely less impressive yells of 'Blind 'em with Science – Stop 'is Breath – Squash 'im Somebody', and other equally picturesque and quaint, frenzied acclamations."

Later in the month, there is more news about football, accompanied, like the Canal Races a year earlier, by the placing of bets.[85] "The football continues as strong and

80) August 31st 1917. Possibly a reference to their time at Khan Yunus.
81) The 38th (Welsh) Division was serving in France.
82) August 31st 1917.
83) Used no other, the famous line from the Pear's Soap advertisement, showing a tramp writing to express his appreciation of the product. Lady Hamilton, the wife of Sir Ian Hamilton, commander of British forces on Gallipoli.
84) September 5th 1917. Headquarters, Khan Yunus. Cap, awarded by sports teams to their regular players.
85) The race across the canal, blacks v. whites is described in a letter of August 3rd 1916.

enthusiastically as ever. There's a game every night. Played last night and lost 2-1. Gosh! Our skipper didn't half raise Cain about it either. You see, there was a lot of money on our side and, unfortunately, the favourites lost, since when we've had our blooming heads chewed off for not 'wading into 'em', as those infuriated sportsmen gamblers are pleased to describe it. But, although we're groaning under the heavy weight of ignominious defeat at present, it won't be for long. The blighters can strut about like peacocks for a few days but after that – Blimey, the very sight of a piece of leather!" Football alternated with games of rugby, played in his mind with the enthusiasm only the Welsh could generate. "Not having enough exercise (?) [sic] we still turn out to play or watch alternately the struggles for the 'Palestine Cup'. Last evening I took part in a match between Sappers and Drivers at Rugger – I played in the pack – Christopher Columbus! Talk about Cf v NE [Cardiff v Newport] wasn't in it. I'm aching all over but it was absolutely lovely – I enjoyed it all thro' and came off jolly lucky – a fat lip and a stiff neck. We weren't out for science, you see, it was 'roughhouse' and, By Jove! they had it. You'd get the ball, run 1 yard and next minute you'd be underneath about umpteen of the blighters. Glorious it was, too. Round the knees with him and down the blighter'd have to come quick. And we won, too – try to nil. As for the scrums, Lummy! I never was in anything like it. Welsh – real Welsh it was all thro' – 'Tackla fo, Dala fo, Spraggo fo, m'yn jawl i'. [Tackle him, catch hold of him, scrag him, by the Devil.][86] Tonight I watched a soccer match but that *was* slow."

A Relaxed Read and a Concert

Reading remained one of his main pleasures, however, and he laments the absence of books from home, no doubt because of the continuing vagaries of the postal system. "You are right about the papers and magazines, Dad – I haven't received anything in that line for ages to my intense sorrow. It's wonderful how one appreciates such things out here – a book is priceless to while away an hour or so and, naturally, I have been forced to be content with second hand material. I should advise you to pack them so that they are unrecognisable as books. Don't send expensive copies of books – paper covers, the cheapest possible, that will do me A.1. Any of Edgar Wallace's, Ian Hay's or Mark Twain's funny 'uns, see?[87] 'Tom Sawyer' and 'Nobby' style, they're just grand."[88]

Concerts and other forms of entertainment continued to prevent the troops, in his words, going 'doolali' with the monotony and the sun – and lack of female company – with Lena Ashwell's visit now only a memory.[89] Often, however, they seem to have involved not much more than a piano and some singers delivering the latest popular songs from back home on a piano borrowed from the YMCA. Musing on one such event at Khan Yunus he writes: "Wonderful how you

---

86) September 18th 1917.

87) Ian Hay, the pen-name of John Hay Beith (1876-1952), Scottish novelist and playwright active in the first half of the 20th century. He served as an officer during the war, ending up as a major. Edgar Wallace (1875-1932) was a popular English crime writer who enjoyed success in Hollywood, particularly with his screenplay for *King Kong*, a joint work with Draycott Dell. Mark Twain, author and humourist, (1835-1910). Nobby, a word Twain uses, smart, elegant.

88) August 7th 1917.

89) September 23rd 1917. Doolally, originally 'doolally tap', meaning to 'lose one's mind', derived from the boredom felt at the Deolali British Army transit camp in India where soldiers could often be stranded waiting to be returned home. 'Tap' may be derived from the Sanskrit word 'tapa' meaning 'heat' or 'fever'.

appreciate these things living out in this 'orrible deserted, uncivilised, barbarous wilderness of the end of the earth. They got on pretty well, did the actors, and made the thing go with a swing, so there was no need for me to go and dig 'em out, so to speak. Besides, I always remember the effect one of my sentimental 'Asleep in the Deep' songs had on that poor unfortunate American hostess of ours last year in Egypt and so now always refrain from inflicting such horrible punishment upon the community at large, except in cases of urgent necessity or ill-fated curiosity as to my vocal powers."[90] The latest music of the day found its way even as far as Palestine, some of which he rather surprisingly thinks may be as yet unknown back home. "There was a deuce of a lot of absolutely new songs sung there, too, which I don't s'pose you've heard in Blighty yet. One of 'em was 'If I was the only boy in the world'. Another of the new songs was 'Tennessee', 'Thora' and 'Man that broke the bank at Monte Carlo' – all of 'em just out, new. I expect you'll hear 'em all in time at the Empire.[91]

The expedition described earlier, when they laid cables under the stars and much of the next day, had been followed, he writes, by a good square meal (?) and a good scraping to remove the dust, and a concert.[92] Parties of men, accompanied by their animals and wagons, threw up clouds of dust, which, mixed with the sweat pouring from their brows, invariably left faces caked. Spruced up, he reports, they made a dash for the Hippodrome – presumably a hastily thrown up concert venue – to hear their fellow soldiers perform as the 'Palestine Pops' pierrot troupe. "It's only an open air theatre, of course, and the audience (which, I may say, rivals even the Cardiff Empire in numbers) squat down on the sand where they like, but the stage is quite posh – electric lights, curtains etc. and the pierrots are dressed in a very becoming costume of black skull-caps, yellow suits and huge black tassels and buttons – not forgetting the piano and chello [sic], of course. Proper swell lot, aren't they? – one can almost fancy oneself back at Weston again, only our pierrots'll knock spots off the silly blighters you find there. The funny man comes from our company and he is a genuine card – real smart at it. As for the 'pierotte', she looks fine, painted up with rosy cheeks and pencilled eyebrows, and long dark tresses. She brings tears to our eyes (tears of mirth, however), when she sings the poignantly emotional ballad, 'If you were the only boy, etc.' with her partner. The appealing way she stretches her arms out and presses her hand on her heart in the song is quite the last word in melodrama. She's got the mezzo soprano falsetto voice absolutely taped off, too. Sometimes it cracks at the critical moment, and either goes up or bumps down about two octaves. (In ordinary life this prima donna is a Sapper of R.Es.)."

These relaxed times would soon come to an end. By late October 1917 preparations for the Third Battle of Gaza were complete and they would be actively engaging the Turks and driving them out of Palestine. It is several months before Dewi writes again. On October 24th after nearly two months in Khan Yunus he reports a new position on the map – Hiseia in Wadi Ghuzza, a staging post for the move they would make towards Beersheba, where the main thrust against the Turkish line would take place.

90) Ibid. *Asleep in the Deep*, words by Arthur J. Lamb and music by Henry W. Petrie, the phrase referring to sailors who have drowned. 'Loudly the bell in the old tower rings, Bidding us list to the warning it brings. Sailor, take care! Sailor, take care! Danger is near thee. Beware! Beware! Beware! Beware! Many brave hearts are asleep in the deep, So beware! beware!' The party at which he performed in front of the American hostess is mentioned in the letter February 6th 1916.

91) Popular songs of the day. Empire, the leading Cardiff variety theatre in Queen Street.

92) October 10th 1917. His question mark is meant to suggest anything but.

(above) The Guns at Gaza. The town was subjected to heavy bombardment during the three battles that took place in 1917.

(left) "Decorating the Heroes on the Field." At least one Victoria Cross was won by Welsh soldiers in the Battle for Gaza.

One of the Army trains operating on lines built by the Royal Engineers. Dewi travelled by train – possibly this one - on his visit to Cairo in August 1917.

18 — L'Arbre de la Vierge à **Matarieh** (1906)

(above) A second visit to Cairo in August 1916 brought a visit to Matarieh to see the tree where Mary and Joseph rested with the Child on their flight to Egypt.

(right) Major-General S.F. Mott, the popular figure who took over as the 53rd's commanding officer after the first Battle of Gaza. The 53rd later became known as "Mott's Detachment".

"The bivouac at the seaside", probably Deir el Belah.

CHAPTER SEVEN

ONWARDS TO JERUSALEM

OCTOBER 1917 – FEBRUARY 1918

The Third Battle of Gaza

B ritish generals commanding troops in France were operating in country that very largely resembled the southern counties of the UK – rolling countryside dotted with farms, villages and towns, large and small – an advantage denied their fellow-officers in command in the Near East. In Egypt British forces had had to learn to come to terms with different, unfamiliar and ever-changing types of desert, as well as unaccustomed heat and the flies. In Palestine another different topography would have to be mastered, though one that would present equal challenges, and in summer, at any rate, no respite from the summer temperatures of the past two years. The country of the Bible is divided into five distinct belts, parallel with the coast and each other, but each very different in character. To the west a three mile wide strip of sand dunes as far as Jaffa lines the Mediterranean, before giving way to the 15 miles wide Philistia plain, a sandy and loamy space, intersected by streams, and full of citrus groves. Water here was plentiful at depth but roads were few, and malaria was present in places.[1] Beyond the plain the irregularly stratified, and deeply fissured, limestone Judaean hills rise in places to 3,000ft and were served by only two, poor roads, Beersheba-Hebron-Nablus and Jaffa-Ramle-Jerusalem. The territory's historic capital occupies a spot 2,600ft above sea level. Water was available in the hills only in underground cisterns where it had gathered after rains. To the east of the hills lay a rift valley, 10 miles wide, a geomorphic formation brought about by the depression in the earth's crust between faults. This is where the River Jordan makes its course 700ft – 1,200ft below sea level, and the setting for the city of Jericho at 850ft below. Further beyond are the mountains of Moab.[2]

Having repulsed two British attacks on Gaza, the key position guarding the coastal route through Palestine, the Turks had not been inactive. They, too, had used the succeeding months to re-group, improve their communications and strengthen their defences. Gaza was now a fortress, and a strong defensive line had been established across to Beersheba 30 miles to the east. The forces available to Allenby had, however, been greatly expanded after a decision in London to take the Middle East campaign much more seriously. In April the EEF had consisted of two mounted divisions and three depleted infantry divisions, with a fourth in the process of formation, a total of probably not much more than 50,000 men, facing an Ottoman and allied army in Gaza of about 35,000. With men arriving from Salonika, East Africa and elsewhere, Allenby's complement by July had reached five infantry divisions and three mounted divisions. For the Third Battle Allenby had at his disposal the 53rd, 60th, 74th and 10th divisions (XXth Corps), the 52nd, 54th and 75th Divisions (XXIst corps) and the mainly Australian and New Zealand Desert Mounted Corps, a formidable force twice the size of that at the two previous battles. The British could put into the field 18,000 sabres, 80,000 rifles, and 450 guns. Facing them, the Turks had two corps and a cavalry division offering 1,500 sabres, 30,000 rifles and 300 guns – plus strong positions from which to ward off attacks.

The dilemma faced by Allenby was that a direct attack on a well-defended Gaza might yet again be repulsed. A wider plan – essentially that developed by Chetwode

---

1) Pritchard, (ed.), p293.
2) A rift valley is a linear-shaped lowland between several highlands or mountain ranges created by a geological rift or fault.

– was, therefore, adopted, which involved attacking the Turks on a broad front across their Gaza-Beersheba line and capturing both towns.[3] This would involve overcoming severe communications problems. The flanking movement that was proposed around the Turkish left would be taking place some distance from the branch railhead and even further from the main railhead the Royal Engineers had been extending through the desert. Deception would be needed to keep the Turks guessing where the main assault would come and prevent reinforcements being moved to threatened points along the line. Two divisions – one of which would be the 53rd – would be deployed for the first part of the attack, which would be from the south west on Beersheba on the British right. A second assault would attempt to break the Turkish lines at Sheria/Hureira, midway between Gaza and Beersheba, enabling troops to advance on into Wadi es Sheria and gain control of water supplies there. The town of Gaza would also be attacked. If successful, the way would be open to push the Ottoman army back through Palestine and possibly all the way to Constantinople. A period of intense preparations now followed. The attack originally planned for September was delayed until later in the year, even though this meant the rainy season might by then be approaching. The risk was considered worthwhile, given the complexity of the operations that now had to be planned, and the need to familiarise newly-arrived troops with local conditions. Just as importantly, water supplies – one of the problems that had caused the failure during the first two attempts to get through – had to be secured. Lack of a plentiful and ongoing supply in the heat of the desert could negate the most spectacular successes in the field. Nor was it only the troops that needed water. Horses, camels, and where railways had been laid, locomotives, all needed prodigious quantities to keep going. Lacking water, animals could become extremely difficult to handle before they finally succumbed to thirst and died. Large numbers of horses did, indeed, die.

Assignment Beersheba

Beersheba, the objective assigned to Chetwode's XXth Corps, was protected by the waterless country surrounding it and by the absence of roads south of the main Gaza-Beersheba road. Available transport – 30,000 camels – was sufficient only for the supply of a corps with food and ammunition up to Beersheba – where it was hoped, sufficient supplies of good water could be obtained – and for one more march. Any assault on Beersheba would, therefore, need to be executed as secretly as possible and to achieve its objective in one day. Otherwise, troops would have to return to their starting points. To supply the 45,000 men, plus 26,000 animals, that would be called upon to move into the forward area to be developed between El Qamle and Hiseia, south of Gaza in Wadi Ghuzza, elaborate storage and distribution arrangements had to be put in place and these operations would have to proceed as inconspicuously as possible. A total of 300,000 gallons a day of water would have to be pumped from Rafa and Khan Yunus to the forward points and a further 100,000 gallons delivered by rail to two new railheads at Shellal and El Qamle. To house the supply, huge concrete and masonry dams would be needed, and camel tank filling areas organized. These were designed with a filling capacity of 2,000 tanks per hour. Facilities also had to include water-bottle filling for the men, and horse watering troughs. Specialist engineers, pumping plants and

147

3) Pritchard, (ed.), p294-5.

equipment to sink wells would also have to be brought up to exploit the Beersheba wells after the town's capture. The Royal Engineers' Ferry Post workshop was moved from the Canal to Rafa and extended in order to repair and manufacture the range of engineering equipment that would be needed to support operations, and in particular water supply. The Rafa-Shellal branch of the railway was extended to Karm, an isolated spot in the desert, construction only starting at the last possible moment to avoid arousing suspicions. The main line was extended to a dummy station beyond Wadi Ghuzza in a further attempt to confuse the Turks. Bridges were put in place by the Royal Engineers in Wadi Ghuzza so that supplies and armour could continue to be sent forward even after the rains had come. Much of this work fell on the Egyptian Labour Force that had been recruited by the British to support their operations.

On October 24th, following a stay of two months for training and rest, most of the 53rd Division marched from their rest camp at Deir el Belah to Hiseia, Dewi among them. Three days later, Dewi, who would now spend the next four months up the line with the 159th Brigade reports another move with the cable wagon way inland to Sebil, south of the main Gaza-Beersheba road, and three miles south east of the new Karm station. The next day he notes in his diary that he had reported to 159th Brigade (presumably to act as a brigade signaller), and two days later reports his position as Wadi Imleih, several miles northwards towards the Turkish lines. On October 30th the British forces were in place. The 53rd Division and the 30th brigade group were at Wadi Hannafish, and the following day the 53rd extended the front to a track running from Tell el Fara to Beersheba. Other 53rd troops continued the line north to Karm station.[4] To deceive the Turks into believing Gaza would be the main target and to prevent a redeployment of troops eastwards, heavy bombardment of the town started on October 26th for eight days, with the Royal Navy joining in from offshore, as it was to do on other occasions during the campaign in Southern Palestine. This was to prove the heaviest bombardment anywhere outside the Western Front. Despite reconnaissance, the Turks failed to pick up British intentions, a separate skilful deception also helping. An intelligence officer, Lt. Colonel Richard Meinertzhagen, deliberately attracted enemy pursuit while reconnoitring, and, feigning injury, dropped a haversack containing a letter to his wife suggesting the attack on Beersheba would be a feint and the first major assault would be on Gaza itself. Clinching the authenticity of the information, as far as the Turks and Germans were concerned, was the inclusion of a £5 note for his wife to pay a pressing account of his. In some ways this ruse prefigured the successful Operation Mincemeat that deceived the Germans in World War Two, when a body containing papers with false information was released from a submarine off Spain to disguise the invasion of Italy from North Africa.

There would be four phases to the operation: the approach march from the right flank and the attack on Beersheba; the exploitation of supplies from the Beersheba wells; the attack on the Turkish left flank; and the pursuit across the Philistia plain. The attack on Beersheba on October 31st was made by infantry and mounted troops from east and west and, remarkably, all objectives had been achieved later the same day, including securing the wells, most of which had suffered little

---

4) Kareim Abu el Hiseia, on Wadi Ghuzza, east of Abu Sitta.

damage. Kress von Kressenstein, the German commander, who had been a thorn in the British side during the defence of the canal in the first two years of the war, admitted in an interview in 1920 they had remained convinced the main thrust would come against Gaza and had failed as a result to reinforce Beersheba. Turkish trenches outside town were overwhelmed (in one of the last great cavalry charges in history), and, despite stubborn resistance, the town itself was taken shortly after, with Turkish forces withdrawing to the neighbouring hills to the north. It was during the battle around Beersheba that Acting Corporal John Collins, of Merthyr Tydfil, a veteran of the South African campaign serving with the Royal Welch Fusiliers, won a V.C. He also earned a Military Cross and a Distinguished Conduct Medal during his army career. His citation declared that "on 31 October 1917 at Wadi Saba, Beersheba, Palestine, he repeatedly went out when his battalion was forced to lie out in the open under heavy shell and machine-gun fire, and brought back many wounded. In subsequent operations he rallied his men and led the final assault with great skill in spite of heavy fire at close range and uncut wire. He bayonetted 15 of the enemy and with a Lewis gun section covered the reorganization and consolidation most effectively, despite being isolated and under fire from snipers and guns".

Capture would not be enough, however, if logistic problems could not be overcome. The British force would need 400,000 gallons of water a day, which would suffice to supply all the mounted troops and two infantry divisions, and make possible the second phase of the operations against the Turkish left flank. This would involve a thrust north west to join up with other British troops coming through the Wadi es Sheria and working around Gaza. With this supply, animals could be watered and every man could have one day's water in hand. Yet, despite the strenuous efforts made to locate and repair wells and to increase storage, demand outstripped supply. Drinking time for camels was reduced with little impact on their ability to survive. The horses, some of which had not drunk for several days, had become thirst-maddened, however, and would have caused serious damage if they had not been restrained. The crisis passed, as new wells were found and pumps were brought up and installed, but even more would have to be found. The 53rd was ordered to move out to relieve the cavalry pickets on the hills to the north of the town to which the Turks had retreated, and to occupy a new line. They were also to search for fresh water supplies around Ain Kohle.[5] The march, according to the Official History, was a difficult one of some 16 miles over rocky, mountainous and largely trackless country, and hard on the feet of men used for months to sand and soft going.[6] To make matters worse the ration convoy lost its way and the men had no food or water. Indeed, water continued to be a problem, the camel water convoys being slow and often losing their way in the hilly country. The men had been issued with two bottles each but in this phase of the operation the horses had to be sent back to Beersheba for the night seven miles away.

A Fierce Fight at Khuweilfeh

149

The Turks, meanwhile, had reinforced their left flank with the aim of attacking the British outer flank and getting around it. Finding the hills immediately north

5) Kholeh Hill in Dewi's itinerary.
6) Dudley Ward, p125.

occupied by British forces, they had moved further back to the Khuweilfeh Heights, 10 miles north of Beersheba hoping to dominate the surrounding countryside from this vantage. Mott, General Officer Commanding the 53rd, or Mott's detachment as it was now known, was told to advance as soon as possible towards Khuweilfeh, control of which had been identified as essential for the continuation of overall operations. The terrain was difficult, however, and troops were now suffering from the heat, and the hot blasts of the Khamseen, as well as from thirst.[7] Khuweilfeh, according to one officer quoted in the history, was a series of difficult-to-cross knolls, offering ample secure spots in which the defenders' machine guns and snipers could be concealed. The Turks were holding the position in greater strength than expected and clearly determined not to cede it. For many men of the 53rd, Khuweilfeh must have brought back memories of trying to dislodge the Turks on Gallipoli from similar elevated positions offering a good field of fire down on assaulting forces. Khuweilfeh was, indeed, one of the bloodiest encounters of the campaign, and a good example of how the best-laid strategies needed to be adapted in the uncertainties of war. It had been expected, after the capture of Beersheba, that troops would be able to move west to support operations in the centre of the line, while other units remained to shore up water supplies in the town.

Although the task at Khuweilfeh had not been completed, the 53rd was given orders to slip away from the foothills it had occupied and support the attacks in the centre of the line. These were aimed at securing the Kauwukah water supply close to Sheria, essential for the further push northwards now planned. Mott, however, resisted, realizing that the abandonment of positions around Khuweilfeh would put von Kressenstein in a position to assemble his reserves and bear down on the rear and flank of the 53rd and the XXth Corps, with possibly decisive results. Mott informed general staff officers at XXth Corps that mounted troops would not be able to complete the job at Khuweilfeh, as headquarters had envisaged when ordering him to move. An infantry division was needed because of the terrain and the artillery required to dislodge the Turks. Allenby himself and Chauvel, the Australian commander of the Desert Mounted Corps, visited Mott at his headquarters and were persuaded. The 53rd should attack Khuweilfeh with the necessary firepower. The XXth Corps' move, in the centre of the line, would proceed simultaneously. With the support of shelling from artillery brigades, battalions of the 53rd moved forward early in the morning of November 6th to mount the attack, each man carrying two water bottles, 170 rounds of ammunition, the unconsumed portion of the day's ration, an extra day's ration and the iron ration. Ammunition was to be fired, however, only on the order of the C.O. Bayonets were to be used instead. The attack was led by the 7th Battalion, the Royal Welch Fusiliers, and the heights were occupied by 7 am, two and a half hours after the start of operations. Turkish counter-attacks saw the hill re-occupied but then taken back again at the point of bayonets, with only fog preventing the operation from being completed without a hitch. A spectacular victory, acknowledged as such by Allenby, had been achieved, yielding among its other results another V.C. – this time posthumous – for one of the participants, Captain Fox Russell of the RAMC, for attending and rescuing wounded men. By tying down Turkish forces it also significantly influenced the outcome of the successful assault the same day on the Kauwukah

7) Dudley Ward, p128.

water supply system. On the next day the Hureira Redoubt, another strong point, was taken. A gap having opened up in the Turkish line, mounted troops operating behind the Turkish left proceeded to intercept or pursue the Turks between Sheria and Gaza.

At the other end of the line, the attack on Gaza had begun on November 1st, two days later than originally planned. Preparations to attack the town's defences had moved up a gear in September. New trenches had been dug, cables laid, gun positions set up, store dumps put in place and roads and water systems laid out, with the front line also advancing in places. The defences had by now been severely weakened by bombardment, with the result that the Turks' forward positions were quickly captured and their trenches guarding the city overwhelmed. The Anzac cavalry were again to the fore, as they had been in the earlier campaigns guarding the Canal and in Sinai. "Forward squadrons [of the Australian Light Horse] galloped over the two front lines of trenches, then dismounted and attacked the occupants with the bayonet. The remainder of the Brigade galloped into the town and captured 1,100 prisoners and ten guns of the Turkish 27th Division. Also they prevented the Turks from destroying more than two of the 17 wells in the town."[8] Although the Turks attempted to drive the British forces back from Gaza, they failed, and on November 7th their defence collapsed. British forces now advanced 8 miles north to Wadi el Hesi to prevent the Turks from occupying a strong position there and after some resistance this point was secured. Over the course of not much more than a week's operations the Turkish defensive line extending to Beersheba had been broken and the town captured. They had been driven out of Gaza, too. British troops were now back where they had been six months earlier at the First Battle of Gaza, before the fateful and misconceived decision to withdraw, but now in much greater numbers. Large areas of Turkish territory had also been occupied, extending east across to Beersheba and north into Palestine. Some fine buildings in Gaza survived but the city was largely destroyed by the British assault and Turkish defensive measures. All wood, including the doors of houses, had been removed to revet the Turkish trenches, and the large mosque which had been used as an ammunition dump by the Turks was detonated by British gunfire and lay in ruins.[9]

On the left of the line, the 54th Division advanced beyond Gaza and on through Sheikh Redwan to the sea. The 52nd Division, also moving along the coast, were in Wadi el Hesi. The 53rd Division at this stage remained concentrated around Beersheba, while other divisions were sent back to Deir el Belah to rest and be refitted. Over the next week the divisions continued moving north in pursuit of the retreating enemy, with orders to capture the strategically important Junction Station where the Turkish railway line from Jerusalem converged with lines from Beersheba and Rafa and from Jaffa and Haifa. Mounted troops would then proceed quickly north towards Ramle and Ludd,[10] and Jaffa on the coast. The Turks made a stand at the village of Mughar, on a line of heights forming a strong defensive position, delaying the hitherto largely unchallenged British advance, but on

151

8) Kearsey, p21.

9) Mortlock, p145.

10) Ludd, the Lod of the Bible and Lydda of the Greeks and Romans, 25 miles northwest of Jerusalem. Ramle, the Biblical Arimathea, also Ramla, 22 miles north west.

November 13th the position was captured at a cost to the Turks of 1,096 prisoners, two guns and 12 machine guns. The victory at Mughar Ridge cleared the way for further advances into Ottoman territory, enabling Junction Station to be captured at 7.30 the following morning. The two Turkish Armies facing the British were split and forced to withdraw separately towards Jerusalem and the coastal Plain of Sharon, north of Jaffa. Their lines of communication had also been broken. The British dispatches presented the picture proudly and more accurately than six months earlier. "In fifteen days our force had advanced sixty miles on its right and 40 miles on its left. It had driven a Turkish Army of nine divisions out of a position in which it had been entrenched for six months and had pursued it, giving battle whenever it attempted to stand, and inflicting on it losses amounting probably to two-thirds of the enemy's original effectives."[11] The Turks continued to try to drive the British from their positions but were repulsed with the capture of hundreds of prisoners. Casualties on both sides were high. More than 10,000 men were killed on the British side in the three battles around Gaza.[12]

On to Jerusalem

The retreat of the Turks had now opened to Allenby a vast canvas leading to Jerusalem and beyond. He was also now facing a new opponent in the person of former Prussian Minister of War, former chief of the German General Staff, and one of the architects of German war strategy, Erich von Falkenhayn. Under von Falkenhayn the Germans had narrowly failed in 1915 to win "the race to the sea", the series of engagements in northern France and Belgium in which each side tried to turn the other's flank to secure the coastline. The Germans had been stopped from achieving this goal – which would have imperilled Britain's control of the English Channel – at the First Battle of Ypres in October–November 1914. In response, von Falkenhayn engineered the massive battle of attrition at Verdun in early 1916, in which more than a quarter of a million soldiers eventually died. He believed a massive slaughter would lead Europe's political leaders to consider ending the war, or that losses would in the end be less harmful for Germany than for France. After the failure of this strategy at Verdun and following incessant lobbying by Field Marshall Paul von Hindenburg and his deputy Erich Ludendorff, von Falkenhayn was replaced as Chief of Staff by von Hindenburg.[13] Von Falkenhayn then led a successful offensive against Romania, leading to the capture of Bucharest, and was sent to take military command in Palestine, with the objective of preventing a British capture of Jerusalem.

Allenby planned an immediate assault on Jerusalem, once Jaffa was in British hands. The port's capture would provide an extra route for supplies and make possible an attack from the north as well as from the south. Despite some initial difficulties, Jaffa was taken on November 16th by troops from the Australian and

11) Kearsey, p25. Quoting from official military dispatches.
12) Bruce Feiler. *Walking the Bible*, William Morrow, New York, 2001. Quoted by Mortlock, p114.
13) After a long career in the Prussian Army, retiring in 1911, Hindenburg (1847-1934) was recalled at the outbreak of World War One, winning the decisive Battle of Tannenberg in August 1914. As Germany's Chief of the General Staff, he and his deputy, Erich Ludendorff, rose in the German public's esteem until Hindenburg gradually gained more influence in Germany than the Kaiser himself. Together they pushed forward the idea of Lebensraum (literally 'living room'), which after the war would be adopted by Hitler. Hindenburg retired again in 1919 but returned to public life in 1925 to be elected as the second President of Germany.

New Zealand Mounted Division, bringing to a climax three weeks of successful campaigning. British forces were now in a position to wheel east to attack Jerusalem from the northeast through the narrow passes from the plain to the plateau of the Judaean range. The 75th Division was ordered to secure a position astride the Latrun-Jerusalem road, with the 52nd Division on its north flank. In difficult fighting passes were secured in the Battle of Nebi Samwil (November 17th-24th) and held against counter-attacks.[14] On November 25th operations were discontinued for two weeks following an adverse break in the weather. Forces were re-organised and given a rest to recover from heavy casualties of the preceding weeks, roads and tracks improved, ammunition and supplies brought up and the water supply developed. Just to keep the Divisions' horses in the field required 100 tons of grain a day to be brought up from Gaza or Jaffa. The Turks, too, had received reinforcements. Though action had had to be stopped, British forces had managed to break through the narrow passes that led to the plateau before the Turks were able to reorganize their defences. This gave them, in Allenby's words, a position "from which the final attack [on Jeruselum] could be prepared and delivered with good prospects of success".[15] "Had the attempt to force the narrow passes from the plain to the plateau of the Judaean range not been made at once [...] the enemy could have had time to re-organise his defences lower down, and the conquest of the plain would have been slow, costly and precarious."

To the west, on the coastal plain, attempts were made to clear an area north of Jaffa. On November 24th the Australian and New Zealand Division secured a bridgehead over the Nahr (River) Auja north of Jaffa, with the aim of containing the Turkish 8th Army and preventing it from reinforcing troops in front of Jerusalem.[16] Sustained efforts were made by the Turkish forces to drive the British back from these positions over the next few weeks, and it became clear larger posts on the south bank of the river would be needed to maintain the bridgeheads on the north. A second attempt would have to be made to push across the Auja a month later. British commanders were not sorry, however, to hear their old foe, von Kressenstein had now been relieved of his command of the Turkish 8th Army. He had been a thorn in the flesh of the British in Egypt and Palestine since September 1914, leading attacks on the Canal, and on British positions in Sinai, as well as commanding the defences at Magdhaba in December 1916, Rafa in January 1917, and Gaza and Beersheba at the three battles there in March, April and September 1917, and during rearguard battles up the maritime plain to Jaffa. With a British attack now expected any time von Falkenhayn had, meanwhile, taken the precaution of moving his own headquarters immediately after the loss of Junction Station from Jerusalem to Nablus, 30 miles further to the north.

Having taken the brunt of the heavy fighting around Khuweilfeh, the 53rd's brigades were not to be called up to join the assault on Jerusalem until early in December. They were to maintain a holding position to the south of the city. Mott had been told late in November that at that time it was not necessary to gain ground along the Hebron Road but that he should make preparations to send a force to

153

14) In British Army nomenclature Jerusalem Operations consisted of the Battle of Nebi Samwil, the Battle of Jaffa and the Defence of Jerusalem. Nebi Samwil was the site of the tomb of the prophet, Samuel.
15) Kearsey, p26.
16) Ibid., p26-27.

Bethlehem and perhaps beyond. He was told to hold back his forces and to accumulate supplies as far forward as the protection offered by his advanced guard allowed. The plan was for troops to reach a position south of Jerusalem from Bethlehem to Beit Jala on the 7th, and, by dawn on the 8th, a line three miles south of Jerusalem. British forces would then close in on the city from the south, west and the northwest.[17] "The two brigade groups, 53rd Division, about Dilbeh, will be prepared to march on the 6th," once ammunition had been accumulated, the orders stated. Mott replied that he would be bringing his left brigade group, the 159th, to which Dewi was attached, up from Burj el Beiyareh to the vicinity of the Dilbeh stream on December 3rd, the 160th to follow a day later. This would bring the two brigade groups to a distance sixteen miles from the Turkish position covering the Jerusalem water supply. He warned, however, that progress would be slow along the exposed road. "Even two brigade groups would require a long road space when entirely confined to the road and, as the enemy is known to possess mountain guns with a long range, it will be necessary to take the ordinary precautions with flanking detachments."

He would not, he said, be able to make any impression on the enemy till the morning of December 7th, allowing for an eight mile advance per day from Dilbeh. "To count on any increase in the distance covered would be inadvisable, as it is useless to try and fight in this country with exhausted infantry. My experience of the fighting in the hilly country at Khuweilfeh is that it is more than ever necessary to fight with small advance guards for information of the ground, enemy's dispositions of machine guns and, if possible, draw his artillery fire before deciding on a plan of attack. If it is required to dislodge the enemy from his position covering the water, the earliest date on which an attack could be launched would be the morning of December 8th."[18] He continued: "It is difficult to make calculations for advance in a strange country, but I would rather underestimate the rapidity of my advance than be later in co-operating with other troops." The road these British forces would have to take was not only open to enemy fire but snaked through the rough and rocky hills in hairpin bends. Dewi's itinerary shows these plans were implemented as outlined. On November 8th he had been at Khuweilfeh, Berya Well.[19] They moved to Dahariya, to Shilbeh, just over half way along the road from Beersheba to Hebron, on December 3rd, and to Hebron itself on December 5th. On December 6th he was at the Russian monastery on the Bethlehem road, almost certainly the spectacular Greek Orthodox Mar Saba monastery 11 miles from Bethlehem in the Judaean Hills.[20] Implementation of plans agreed at a further Corps conference at Latrun on December 2nd, which Mott attended, would depend on the reaction of the Turks. Mott's instructions received on December 4th detailed their dispositions and concluded Turkish defences were not deep. Once they had been broken the main problem would be terrain. If the Turks pushed troops south, to ward off the attack from this direction, the 60th and 74th divisions would drive in from the Jerusalem-Nablus road to the north. The Turks, however, would be

17) Ibid., p48.
18) Dudley Ward, p143.
19) Berya, also Burj el Beiyareh
20) Mar Saba, founded by St. Saba of Cappadocia in the 5th century. Over the centuries invaders razed the buildings but it was rebuilt by the Russian government in 1840 when the superpowers were all keen to demonstrate their interest in and stake their claims to the Holy Land.

alert, it was thought to the dangers of succumbing to an attack from the north and would not move troops south in numbers to head off a British attack, as this could result in their retreat being cut off.

The country through which the men of the 53rd had to advance was a moorland plateau, full of boulders, with stony fields and dry torrent beds in the hollows. Olive groves, fig trees and a few vines skirted the occasional grey stone native village. Though there were no big hills, gradients were steep for wagons and transport animals. To get down a hill two hairpin corners sometimes had to be negotiated, leading Mott to recommend he should stop north of Hebron on the 5th rather than push on to the outskirts of Bethlehem, permission for which was granted. An able commander, much appreciated by his men, Mott took a more realistic view of his likely progress than Corps headquarters and the next few days saw a sometimes testy interchange between him and Chetwode, who was determined to keep to his timetable. Zero Day, when Jerusalem would be attacked, had been set for December 8th, with Mott's Detachment to be in the Bethlehem-Beit Jala area the day before in order to lead the assault. The difficulties in keeping men of Mott's detachment supplied during this long advance – one of the reasons for his caution – are acknowledged in the Division History. Though troops in the West operating along the coast could be supplied by the advancing railway, the 53rd further east was dependent on the Karm railhead in Wadi es Sheria. Supplies, including bread from the Royal Engineers' bakery in Port Said came from the Kantara railhead on the Suez Canal, to Karm. They were then conveyed by caterpillar tractor over sand and broken country to Irgreig, thence on the old Turkish narrow gauge railway (the trucks being drawn by mules) to Beersheba, where G.S.[21] wagons of the Divisional Train and their mules took the supplies a stage further north. Motor lorries conveyed them to a dump three miles north of Hebron, where they were loaded on to camels and taken to the forward Divisional dump, either at Solomon's Pools,[22] or, as the advance extended, Bethlehem, Jerusalem, or beyond. The first line transport of the units took them to the line." Many camels – and native camel drivers – suffered in the process, not being used to the conditions experienced in the Judaean hills. The camels, whose feet were adapted to walk on Egypt's sand, had great difficulties gaining a grip on wet and slippery soil, and no doubt became even less agreeable than usual to their handlers.

Jerusalem Secured

The columns of the 53rd began moving forward from 6 o'clock in the morning on the 6th, picking up information from native villages on the way about Turkish movements, and gaining control of key points. Clouds, however, descended on the hills. Where previously it had been possible to see Bethlehem and Jerusalem ahead, visibility in a deluge of rain had been cut to no more than 200-300 yards. The advanced troops camped overlooking Burak, or Solomon's Pools, were now close to the main enemy positions defending Bethlehem and had to endure the wet and cold with no more than waterproof sheets over jackets and shorts. Mott wired the

155

---

21) G.S., probably General Support.
22) Dudley Ward, p163. Solomon's pools, three huge rectangular cisterns fed by springs cut in the rock in steps two miles south of Bethlehem, were designed to supply water to Bethlehem and Jerusalem by gravity. Though attributed to Solomon, they probably date from the Maccabean era in the 2nd century BC, with further work by Pontius Pilate in the time of Herod.

XXth Corps to say he could not move until the weather cleared, only to be told the advance would proceed as arranged, regardless of the weather, so that the attack on Jerusalem could take place at 5.15 am the next day. After running into stiff resistance from the Turks defending Bethlehem, Mott decided to skirt the town and to deploy four battalions to seize the heights of Beit Jala to the northwest, calculating that the enemy would not remain in Bethlehem once this commanding position had been secured. Wires from Chetwode now reported the 60th division was being held up and could not continue until the 53rd caught up. "It is imperative that your advance should continue with the utmost energy and that you report progress." "I'm doing my best," Mott cabled him back in response. Chetwode, to the northwest, was able to tell Mott that the Royal Flying Corps was reporting that the Turks were beginning to pull out of Jerusalem. As they pulled back, however, they offered stout resistance to the 74th and 60th Divisions, helped by country ideally suited to defence and by the bad weather. This had made it difficult for artillery to be moved over sodden ground. Despite the impatience he had shown, Chetwode later paid tribute to the performance of the 53rd during the advance, writing to his wife: "Tell Wales my Welsh Division fought magnificently and stood up to superior numbers for three days."

At the end of the first day of the renewed attack on December 8th all the dominating positions west and northwest of the enemy's main line of retreat had been captured. The Turks made no attempt to regain their lost positions and by the end of the second day the city had been completely cordoned off. Waving a flag of truce and carrying a letter of surrender from Izzat, the Mutasarrif (the Ottoman Governor of Jerusalem), the Mayor, Hussein Salim al-Husseini, handed over the keys of the city the same day, according to some reports, to two sergeants, Hurcomb and Sedgewick, who happened to stumble across the surrender party. Another version has the mayor and his group meeting a cook sent out to find eggs for breakfast, who ran back with the news to his commanding officer. Actual photographs of the two sergeants suggest, however, the first story is the most probable. The surrender document read: "Due to the severity of the siege of the city and the suffering this peaceful country has endured from your heavy guns; and for fear that these deadly bombs will hit the holy places, we are forced to hand over to you the city, [...] hoping that you will protect Jerusalem the way we have protected it for more than five hundred years." Allenby was aware of the sensitivities of the situation. Having secured Jerusalem without a shot being fired, he put Indian Moslems to guard Islam's sacred sites. Five hundred years of Ottoman rule – and indeed Turkish leadership of the Moslem world – had been brought to an end.

There were Europeans living in the city for whom the British arrival came only just in time. A date had been set by the Turks for the deportation of all European men, and they might not have survived, the Turks not enjoying a good reputation for their treatment of prisoners of war. On hearing about the capture of Jerusalem Allenby is reported to have sent a telegram to General Shea, commanding the 60th Division, (and possibly to the other commanders as well) stating simply "Congratulations. Psalm 122. v2." In a bible-literate age, many would have recognized the verse – "Our feet shall stand within thy gates, O Jerusalem". British troops now mounted guard on the city's gates, working with Turkish police, who had surrendered. On December 9th, the detail for manning the Jaffa Gate was given to No. 11 Platoon, C Company. 5th Welch Regiment, from the 53rd (Welsh) Division, many of them, no doubt, like Dewi, Sunday School boys, who could hardly ever have imagined they would stand in the Holy Land at Christmas, guarding the city where the Crucifixion occurred. The British had mounted their assault in such a way as to minimize the threat to Jerusalem and on Allenby's orders the British flag was not flown over the city, only that of the Red Cross. Allenby, entered Jerusalem two days later on December 11th, a scene that will have gladdened the hearts of the by now war-weary British public, including Dewi's parents, when it was shown on cinema newsreels early the next year. With due modesty, Allenby chose to enter via the Jaffa Gate on foot, going past the wide breach in the walls that had been made for the Kaiser's more bombastic entry in 1898. Here he was greeted by men from the four home nations and from Australia and New Zealand, and accompanied by the French and Italian commanders of the contingents those countries had supplied men to the campaign.[23] At the base of the Tower of David the Proclamation of Military Law was read declaring the right of every person to pursue his lawful business and offering protection to every sacred building, pious foundation, or customary place of prayer, whether Christian, Hebrew, or Moslem. Allenby then moved on to receive notables and the heads of all the city's religious communities.

In letters sent the following year we learn that Dewi's parents had been to see newsreel of the capture of Jerusalem and were keen to know where he had been in the scenes they saw. "I was much interested to hear of your having been to see the Entry into the Holy City on the bioscope. Gosh! I should have liked to see that with you and I can quite understand the enthusiasm when the orchestra struck up that very appropriate march."[24] The pictures did not, however, tell the full story, he explains, the generals organising their own entry so that the important part they played in these events could be acknowledged. "And, now, you want to know why you didn't see me there. Well, that's simply explained. I wasn't there, you see. Nunno, what you saw was all the pomp and ceremony of the official entry of the C. in C. – you didn't see the actual occupation by the old un cant pum deg a naw (159s).[25] I went in there with the boys of the old brigade two days before that, and there were no bands playing. Still, I wish to goodness you could have seen me in it – guess you'd have gone clean crazy, eh? So, you see, Dad, there'll be no need for you to pinch that film after all – Shame isn't it? It's wonderful when you come to think of it, tho'. Fancy you having seen the Jaffa Gate and the streets I passed along but a few days before and also to see the fellers marching in. Very glad, indeed, you took the opportunity and pleased you enjoyed it, although not spotting me must have been a terrible disappointment for you. No doubt, you went to the Gaiety that night fully expecting to see my ugly dial confronting you from the canvas?[26] Never mind. As long as you see my triumphal entry into the approach via no. 3 platform,

23) Under the Sykes-Picot agreement reached when the possibility of a British invasion of Palestine was first raised, British diplomat Sir Mark Sykes agreed with Francois George-Picot, former French consul at Beirut, that Britain would occupy Palestine and France take Syria. They also agreed an all-arms French contingent would be attached to the Egyptian Expeditionary Force.
The Italians had petitioned the British and French to be allowed to participate in negotiations on the government of Palestine after the war and were allowed to send 500 men for 'representative purposes only'. Their interest was in asserting 'hereditary ecclesiastical prerogatives in connection with the Christian churches in Jerusalem and Bethlehem'.
24) April 29th 1918.
25) C. in C., General Allenby.
26) The Gaiety Theatre in City Road.

everything'll be OK, won't it? That's the only 'entry' I'm waiting or troubling about – and a single decker from the Monument."[27]

In a later letter he recounts a humorous incident that happened not long after the men had arrived, and, like all victors, found themselves going through the quarters of the defeated. "All of which reminds me of the way in which you say people made fun at home of the Jordan water some fellers sent home. If I remember correctly, you said they imagined their legs were being pulled and suspected the fluid to be only ordinary common or garden Jerusalem tap aqua pura. Glad to say, I can put their minds at rest. All or most of those bottles sent home contained Honest Injun Jordan water, altho' the senders hadn't seen the famous river. You see, this is the explanation – when we entered Jerusalem we found 'em in the houses, all ready packed up and labelled to various addresses in Der Vaterland, 'cos those Germans had been in such a terrible hurry to get away when they saw the old Welsh coming over the hill at Bethlehem that they quite forgot to take the bottles with 'em, and which naturally came in handy for our fellers. One of the chaps in the company sent one to his fiancée and the letter she wrote him back caused us much merriment as she accused him of being rather previous, gently hinting that they weren't married yet. You see, it had quite slipped that indiscreet young man's memory that the liquid was universally used at Christenings. He did feel an ass, you bet."[28]

Jerusalem, nevertheless, disappoints, and he says his father is right in assuming it was not the El Dorado they had imagined it to be. British soldiers attributed this to Turkish neglect. "It suffered from the same complaint as any other city which has long been under the lazy old scoundrel, Johnny Turk's rule and looked just as tho' the corporation officials had a very soft time, indeed, a Bobby's job, in fact.[29] I must say, tho', that, advancing along the road from Bethlehem, it made a very beautiful and thrilling picture, with the sun shining on its historical old walls and innumerable mosques and minarets, a typically enchanting city of the East. It has improved immensely in appearance, so I am given to understand, since we pinched it, and every man, woman and child of the inhabitants who cared to earn an honest piastre were soon set to work road-making and generally renovating the place." He much prefers Bethlehem, not least because they had had a good reception there from the locals. "Nestling in the hills, it looked almost like an ordinary clean, healthy English village and, moreover, I shall always treasure memories of Bethlehem as possessing much the prettiest, choicest, daintiest demoiselles it has been my privilege to feast my eyes upon during the whole of my extensive travelling in the Near East, who smiled most charmingly over their vineyard walls at us travel-stained ruffians, as we marched thro', wishing us 'Bon Fortune' in a delightfully encouraging fashion. Nor were they shocked and insulted when we gaily blew them kisses – you see nobody could but fall in love with those gay, laughing, victorious Welsh battalions. They'd seen so much of those ragged, down-at-heel, dirty, miserable looking Turks, was it any wonder their feminine hearts beat a little faster to see those stalwart, clean-limbed, ridiculously boyish-looking warriors come swinging past their garden walls?"

27) No. 3 Platform. Cardiff General Station, now Cardiff Central. The Monument, the statue of the 3rd Marquess of Bute then on a roundabout at the bottom of St. Mary Street in Cardiff, now in Callaghan Square, south of the station.

28) April 14th 1918.

29) Bobby's job may refer to the supposedly comfortable life of policemen of old, hands behind back, rocking back and fore and possibly whistling, too.

The next important step for British commanders was to determine whether or not to push further forward. Though there were some arguments for halting at this point, and ensuring all resources were concentrated on the Western Front, the War Cabinet decided offensive operations should continue, with the aim of knocking Turkey, and possibly Bulgaria, as a consequence, out of the war, and perhaps persuading the Germans their Eastern policy had been a failure. On December 13th the 53rd advanced north east of Jerusalem and other divisions advanced northwest. The following day they were given a new position to hold after improvements had been made in the XXth Corps' communications and supplies – an east-west line 12 miles north of Jerusalem. The retreating Turkish 7th and 8th Armies were 20 miles apart, their only lateral communication coming through a road 30 miles north of Jerusalem. The advance from Jerusalem was delayed, however, by intelligence that a Turkish counter-attack aimed at recapturing the city was planned. Although the Turks had not mounted full frontal resistance at Jerusalem they were still present in the area, and this had to be secured so that Jerusalem could be held against attempts to retake it. Mott was given permission to shell the Mount of Olives, where a large body of Turks was still encamped. A postponement providentially intervened, however, enabling it to be taken unoccupied the following dawn. The 53rd's commander was then given the order to cover Jerusalem from the east and northeast and to advance down the road to Jericho.

The Turkish response came on the night of December 26th-27th and was contained by the 53rd and 60th, while two other divisions, the 74th and 10th, counter-attacked. Some outposts fell initially to the enemy forces but an advance across a six mile wide front by British infantry brought El Jib, a previous objective, together with Er Ram, birthplace of the prophet Samuel, and Rafat into Allied hands. By December 30th, the British had a new line astride the Nablus road beyond Ramallah and Bireh, eight miles north of Jerusalem. The Turks sustained heavy casualties over the next three days and the fight for Jerusalem, a Turkish-held city for 400 years, was finally over by December 30th. The two British Corps, the XXth and XXIst now had a strong line running from Jaffa through Ramle to Jerusalem, the EEF having advanced 60 miles in the previous six weeks. There would now be a pause in offensive operations until February, while roads and railways were improved and brought closer to the front. To the west, three divisions of the XXIst Corps had been put into position on December 7th on the coastal plain for the second attempt to cross the Auja river, a formidable obstacle forty feet wide and ten feet deep in places, bounded on both sides by soft and muddy banks with a current growing stronger from the autumn and winter rains. On the night of December 20th-21st three British brigades from the 52nd Division crossed the Auja on rafts built for them by the Royal Engineers. The crossing had been preceded by a reconnaissance by two infantry officers who had swum across to the other side to examine the ford at the bar. The Turks were again caught by surprise, having expected the crossing to be attempted in a different location. The Turks were driven back eight miles, the port of Jaffa now finally safe.

Billets near Calvary

No letters from Dewi survive from the period of campaigning leading up to events in Jerusalem, whether because he had been too busy or because enemy submarine action had sent mails to the bottom of the sea, is not clear. Early in the New Year he commiserates with them for the absence of mails, the last he appears to have sent being dated October 17th. "As a matter of fact," he tells his sister, "the mails both ways are something atrocious. They're all complaining about not having heard from me for a deuce of a time, and, of course, it isn't any fault of mine."[30] On arrival in Jerusalem Dewi and his companions were billeted at first near Calvary, where Christ was crucified, just outside the walls of Jerusalem, but on December 17th they moved into new quarters on the Mount of Olives, where Christ had preached to his disciples. Here, they stayed in a monastery previously occupied by the Germans, as he tells Doris in a letter the following year, after she had evidently commented on a postcard he had sent. "Very glad, indeed, you liked the P.Cs. Re the Hun building on the Mt. of Olives, as you have asked for its name, I may tell you it is the Kaiser Wilhelm Augusta Victoria Sanatorium – quite a mouthful, you observe. Not only did he call it after himself either but the old blighter had photos and statues etc. of himself hanging about all over the shop. Guess he thinks he's some personage. One picture of him – moustache and all – covered the roof of the church inside and depicted him holding a miniature church in the hollow of his hand, Defender of the Faith, I s'pose?"[31]

The complex he refers to was named after the Kaiserin, Augusta Viktoria of Schleswig-Holstein-Sonderburg-Augustenburg, wife of German Kaiser Wilhelm II, and was one of a number of religious sites the Germans had built in the Holy Land over the preceding century. The architect, Robert Leibnitz, was inspired by German palaces, such as the German Hohenzollern Castle, and after the Kaiser's visit, he commissioned the construction of a guesthouse for German pilgrims, making extensive use of building materials imported from Germany. A 50-metre high church tower was constructed with four bells, the largest of them weighing six tons. To transport these bells from Jaffa, the road to Jerusalem had to be widened and paved, an exercise that cost more than double that of transporting the bells from Hamburg to Jaffa. The Augusta Viktoria was the first building in the country to have electricity (provided by a diesel generator), offering amenities doubtless welcome to the British soldiers staying there after months of living outdoors. The compound now became Allenby's EEF headquarters and that of the British Military Administration of Occupied Enemy Territory. Other German religious buildings of the era included the Protestant Church of the Redeemer, built on the site and on the ground plan of a church belonging to the Knights of St. John, the new Roman Catholic Church of the Dormition on Mount Zion, with an adjoining Benedictine convent, a Roman Catholic hospice outside the Damascus Gate, and the Protestant Johanniter Hospice. A curiosity was the German colony, the Friends of Jerusalem, a group of pious Swabian families who had fallen out with the Evangelical-Lutheran church. They had emigrated to the Holy Land, where they declared themselves the German Temple, an independent religious sect. Dewi had been extremely proud to tell his sister about their advance into the Holy City – a victory that elevated Allenby to the status of national hero, his Army's exploits commemorated in newspaper supplements of the time. His advance had not only secured considerable territorial gains but had also helped Britain secure

---

30) January 4th 1918. He had many correspondents back in Wales.

31) April 29th 1918. The title Fidei Defensor, Defender of the Faith, was granted in 1521, by Pope Leo X to King Henry VIII of England and has been used subsequently by all by British monarchs. It appears on British coinage as Fid. Def.

Baghdad and the oilfields in Basra in Mesopotamia. The other news at this time had not been nearly as good. The November offensive at Cambrai on the Western Front had brought heavy losses and no gains, and the French Army was still recovering from a serious mutiny. Russia was no longer in the war, following the Bolshevik revolution, and United States troops had only recently begun to arrive in France.

Paying for the War

Alongside these setbacks in Europe, the cost domestically of the war was also being brought home to the British public and even to those not affected by casualties. The British Government was finding it necessary to borrow heavily from the public through the sale of £5, £20 and £50 War Bonds and War and Savings Certificates. Bonds could be purchased not just from Post Offices and banks but through businesses, many of which had entered enthusiastically into their sale, in some cases entering purchasers into draws to win prizes. The leading Cardiff department store, James Howell, was among those that offered bonds for sale. Other retailers were willing to accept War Bonds in payment for goods. A contemporary advertisement shows a man standing expectantly over his elegantly gowned wife, who is refusing to give him his Kenilworth cigarettes. "You said you should buy some War Bonds this month, and here's the cheque all ready. Now that you've given up the car and I've forsworn new furs, we can manage it." The threat works. "Very well, my dear," he replies "It's no good leaving the money in the Bank." He agrees it would be much better to buy a War Bond.

Six tanks – at the time a technological novelty – toured Britain to sell bonds and certificates, and appeals were made from the gun turrets by civic dignitaries, politicians, businessmen, musicians, actors and others for the public to sacrifice something from their savings. In Cardiff the honours were done by coal and shipping magnates, the Marquess of Bute, Lord Treowen, Herbert Cory, and Sir Edward Nicholls. The tank was accompanied by soldiers and artillery guns, and sometimes an aircraft would drop pamphlets over the town or city before the tank's appearance, exhorting the people to invest. The tank would usually put on a show for the crowds – riding over obstacles such as old cars – in order to demonstrate its capabilities. For the visit to Cardiff in December 1917, a tank was put on a train at its previous stop in Gloucester and parked outside the City Hall before moving on to the Docks, where a cheque for £50,000 was received from one business in the area. Two daughters of Cardiff shipowner, Samuel Instone, arrived on Shetland ponies to buy their bonds, an event the *Western Mail* considered significant enough to offer for sale prints of the pictures its photographer took. The tank bank then moved on to Bristol and Birmingham. Large crowds gathered around the tanks in the towns and cities they visited and the newspapers of the day tried to whip up intense competition between rival centres to see which could raise the most money per head. In Swansea the sum raised came to just short of a remarkable £2.2m.

The war was being felt in other ways, too. Rationing had had to be introduced to deal with the growing shortages of food as a result of losses incurred by merchant shipping bringing supplies from the US, Canada and elsewhere, following the resumption of unrestricted German submarine warfare earlier in 1917. Lloyd George's associate, Lord Rhondda, had been appointed to the important post of Food Controller in June. The nation at the end of 1917 was being urged to eat one-fifth less food to ease the food crisis and food suppliers, such as Bovril, were stressing the benefits their product could offer as an alternative to more substantial fare. Shortages of food meant queues for even basic products, such as sugar and butter, and there were accusations of cheating or worse. Sir Arthur Yapp, the Government's Director of Food Economy, at a meeting with refractory postal workers, was accused by one heckler of having had a side of bacon delivered to his house, the carman having apparently divulged this piece of information.[32] Sir Arthur went on to deny he had had bacon for weeks and to offer a reward of £100 to anyone who could make this charge stand up. Shortages of butter and tea and high–priced eggs caused particular annoyance and sometimes led to disturbances at the queues that now formed outside shops. The police in Newport were accused of seizing butter supplies in the market for their own consumption. Some of those who needed food most, such as munitions workers, were unable to find sufficient, while the better off could go to the black market.

In January 1918 sugar was rationed and by the end of April it had been joined by meat, butter, cheese and margarine. Ration cards were issued and everyone had to register with a butcher and a grocer. Other consumer products, including clothing, were also in short supply, as a result of the need to divert labour, both male and female, away from meeting consumer demand to fulfilling War Department orders. Strict petrol rationing had also come in by late 1917, netting as miscreants some well-known personalities. In December, the actor Fred Terry, brother of the even more famous Ellen Terry, and his chauffeur were both fined £5, with the alternative of a month in prison, for driving from Cheltenham to Cardiff when they could have taken a train, an eagle-eyed policemen spotting them in Tudor Street. Terry plaintively, and not unreasonably, asked the magistrate how he was to get his car away, if it could not be driven, but received no sympathy, despite his plea that a heart condition made him a special case.[33] Lower down the social scale a Cardiff fish merchant was fined for using his motor bike to collect fish from the docks. It was pointed out to him by the court that a tram passed his house. Nor was it just the Government that was seeking to raise funds from the public. The YMCA, whose facilities Dewi had found so useful in Egypt, was also raising money to support its activities at home and abroad in support of soldiers at the front or back for rest and rehabilitation from injury. Its appeal for £500,000 in donations urged Britain's then many trades to match each other in their generosity. An appeal in the name of Boer War victor, Lord Roberts, for funds to help returning servicemen also called on the generosity of the public.

Britain's Christmas Present

The news of Allenby's success proved highly welcome at home and was seized on by politicians anxious to give the public some seasonal good news. Lloyd George famously described it as a "Christmas present for the British public". On Monday

32) Carman, archaic expression for van driver.
33) Ivor Novello, composer of the popular World War One song, *Keep the Homes Fires Burning*, was to suffer a similar fate in World War Two, going to prison for eight weeks for breaking petrol regulations.

December 10th Bonar Law, the Conservative leader, who at this time held the relatively minor position of Colonial Secretary in the Coalition Government, told the House of Commons that Allenby had reported that on the previous Saturday he had attacked the enemy's positions south and west of Jerusalem. "Welsh and Home Counties troops, advancing from the direction of Bethlehem, drove back the enemy and, passing Jerusalem on the East, established themselves on the Jerusalem and Jericho road. At the same time, London infantry and dismounted yeomanry attacked strong enemy positions west and northwest of Jerusalem and established themselves astride the Jerusalem – Shekem road.[34] The Holy City thus being isolated was surrendered," the report continued. King George V sent Allenby a message of congratulation, extending to all ranks, in which he declared the occupation of Jerusalem would be received with the greatest satisfaction "throughout my empire". "Such an achievement," he went on "is a fitting sequel to the hard marching and fighting of the troops, as well as to the organisation by which the difficulties of supply, transport and water have been overcome." He praised Allenby for the "skilful dispositions" which had preserved the Holy Places.

The *Western Mail*, enjoying the added bonus of Welsh involvement, was able to declare the success one of the outstanding events of the war. "It will be seen that Welsh troops have again shared in a great victory in Palestine. They displayed fine dash on previous occasions when Gaza was captured on November 7th and Jaffa on November 17th. A glowing tribute to their splendid work has been paid by Sir Philip [Chetwode] who says they harried the Turks off their legs. The Australians have christened them the Welsh Gurkhas".[35] In a highly partisan view of the enemy, the Cardiff morning averred: "The Turk is a Moslem by adoption only. He inherited the country of the Saracens but not their spirit and character. The events of the war have marked in the Turk the survival of a primitive barbarism in which Islam had no part and the Turkish policy towards the native Islamic population both of Palestine and Arabia has been contemptuous and oppressive. Under the Turkish sway Palestine has become almost a desert. It must be part of the war settlement to destroy the power of those who made the desert and restore to the country the wondrous fertility and opulence of ancient times." To emphasise the difference in the approach the British would bring, the paper's leader writer refers back to the "insolent ostentation" of the Kaiser's entry into the Holy City a decade earlier "surrounded by a bodyguard of Turkish troops after bribing the Ministers at Stamboul for military and commercial concessions". General Allenby, by contrast enters on foot "as a simple English gentleman".

The picture papers were quick to rush out news of the great victory in time for the public to read about it before Christmas. *The Graphic's* page 3 title page (there were advertisements on the front and inside front covers) for its issue of Saturday, December 15th featured a picture of General Allenby, 'the Captor of Jerusalem', and a two page relief map of Judaea showing the surrounding country. Because detailed reports would not by then have reached Britain, readers had to make do with a scene-setter by Estelle Blyth, billed as the acting Secretary of the Palestine Exploration Fund, telling readers about the city she knew, then a busy entrepôt

163

34) Shekem, or Nablus.
35) *Western Mail*, Tuesday December 11th and Wednesday December 12th, 1917.

with a population of around 50,000. It was an impression that will have chimed well with the British public, reinforcing their view of both Turk and German. After describing the geographical position of the city, high in the hills, and its landmarks, the Dome of the Rock (Mosque of Omar), the Church of the Holy Sepulchre, the Tower of David, now the citadel, and Omar's Minaret, she declares the blot on the appearance of the city has to be the ungainly tower of the German church, designed by the Kaiser, who insisted it be higher than the venerable Church of the Holy Sepulchre, "which it certainly is". She continues: "A network of narrow, dirty but picturesque streets leads in intricate ways from one point of interest to the other. You meet history at every turn; the glamour of a storied past enfolds you; while in the varied crowds of East and West commingled you realise an entrancing present. Russians, Persians, Afghans, Armenians, Jews of all nationalities, Greeks, Sudanese, Europeans, Americans – all pass freely in and out of Jerusalem; diverse in every other way, they are one people within her gates. Arabic is the language of the country, but forty-eight languages and dialects are spoken daily in Jerusalem. Separate quarters are assigned to different trades; there are the spice market, the grain, the leather, the silver markets and so on." It suited British propaganda – keen to establish that Jerusalem had been liberated – to assert that the Holy City had suffered much under Turkish rule, though there is good reason to doubt the accuracy of the picture painted. In a piece of lyrical writing that now seems particularly dated, Blyth continues: "What she has suffered during the war we can only guess at; but even before 1914 the people of Palestine were longing openly for English rule; and Germany was the most disliked of all the European Powers. To this sinister partnership Palestine has been delivered over, body and soul, through no fault of her own, for three years – a cruel fate indeed! The name of England has always stood for liberty to her, from the day when Richard tried his best to free her, down through the ages to the present. And now England is drawing near, bringing to Jerusalem a deliverance bought by war, but through the clouds the Holy City sees the breaking of the day that brings her Peace."[36]

The division's arrival in Jerusalem brought a stay in billets, a welcome development after months on the march and camping, as best they could, in the Judaean hills. Their stay in proper accommodation does not last long, however, and they are soon on the move, marching on to reach Er Ram on December 29th, after the Turks" attempts to retake Jerusalem had been repulsed, and Ramallah[37] five days later, where they again have to contend with poor weather. "We have trekked once again," Dewi writes, "leaving Jerusalem behind – you see, 'Ymlaen' [Forward] is the watchword and at the present moment [we] are stationed in a native village with four walls and a roof to keep dry, thank goodness. Last night we spent in bivvies and got washed out, 'cos the weather is still very wet indeed – mud and slush as per usual and cold as old boots. The sooner March is here the better – I could revel in a real good day of scorching, blazing sunshine. We're like hot-house plants now, you see, without the sun – much more of this and we shall just pine away. (!) Don't know how on earth we shall fare in Blighty – just having a taste of the sort of weather you put up with there, and it's *most* undesirable, I assure you."[38]

36) *Western Mail*, December 24th 1917.
37) Ramallah, literally Height of God, 17 miles north of Jerusalem.
38) January 4th 1918.

There is, however, news of a parcel from home to report, though once again its contents seem to have been quickly devoured. "It was on the last little trek before arriving here that the parcel (dated October 13th) arrived, and, seeing that bully and biscuit rations are still the order of the day with us, you can easily imagine how welcome it was. We played havoc with it in about ten minutes and really, Mum, if you only saw the boys necking into your cakes, it would do your heart good " Morale has clearly been boosted by the events of the past month. Their Ottoman enemy, with its stiffening of German officers and men, is regarded with some respect, though the superiority of the British fighting man is taken for granted. They are "blighters" for what they did at Gallipoli and, by 1918, are paying the price. The Turks, having retreated from Jerusalem, are pictured as being in full flight and responsible for the problems of getting letters through, so fast is the British Army moving after them. He complains: "That's one of the disadvantages of being top-dogs and cock of the walk, as you might say. Indeed, I sometimes wish old 'Johnny' wouldn't go back so blamed fast, 'cos it only means us following his dainty footsteps all the time. Then again, there's no railways over these blessed hills – result, us trekking, base umpteen blooming miles away, and getting farther every day, everything got to be brought up by camel convoys (*mails* and *grub* included, of course), so you can imagine it's glorious prospects for regular mails. However, there you have a fairly good idea of our excellent improved postal service, which should explain matters a great deal – keep smiling, tho' and your peckers up, we'd like letters, allus [always] do, don't us? – but Lummy we're not going to let little things like that put the kybosh on our spirits – not on your life, eh? Anyhow, there's one thing about it, the very cause of the delay on our letters is making huge strides towards me coming home, what do you say? – sooner Johnny's fed up, the sooner that'll happen. Gee! Dolly, we aren't half having owns back and a little bit more for events of Dec. 1915.[39] Forgive me, won't you, if all this sounds rather swankish, but I've got to say it, so, there we are – goodness knows, we've been poor unfortunates before."

A Low-key Christmas

Despite the lift they had received from capturing Jerusalem, Christmas 1917 itself had been a low-key affair, with little opportunity to celebrate being in one of the world's most famous cities, sacred to three religions, Judaism, Christianity and Islam. Early in 1918 he writes to thank his sister for a telegram he had received, the first ever, he tells her, and to describe a not very festive time that he would have preferred to have spent at home. "Very many thanks, firstly for your wire – it was very thoughtful of you and is an excellent New Year's card. First wire I've had, so you can guess I didn't exactly know what the deuce to make of it at first. Telegram for me, thought I, most remarkable. However, altho' it was absolutely imposs for me to send Xmas Cards or telegrams, Dolly, you may be sure I was most thankful for the greetings and good wishes and returned them most heartily per wireless. I hope you had a good Xmas this year again, and, I tell you, I wasn't half wishing myself back at 76 on the 25th ult." They had not had a proper Christmas, or at least preferred to forget all about it being the festive season, he tells her. "You see, it was the biggest washout of a Xmastide I ever had – and hope to goodness I don't have

165

39) The retreat from Gallipoli.

another like it – Ugh! Blooming awful it was. No wonder it got on our nerves – bully and biscuits for a Xmas dinner – Phew! 'nuff to drive a feller loopy, I should think – *we* didn't feel like singing carols, you can betcher your life. So, as I was saying, we kind of naturally forgot all about Xmases in general and this one in particular. Last Xmas, now, was a blooming good 'un – a concert and plenty of grub, Xmas before that, well, we had a decent time at Salonica but this 'un – O! absolutely too impossible altogether – never no more – turkey, not bully, next one, I trust."[40] Some active servicemen will have been the recipients of the 10/- Christmas boxes that the Dutch and Dorothy cafes in Cardiff – and no doubt restaurants in other towns – invited their readers to send to 'your boy' in France". Being so far away in Palestine it is unlikely any of these reached the E.E.F.

His spirits soon rose, however. "We didn't worry – norrabitofit – care? Phew! I don't think. Too much blooming trouble to worry over that sort of thing. Anyhow, we did manage to wind up the evening in a fairly decent manner after all. Managed to get some wine from the town to drink a few toasts, as you might say. We were in billets, luckily for us, out of the cold and wet, so it wasn't so bad. The singsong afterwards was very spirited – no doubt about it, our choir can give it socks when they start." He cannot resist a little boasting, as any brother might, to a younger sister about his own part in the events. "Excuse me blowing my own trumpet, won't you, but really my little recitation made a great hit and was top of the bill a bit easy, too – I do break out rather rashly like that now and again, you know. I may say that the applause was terrific and you can picture the artist (ahem!) bowing his blushing acknowledgments to the very select audience composing of sappers, pioneers and divers other rank and file." He explains in detail to his sister how he had apparently managed to charm his listeners. "You see, Dolly, to make big hits in cases like that you have to study most minutely the audience, the times and the general condition of their hum-drum existence. Well, I played upon their feelings in a very masterful manner, causing the most poignant emotions and delivering my little address with great eloquence and expression – appealing to them as one of their noble suffering fraternity. P'raps you are just a little curious as to the nature of my famous appeal, so I will set it down forthwith, word for word, as it issued from the lips of the renowned orator. Silence – dead silence – except for the gulps of a few belated 'toasters'.

> 'O! Don't the days seem dull and long
> when all goes right and nothing wrong?
> And isn't life extremely flat
> when you've nothing to growl or grumble at?'

Only four lines, as you perceive, but you can't imagine what a complete success it was – went right to their hearts, it did, believe me."

166

He was looking forward, after three Christmases away, to next year, though once again he would have to spend that away from home. "I have, however, decided to chuck speechmaking etc. till next Xmas when I sincerely hope to raise the roof of the front room No. 76 with a couple of similar spasms, so get the old Johanna tuned,

40) January 4th 1918.

Dolly, 'cos I dessay I might condescend to send you into transports of ecstatic joy with my silvery melodious notes."[41] He had tried, it seems, to be there in spirit, expressing the hope in a letter in February that his sister was not too disappointed he had not been able to send her a present for Christmas. Having moved, from Egypt to Palestine, he is, he explains, miles from amenities and the merchandise in Jerusalem had not met his expectations. "These people are miles behind the times, as regards shops and all that. Gave it up as a bad job eventually 'cos, really, the miserable paltry specimen of the Birmingham jewellers' art (overseas department, remember) that I inspected were a gross insult to the average man's intelligence and would [not] have deceived even the dullest member of a West African missioner's flock. Never mind, don't worry, let it slide till I go on leave to Cairo again, will you? I'll make up for it then, Doll, not half."[42]

Turkish counter attacks having been successfully repulsed at the end of December, the XXth and XXIst Corps were in command of Jerusalem, Ramle, and Jaffa and the road connecting them. With the midwinter weather making further operations difficult, attention turned to improving the roads and to bringing the railways, and the supplies they could transport, closer to the front. The British had a strategically strong defensive line behind which the further advance towards Damascus and Aleppo could be planned, the success of which would roll the Turks all the way back to their native territory. Already stretching from north of Jaffa to Jerusalem it would be extended in February to the Dead Sea with the capture of Jericho. The campaign, according to American historian, John D. Grainger was the first military defeat of a Central Power that led to a substantial loss of enemy territory. In particular, he notes, the fighting from October 31 to November 7th against the Ottoman Gaza-Sheria-Beersheba line resulted in the first defeat of entrenched, experienced, and, until then, successful Ottoman armies, supported by artillery, machine guns, and aircraft. "During these attacks the Ottoman defenders were well-established in trenches, redoubts and other fortifications, requiring a Western Front style of battle, as the attackers were forced to approach over open ground."[43]

The year 1918 would be momentous for the EEF, culminating in the collapse of the Ottoman forces in the Near East and their surrender after the Battle of Megiddo, the crowning glory of Allenby's career, the name of which he took for the peerage he was awarded after his triumphs – Lord Allenby of Megiddo. Dewi was duly proud, though the full impact of what they had achieved at the end of 1917 would not have been apparent to him. "Our brigade, let me repeat, were the b'hoys [sic] who did the trick – 'Y Ddraig Goch a Ddyry Cychwyn' [The Red Dragon, Ever Ready] – it was never more true."[44]

41) Dessay, daresay.
42) February 3rd 1918.
43) Quoted in *Wikipedia*, The Battle of Jerusalem.
44) January 4th 1918.

(top) Infantry advancing through the wheat-fields. The change of landscape once they had passed into Palestine had come as a welcome surprise.

(above) "Our camp in the Wadi, Palestine". Dewi spent much of his service in bivouacs, crude shelters of canvas or other material built into the sides of available slopes.

(right) Memorial to the fallen of the 53rd Division, probably in the battles for Gaza.

(below) The great trek – the advance on Jerusalem through the steep and rocky Judaean Hills in late 1917.

(above) Bethlehem, which the 53rd reached in
December 1917 in the march on Jerusalem.

(left) The famous walls of Jerusalem, the ancient
city's limits until modern times.

Jaffa Gate. The main route through the walls of
Jerusalem from the south.

Jaffa Gate. Camel convoys entering Jerusalem after
its capture by British troops in 1917.

CHAPTER EIGHT

CAMPAIGNING IN JUDAEA

FEBRUARY 1918 – APRIL 1918

Allenby's next plans

With Jerusalem now securely held, Allenby laid plans for the next stage of his campaign. Early in January the 53rd had taken over the line north of Jerusalem, the 158th Brigade on the right, and the 159th on the left. By now, the Turks had no settled front line of their own but were occupying a succession of positions, rocks and village edges.[1] As such, they remained a dangerous enemy, and the next stages of the advance had to be carefully planned, if the gains made over the preceding months since the capture of Gaza were not to be overturned. Allenby's original intention had been to advance north and east of the low-lying Jordan Valley but, with the necessary supplies for such an operation still awaited, communications poor, and the weather less than favourable, he decided to advance east only as far as the Jordan while securing the line north up as far as the Nahr Auja three miles north of Jaffa. The infrastructure that would be needed to support a successful campaign was largely lacking, with the result that troops needed to spend much of the next few months laying down roads, rail lines and cables – and in drenching rain, too. Lateral roads running east – west would be particularly important – the only means of moving men from one flank to the other being the winding Ramle-Jerusalem road. The scale of the exercise was immense. The native paths could not be navigated by laden mules, the steep, rocky ridges were often terraced for cultivation, the local stone was too soft for surfacing, and steam rollers, when they arrived, were too few for the long mileage under construction and repair. Large infantry parties had to be put to work on building roads, supplemented by the Egyptian Labour Force and local labour. Water was also now in short supply, making it necessary to develop a large watering station near Junction Station.[2]

Dewi settled in for a two month stay in Ramallah 17 miles north of Jerusalem, while the railways were extended and preparations put in place for the advance on Jericho and east of the Jordan. He is keen to tell his parents, however, that they have come to a full stop not because the Turks are putting up any stronger resistance. "Not obliged to, you know. O! dear me, no – old Johnny needn't kid hisself 'bout that – he ain't got a leg to stand on, not 'im – beaten to a frazzle now, so we've stopped for a breather and are taking advantage of it, too, you bet. We can appreciate a halt now, you may be sure, after our recent flying column job. That's the worst of being old reliable, fire-eating veterans [...] any job which needs *some* doing – shove the old 53rd on it – you can rely on them any old time. But now, since we're satisfied with things in general for the time being, we're sticking here for now, halted and blooming glad of it, too. S'pose we'll be off shortly again, tho', as soon as the fine weather shows any signs of coming to stay for good. We don't mind getting a move on then, of course, 'cos it's not too bad, after all, trekking in good weather but as for nightly pitching our moving tents in this – O! Dear, no. Don't mensh' please – it's worse than awful. I tell you, I never was more thankful for being in billets. No, By Jove! – we do bless our lucky stars for it every day, and pity the poor blighters who have to be out in bivvies in it. They have my deepest sympathy – it's cruel. Raining and blowing as cold as anything, or even worse than you're getting in

---

1) Dudley Ward, p183.
2) Pritchard (ed.), p346.

Blighty. The roads are swamped and each side is like a quagmire. You get drenched only being out for about half an hour. It's these blooming clouds, you see – us being so high up in the hills and the clouds coming right down on top of us soon soaks thro."[3] Ramallah – literally hill of God – was indeed, an elevated location, some 2,950 feet above sea level, not far short of the peak of Snowdon, Wales's highest mountain, which climbs to 3,500 feet.

They were experiencing weather not encountered since they had left Gallipoli after the violent storms of November 1915. In Egypt and Sinai the problems had been the exact opposite. "Strewth! there was a time when we hadn't had a drop of rain for about nine months or so but 'pon my word! we're getting all our back pay now with a vengeance. There's such a thing as having too much of a good thing, as you know, and, well – we're getting it in the neck now for being so greedy with the sunshine all those months. By Jove! Won't it be absolutely delightful when it comes again? We're longing for it, believe me. I expect this stuff'll last for the remainder of this month [February] now and after that, well – we're hoping as much as we can for the best. March should see us basking under Old Sol's warm life-giving rays and we – hot-house plants, 'cos we have most assuredly become, since our sojourn in the East began – shall hail his appearance with ecstatic joy and delight. Gimme my old shorts and my Wolsey sun bonnet and my shirt sleeves and I'll – well I'll blooming well 'sing thee songs of Araby'."[4] At the end of February, the weather was showing signs of improving, he was able to report, though it remained changeable. "Now and then we experience weather such as you are now having, and it is welcome after the wet. We are getting some of the former at the present moment after five rotten days. In fact, this is most desirable weather, the sun shines, it's fine and dry and just a little bit brisk – no heat at all to speak of. Then, all of a sudden, the sky'll get as black as the ace of spades and it'll fairly drown you, if you're out in it. We're still in billets, thank goodness, and consider ourselves lucky when these deluges occur. Don't suppose we'll enjoy this luxury much longer and are expecting to move out any day now into the bivouacs again. That won't be so bad, as long as it doesn't rain much. If it does, well – have to make the best of a wet time, that's all. However, I think the worst weather is over now and I sincerely hope that very soon next month we shall be enjoying the sunshine every day once again."

The conditions demanded essential supplies from home other than food, which the Army was obviously not capable of providing. "Socks, I may say, are truly a godsend out here at present while this weather lasts. One wants a few changes in these deluges and they are, as you may well imagine, a most important item under the circs. The scissors, well that's just what I was in urgent need of, so it comes in jolly handy indeed. Of course, we haven't got much time to pass away at the moment at the manicure and chiropody stunts but – well, you understand, it is desirable and necessary now and then to attend to one's talons. A pair of scissors, I may say, is a very essential article of kit in the Welsh Division – the flying column, the forced marchers of world renown, the boys who advance so swiftly that it blinds 'em. You see how important our fairy tootsies are to us – my best thanks for 'em, they'll do O.K."[5]

---

3) February 6th 1918.
4) February 6th 1918. Victorian song, Music by Frederick Clay; words by W.G. Wills. From the *Cantata Lalla Rookh*. 'I'll sing thee songs of Araby, And tales of fair Cashmere, Wild tales to cheat thee of a sigh, Or charm thee to a tear.'
5) February 27th 1918.

Dewi's service during this period had started with a return to Signal Office duties after their arrival in Jerusalem in December but he is soon moved, much to his disappointment, from brigade back to company duties and away from his best friend Frank and the "b'hoys" he had been with since "the stunt" – the march on Jerusalem – began. From the middle of January there is also a change of routine to get used to in Ramallah, and an unpleasantly early start. "It is a bit of a change going back to the old life of the stables again, and I find it most unattractive at 5.30 am every day on being hauled out in the dark just for the sake of some sly, vicious and elegant mules. As I say, it is a bad shock after a few months of getting up for brekker and living in general the lordly life of a brigade signaller." He is pleased, however, with his new quarters. "We're billeted in a tophole place, tho', beats many of the native dwelling places I *have* experienced, all to fits. It is above an American Mission Church that used to was [be] before '14 and you couldn't wish for a better place to hang out."[6]

He sympathises with Doris for wanting a lie-in on Christmas morning, telling her that getting up before dawn finds him too disgusted for mere words. "It's so blessed cold turning out at that unearthly hour. But thank heavens there's no rain with it now, and then, again, we're in billets. Indeed, I shudder to think of bivouacs while this cool weather is on."[7] In his next letter he reports that he has been given the not very pleasant duty of washing down the passages of their billet every morning. "Glad I haven't got an outdoor job in it, I can assure you, know when I'm well off, don't you worry, having had some before – I've clicked since this trip alright, and am lying low as long as I can. I don't want a change of occupation till this rotten weather's over and done with – not likely, although, unfortunately, I have to soil these h-hands of mine, donchknow, and it does go against the grain, as you might guess. Not being used to hard duty work, of course, I have naturally a perfect horror of it, what?" He has the makings he says of a very thorough and competent charwoman. "It's no light task with these careless lads bringing in all the mud of Palestine on their boots every time they're dismissed, you can bet your life. It needs plenty of water and elbow grease on my job but I don't worry a jot, for it's no parades for me – (see me wink) and I don't shove my blooming nose outside till the weather clerk sends a plumber to see to this blessed leak."[8]

The Turks in Retreat

During February Allenby was able to put into effect the plans he had drawn up for securing his eastern flank and proceeding further north. If the crossing over the Jordan could be held, he would be able to prevent the enemy from raiding the country west of the river and he would also gain control of the Dead Sea. Instructions were sent out on February 9th for the operation to begin on the fourth fine day after the spell of bad weather ended. The 53rd was given the task of advancing their line north east of Jerusalem on the Nablus road to take Ras et Tawil and the high ground between Wadi el Ain and the Taiyibeh-Jericho road.[9] The attacks were eventually launched on February 19th and, despite heavy resistance

6) January 29th 1918.
7) February 3rd 1918.
8) February 6th 1918. Blessed leak, the wet weather.
9) Taiyibeh, Tyiber in Dewi's itinerary.

in rough and hilly country, the objectives were achieved within two days. Jericho, 13 miles north east of Jerusalem, was taken on February 21st by the Australian Light Horse Brigade, who also cleared the plain west of the Jordan for six miles north of the town. At the same time, the New Zealand Brigade occupied the Turkish base on the Dead Sea. Further moves east, and a link with Feisal's Army to the south east, which was advancing from its base at Aqaba and attacking the Hejaz railway, would now become possible. The next advance was ordered on March 8th. The objective given to the 53rd was the 3,318 ft. stronghold of Tell Asur, the highest point in Judaea and a position the enemy would be sure to cling to tenaciously. "The effort to move forward was tremendous. The succession of high rocky ridges and deep valleys contained many places where men must hoist themselves up or lower themselves down, and, as was afterwards discovered, the conformation of the ground frequently confined troops to one ledge on which the enemy could concentrate his fire. Roads had to be made in feverish haste for the artillery so that the infantry might not move beyond the support of their fire; and also to bring up food and water for the troops."[10] The enemy forces were now also under new command, General Liman von Sanders, whom British forces had first encountered in Gallipoli, replacing von Falkenhayn on March 1st. The battle started on the morning of March 9th, with the Herefordshires and the Royal Welch Fusiliers instructed by Mott to capture Tell Asur from the east, "a steep, rocky hill" according to one officer's account, "going straight up out of the valley at its foot". Its other side was the edge of a high plateau.[11] The leading battalions began their advance at 2 am, with the prospect of a tiring trek over the rocky lower hills even before they engaged with the enemy. Fog intervened to hamper operations and make visual signaling between units impossible but Tell Asur was taken by the 5th Royal Welch Fusiliers, who were relieved by the 6th, only to be driven off by a Turkish counter-attack before regaining it later. Other hills were similarly captured and lost and then re-taken in heavy fighting, with neighbouring Chipp Hill the scene of some of the heaviest action and most determined resistance. Fighting continued until March 12th, by which time the British line had advanced north-east beyond Tell Asur to Abu Fela, its new occupants giving its points new names evocative of home – Cardiff Hill, Rock Park and Beachey Head among them. Other divisions captured important positions at Abu Tellul, Wadi Jib, Wadi Ballut and Ras el Ain to extend the line further.[12]

The next task was to clear the Turks from Ghoraniyeh, a Jordan crossing 15 miles north of the Dead Sea on the Jericho to Es Salt road. This was achieved on March 23rd, enabling the 60th Division to cross on three new bridges that were quickly built and to occupy Es Salt situated on a steep escarpment on the road to Amman east of the Jordan. Australian mounted troops were instructed to carry out raids on Amman, at the time only a modestly-sized town 30 miles from Jericho on both the Pilgrims' Road to Jerusalem and the Hejaz railway. Allenby himself described the country beyond the Jordan leading to Amman as flat and marshy for a mile leading to a clay ridge, beyond which was scrub and numerous wadis. For the first five miles the total rise was 500 ft., climbing, however, over the next 12 miles to 3,500 ft. until the edge of the plateau of Moab, east of the Dead Sea, is reached.

10) Dudley Ward, p190.
11) Ibid, p195.
12) Wadi Deir Ballut separated Judaea from Samaria in Biblical times.

Amman itself lay in a cultivated plain, extending some 12 miles west and four miles northwest of the town, intersected by deep wadis that were difficult to cross. The attack on Amman on March 28th was successfully resisted, however, by the 4,000 strong defending force, and with Turkish reinforcements arriving from the north, a decision to retire west of the Jordan was taken, leaving only the bridgehead at Ghoraniyeh. Troops were withdrawn, too, from Es Salt. The Turkish withdrawal of troops for the defence of Amman, however, meant Arab forces were able to cut large sections of the railway line north and south of Maan 135 miles southwest of Amman. The raids also obliged the Turks to maintain forces east of the river because of uncertainty as to where the next British assaults would take place.

Further Advance

The advance north and east had required the laying of further communications links over some of the most difficult country the division had yet encountered, and Dewi found himself plucked from his indoor job, though not entirely unwillingly. A letter home at the end of February describes how he has been shifted from his responsibilities as "charwoman" and no longer enjoyed its privileges and easy hours. His new tasks have much more excitement attached, however. "You bet, I was terribly cut up about getting the poke from that job and the unkindest cut of all was getting shoved back in the office. That just about killed my pig, you may imagine. I didn't stay there long tho', thank heavens, and soon clicked for another job at which I still exercise my skill. It's not bad y'know – bit stiff at times, mind, but suits me down to the ground. You see, it's out in the open air all day laying cable, and another day repairing cable for a change. Some fun, too, laying cable through the villages, climbing up on trees, roofs of houses, shoving up poles and burying the cable where it crosses the roads – not half bad, don't mind it at all. Plenty of pick, shovel and hammer work. (!) If I ever forget how to work a key when I come home, I can easy apply for a job in the engineer's department now 'cos climbing forty foot poles etc. will be child's play after this little lot."[13]

Dewi's log reports his leaving Ramallah on March 2nd for Beitin, Rummon, and Tyiber, which he reached on March 8th, the day the battle of Tell Asur began. A day later he was in Dayr Ibzi, then at Advanced Brigade Headquarters on March 11th, and back in Beitin on March 13th. "Had a deuce of a job on a few days ago, tho' – Phew! I never did, not in all my blooming natural – 'twasn't half a holiday, I don't think. We couldn't take a cable wagon to the lines, 'cos the country was too rough and had to carry those blessed drums for miles, laying out by hand, so you can just guess what it was like. We went out on horseback so far and carried on on foot from there. As for the country, well – Gee Whiz! you never saw anything like it in Wales, Switzerland or Italy. Great, big, rocky hills, and steep ravines, dropping down sheer for hundreds of feet. I think I have liked us unto 'Alpines' before in one of my missives but, By George! this stunt beats anything I've yet come across. Imagine us crawling up the sides and hanging on to those sides of the ravines like flies – couldn't even take mules there, and I doubt whether a blooming goat would escape breaking his neck there. They are real Highlands in every sense of the word

13) February 27th 1918.

and the only way I can account for the fact of 'our boys' – y bechgyn dewr [the brave boys] – shifting Johnny Turk from there is that they have inherited some of the old hill-fighting art from their ancestors of Owain Glyndwr's day who were such adepts at the game, what say you, Dad? If you ever see the *Daily Sketch* nowadays, p'raps you have admired the vivid manner in which that chap Matania (I think that's his name) draws those pictures of the Italians hauling up guns by hand over beetling precipices.[14] Well, all I can say is that the Isonzo isn't the only place where that happens.[15] Pretty tough on the whole, and I may tell you that I very often wish I was back on the old desert again, where everything is, for the most part, at any rate, as flat as a pancake.(!) Hope it won't be like this all the way we go, 'cos it won't be any joke climbing up and down those places with a blessed pack weighing you down – B-r-r-! not 'arf." The exploits of the Italians, as portrayed by their London-based fellow-countryman, had no doubt thrilled the British public, keen for tales of heroic deeds of derring-do by their allies. The Italians had been drawn into the war in 1915 as both sides brought pressure on neutrals to join in. Persuaded by secret offers of Austrian territory down the Dalmatian coast and of Turkish territory, Italy had forsaken its alliance with the Central Powers and declared war on Austria in May 1915. Twelve battles were fought at Isonzo between June 1915 and November 1917, as the Italians pursued the dream of their commander, Field Marshal Luigi Cadorna, of breaking through into the Slovenian plateau, taking Ljubljana and threatening Vienna. As an example of just how difficult were the conditions the 53rd encountered, the division's historian cites the experience of a Field Artillery Battery which took 36 hours to cover a distance of only eight miles on the map to reach the village of Neby Musa. According to other reports, the rocky hillside was so steep the sole task of some men was to support others drilling holes for blasting.

As usual, he is rueful but resigned at the impositions being placed upon him. "I think the last letter I was guilty of proved to be nothing more or less than a prolonged harangue bemoaning the fact of our having been given the poke from our comfortable billet to experience once more the exquisite delights of bivouacking on a bleak and barren hillside amidst these benighted Judean highlands in the month of March – B-r- r! specially at nights.[16] Well, the very next morning, after writing that letter, observe me parading in full marching order in the pale uncertain light of dawn, feeling highly indignant and not the slightest particle enamoured with this rude interruption of my beauty sleep, the pulling down of our bivvy, and all this apparently unnecessary hustling. As for my corporal – well, as far as he was concerned, I felt in a particularly murderous mood for was it not he that had come up to me shouting, 'Dewi – Dewi, come on, rise and shine, my lucky lad – we move off in 20 minutes'. You see, I am a firm believer in that good old motto 'Deffro, mae'n ddydd' [Awake, it is day]'mae'n wyth o'r gloch' [it's eight o'clock] for preference, like, you know, and any contradiction of that motto, such as in this case, 'Deffro cyn y wawr', [Awake, before the dawn] – well, makes me feel most terribly

14) February 27th 1918. Born in Naples, Fortunino Matania, (1881-1963) established himself through the pages of *Illustration Française* before being invited to cover the 1902 coronation of Edward VII for *The Graphic*. He covered many royal events over the years for *The Sphere* and was hailed as one of the finest World War One artists.

15) The Battles of the Isonzo were fought along the 60 mile long River of the same name on the eastern sector of the Italian Front from June 1915 to November 1917. Most were fought on the territory of modern Slovenia, the remainder in Italy.

16) March 23rd 1918.

bored, what? However, to continue – observe us then flitting away on the wagons at that unearthly hour lock, stock and barrel, rations, water, all dressed up, in fact, and somewhere in Palestine to go to. "Your humble, if you look closely, you will easily recognise in that half-awake looking individual seated amidships, in the act of lighting one of your own very excellent Gold Flakes, as a desperate attempt to stave off ennui, donchaknow. You will notice I was most particular to mention for your benefit that I was seated amidships – for a very obvious reason, for, you see, I still remain true to my character as Jack of all trades and have consequently been appointed to the very responsible post of official brakesman on our wagon, who, in addition, as you perhaps know, has charge of the winding gear, clutch, chains, wheels and drums on those mysterious chariots which are to be seen in various parts of the universe employed on that ridiculously complicated business of cable-laying in the field."

After a long and very rough passage, which "would leave those unused to such trips decidedly saddle-sore", they come to a halt. Their trek, he reports, had taken them over boulder-strewn hills and valleys, precipices and chasms, wadis "which you might fancy would surely defy the most intrepid cinema actors, Alpine climbers or even goats, much less a cable wagon where all hands hang on by their very eyebrows to prevent being hurled to destruction or washed overboard". There was relief in arriving, however, at what he describes as his "ancestral home". This is the 159th brigade, "the un cant pum deg a naw, where we off-saddled and had a dixie merrily in no time – O! the joy of these al fresco breakfasts."[17] The interlude, however, was brief, – the battle for Tell Asur is soon joined. "That very afternoon the boys moved out and our old wagon moved thro' the Welsh battalion paying out cable for dear life long after dark.[18] I expect you can guess what's coming now – it was Heigh-ho! for another little stunt, and, thought we to ourselves, another little stunt won't do us any harm. We came to the end of our tether at a little village without a soul about at somewhere near 10 p.m. and, the job done, sat us down to await events. 'Twasn't long either, before they did happen and soon you could hear a faint rattle of equipment, as the shadowy figures of 'Y bechgyn dewr' [the brave boys] crept silently into view behind the hill. On they came scores upon scores of 'em boding no good for old Johnny – he couldn't have had the foggiest notion of what was in store for him. Round in front of the village they filed and Biff!! Rattle!! Bang!!! it started – Blimey! didn't half give 'em socks, the blighters. It lasted four days and after chasing Johnny Turk 12 miles approx we've stopped for a rest. Not bad eh? Strewth! they know who's top dog out here, don't you worry. Didn't half have our work cut out during those days either 'cos, you see, we had to leave the old wagon behind miles away 'cos of the country, – Gee Whiz! worst country yet, believe me, great big hills, covered with boulders and deep wadis and 'twas a sight to behold to see us slipping, sliding and stumbling all over the blessed [place], reeling out cable behind the old pack mule – advancing ever advancing. They fairly blew the blighters out of those hills and as they got up to run our boys let 'em have it thick and heavy in the rear. The pace was fast and furious, I can tell you – first they can't half hop it, and then, of course, they're in the soup again, 'cos the boys on our gee-gees canter after 'em then. – O! it is a game, and we naturally feel highly elated after this big success again."[19]

---

17) Though the sequence is hard to reconstruct, cable-laying operations appear to have brought them up to the front line, close to the troops about to engage in the Battle of Tell Asur.

18) He had moved on March 11th to Advanced Brigade Headquarters.

19) March 23rd 1918.

They were clearly close enough to the enemy at this stage for the two sides to taunt each other and Dewi seems himself to have shared the feelings of his comrades for their opponents, with comments perhaps understandable from the pen of a 20 year old by now keen just to get home but also to tell his readers there were real fights going on – and against German as well as Turkish troops. "When the Welsh got to business they were greeted with shouts of 'Come on you, Welsh so and so, and so and so, not Turks this time, you got Germans'. And so it was, too, there was a plentiful sprinkling of those vermin in front of us but that only made those mad, reckless, splendid Welsh madder than ever and those Huns ran even faster than old Johnny. Y'see they can't skulk in concrete dug-outs out here – it's all plain fair and above board hill-scrapping and they *don't* like that – not they. When they see the Welsh coming up over the hill like cats from stone to stone, with the sun playing on those shining little things, it's either 'Kamarad', 'Allah!, Allah!!' or a sprint towards Constantinople. I simply have to tell you all about this, 'cos the glorious old 53rd gave 'em of their best and you know what that's like – bless 'em. Proud of 'em? – why there's nobody to touch 'em. Anyhow, they're wonderful, they're marvels, they're Welsh! If I had my way I'd give 'em all a V.C. and a 1,000 piastre's worth in the canteen. However, directly after the dirty work was done we were relieved and I have been terribly busy engaged in that pleasant pastime of picking up all our cable. Blooming hard work and, worst of all, the blessed weather broke again and it simply poured down. When it pours here you can betcher life it does pour some, and there we were washed out of house and home – or rather bivvy – out on those blessed hills trying to pick up blooming cable thro seas of mud and lakes of rain water. Gee Whiz, it was! it was a rough time, believe me, 'cos the blessed wagon was over its axles in mud and water, the horses floundering about, the winding gear choked up and in consequence us poor blighters had to wade thro' it all and wind up [the cables] by hand."

After a few days working in poor weather and difficult terrain, they returned to their bivvies to sleep in wet and muddy blankets. One of the officers seems to have decided enough was enough and a halt was temporarily called to further cable retrieval expeditions. On March 17th they return to their former quarters in Ramallah. "I'll never forget my triumphant entry into that billet – back to the old room and the old boys again. I was a sight, and no mistake, mud from head to foot – inches thick and soaked right thro'. You wouldn't believe what a delicious experience it is to go under a roof in shelter again. I really can't describe it, never had a dry thing to my name, my blankets and clothes dripping wet. But, there again, what a thing it is to have pals – real pals – one gave me shorts, as a dry rig-out, another shoved Maconochie into my hand, and hot at that, and another feller boiled up some 'café' and last, and finally, I got in between dry warm blankets with my old sleeping pardner. I couldn't have thanked 'em if I'd tried – if ever a chap was grateful it was this chicken – O! the joy, the utter deliciousness of being in a dry bed feeling as warm as toast."[20]

He is soon, he tells his parents, no longer a miserable, desperate, weather-beaten ruffian but a smarter sapper, fit to grace parade ground, or even a ball room, at a pinch, none the worse for the recent picnic and feeling tophole, thanks, despite

20) March 23rd 1918. Sleeping pardner, cigarettes.

what he is sure his mother might be fearing. "Remarkable how we recover, is it not? No, Mum I cannot lie and regret to have to confess that it was utterly impossible to air shirts and chest protectors during that period but don't you worry your head about that – doesn't have the slightest effect on me, y'know – think I'm pretty tough now, anyway. However, we're having a pretty quiet time now, and am using up my spare time getting off answers to that pile of letters, which I am hoping against hope to get finished some time or other. Yes, a quiet time but, nevertheless, very busy – repairing cable for all we're worth – miles and miles of the blamed stuff. So, you can bet, since we're at it all day, what spare moments I do get are very scanty. Anyhow, I feel sure of your pardon for not writing before and know that you quite understand – it has been really impossible amidst all the recent hustle, and that if I could possibly have managed it, I certainly would have done so. I hope in the near future to be able to write more regularly and oftener, 'cos it's practically a dead cert that we go down on the plain for a fairly long rest shortly. About time, too, I should think, seeing that the poor 'Invincibles' have been in the line since last October without a blooming break – the only ones that haven't had a rest yet, 'cos you see they simply can't do without us. Think of it – canteens, football, concerts and plenty of time to write – By Jove! won't it be glorious? You can just bet we'll give it socks after this." The weather remained changeable, however. "After the recent storm we have had a spell of a few days of glorious sunshine but now again yesterday and today it has rained intermittently all day, which makes us thankful to be in billets, I can tell you. I fear sometimes, in fact, that it's making us somewhat soft – luxurious blighters, y'know. I thought March would see us well out of the rainy season but so far, anyway, we have had a rude shock and it certainly doesn't look very hopeful. I s'pose it's these blooming hills, they are the cause of all the trouble but once we are down on the plains for that rest over Jaffa way it'll be all merry and bright – don't get much rain there, they say, and it's fine and warm."[21]

A few weeks later, with 159th Brigade at Hadeitha, a village further to the west in Wadi Ballut, five miles north east of Ramle, close to the Jerusalem to Jaffa road, the immediate need for cable-laying had ceased, and Dewi found himself once again looking after animals. "I now hold the responsible and horribly arduous job of groom to the corporal's nag – a dear fine old bay – Patsy by name and quietly Irish by nature.[22] In fact, he'll follow me about all over the show, rubbing his old nose on my shoulder, pricking up his ears if I just come by and whisper 'Patsy, – Patsy old man.' So, you can bet he knows me some – all this may, it be said, to the amusement of our wagon crew – in fact the corporal swears I feed him on oranges – anyhow, he gets all the peel. Naturally, I take him for water twice a day with the rest and, as it's a long way to the troughs at the farm and we're only eighty men, all of which have either a pair of mules or a horse apiece, we do have a gorgeous time on those rides."[23] The weather has taken a more decided turn for the better, now Spring has arrived. "You will be pleased to know that at last mud and rain and cold are but the memory of a horrid nightmare and lately we have been treated to the old kind of weather – the stuff I'm used to and pine for, if I can't get it – a glorious, scorching, blinding sun in a perfectly cloudless sky of azure blue and the nights typically, splendidly Eastern, with myriads of magic stars and scarcely a puff of air

21) March 23rd 1918.
22) Bay, a reddish-brown horse.
23) April 14th 1918.

– no wonder my heart rejoices, I can't do without it – it takes me back to Egypt and the mysterious grandeur of the desert, which, when I come to think of it, wasn't so bad after all. I feel satisfied, content and more at home in this and khaki drill shorts and shirtsleeves, for we've had our summer clothing. Gee! wasn't I glad to climb out of breeches and a rotten old sage tunic, which always seemed to cramp and stifle me. Guess we're all serene now, everything in the garden is superb. Your conjecture as to my whereabouts, you see, were somewhat wide of the mark. Although some of our boys were out Jericho way, Frank's lot, however (including, of course, your humble) were rather busy elsewhere, helping 'em on their left – indeed we had a good view of the Dead Sea, that dark, forbidding waste of water of evil repute, so you can imagine we weren't very, very far away. Indeed, I am not at all cut up at not seeing that place, Jericho – by all accounts it is a dreadful hole, and, being on a level with the Dead Sea, is unbearably hot, enough to stifle one."[24] Others seem to have found Jericho more amenable. Contemporary reports describe white and yellow daisies and scarlet poppies, partridges nesting and nearly tame storks, the scent of orange blossom, and plentiful water from little streams making their way to the Jordan.[25]

Brass Hats and Bungled Leave

By April of 1918 his letters, though still enthusiastic, particularly about the japes they get up to in periods of enforced idleness, are also interspersed with a few bitter remarks about the ways of the Army brass-hats. In particular, it would seem men in his own unit were fed up with leave promised and cancelled, and prepared even to decline what they seem to have regarded as not very serious offers. Wearied by their very busy stay in the wet and bleak Judaean hills, they had been buoyed by rumours in March of a rest on the plain at Ludd. "There was a general feeling [of] scepticism in the air and injured innocence at having our legs pulled in this unmerciful fashion. Little did I think at the time that such an event would ever happen, and, if it did, that it would prove such a ludicrous fiasco. [...] Imagine our amazed delight, then, not so very long ago, at having our fondest hope come true and being ordered to pack up. There was no doubt whatever about it this time – the old division were going to enjoy the fruits of their many weary months of hard toil, and rest as hard as they could. Far away from the maddening crowd and those rotten hills, we'd loll and bask in the sun, at peace with all the world, and well content to remain undisturbed, to make the most, and enjoy every moment, of that hard-earned sweet repose. Two days' trek, and we arrived – two days trek down and down – always downhill with all breaks [brakes] on for hours at a stretch, and reached our destination, the plains. What a delightful change it was after months of no better landscape than those greyish-brown rocky ridges I will leave you to imagine. The sight of these stretches of green fields and cultivated areas, dotted about with farms, and, here and there, clusters of trees resplendent, clothed in spring-time foliage, was positively soothing to the eyes and balm to our tortured feelings, when we thought of those dark, frowning, sombre hard hills. This was enough reward in itself for our recent gruelling, and I should have been quite content, if a short stay in that smiling countryside had been our only relaxation, and I hied me away in my imagination to the fields and woods of the happy Vale of

181

24) The 158th had moved from Jerusalem to Jericho.
25) Dudley Ward, p204.

Glamorgan, the better to drink in its beauty."[26] This was not the only charm held out by the prospect. The men were looking forward, too, he writes, to being able to relax, have better food and entertainment. "Much as I was in sympathy with the author of those words, 'O! to be in England (preferably Wales, of course), now that April's there', I was bound to admit that there were heaps worse places than this overseas idyll of spring.[27] What a narrative I should be able to write, which would stir your imagination to the extent of enjoying with me this glad, joyful holiday. The tales of Rugger Cup-ties I should have been able to unfold, and the anything but reticent communiqués regarding these new and wonderful performances of our 'Welsh Rarebits'[28] I should have been delighted to dwell upon – the canteen stores I should have given a better home, with which I was to aid my vivid imagination and sharpen my wits in order to paint you this brightest of pictures."

The scene he paints is, of course, the opposite of what happened. "O! it was indeed too good to be believed – Dame Fortune had never smiled upon us so sweetly. She, being a woman and so, full of whims – capricious to the core, like the rest of her sex, I might have known something was going to happen. Indeed, I felt a restless gnawing fear at the time that some ugly catastrophe was imminent and that we should fall victims to that whimsical streak in her nature. How shall I deserve it? – what need is there to cause myself unnecessary torture by recalling such bitter memories, which would be far better left alone, forgotten, buried in the special receptacle of my mind, reserved for the interment of past incidents such as this – sad, cruel, and unutterably rude awakenings. I cannot, however, but admire the lady's subtle, villainous sense of humour in a grudging kind of way – it attracts me in something the same manner as the most repulsive, sordid thing attracts one's attention. She chose a most appropriate day for the foul deed – and the more I think of it the more uncanny it seems – the more it savours of the occult. March 31st we arrived for the 'rest' – our 'der tag' believe me, and she beamed on us.[29] And we, like unsuspecting, blithering idiots, basked in her smile, like children off for a treat, full of her praises. April 1st …Forgive a strong man's weeping – p'raps in pronouncing it you realise how ominous and forbidding that date sounds – April 1st – Heaven help me to forget it – and she frowned darkly and terribly – we were out of favour and found, ourselves, after only one night's stay, packing up to go back where we came from again. What a beastly rotten sell it was – could you possibly imagine anything half so maddening? Gosh! It was a proper knock-out blow – fairly left us gasping for breath and in a complete trance. Don't you think it's just the cruellest practical joke – the hugest, meanest hoax ever played on All Fools' Day? Can you wonder at us feeling rather desperate and nearly bubbling over with justified rage? What a pack of prize fools they did make us look, to be sure, the rotters. What benefit can it possibly afford anyone, I should like to know, by heaping ridicule upon the heads of us poor innocents? Anyhow, it only just goes to prove that there's no other boys like our little rascals to scrap in those blamed hills – simply can't do without the old 'Fighting 53rd – the flower of the British Army – second to none.'"

26) April 14th 1918.

27) 'Oh, to be in England, now that April's here', a line from *Home Thoughts from Abroad*, poem by Robert Browning (1812-1879).

28) The *Welsh Rarebits* were a concert party founded by Cardiff-born musician, band leader and impresario, Wally Bishop, who served with the RAMC in the Middle East. Bishop continued his career after the war as a cinema musician, until the talkies made his job redundant. Known as Cardiff's Mr Music, he survived the Great Depression by forming an orchestra from out of work musicians, Waldini and his Gypsy Band, who played daily in the city's Roath Park, dressed in Romany outfits.

29) Der tag, the day.

On his return from their abortive trip to the plains, the reason for which lay in less than favourable developments on the Western Front, Dewi is placed on Brigade duties in Hadeitha. He is separated again from the companions he had enjoyed being with over the past few months but he remains cheerful. "So they've gone back – at least most of 'em – over the hills and goodness knows where, wherever they are. I want to be there, too – guess I'm an old member of that glorious brave old family and don't feel at home away from 'em, somehow. I want to hear the question "Shwd mae heddi, iawn?" [How's it today, All right?] and the grinning reply "Fel y jawl bachen" [Like the devil, boy] – that's music to me, you betcher life. Unfortunately, however, our old wagon never went with the majority but got left behind with Frankie's lot and are still over this side. We have moved, of course, it wouldn't be us if we hadn't, and are now sitting tight till any old thing crops up to demand our presence. Funny thing, but altho' idle, we don't give way to despair during this time hanging on our hands and never show an inclination to brood over the recent most regrettable misfortune. Nunno, we're a queer set and can – would you believe it – by now actually laugh at the way our legs have been pulled. Downhearted? Fed up? – 'Strewth! norrabitofit – take more than a measly old rest missed to make these fellers sulk. Like a lot of sandboys – don't care tuppence if it snows green bluebottles. Philosophical? – why yes – By Jove! this is the finest training school for philosophy in the whole wild world, Dad, and we're all unconsciously industrious students."

Even after this charade the Army continues to raise hopes. Dewi goes on to describe how the day before his letter, names were taken for Blighty leave. "As another irresistible humourist remarked, since this is only about the umpteenth time they've done it so far, it won't' do us any good but it certainly won't do us any harm, so we'll just humour the powers-that-be – kid 'em on we're biting again. Of course, sometimes we turn round on them and enjoy having them for a change, same as one Welsh battalion who were recently offered leave to Cairo. 'Any chance of going home for a change?' they queried very politely. 'O! no – I'm afraid' – 'then blow Cairo, sell it to someone else,' and they didn't go either. Very well, they took their advice and did try to sell it somewhere else. Unfortunately, everyone took the Welsh lead and refused also to purchase – same reason. Independent? – not 'arf – you see we still have some slight self-respect left, even tho' we don't part our hair in the middle now this ages. It'll come round again in all probability, and why – then they'll all decide there's no harm in seeing civilisation again and they'll take advantage of the offer to visit that city – come back broke to the wide, p'raps, but never broken spirits. 'Course, as you say, it would be very nice if I happened to be one of the lucky 'repatriated' ones – it's a long time since, as you might say. Anyhow, to tell you the truth, I'm not exactly pinning my faith to such a scheme – guess it's only a joke of Sir A. Geddes, after all – I'll be mighty surprised if anything comes of it."[30] Besides, he writes, even if he did have such luck, he would look a prize ass on a circuit in the Instrument Room. "A linen collar, shot tie fancy socks, and my hair plentifully besprinkled with Anzoic, and parted in the middle, clean, polished boots, a snowy white handkerchief, cuffs, gold links and a button-hole, sitting down on the Glasgow duplex with some fragile flower of a fair maid, trying to be painfully polate [sic] and sounds my aitches – dear Heaven – what a catastrophe."[31]

---

30) Sir Auckland Geddes, appointed Britain's director of recruitment in 1916.

31) April 14th 1918. Glasgow Duplex, a system by which one telegraph wire transmits messages both ways; Anzoic, possibly a hair dressing; shot, silk.

He is soon back where he wants to be with his closest pals. "You have no doubt by now received my last containing the news of the great "April 1st Rest Hoax" and of my being with Frank's brigade over on the other side away from the division. [...] We were all greatly relieved about a week ago to receive our marching orders. March we did, and now after a few days trek right back across country we find ourselves once more amongst the hills with the old div. So, I'm perfectly satisfied now – everything in the garden is lovely now we're back with the boys and, please heaven, they don't send us on any more farce rests. That's all we ask."[32] He had spent two and a half weeks with Brigade in Hadeitha in early April, moving on April 19th to Rentis, then on the following day back to Hadeitha, followed by Latrun and Ain Duk, north of Jericho, to a location identified only as Home Counties Road, which they reached on April 25th. The task assigned to the 159th during this period had been to protect the right flank of the 75th Division as part of a plan to win new positions further north covering Nablus and Tulkeram. In the event the attack, which was to be carried out by the XXIst Corps, was cancelled, partly because of unexpected opposition but also because of events in France. Extra divisions needed to be sent to France and would be substituted with Indian Divisions. They remained at their new location until May 8th when they moved to Ain Sinia, 20 miles north of Jerusalem. Allenby had already been told in February that because of manpower requirements in France British troops would be replaced partly by Indian units. On March 23rd after the success of the German Spring offensive on the Western Front he was ordered to release one British division and a few days later to substitute a policy of active defence for the offensive previously planned to drive the Turks out of the whole of Palestine and their other Near Eastern possessions. Unbeknown to the men this was the reason for the sudden cancellation of their leave on April Fool's Day. The 52nd Division from the XXIst Corps and the 74th from the XXth were chosen for France. The EEF itself was re-organised as an Indian Force, its supplies henceforward to come from the sub-Continent and, therefore, less liable to attack by German submarines.

Always happy to look on the bright side, Dewi writes in late April to say he is glad, despite all the hardships of laying cable a month or so earlier, to be back in the hills, declaring that the plains did not suit them. "The sun was very nice, of course, to start off with but, By Jove! it got to be positively stifling – no air, you understand. So, that's why we're so glad to be where the breezes blow a little, up here on high. The weather still continues to be delightfully warm and this suits us absolutely down to the ground and no mistake – it's a real treat after that horrible mud, which I abhor. Things are pretty quiet now, too, and we're not having a hard time at all – just carrying on easy, like, cable-repairing and fatigues, the jobs we love (?) [sic]."[33] A further trans-Jordan raid was carried out in May, to divert the Turks' attention from the coastal plain where Allenby's final offensive was planned and, more immediately, to destroy Turkish forces south of Es Salt. The operation would also seize the grain harvest and gain summer bivouacs for the men, out of the stifling Jordan Valley heat.[34] Es Salt was again taken briefly but evacuated when the position of the troops there was considered to be dangerous. The raid was a tactical failure but the wider plan had succeeded again. One third of Turkish forces were henceforward always kept east of the Jordan.[35]

32) April 29th 1918.
33) April 29th 1918.
34) Pritchard, (ed.), p359.
35) Ibid, p361.

Dribs and Drabs of Mail

Despite his reassurances that he remains "philosophical", and the disappointments of leave denied, war-weariness was clearly beginning to affect Dewi. By early 1918 – by which time he had been away from home for more than two and a half years, resentment seems to have been building up, not only at the boredom and futility of much of what they were being called upon to do but at the lack of understanding and respect back home for their efforts. His mother seems to have been worried that he was suffering from the "blues", which he is keen to deny, but he ends with a pointed reference to a comment his father had made that the old "Indomitables" [the 53rd] were getting the praise and encouragement they deserved in Britain, presumably after their success at Jerusalem. "They deserve it, too, more than anyone at home will ever know – especially those that think that, France and only France, is the solitary instance of hell upon earth. I shall be proud – aye, more than that, to my dying day that I was with the Llanelly and Pontypridd boys when three divisions of the "blighters" [the Turks] were turned loose upon 'em and failed miserably to break thro'. Proud, Dad? By Jove, yes. They are splendid and glorious. God bless 'em, God rest 'em."[36]

The irregularity of the mail and the poor Army food cannot have helped, so the better fare while at Ramallah in February would have been welcome. Letters often took months to arrive and were not always in the order they were sent. "The mails at this end, of course, have also been most exasperatingly scarce, coming in, in dribs and drabs fashion, calculated to make the most philosophical of us almost lose heart. They are, however, [...] improving hand over fist of late – Huzza! for that, say I – and will, I sincerely hope, gradually and very soon return to their normal and regular condition. F'rinstance, I am getting (and everyone is just the same, of course) letters dated in the beginning of January one mail and those dated somewhere in December by the next. It cannot be helped, I suppose, the dumps further down the line must be in a terribly neglected state. During a spell of fine weather (which we do get now and again, a few days at a time) they are able to send up as much as possible and get rid of the outgoing letters to a certain extent. But when the rain comes again, well, things are practically at a standstill once more – camel convoys are [...] anything but an ideal postal service. If you could only see them moving you would understand and, of course, not being used to wet and cold, they are painfully useless under such conditions." Even if the more personal items – such as toothbrushes, combs, books or socks – were retained by the intended recipient, food was generally shared with the other men in the same tent or bivouac. He writes appreciatively to Doris of a parcel just received, "Shall I ever really be able to make you understand the feelings of delight and exquisite joy in which I opened that bundle of delicacies? It was dated November 14th and its totally unexpected arrival, combined with the sheer joy I experienced, was almost too much – it overwhelmed me. A thousand thanks from me and all the rest of the room – 17 very grateful sappers and drivers who thought that pudding the very best they'd ever tasted. You see, that's the first we'd had this year, and we made that dinner a regular red letter affair, believe me."[37]

---

36) January 29th 1918. The then spelling of Llanelli, the tinplate-producing and rugby-playing town in Carmarthenshire.
37) February 6th 1918.

The exaggerated words of gratitude he offers suggest food was almost always in short supply, given the difficulties of ensuring provisions kept up with the advance. "There was resentment, too, that soliders in France were receiving Christmas treats, as he explains when a parcel brings him a Christmas pudding early in 1918. "Not being entitled, of course, to the half a pound of Xmas pudd'n, which I read in the paper was to be sent to all troops at the *Front*, you may easily imagine we were longing for some to turn up. When it did well – we gave it beans, I give you my word. Five minutes to cut it up and distribute the prizes amongst those ravenous appetites and, you can take it from me, there wasn't a single crumb to be seen anywhere. [...] Never even had time to act upon your suggestion to warm it but scoffed him out of house and home, right swift. Best thanks to your ma, they said – 'Tophole – real goods – O.K. – A1' - and umpteen other expressions which signify that it was, well – absolutely the 'gear'. I can never thank you sufficiently for it, and, altho' it was bully and biscuits for dinner Xmas day, with not a smell of puddin' after it, you can bet your bottom dollar we had an Xmas Dinner the day after the parcel came. [...] "That box of 18 carat biscuits wasn't long either in following the puddin to a good home, you can bet your life. They just melted clean away soon as you shoved your teeth into 'em and they beat those we get as rations into a blessed cocked hat. They don't have a leg to stand on in comparison. Good old Crawford – I back him against those shameful old rascals H & P any day of the week after jerking those toothsome dainties back."[38]

As the advance north continued, food was again scarce, and parcels doubly appreciated, as a fulsome response to one of their dispatches reveals. "Talk about a feed – Tut-tut – it was a feast for the Khedive himself and, anyway, it's only when your parcels arrive I get the chance of a real good blow-out.[39] We haven't seen the likes of canteens for ages – just a little bit now and then – 'nuff to satisfy a sparrow, sort of style, you know. There's only a tin of beef paste left now, he explains, "worse luck, 'cos it all went just as quick as all of 'em do and that'll go, too, for brekker tomorrow morning. You see, we're getting bread now, so it'll just go down A1 on that. 'Bout time, too, – we sure have had our fair share of them hateful H&Ps. Jolly glad I got a decent lot of ivories to tackle 'em, 'cos fellers with false ones don't half cop out – blooming near starve, and got to break 'em up with pliers to nibble at 'em."[40]

After food, Dewi's greatest wish, as we have seen, was for constant supplies of his favourite cigarettes. The Army supplied men with its own issue of cigarettes – Tabs – but these were regarded, as he mentions several times, as very inferior, compared with the leading brands. It is not clear when Dewi started smoking, or even whether he did so before leaving home, but by this time in his Army career he was clearly addicted to these comforters. As he tells his sister in an earlier letter: "As for the fags – well Gosh! You may be sure they're always a bull's-eye. Never need to worry about them not getting a right royal welcome. Gee whiz! – taste like nectar, if fags can possibly taste like that, and smoking these, well, I guess it gives you inspiration to write pages and pages – soothing? – you bet – not 'arf My Lady Nicotine – you see, we quite lose our heads over her – a lady of unlimited allurements. [...] I should send 'em always like this in an airtight tin. They keep O.K. and are much better for it.

38) February 6th 1918. Crawford's and Huntley & Palmer's were rival brands. Dewi seems to have had a particular aversion to the latter, possibly because they produced the hard biscuits that were part of their regular Army diet.

39) Khedive, the name given to Turkish viceroys ruling Egypt from 1867 to 1914. French khédive, from Turkish hidiv, lord.

40) April 29th 1918.

You see, the last lot you sent were not, and had gone slightly mildew, owing to the parcel having been on the way for such a long time. Anyhow, these are the genuine article – absolutely the pure root – the old favourite 'Waverley'. Always takes me by storm.[41] We had café au lait tonight, too, after tea and By Jove! it's A.1 with your rum ration – that's the stuff to give the troops these cold wet nights. The beef paté I shall devour in a most disgusting manner, I fear, for brekker tomorrow morn. It won't be too much with one miserable rasher of fat bacon, you bet. I'll just about scoff that and not turn a hair, 'cos you see we happened to have a full bread ration today – a whole loaf – bit unusual these days – but it'll go O.K. with that paté 'bukra' (sorry, tomorrow, I should have said – you don't savvy Arabic)." The previous month he had given a strong indication of just how desperate they were for cigarettes. "Send socks, blades and scores of *fags* 'cos I'm absolutely starving for a smoke – send couple of hundred quickly, as an Xmas present *please* [triple underline] – don't delay one moment after you've read this – we are in desperate straits and I want to be soothed by my Lady Nicotine – she *is* a stunner, so pack a few tins together right away, dear Dolly, and you'll have my eternal blessing."[42]

There was always the danger parcels might have gone to the bottom of the sea. "Here have I been enduring an ominous silence on your part with most remarkable fortitude (tho' I say it), and in meditative moments consigning 'U' boats and all their ilk to depths far greater than those ever shown on Admiralty charts and confounding their nefarious methods and interference with every breath. What 'yn enw dyn' [in the name of man] had I done to deserve such rotten luck?"[43] In July, however, he is again reporting ecstatically on the latest food parcels he has received from home. "After a pretty annoying time of nixes doin' in the mails I have been rewarded beyond my wildest dreams – a feast of words and (yum-yum) a feast for a king. [...] Well after receiving those two epistles with the pleasing intimation of the despatch of that there cake I just about could think of nothing else and went thro' untold agony in thinking out the chances of it being served up at some Mediterranean piscatorial banquet.[44] Even the salmon I ate for dinner that day grated on me. You see, I was, as it were, at daggers drawn with the whole species. Phew! It's a terrible feeling, I assure you, is that great debate which I so often go through – the "To be or not be – torpedoed" debate I call it, and I feel sure we are four minds but with a single debate very often. Well, next day, dog my cats, if another small consignment didn't come rolling up from the P.O. by limber and they'd scarcely unloaded when your humble, whose hawk-eye (it's always a hawk's eye when mails are kicking around, you betcher bonnet), espies one single, solitary, forlorn, little (only it was big) orphan of a parcel there, which seemed to be shouting out at the top of its voice (fairly bursting would be more appropriate, I think) 'I want to be somebody's baby – likewise joy.' Couldn't see the fateful address on it but I thought to myself, 'If that isn't about the size, build, complexion, figure and general physique of my little old age pension I'm expecting, I'll – well, swipe me, if I don't go to the cookhouse for my tea'. Anyway, after another dekko I chanced me with and politely requested the nearest loafer to be careful in slinging my personal effects across. He obliged and – (well, I didn't spend evenings over the Acres at

41) February 6th 1918.
42) January 4th 1918
43) June 28th 1918.
44) July 27th 1918. Served up at a piscatorial banquet, that is, torpedoed, sunk and eaten by fishes.

baseball without learning how to 'ketchit', you may lay to that).[46] Once within my embrace and Eureka! I'd clicked. – 'Bully for you, kid', says I to my best friend.

His praise for his mother's cooking is again highly exaggerated but no doubt served the purpose of encouraging her to continue baking for him. "Of all the gorgeous, tophole, 18 carat, first water, absolutely *in*-comparable triumphs of the culinary art, this is IT – without the least shadow of a doubt I never tasted such a sublime morsel in all my blessed puff. [...] *Some* cake that, my oath, and some appetite to deal with it, too – why I'd scoffed half of it before you could say knife. You never got that recipe from 'a country gentlewoman', like it says on the sauce bottles. I know that's your very own. 'Strewth! It's worth something, too – don't sell it 'cos I've altered my one ambition in life now from joining the Force to come home and eat your iced cakes one a day ad finitum [sic]. "Mum, you're a peach – you take the palm, the bouquets, the laurel wreaths, the daisy chains – in fact all the Royal Horticultural Shows rolled into one. I've never forgotten that iced cake I had just a year ago but, strike me awkward, this 'un beats it into a cocked hat abso-entirely-utely. Of all the bricks, Mum, you're the brickest. [...]. Here's looking at you – champion gold medallist and platinum diploma studded with diamonds holder for second to none masterpieces of palate-tickling confections."

While the British were successfully bringing their campaign in the Middle East to an end, the battle in Europe remained on a knife edge. In Russia, the Bolsheviks having assumed power negotiated a peace treaty with the Central Powers on March 3rd followed two days later by Romania. The Germans started their great offensive on the Western Front two weeks later, prompting the C-in-C, Haig, to issue a Special Order of the Day – the famous "backs to the wall" order – to troops in France on April 12th. This urged the British Army to 'fight it out' to the end, and stated that the war's victor would be "the side which holds out the longest".[47] On April 14th the Allied Armies were put under the unified command of the French Marshal, Ferdinand Foch. The German offensive was halted and ultimately turned back at the second battle of the Marne in July, inflicting such damage as ultimately to bring about Germany's defeat.

46) Baseball, the British version played in leagues in public parks in Cardiff, Newport and Liverpool. Ketchit, catch it.

47) The text stated: 'Three weeks ago to-day the enemy began his terrific attacks against us on a fifty-mile front. His objects are to separate us from the French, to take the Channel Ports and destroy the British Army. In spite of throwing already 106 Divisions into the battle and enduring the most reckless sacrifice of human life, he has as yet made little progress towards his goals. We owe this to the determined fighting and self-sacrifice of our troops. Words fail me to express the admiration which I feel for the splendid resistance offered by all ranks of our Army under the most trying circumstances. Many amongst us now are tired. To those I would say that Victory will belong to the side which holds out the longest. The French Army is moving rapidly and in great force to our support. There is no other course open to us but to fight it out. Every position must be held to the last man: there must be no retirement. With our backs to the wall and believing in the justice of our cause each one of us must fight on to the end. The safety of our homes and the freedom of mankind alike depend upon the conduct of each one of us at this critical moment.'
(Signed) D. Haig, F.M., Commander-in-Chief British Armies in France.

(above) Bivouacs – temporary shelters built into the side of the hills – on the campaign in Judaea.

(left) Cable wagon. Lines were reeled off to link forward positions with headquarters further back.

General Otto Liman von Sanders, the doughty opponent encountered by Allied forces on Gallipoli and later in Palestine. Bundesarchiv Bild 183 R02991

General Sir Edmund Allenby, leader of the British and Allied forces that drove the Ottoman forces out of their possessions in the Near East.
National Portrait Gallery

1914 – 1915 Star and ribbon awarded to men who had served in any theatre between August 1914 and December 1915.

CHAPTER NINE

VICTORY AT MEGIDDO

MAY – NOVEMBER 1918?

Back in the Hills

Over the months of April and May the EEF forces were re-organised, as divisions were transferred to France to counter the big German offensive launched on the Western Front on March 21st. Like the other divisions in the XXth and XXIst Corps, the 53rd would be re-constituted with Indian brigades to replace those sent away. Early in April the XXIst Corps was ordered to drive through Turkish defences near Jiljulieh and push the British line further forward. The 159th Brigade, now made up of the 4th and 5th battalions of the Welch Regiment, (a unit recruited mainly in south Wales) and two Indian infantry battalions, was tasked with protecting the right flank of the 75th Division in this operation. An attack was launched on April 9th but, despite some success, Turkish resistance proved stronger than expected and the wider assault was called off. Hostilities rumbled on, however, as the Turks attempted to reclaim ground from the British, and a serious encounter took place later in April when a battalion had to be deployed to expel Turkish forces from a village they had recaptured near Tell Asur.

Dewi spent two weeks at Home Counties Road, (probably in the vicinity of Tell Asur), until a move on May 8th to Ain Sinia between Bir Zayt and Silwad, 20 miles north of Jerusalem, where a new Divisional headquarters had been opened. On May 15th Dewi is with Company for a few days, where life had resumed its normal pattern of multiple job changes – cable laying, boss of the camel water convoy, and postman. "Only had the last job three days and, s'welp me Bob, if I didn't bring the boys the same number of mails. The first day I took it over was the first mail they'd had for about a fortnight and you should have heard 'em yell each of those three days when I pitched the bags out. Tell you what, I'd brought 'em such good luck, they swore I was a jewel of a postman and actually were on the point of organising a deputation to the O.C. to ask him if I should be allowed to remain permanently in the mail line.(!)"[1] The band plays for them occasionally, so, altogether it was, he says, "a delightful return."

On May 20th he is off for a spell with the 158th Brigade, now comprising the 4th and 6th Royal Welch Fusiliers, mainly recruited from north Wales, and a Gurkha Rifles and Indian Infantry battalion. He is back up in the line, he reports, in his old capacity as a signaller, "not with Frank's bde [the 159th] this time, tho', unfortunately, but with a N. Wales crush – The Fusies, you know, 'rwan' like, and am more than satisfied – whyfor? Well, I'll tell you – I'm getting tophole chuck up here – better than within the coy [company] – not 'arf.[2] They feed you when you're in [the line] alright. The fellows are sports and, altho' strangers to me at first, I know 'em alright now. First time I've been with 'em, you see, since 'ghastly Gaza', as Horatio says – un cant bump deg a naw [159th] is my usual lot as you know – this is the 'wyth' tho'.[3] We're right up in the mountain fastnesses [...] it's O! so quiet

1) May 28th 1918.
2) Royal Welch Fusiliers. Recruited predominantly in north Wales. One of the linguistic differences between north and south Wales is the use of different words for the English 'now'. 'Rwan' in north Wales and 'yn awr' in south Wales.
3) Wyth is Welsh for eight. Reference is to the 158th. He was posted to the Brigade on May 20th.
   The quotation is possibly a reference to Thomas Macaulay's poem, *Horatio at the Bridge*. 'And, from the ghastly entrance where those bold Romans stood, All shrank, like boys who unaware, ranging the woods to start a hare, Come to the mouth of a dark lair where, growling low, a fierce old bear Lies amidst bones and blood.'

after concerts and bands especially. I've never experienced such a terribly lonely place. The 'Vale of Clwyd' is close at hand and we are somewhere near 'Bettws-y-Coed Road'. Frank's lot are on our left in 'Welsh Wood' and on 'Cardiff Hill', (a home from home). Selwyn's lot are ready, aye ready, always behind the wyths but I haven't seen him."[4] Cardiff Hill was close to a fork in the Wadi el Kola on the right flank of the British line. In North Africa in World War Two a famous defensive position adopted by the Guards in the Battle of Gazala was named Knightsbridge,[5] a reminder of their London barracks.

Conditions remained tough, however, and the enemy were still close, as he reports at the end of May. "The only trouble is the water which, altho' plentiful, is, as it were, so near and yet so far. [...] You see, there's a well about a few hundred yards away but we can't go out of the depression in the daytime to it, 'cos Johnny's got his eyes skinned and has it taped. So, we sneak out at night like blessed criminals to get the precious fluid."[6] The Turks are praised later, however, for a humanitarian practice in wartime, which is helping to make their life somewhat easier. "Gosh! I've thanked the Koran many times for giving old Johnny 10 commandments, one of which forbids him to poison water – he sticks to it, too, fair does [do's], which is a jolly lucky job for us, I can tell you. Water! – Gosh! d'you know what happened yesterday? There was one biscuit tin of water, three men washed, two men bathed (one was myself) and then I washed a shirt, towel, and socks in it. Well, you can imagine it didn't exactly need a razor to cut that water in the finish. (!) Why, you've got to scheme and economise and save up like old boots for a clean shirt, and it's produced such an effect that I feel sure I shall hesitate before using two little bowls full, when I come home, for fear of wastage. As for throwing it down the sink after only one wash – O! dear! Mum, I couldn't think of it." The British failed to show the same grace when it came to competition for wheat, his report a month later suggests. "They played old Johnny a dirty trick last night out in front. You see, the wheat fields are just in their prime now and, s'welp me Bob, if he didn't, with his usual cheek, come out at night, sneaking up with scythes and start reaping the blooming harvest for his own tummy. He won't do it any more, tho', simply because last night there was a bonfire – a couple of tins of petrol and trails did the trick. Serves him right. Let him go to his own blessed supply dumps, same as we gotter do for chuck."[7]

By now the forces preparing to confront the Turks near Megiddo in the Plain of Sharon[8] in the last great engagement of the campaign, were a mixed bunch of nationalities, the original English, Scottish, Irish, Welsh, Australian, and New Zealand contingents being supplemented by French, Algerian, and Armenian, as well as Indian and Burmese, though, apart from one reference to Gurkhas, he makes surprisingly few references to troops from the then Empire. Indeed, he is more amused by the north Walians he meets, as his comments on their distinctive

4) May 28th 1918.
5) The use of familiar names from home to identify landscape was common in both world wars.
6) May 28th 1918.
7) June 8th 1918.
8) Megiddo, historic site 20 miles south east of Haifa, on the trade route between Egypt and Assyria in ancient times, and the scene of a number of important battles. The Battle of Megiddo (September 19th – 25th 1918) was fought in front of Tulkeram in the Judaean Hills, as well as in the Plain of Esdraelon at Nazareth, Afula, Beisan, and Jenin.

Welsh usages indicates. He is more than content up the line, now that British forces were well on top, hoping against hope they won't call him back this time. "We've still a little time to do before being relieved, meanwhile the solitude is as deep as ever, only the rocks and trees for company but I'm not bored in the least. Nunno! In fact I have a sneaking regard for its grandeur."[9] His next move – his precise location at this point is unclear – came on June 30th when he is on the Nablus Road again, a location he would become very familiar with. While the British maintained their preparations and ensured troops remained in a positive frame of mind, the Turks were under growing pressure from their Arab opponents further south. In July these forces managed to isolate Medina with the demolition of a section of the Hejaz railway. The British, for their part, were busy connecting Jerusalem to the railway at Bireh, and Jaffa was linked up with Ludd and up to a point close to Arsuf further north along the coast. Roads were also widened, a large bridge was built over the Jordan at Ghoraniyeh and water supplies improved, all with the aim of ensuring troops remained supplied as they pushed further north.

Back home they were still trying to follow him on the map, possibly through newspaper reports of Allenby's progress. Writing in June he has to disillusion his sister about billets, which she thought he was enjoying again. "Billets have been bygones for O! – letters ago. […] Yes, it's the old bivouacs and funk holes for us every time now, 'cos, don't you see, there's no such a thing as wet weather now.[10] It's all over this long time and a blessed good job, too – I can't stick it or, rather, I don't like it. (!) Nunno, it's all sunshining now but, please, Dolly, get that idea out of your head about us basking in the sunshine. When I read it, I start to perspire more fully than before. I can assure you, Doll, there's no need to bask out here to get sunburnt, as the belles do on the sands of P'Cawl. If they tried that on in Palestine they'd be deficient in kit to the extent of one complexion, peach and milk." There were severe penalties for ignoring the sun's harmful rays and risking a Field Hospital confinement. "If one is caught [not] wearing a cap after 8 am, you can reckon yourself on the peg next morning a bit easy and a few hard-earned days' pay stopped in the bargain. All for a harmless bit of basking, you see, but, of course, the sanity of the troops must be one of the first important considerations. That, and being out 3 years, is, you will agree, quite sufficient to justify any man going berserk. Being up in the hills, as we are, tho', and pretty high at that, tempers it a great deal, and we are blessed with some cooling breezes and vicious dust storms alternately. One of 'em came on two nights ago – 'bout 3 am and blew the blamed bivvy down on top of us – poles, canvas, blankets etc. etc. all in one glorious mix-up and me and ol' Bill out in our shirts in the middle of it trying to peg it down and wrestling frantically with the flapping sheets. O! what recitations – an ode to a bivouac sort of style, you know."[11]

A Sapper to the End

At the end of the war, despite his many jobs, Dewi had not advanced beyond the lowliest rank in the Royal Engineers, that of sapper, whether as a result of lack of

9) June 8th 1918.
10) Funk holes, trench dug-outs.
11) June 8th 1918.

ambition or his still comparatively young age, we cannot tell. (He was still a mere 20 in 1918.) His one small period of command – other than over the animals he was intermittently in charge of – does not seem to have shown much evidence of the leadership qualities the Army might have been looking for. After three years away from home, Dewi was almost certainly just anxious to finish the war and forget about the military, and he describes his modest promotion in the jocular yet world-weary manner that characterised many of his later letters. "Time and oft has it been my sad lot to inform you of the fate, which, try as I might, I cannot elude and which seems to stalk me as faithfully as my own shadow – i.e. my seemingly inborn aptitude for getting collared for novel and very often ludicrous (when you think of them as handled by me, of course) jobs. Jack of all trades, I seem to have been labelled, and Jack of all trade, I s'pose, I'll continue to be, whether it's charring, packing up the 'dead marines' at the Company canteen, camel convoy 'effendi', or Fire Brigade 'water officer' [sic] and medical advisor.[12] To put the whole matter in a nut-shell, my misfortune has, I regret to say, once again overtaken me and, as I have long ere this become quite resigned to my fate, I have seen this instance through once again with the serenity of long experience. T'other morning, whilst in the middle of my ablutions, our worthy sergeant appears and says, 'O! Dewi' – 'Hulloh-o! Phew! P'shaw!',[13] I said, having swallowed more soap than you'd find in umpteen boxes. 'Hm!' he says, 'it's like this – you gotter start this afternoon as Signalmaster with Ned, Bill and Dai as your shift.' [...] 'Excuse me, sergeant,' I says, very polite like, 'but what the devil for? – have I ever so much as raised my voice to you, that you should thrust this thing upon me?' but he was gone as quickly as he'd come."[14]

It does not seem his new charges took their responsibilities any more seriously than he did, perhaps reflecting the more relaxed time they were now enjoying while awaiting the next push forward. Dewi's own morale at this point certainly seems to have been good. "So now you perceive me acting in the highly exalted, immensely important and dignified capacity of Signalmaster i/c of no. 3 Shift, – the Brigade Signals', whose merest word is law to my staff, comprising of Ned, Bill and Dai (3 incorrigibles who can perform wonders with the Morse code and a buzzer), sundry orderlies and divers despatch riders. Lord of all I survey, in fact. At least, that's what I'm supposed to be but, bless you! I never quite realised before what a deuce of a rotten job being a corporal is, or how absolute a failure I should be at that dizzy height of fame. What's the use of my trying to assert my authority? – not one iota, I assure you – why, they'd laugh in my blessed face, if I carried out my duties as Signalmaster with the firmness and decorum required of such high and mighty ones. As it is, I've got about the very worst set of rogues in the Signals for my shift, who require such stern handling as I could never hope to be capable of, and who have broken the spirit of more than one Signalmaster in their career of crime. In fact, I fear me, my particular shift, together with its grey-haired, worn out, worried chief, is the very last word in 'ragtime',[15] and, indeed, I entertain the gravest doubts as to whether I can possibly last out another week on it in possession of all my faculties."

195

12) Dead marines, Army slang for empty beer bottles. Effendi, Turkish title of respect applied to government officials.
13) P'shaw, interjection expressing contempt or impatience
14) June 28th 1918.
15) Ragtime, disorderly, as in Ragtime Army.

He goes on to describe a "couldn't care less" approach possibly common by now among the men. "Bill has a positive mania for translating code times in the most unorthodox and weird manner possible, while Ned's little weaknesses are 1) language calculated to fuse the whole system of communication and 2) an absent-mindedness which causes me grave alarm in always sending the prior codes last of all, if he can possibly see his way clear.[16] The third playful humorist has nothing but contempt for his superiors and will persist in utterly ignoring conversations between brigadiers, colonels, adjutants etc., considering his messages referring to 'the names of any skilled cobblers in your battalion' or 'English mail arriving at Jerusalem at such and such a time' or 'one limber of canteen stores awaiting your collection' of infinitely more importance, which zeal causes these worthy gentlemen much waste of breath and fiery eloquence in their appeals to 'Stop that infernal buzzing'. Is it any wonder then that the Signals are granted innumerable free passports to the warm regions when our shift is on, or is it in the least difficult to understand why I am so pessimistic concerning my ability to stand the anxious strain of squaring all these little oversights to the mollification of these dread fire-eaters? As for writing letters on such a duty – my only helmet [sic] – it's more than hopeless, it's heart-breaking."

Concert Parties

Efforts were clearly made to ensure troops remained motivated after their long period away from home. At the end of June Dewi writes to say they are now back in reserve for a short time 'and it's a blooming fine change, believe me.'[17] For a start, they seem to have been given decent supplies, the advancing railway lines and the capture of Jaffa no doubt making it easier to keep the troops fed. "Here I am in the old bivouac with a box full of milk, tomatoes, eggs, everything they sell in the canteen as a matter of fact, and an old Primus stove buzzing away merrily, drumming up café au lait for supper. O! we do live, but I've forgotten one thing – don't grin when I tell you that in the bargain I'm smoking a 'Romeo y Julietta Habana' cigar – $2^1/_2$ piastres a time – could you possibly imagine anything more romantic – what? Bar Jove! no – I always make a point of leaving the band on 'em too."[18] Normal rotation for troops in World War One was a period up the line, followed by a period in reserve, followed by rest, though men often had to work as hard on rest – on fatigues or in training – as when they were facing the enemy. Physical exercises to keep the men occupied and fit for the next stage of the campaign continued, and men were being put through what appears to have been a training ground version of a popular Edwardian parlour game. "In fact, the only fly in the hair oil is that we've got to turn out so awfully beastly jolly early in the mornings and kow-tow[19] to a hoarse-throated individual wearing cross-swords who shouts 'Move' in a most disconcerting manner – physical jerks of course – Gott strafe Sweden.[20]

16) Bill appears to have reversed the order of priority for messages, sending the least important first.
17) June 28th 1918. He gives his position on June 30th as Nablus Road.
18) Cigar smokers were divided on whether or not to retain the decorative paper band with the maker's name on it while smoking. Some regarded it as boastful to draw attention to an expensive brand. Purists, however, argued that removing the band could damage the wrapper leaf, to which it was attached by a spot of glue. Once lit, the glue would melt, making it easier to remove the wrapper when the smoker had reached this far along the cigar in his smoke. Cigars were not cheap, retailing at the time in Britain at 100 shillings (£5) for one hundred.
19) Kow-tow, Chinese custom of touching ground with forehead as a sign of submission.
20) During World War One a popular slogan of the German Army was 'Gott Strafe England' – 'May God Punish England'. The reference is perhaps to an association between Sweden and physical jerks. A cross sword and baton in the British Army indicate the rank of General.

And before breakfast, my dear – shocking really isn't it? But there, I mustn't grumble, tho', it does wake one up most effectively, 'cos we do get some fun out of it after all. Leap frog and – er – kiss in the ring – a most exhilarating pastime, the latter, but not played exactly on the 'Marquis of Birthday Party Rules,' you know.[21] One does get kissed, it's true, if one doesn't 'move', as my imitation 'Field Marshal' cross-batoned friend says. You see a rather painfully thick belt is responsible for the osculatory salutations[22] and the most tender part of your anatomy is that which is saluted. And, as there are about 4 straps on the go at a time, well, it's rather a strenuous time running the gauntlet, if you don't happen to have the 'gift of the move'. The 'powers that be' generally turn up, too – to get rid of a fat head, after Johnny Walker's acquaintance at mess the night before, I expect.[23] Anyway, I managed to get five lusty swacks in this morning upon an aristocratic figure – it was a delightful sensation for both of us. S'welp me Bob, tho', if he didn't make a blamed good effort to have owns back a few minutes later when the position was reversed but, bless you, – I saw the old 'Field Marshal' shove the buckle into his hand out of the corner of my eye and you couldn't see me for smoke going round that ring. Foiled again – aha! – Percy, your luck's out, old chap – besides who couldn't run on bags of canteen stores, eh? Pooh! simple, old thing – nothing in it."[24]

Entertainment of a different sort was available from time to time at their various camps. At Wadi Ballut in April he had seen 'those marvels, the 'Welsh Rarebits'.[25] "By Jove! Dolly, old girl, you simply can't believe till you've seen 'em. A real tophole stage with quite the latest footlights and lime-light effects – plush curtains with the arms of the party in gold upon it – two rabbits rampant – but all this is by the way – it doesn't really count when the artists come on the scene – O! no, most decidedly not." A hint at the frustrations vigorous young men must have been experiencing from not seeing any girls they could talk to or date – having to rely instead for their amusement on their fellow-soldiers in drag – comes across in his description of the performance. "Did I tell you that Flossie has a sparring partner of her own sex now? Well, it's right – and they do look positively plums – real peaches. Talk about the light fantastic, too – my word! they're real experts at the 'trip it lightly' game and such ankles, Dolly – sublime, believe me – make many a real demoiselle turn green with envy. They've got that trick, you know, of looking so absolutely frail and timid and – well, I dunno, 'glass, with care' sort of thing – got it swung, I tell you, and as for walking, well, they simply have forgotten how to walk, and when I say 'walk', I mean a clumsy slouching forceful tread, like any other self-respecting fellow.[26] Forgotten it altogether and, in accordance with their role, they kind of float along with those ridiculously short steps, like you see in Queen Street any old day of the week."[27] The Welsh Rarebits, he explains, "were the only demoiselles we've got, barring the charming Buddoo [Bedouin] damsels who are now millionairesses on the 15 tomatoes for 5 piastre touch and, of course, it's only

21) The Marquis of Queensbury Rules govern the sport of boxing.
22) Osculatory, of kissing.
23) Johnny Walker, the Scotch Whiskey.
24) June 28th 1918.
25) *Welsh Rarebits*, the Divisional Concert Party.
26) Glass with Care, the warning placed on packaging.
27) June 28th 1918.

natural that a feller likes to be deceived and feel like straightening his imaginary tie and parting his hair before he goes to a concert. Best thing a fellow can do in the E.E.F. where leave is almost extinct as a rest eh?" He concludes, "O! well, supper and then to bed and more 'kiss in the ring' tomorrow morn."

From Bivvies to Billets

On July 21st the Division was sent to rest billets, a date marked in Dewi's itinerary as a move to Ain Duk and reported to his parents and sister as a reason for some satisfaction. "The whole division has come out of the line and we are at present taking a well-earned rest midst much more pleasant surroundings. You can guess what we felt like when leaving 'yon ugly lump of rock and dirt'. Says I to that hill, 'never again shall I see thee once more for a long time – at least I hope not'. Parting is one of the great tragedies in life, so they say, but there are partings and partings and that one was a big-ootiful one – better than the best I ever accomplished with Anagora even.[28] The only fly in the ointment, though was – well, you try and start off for a 17 mile march at 11.30 *am* in *Palestine* under a bloke on horseback who knows sweet nothing about marching and, saint or no saint, you'll have the very deuce of a job to refrain from allowing your eloquence to run away with you beyond the drawing room phraseology of fly and ointment. By Jove! It was wicked at that time of the day, too, when the sun was still frazzling and the road underneath your tootsies felt like a long, long lane with no blessed turning, composed entirely of red hot steel plates and on top of that, which was O! Tut-tut! awfly mild, (Phew!) he must take us round an extra six miles to comply with the order that no troops must march thro' a village, if it can be avoided. He avoided it alright – he was on a horse, the...the-- (give us a dictionary). Well, it was a footsore, weary, done-up crowd of miserable unfortunates we were before we passed the 12 mile limit with a thirst that could have been called beautiful, if we'd had any water in our bottles to quench it. I'll march all night willingly when you've got to go, tho, no baking oven stunts, coals, fire and w.. (but there, as I have said, there was a slump in the liquid) but, bust me, if I want another little jaunt like that one – managed it somehow, tho' – heavens knows how, and arrived whacked to the wide world with blisters as big as saucers to let and once on the ground stretched out like a limp dish rag. Allenby hisself couldn't have made me stand to attention under half an hour. When that time had elapsed the sight of a canteen, a quarter of a mile away, proved too much and with the aid of a bivvy pole I succeeded in hobbling painfully across the remaining space and between me and you, wild horses wouldn't have dragged me from there until I'd gone right through the menu from lemonade at 1 piastre a glass to 'No responsibility for caps and badges'.

Anyway, here we are all settled down in a first class place for an ideal rest.[29] Plenty of canteen stores, no parades, native market with tomatoes, cucumbers, water melons and grapes (Smack!) and last but not least, O! Listen here for I bring glad tidings of exceeding joy! tons of water in the wadi – very cold from a spring where you can use umpteen buckets full for one shirt, if you feel so inclined, and, above

---

28) July 27th 1918. Anagora, possibly a hair oil.
29) Ain Duk, a natural spring, the waters of which supplied Jericho.

all, an ancient Roman bath as big as the Cardiff bath, where you can swim, dive, splash, kick and blessed well drown, if you feel that way inclined.[30] But, you see, life is worth living under these circs. I'm just about landed or rather submerged – it's absolutely the blooming goods and I revel in this heaven-sent delight. If I ever qualify in the Angels' Choir, I should pick out old Julius Pilat Brutus or whoever it was in charge of the fatigue party who built that bath and say, 'Put it right there, yr hen gŵr [old man], – what's yours?' Every night about 9 we go down and swim by moonlight and the ghosts of the old Johnnies around here are sure to have the breeze up when they hear the splashes and churnings and clamorous shouts of fellas in the seventh heaven of delight. To fellows like us who have been used to one bottle full per diem perhaps you can just imagine what a perfect holiday this is and why plunging into 6 foot of water and fetching across to the other side for as long as you please is bliss unalloyed. Come back about 12 and sleep like a blooming log, mosquitoes and ants and all 'till brekker."

The break would give them a chance for sports, too, including boxing and football. "There'll be plenty of opportunities for the bloodthirsty. [...] I've seen two rival Welsh regiments, during a rest, play Rugger for ten minutes and then suddenly draw mallets from their shorts and carry on with the game, all in fun, bless 'em. They really don't mean to do harm, you know. I have already declined with thanks to act as wheelbarrow in the races, giving place to a man who is in our opinion far more fitted to act in that capacity. You see, when the barrels are tapped here in rest he is a devout worshipper at the shrine and blossoms forth as an actor of no small dramatical powers, 'Aha!', he is wont to say, 'I am not the Silver King.[31] I am the Cottage by the Sea'. Therefore, thought I, is not such a human bundle of contradictions far more suitable for the vacant position and is [it] not a trifle for such as he to go one better and become a wheelbarrow or possibly a steamroller, if needs be?" Other games took the place of those with which they had become bored. "This is the first time our old div. has been out of the line since last October and we intend making the very best of it, don't worry. The spot is very quiet and the fig and pomegranate trees around here show great promise of bearing luscious fruit in the near future. Just as the ping pong craze took Blighty by storm some years ago, so do we become engrossed from time to time with novel means of killing time. You recollect very readily our exploits in the jackstone and jam tin bombing championships and this letter would scarcely be complete without some mention of the very latest prevailing pastime.[32] O! no, nothing unusual, I assure you, but this time it is a very refined and genteel game, indeed, which, nevertheless, is often the cause of heated arguments. This time it is 'Draughts', and 'Draughts' it is with a vengeance till we tire and sigh for new worlds to conquer. I am, you may be sure, an ardent devotee and bring all my prowess and subtle cunning acquired and exposed at those far off games of 'Animal Grab' to bear on my victims in order to swap 3 and get a king."[33]

---

30) Guildford Crescent baths, opened in 1873, demolished 1985. Now the site of the Ibis Hotel, Churchill Way.

31) Silver King, possibly a reference to the 1882 popular, melodramatic play by Henry Arthur Jones and Henry Herman.

32) Jackstones, a traditional children's game involving throwing and catching a series of stones. Jam tin bombing, another boys' game.

33) Animal Grab, a card game where players competed to be first to spot two identical cards. Get a 'King', the reward for moving one's counters across the draughts board.

Card games provide an excuse for him to tell an elaborate story of his own good luck – though not in one of the hands he had been dealt. Not having received letters for a while, he gets six "nice, plump, heavy envelopes, speaking of untold delights and by far the most joyful hour I'd spent for many a weary day. The Poker School in our bivvy, with tightly drawn anxious brows and all 'eyes down', were far too busy watching the dealer and the 15 bob in the 'kitty' to worry about me," he writes. "Presently, having picked their respective 'hands' up and shown their luck and emotion, either by cunning superior smiles or resigned hopeless sighs, I observed them to be looking askance in my direction and, coming to earth, I realised it must be my turn to call, and so, clearing my throat, I spoke my mind honestly – 'Chaps,' I says, 'don't get in the leastwise alarmed, likewise exasperated – take it cool, we don't want a scene and above all no shootin', mind.' (Gee! you should ha' seen their jaws drop.) 'Some lily-livered skunk,' I says, 'some lily-livered skunk have been monkeyin' with this 'ere blamed pack'. (Jumping Ju – hosaphat! you should ha' seen them eyeing each other up and down – 10 seconds more and they'd ha' been at one another's throats, so I hurriedly continued 'or else,' says I, 'or else it's the pee-culiarist phenomenon as never was – call it what you like, 'running flush' or any other happellation [sic] but (and here throwing my bee-utiful hand with studied effect upon the blanket, I concluded) 'there's my deal – six blamed aces, as never was, and where's the cove to deny it.'[34] Well, believe me, them fellers was wringing with the perspiration of excitement by the time I finished, and I consider myself extremely fortunate to have escaped unscathed after putting the wind up 'em with such a rotten trick. I fully expected my deserts, which would have meant 'em falling upon me and smiting me hip and thigh, even as did Moses, I think, with the Amalekites.[35] As it was, I really don't fancy they had breath enough left to perform such violent exercise. Anyhow, their idea of severely admonishing a person is in itself a fearful, shocking ordeal to even a less modest sapper than myself, and so now you know the real reason why I never won that 15 bob kitty and played in a ridiculously ecstatic, pre-occupied dream for the rest of the game."

He goes on to shower his usual exaggerated praise on their letters. "Amongst that inspiring avalanche of treasured volumes were two of your incomparable productions, Dolly, and two of Dad's enthusiastic efforts, of May 8th and 20th and 11th and 22nd of the same respectively. Gosh! what a feast. I could never describe it to you to my satisfaction – how whilst performing my favourite gymnastic ("back" exercises) I devoured with ravenous appetite those top-hole budgets written in the well-known hands, oblivious to all, flies included, save one of Auntie's 'Players' and the classics before me.[36] You talk of what sense of gladness takes place on the arrival of mine in every letter and, as I have said time and again – Ah! I can imagine the scene but it cannot possibly be compared with the raptures of this chee-ild. And, now, I shall be busy – terribly busy in all my spare time,

34) June 28th 1918. Jehosaphat, fourth king of Judah in the Bible

35) 'Then Amalek came and fought with Israel at Rephidim. So Moses said to Joshua, "Choose for us men, and go out and fight with Amalek. Tomorrow I will stand on the top of the hill with the staff of God in my hand." So Joshua did as Moses told him, and fought with Amalek, while Moses, Aaron, and Hur went up to the top of the hill. Whenever Moses held up his hand, Israel prevailed, and whenever he lowered his hand, Amalek prevailed. But Moses' hands grew weary, so they took a stone and put it under him, and he sat on it, while Aaron and Hur held up his hands, one on one side, and the other on the other side. So his hands were steady until the going down of the sun. And Joshua overwhelmed Amalek and his people with the sword.' Exodus 17. 8-13

36) June 28th 1918. 'Back' exercises, lying down resting.

repaying with a consuming zest for the pleasures these half dozen delightful epistles have occasioned me in this deserted hole, which well might be the last place at the end of the earth before stepping off into space. Forgive me, if in my childish excitement I fail to repay in full measure – indeed my most sanguine hopes only lead me to expect an indifferently well-off bankrupt's effort – 15/- in the pound.[37] In this I confine myself only to answering yours, Doll, as I realise you to have denied yourself much respite from Mr Aitkin and his blessed P'Cll [Porthcawl] sand and gravel to afford me these luxuries, whereas Dad – well, he does nothing, of course – nothing at all, bless you! except saunter up and down indulging in little pleasantries with his fair charges on the L.V. and T.S.[38] which is a blooming paradise of an existence, compared with daily pleasantries à la Aitkin[39] bounder, isn't it? Besides, it's only what I expect from Dad (altho' I let him off very light), seeing that not leading your strenuous life, respite from his labours is a farce and nothing more."

Homesickness and Disillusion

At times he could lapse into sheer sentimentality – occasioned no doubt by keenly-felt homesickness – when meditating on his lot stuck out in Palestine, so far from his family back in Cardiff, as in a letter in May. "Heavens! how I do devour 'em [their letters] – altho' to the ordinary eye those words are mute, just mere unconvincing black and white, to me, and only me, they speak. I do not as a general rule dwell exclusively upon my most sacred thoughts – of home. That is a common error with not a few chaps. It is the chief cause of many long faces, most mopishness and positively disastrous to good spirits (without which invaluable asset one cannot pull thro' on this job.) But on those occasions on which I have just spoken I must confess that unwittingly almost, that vague, mysterious something grips, and grips hard, and by the time I arrive at that beloved signature, Mum, Dad and Doll, gone is the careless, irresponsible air of that small photo and I find myself smiling just a wee bit wistfully and thinking *some*, while I see my surroundings with unseeing eyes. Then, suddenly, I come to earth with a rude shock, as some blighter lounges up with the mundane question, 'Go halves in a tin of sardines for tea, old man?' which puts an end to my castles in the air more or less effectively and I wait patiently for the next letter (and goodness knows I'm an old hand at that by now)."

This angst, it appears, is not uncommon. "There is something pathetic I have always thought about a fellow reading 'one from home' three thousand miles away. I have watched the little episode many times and conclude from the study that mine must be equally pathetic to another. That far-away look, that breuddwyd [dream] must be there, too. At the age of 10 I imagined there could be no more thrilling sensation than being presented by Dad with a loco or a telescope, at 14, I was just as much convinced that there was nothing more delightful and precious in the whole universe than a $5^1/_2$d [five pence ha'penny] 'chuck-out' presented by Daddy Howe.[40] But from the 17th unto the 20th year of my existence I realise that all else

---

37) A bankrupt is expected to repay his creditors as much of his debt as he could – in this case a sum of 15/- in the £.
38) Telegraphy terms.
39) Doris's first job was with Aitkin and Morcom, a firm of timber merchants at Merchant's Exchange, Bute Street. Vd. Chap 12, p269.
40) Daddy Howe, presumably a Telegraph Office supervisor.

that has been before counts for nought, that letters from home are far and away the most priceless of this world's goods, and that every other experience which is to be mine in the future will pall before that eventful thrilling day of days when I shall literally hurl myself from the Paddington express towards that trio which I know will be waiting on No. ... O! never mind the number of the platform. If it's No. umpteen I'll be right there, 'cos I think I've just about paid my fare."[41] He could, nevertheless, puff his chest out in pride at sticking it so long in difficult surroundings, as in one of his last letters, when he comments on a visit his father had received from one of his colleagues, Sgt. Pace. "Had his chevrons[42] up, too, did he? – well, we haven't got 'em yet and it doesn't much matter 'cos there's only a lot of Bedouins begotten of centuries of unwashed ancestors to be interested in the length of our sojourn together. I've been shoved down for four anyway, which will look très chic if there's any truth in the rumour that a Dardanelles ribbon is to be issued, too. *Then* I come on leave, *when* I'll stick my chest out and swing my arm and the first frog-hearted, stiff-necked cross between a Spitzbergen sea-cook and a muzzled oyster, mealy-mouthed son of a doormat who cocks his nose at that'll be handed a bunch of double fives good and hard."[43]

Onwards to Megiddo

Allenby's aim in the autumn of 1918 was not merely to beat backwards but to encircle and annihilate the enemy forces in Palestine, a campaign he now planned and mounted with real military skill. Indeed, according to Mortlock, "the Battle of Megiddo was a brilliant operation, of a kind supremely satisfactory to an army commander". Perhaps somewhat hyperbolically, he goes on to argue it rated alongside great military triumphs down through the ages, such as Agincourt, Austerlitz, Blenheim, Cannae, Crecy, Hastings, the Heights of Abraham, Marathon, Naseby, Omdurman, Plassey, Poitiers, Rourke's Drift, Thermopylae, Waterloo and Yorktown among others. The campaigns by Allenby, one of the most admired generals of World War One, are, nevertheless, still regarded as textbook examples of how to conduct military operations, destroying, as he did, several Turkish armies and bringing Palestine operations to a triumphant conclusion. When they agreed an armistice at Mudros on Lemnos, the base from which Dewi had started seriously on his overseas military adventures, the Turks could no longer put an army in the field in Palestine, their troops having either melted away or been taken captive. Out of total remaining forces of 90,000 men, some 75,000 would end up in British hands, as, too, would the remaining key towns of the Ottoman Empire outside Turkey, Amman, Caesarea, Damascus, and Aleppo, not to mention those captured in earlier successes – Jerusalem, Gaza and Jaffa. The final stages, too, were accomplished in a matter of weeks.

41) May 28th 1918

42) Four chevrons is the insignia of a sergeant, commander of a platoon. Corporals, in charge of a section, wore three chevrons, and their seconds-in-command, lance-corporals, two.

43) July 27th 1918. Spitzbergen sea-cook, a quotation from *The Champion of The Weather*, a short story by O. Henry. One of a party of hunters recounts how he knew from just two words, 'Nice night', that another individual was from New York. The hunter objects to the use of such pleasantries when they lead nowhere in conversation and tells the story of how he had forced a cafe manager, by showing him his gun, not to use the weather as a meaningless greeting.

Allenby knew by the middle of the year that his superiority in numbers and resources would enable him to take the offensive at a time of his choosing. The area for these operations was to be west of the River Jordan. The country was more suited for mounted action than in the difficult and hilly country east of the River Jordan so in early August Allenby informed his corps commanders that he intended to pierce the Turkish front near the coast and to pass mounted troops through the gap to reach the Tiberias-Acre line several miles further north, deep behind Turkish lines. Five infantry divisions of the XXIst Corps under Bulfin would lead the initial breakthrough on an eight mile front between the railway and the Mediterranean. The aim was to cut off all road and railway communications behind the Turkish forces south of the Der'a, Beisan – El Afule railway in the Plain of Esdraelon (or Megiddo), stretching southeast from Haifa.[44] Arab forces were given the task of capturing Der'a Junction and the XXth Corps would attack northwards along the Nablus Road and block the exits to the lower Jordan valley.

Dewi had spent much of the preceding months camped around this road, as he had explained to his father in a letter at the end of July. "Been having a good look at the map then, Dad – well, from the place you mentioned, I will tell you you've hit the nail on the head. I know that blessed road like I do Moorland Rd by now and shan't forget it either. There's been some ugly scuffles along it, you bet. Pace's lot were on our left in those times of April showers.[45] Though not part of the main thrust along the coast the XXth Corps' position was, nevertheless, of key significance. The Turks could be expected to defend their position on the Nablus Road very strongly, as it was the pivot on which any retreat would depend, their troops further west towards the coast having further distances to cover in order to retire. It was also where the strongest counter-attacks could be expected. Concealment was necessary, however, if the Turks were not to reinforce their positions. It was essential they believed an attack was most likely to the east in the Jordan Valley, yet troops would have to be withdrawn from that area for operations in the west. The measures taken were extraordinary. Staff officers and orderlies went around Jerusalem painting departmental names on the doors of buildings so that word might get back from informers that this would be the British headquarters for an attack eastwards; Decauville[46] rail lines and bridges were built and rows of dummy horses erected, and West Indies troops were marched up and back the Jordan valley every night, the dust they kicked up intended to suggest large concentrations of troops were being positioned for a move east. The gathering of forces in the west also had to be kept secret, a task made easier by the British mastery of the skies, with British aircraft at this stage superior to German machines, as von Sanders recognised in a despatch. German air losses hindered their reconnaissance and had become so serious flying operations had had to be suspended. Allenby himself noted that, whereas 100 hostile aircraft had crossed British lines in June, by August the number had reduced to 18, and, after a number had been shot down, only four ventured out during the period of concentration. Roads, bridges, water, camps and defences were all worked on where the main thrust would take place. In the 53rd Division's sector to the east of the main attack area the Nablus Road was improved,

---

44) Pritchard, (ed.), p380.

45) July 27th 1918.

46) Decauville, ready-made sections of light, narrow gauge tracks fastened to steel sleepers, capable of being disassembled and transported. The French military began using the system as early as 1888 to equip its strongholds and carry artillery pieces and ammunition.

as were its bridges, and new storage for water installed at Tell Asur. Maps – 8,800 copies of 32 different maps – also had to be made of the unfamiliar country ahead, based on air photographs and intelligence reports.

The Battle of Megiddo – the Armageddon of the Bible – opened on September 19th. The XXIst moved ahead at 5.30 a.m. supported by heavy bombardment of Turkish counter-battery defences by artillery. The day proved outstandingly successful, even though some divisions faced determined opposition and strong defences. The XXIst managed to advance fifteen miles over the coastal plain, and swing right, destroying the Turkish right wing and opening the way for the cavalry to execute its intercepting movement. The XXth Corps in Judaea also moved on the night of September 18th - 19th towards Nablus, making a converging attack with two brigades. North of Jericho, a group known as Chaytor's Force harried the Turkish retreat across the Jordan and secured a bridge across the river, before advancing through Es Salt – scene of actions earlier in the year – to Amman. The town that was to become capital of Jordan was taken on September 25th with thousands of prisoners and much material.[47] Operations continued on succeeding days.

The 53rd was engaged in tough fighting on September 20th, as roads could not be built quickly enough to enable the artillery to keep close behind the infantry. Mines, too, had to be removed from the Nablus Road so that motor vehicles could pass along, bringing the artillery up, and some road work had to be undertaken under fire. Driving a road through that would be big enough for artillery required rock blasting, too, in some places. The task assigned to the 53rd was to cross the considerable obstacle of the Wadi es Samieh basin to reach a position along the line Valley View-el Mugheir-Hindhead – Narn Ridge, an objective that would also bring with it the Wadi's unlimited supplies of water. General Mott in charge of the XXth Corps decided to attack the Turkish positions by sending two brigades, the 159th and 160th, in opposite directions around the rim of the basin, meeting on the other side. This was a difficult exercise as the latter, who would have to cover two–thirds of the rim, would have to make a night march over difficult country, followed by a steep climb on the other side of the basin before fanning out to attack a fortified position.[48] The other brigade, the 159th, would have to make a series of frontal attacks. Turkish reconnaissance failed, however, to detect the British forces moving into position and indeed issued a wildly erroneous map on September 17th of where they believed British forces to be, suggesting British deception had proved wholly convincing. The 158th Brigade, following through between the two other brigades, was ordered to concentrate at the position that British forces had named Hindhead from where they were to occupy a line of hills across the plateau beyond Hindhead, a strong defensive position where the Turks had machine guns in number.[49] As elsewhere on this front, progress was made but, inevitably, delays occurred when, in country difficult for wheeled vehicles, the infantry outpaced the supporting artillery. After Hindhead had been taken the 158th brigade was ordered to advance north on Akrabeh, the 159th proceeding on its left and the 160th protecting its right flank from any attacks by Turkish forces still in the Jordan Valley. Over the next few days, as the Turks escaped as best they could, the 158th

47) Pritchard, (ed.), p387.
48) Dudley Ward, p230-1.
49) At 800 feet, Hindhead is the highest point in Surrey.

advanced past Ras Tawil and Kustrah through Akrabeh, 12 miles southeast of Nablus, and on September 21st, in what proved to be the last action of the campaign, secured Kholeh el Kerum in a sharp encounter, before marching on to El Tewanik and Beit Dejan where they halted. Dewi gives his own position as Hindhead on September 21st, and Akrabeh on September 22nd and finally Yanun, (eight miles southeast of Nablus) and El Tewanik on September 23rd. On September 26th the division was withdrawn for rest back to Tell Asur and he reports his position the following day as Hawaida. To the west the main constraint on the infantry's advance was the difficulty in getting enough water forward and in developing supplies sufficient for the large body of men now on the move. The Desert Mounted Corps' divisions had pushed on to their objective El Afule and one brigade raided Nazareth before withdrawing, having narrowly failed to capture von Sanders – now a marshal – who escaped to Tiberias. "The bulk of the Turkish armies was disintegrating and the few organised remnants were being driven into an ever decreasing area around Nablus. Their escape routes were being rapidly stopped by the cavalry and subsequent operations consisted primarily of collecting and disarming the demoralised enemy."[50]

The scale of the victory was clear. Two Turkish armies west of the Jordan had been destroyed and a third east of the river was in full retreat, its rail communications severely compromised by Arab attacks on its left flank. Allenby decided as a result to advance on Damascus. The 4th Cavalry Division was ordered to move forward east of the Jordan through Der'a, with other mounted troops proceeding west of the Sea of Galilee. An Indian Division marched along the coast to Beirut. With Damascus 150 miles from the main British supply base at Ludd on the Jaffa-Jerusalem road, however, supplies would depend on linking up the advancing British railway with the Turkish lines at Tulkeram, and opening the Turkish railway from the more northerly port of Haifa. Water supplies would also need to be found for horses and men on the advance. Der'a was taken by the XXIst Corps on September 28th, as the pursuit continued, and Damascus on October 1st. Despite supply difficulties Allenby was keen to press on, and on October 3rd he ordered the capture of Riyaq, an important rail centre 30 miles northwest of Damascus, where the narrow-gauged lines from Damascus and Beirut joined the standard gauge to Homs, Aleppo and the Taurus mountains. Homs was captured on October 5th and Aleppo three weeks later, forcing the Turks to seek an armistice on October 31st, just 11 days before the end of the war in Europe. In the course of five weeks the EEF had managed to destroy the Turkish Army, taking 75,000 prisoners, 360 guns, 89 locomotives, 468 railway carriages and trucks and vast quantities of stores at the cost of 5,700 casualties of its own.

Christmas in Alex and Home

Four years of fighting were over for the EEF but for men like Dewi another few months would elapse before they reached home. After their successes in Palestine, Dewi and his colleagues began to pull back, first on October 10th to Ain Duk, then to Latrun and Ramok on succeeding days, and finally to Alexandria, which he reached on October 20th. He and his colleagues spent the following two months in Alexandria, the one noteworthy event in this period in his log being "Metropole",

205

50) Pritchard, p391.

a visit, one has to assume, to the five storey hotel of that name, an 18th century building overlooking the Mediterranean. Two weeks later he attended a dinner and concert given by the 100-voice strong 53rd Division Welsh Male Voice Choir on January 10th and 11th, items including *The Sailors' Chorus*, by the poet Mynyddog, set to music by Dr. Joseph Parry, the Welsh composer, and those other male voice favourites *Myfanwy*, *Men Of Harlech*, and *Martyrs of the Arena*, plus vocal, piano, and violin solos by serving men. His programme is signed by a large number of colleagues, the sort of post-war memento many of the men will have collected.

He was to have one more interlude in Palestine before returning home, moving to the railway junction at Kantara in February 1919 on his way north to Haifa. Here he spent a period of time on secondment to the North Palestine Signal Company on the North Palestine Line of Communication. He left Haifa two days after attaining his majority on March 3rd for demob. camp at Kantara before embarking on March 8th on *Malwa* at Port Said, en route to Taranto and the train to Le Havre. *Malwa*, a 10,986 ton P. &. O passenger ship, had been diverted to Mediterranean transport duties from its usual Britain to Australia route via the Suez Canal and India.[51] Taranto had at this time become an enormous transit camp, developed during the war as the port of embarkation for all troops proceeding to Salonika, Palestine, Mesopotamia and India and back from there at the end of the war as well. Trains from there travelled along the east coast of Italy and thence through Bologna to Genoa, and on to Le Havre, which Dewi reached after six days' travelling.

After the war Dewi returned to the Post Office in Cardiff, where he remained until his retirement, and, apart from an extended visit to the United States in the early 1930s to see the sister he had written so fondly to and her husband and two sons, his four years away from home seem to have cured him of any wanderlust. He remained a great reader, became an accomplished pianist, particularly of works by Chopin, which he played most evenings, and a supporter of Cardiff and Wales rugby. He married Prudence Williams, a native of Abercynon, 15 miles north of Cardiff, who also worked in the Post Office in 1939, shortly before the outbreak of World War Two. They had two children, Mari and Rhys. He died on the eve of Easter Sunday, April 15th, in 1963 not long after his 65th birthday. He talked little about the war, meeting men he had served with for a reunion just once a year until the early 1960s, though he remained friendly all his life with Frank Somers, the school friend mentioned on a number of occasions in the letters, whose own enlistment encouraged him to join the colours, and with Aubrey Mills, Sam Milner and C.G. "Pip" Pippen, three other Post Office friends. His service had a profound effect – his four years away from home at a very formative age perhaps persuading him to value all the more a quiet domestic life in the city he loved.

---

51) Built by Caird & Co., Greenock, in 1908, *Malwa* could carry 350 first class and 160 second class passengers but no doubt many more troops were carried on the passage across from Port Said to Taranto.

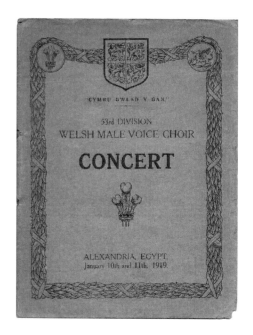

Back in Alexandria for Christmas 1918 the men were entertained at a concert by their fellow-soldiers.

The extent of British influence in Egypt can be seen in an advertisement in the programme Davies, Bryan, "the old-established British firm" of kit suppliers.

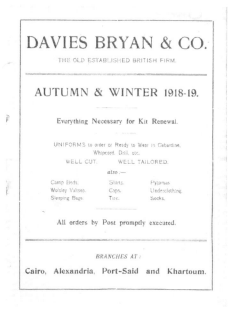

(right) Roberts, Hughes, a Welsh business in Alexandria, similarly advertising in the concert programme.

(below) Haifa. Dewi's last posting in March 1919 at North Palestine Line of Communications in the seaport to the north of Jerusalem.

ROBERTS, HUGHES & Cº

for

Everything in the Sporting Line.

TENNIS, CRICKET,
FOOTBALL, BOXING,
ETC., ETC.

Also BOOTS AND SHOES
FOR
GENTS., LADIES AND
CHILDREN.

RUE SESOSTRIS - - - ALEXANDRIA.
Also Branches in CAIRO and MANSOURAH.

(left) British soldiers parading at the end of the war, probably in Alexandria.

(opposite) Christmas was celebrated at the Grand Hotel, Alexandria, with comrades signing each other's menus as a memento. Men will probably have eaten better food than at any other time in the previous four years.

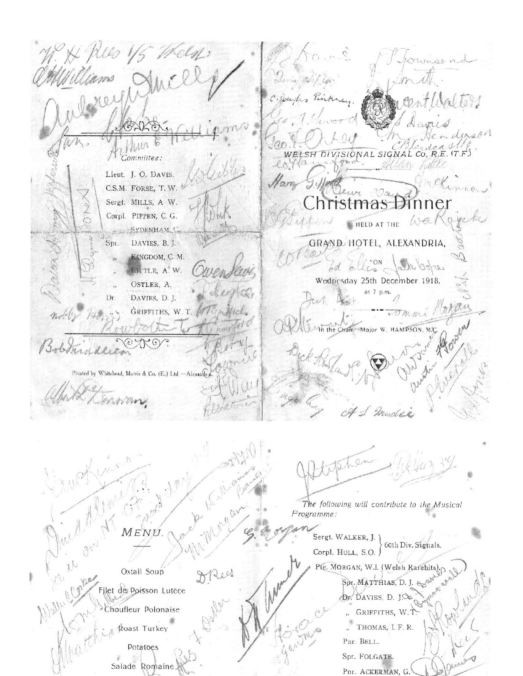

(above left) Certificate of Employment, listing the duties carried out during service, supplied to soliders to help them return to work.

(above) Protection Certificate. The document handed to soldiers "not remaining with the colours" on dispersal.

(left) Certificate of Transfer to the Reserves. Dewi could still be recalled if needed.

CHAPTER TEN

THE BEST BUNCH OF LADS

Friends and Cousins

During four years' continuous service abroad – a period of time and at an age when many young people today would be enjoying university as their first break from home – Dewi undoubtedly grew up. His letters tell us of a carefree pre-war existence in Cardiff, taking part in teenage activities that would make many parents shudder in the twenty first century. Much of his youth was spent taking long cycle rides, learning to swim in the open air pool in Splott, diving into Roath Park Lake on the city's then northern outskirts and even mud-wrestling on Pengam flats.[1] Dewi had joined up in 1915 because so many of his friends, many of them only a little older than he, had already enlisted. For much of his war, therefore, he was with people he knew, or knew where they were, and he would occasionally bump into them. He also had cousins and other relatives serving in the forces, as has been mentioned already, including four cousins on his father's side, Selwyn (who left for the Near East at roughly the same time), Arthur, Walter, and Alfred, and another cousin, Tom Jenkins, on his mother's side, and Hugh Mowbray, fiancé of Tom's sister Beatrice. Beat's sister, Janet was engaged to (and later married during the war) Eddie Richards, who served in the merchant marine. Dewi's best friend, Frank Somers, one year older, whose family had migrated from the West of England to Cardiff during the city's Coal Rush era in the latter years of the 19th century, was also posted to the Near East, and they met from time to time, and corresponded with each other. At times, too, they served alongside each other. Frank was but one of a number of Post Office colleagues, neighbours and other friends whom Dewi refers to regularly in his letters, an indication of the extent to which the young men of Britain were mobilised during the war and the impact this must have had on communities throughout the country.

In one of his first letters home from Gallipoli he gives his parents the doubtless re-assuring news that he has met up with several of his old chums. "We were very much surprised at the intermediate base to run up against Collett, who I thought was at home. I have seen most of the P.O. fellows here but some of them are in another part or else sick. Somers, I hear, is in hospital with some fever or other, so I was disappointed at not seeing him here."[2] The sea trip had apparently upset some of the men, though not Dewi. In his next letter he reports on the return from hospital of another of his friends and on the difficulty of finding and meeting people he wanted to see. "All the P.O. fellows are well and Pippen re-joined us a few days ago from hospital at Alexandria.[3] A recent copy of the Record giving his history found its way here and caused much amusement and he came in for a lot of chaff. I haven't come across him yet. It's a harder job than I thought, as he is a good way off, and we are not allowed to stray from camp."[4] Writing a few weeks later from the Signal Office at Suvla Bay, where he was now established, he reports the sea was

1) The land on which Roath Park was built was donated to the borough of Cardiff by the Marquess of Bute in 1887, and a 30 acre lake, formed by damming the Nant Fawr stream, was opened in 1894. The lake was popular for swimming and the venue for many years for the annual Taff Swim, an event attracting competitors from all over the British Isles. It was last held in 1961 when pollution fears resulted in swimming being stopped.

2) October 25th 1915. Young men would habitually refer to even close friends by their surnames in this period, a practice which probably only started to die out several decades after World War Two.

3) C.G. "Pip" Pippen, another friend from the Post Office, who had perhaps been laid low by his Gallipoli experiences.

4) October 31st 1915.

quite calm and sun shining, and two Cardiff colleagues his parents will have known were on either side of him.[5] "Edwards has the circuit on my left and Townsend occupies the one on my right. Contrary to my expectations, I have not yet met either Somers, Mac, or Hughie. However, I hope they are in the pink and that I will drop across them some day."

He is pleased to meet up with Hughie who came down to see him at his base in Suvla Bay. "He had made enquiries as to the whereabouts of our company and, happening to pass by, called in. We were both glad to see one another and I had a fairly long chat with him. He is looking O.K. but has had a pretty rough time of it. He says that I have come out at the best time."[6] Hughie had clearly been on Gallipoli for the earlier stages of the battle, before the reinforcements to which Dewi belonged had arrived. He was several years older and seems throughout the war to have taken an elder brother interest in Dewi as one of the youngest men serving in the Near East. Hughie died shortly after the war, leaving Beatrice, his widow, with a young son, Leighton, who went on to fly Spitfire over Europe, the Mediterranean and the Far East during World War Two. There is further mention of Leighton's father in a letter just before Christmas. You can bet, he says, that he is going to invite Hughie "to a feed, if he is anywhere about", when a certain parcel containing Christmas pudding arrives, he tells them.[7] Later that month writing after the severe November storms that flooded trenches on Gallipoli, Dewi reports: "I saw Hughie again a few days before I left our last address and had a long chat with him. He is quite OK but had a pretty rough time during the blizzard. He seems to have given you a fearful account of the flies etc."[8] His cousin's husband – clearly a family favourite – crops up again early in 1916 when Dewi, now in Egypt in Wardan, in Beni Salama Camp, 25 miles north of Cairo, drops by to give him a slice of his mother's Christmas cake, and talk about the happenings in Gallipoli, where they had last been in touch. "Hugh is O.K. and, of course, I had a lot to tell him of the life at our last address. He seemed glad that I have come away from there and thinks there will be "high jinks" there soon. I also was pleased to find Mac here and he tells me that Frank is about 15 miles away." A few weeks later he is writing to his parents thanking them for sending him out cigarettes, some of which he has passed to Frank who was "clean out" and "very grateful for them". All his P.O. colleagues were with him at this stage at their temporary new base Fayoum, except for Frank, who was still at another station some miles away and later up the line with the Brigade.[9] In November 1916 Signal Office duties bring him together again with Frank and another Cardiff colleague, S.V. Lewis.[10]

Other friends who had taken different military paths were also in touch. After arriving in Egypt, he mentions Billy London, as one of several people he had heard from that week, now somewhere in Norfolk and a bandsman, suggesting young people kept in touch with each other through letters in a way we perhaps thought had only become possible in the age of electronic communication, albeit much less

5) November 8th 1915.
6) November 11th 1915.
7) December 6th 1915.
8) December 20th 1915. Last address was Gallipoli.
9) January 24th, February 6th, 3rd, 29th 1916.
10) November 27th 1916.

frequently.[11] Another correspondent had been Cecil London – presumably Billy's brother – also in the Army, who had written to him from Italy while he was in Gallipoli.[12] Back home they were clearly confused as to where he and his former office colleagues all were, particularly at the start of their service. Writing from Egypt not long after they had withdrawn there from Gallipoli, he writes to put them straight. "In several of your letters I see you are enquiring about my companions and seem to think the company distributed [all] over the place. That is not so, all our company is together now in this camp and excepting one or two brigade sections, one of which, unfortunately for me, Frank Somers is attached [to]. However, all the P.O. fellows are here with us, Bully, [Sam] Milner, [Aubrey] Mills, Ropke, and that crowd, and Dai David, Collins and Edwards, so you needn't worry about my companions, we are all pals. In my tent are A. J. Thomas, Charlie Hardcastle, who by the way is quite changed and quite a noisy chap now, a postman from Tonyrefail, who is my champion when we have good humoured arguments about Wales and Lloyd George etc. and I may tell you also that we are able to hold our own. There is in our tent a farrier corporal from Maesteg and a telegraphist from Port Talbot. All decent fellows and good sports. Of course, I get a lot of chaff about being the "boy" of the tent. We also had two fellows from the S.E's office Cf [Cardiff] in the tent up till a week ago but they have gone out on telegraph duty with H.M. Price further up the line.[13] Hansford was one of them, I expect you know him, Dad, a very comical chap."[14] In May he reports that he has not seen Frank but has been corresponding with him, and they do finally meet up. "I forgot to tell you in my last that Frank Somers came to see me about a week ago and we had a few hours together. It was the first time I had seen him and he looks in the pink. He's a jolly decent chap (stood me a feed in the canteen). He's off to an awfully out of the [way] place, so I hear, and I had to send him some fags to console him."[15]

He continues to meet and correspond with Hughie throughout the war, frequently writing home to say he had either met with him or corresponded with him, or perhaps not seen him for long periods.[16] Writing from Fayoum, he says he does not know where he or cousin Selwyn are but expects to drop across them again during their "tour". "You see I owe Hughie 10 piastres." Later in the year he writes: "Had a card from Hugh yesterday also. Doesn't say where he's at but says there's no bathing there, so it can't be anything great. He says he's writing me in a few days and mentions that G. Davies is with him."[17] In November Hughie stumbles across him in the big Army camp in Moascar, while he is "keeping the desert tidy" and jocularly calls him to order for leaning on his shovel.[18] They met up again later that year, Hughie's familiar face seeming to re-assure him and remind him of home.[19] "It was at our first port of call that I met Hugh but not until my search for that worthy had extended through five battalions of infantry. I told him of this, whereupon, like the

---

11) February 29th 1916.

12) November 4th 1916.

13) S.E., possibly superintendent engineer.

14) March 2nd 1916. Hansford was several years older. He had qualified by examination to become a Post Office male learner in 1897, as did Dewi 16 years later.

15) May 1st 1916.

16) February 29th 1916

17) September 9th 1916.

18) November 27th 1916.

19) December 13th 1916.

buck he is, he suggested the canteen as a 'pick me up'. I was not averse to this, consequently we supped off pineapple chunks and 'Thin Lunch', our wines consisting of the juice at the bottom of the tin. Very much to my surprise, I met Dick Williams from Eyre Street [in Splott] while at this feast, and he wishes me to remember him to you with his kind regards. He recalled the Sundays of the past, when Dad was his "athraw" [Sunday School teacher] with Sydney and the rest, and seemed astonished that I had grown since those days of Whitsun treats and Gymanfau Ganu.[20] I can remember him clearly now as one of my favourites when in sailor collars, for he was an excellent fellow to talk about the approaching St. Mellons treat."[21]

Other meetings with Hugh and with his cousin Selwyn occur by chance. While on the tramp through Gaza in 1917, he meets Hugh at a well where his unit was gathering water. They meet at the same place again a few weeks later, and in a later letter he is able to send a picture of it home.[22] Several months follow when he does not see Hugh, though he does meet Selwyn. He hopes Hugh is not lost but thinks he may have been down in Cairo on leave, as Dewi himself had been about this time. Their next meeting that year was in September where Dewi's account suggests he thought he was being greeted by a new officer. "A few days since no other than Hughie presented himself in person at our camp. As he was in shirtsleeves and, therefore, no ensignia [sic] of rank or office, I may be excused for springing immediately to 'Attention', clicking my heels together smartly and bringing the right arm to the 'Salute' (badly wrenching my collar bone in the process, let it be mentioned). The broad expansive grin which spread over his countenance sufficiently intimated to me that we were still 'equals' and I was sorely tempted at being made the victim of such a scurvy trick, at the extremity of my resentment and confusion, to 'dot 'im one'. But thoughts of the grief of my esteemed kinswoman, Beatrice, served to dispel my determination for revenge and violent vindication of my honour and I quickly forgave the varlet. He has been on leave as well, so you can imagine the chin music was fast and furious while it lasted."[23]

Dewi's deep admiration and affection for his cousin's intended again comes through strongly when he is next mentioned the following year. "I had a caller from the Ambulance the other afternoon – a pal of Hugh's who showed me a letter he had received from the latter – in which he had requested this chap to inform me of his whereabouts and good health. I was jolly pleased with that, you may imagine, as having not seen him all this time I was wondering what had become of him. It seems he is with some Eastern County troops undergoing a course for his commission.[24] Bit of a surprise, I can tell you, 'cos I had left him at a very different occupation, pen pushing in a CCS.[25] By his letter I should judge he is highly delighted with everything and everybody around him where he is now. It was written in the inimitable 'H.M.' style and strain!, which always tickles me, and makes me grin hugely. It was jolly good news, anyway, and by the way he winds up, I should guess he had landed where 'Health and plenty cheer the labouring swoddy'.[26]

---

20) Gymanfaoedd Ganu, Non-Conformist church religious singing festivals.
21) 'Sailor suits' were a standard dress for young boys at the time.
22) March 30th, May 17th, June 10th 1917
23) September 5th 1917. Chin music, conversation.
24) The 54th (East Anglian) Division. Hughie undertook this course back in Cairo.
25) C.C.S., probably Casualty Clearing Station.
26) Health and Plenty, a quotation from Oliver Goldsmith's poem, *The Deserted Village*. 'Sweet Auburn, loveliest village of the plain, where health and plenty cheer the labouring swain.'

It filled me both with admiration and envy – judge for yourselves – 'Shall always think of you when I go to a pub' – doesn't that reveal to you the truly noble, affectionate side of his nature. Drinking a pal's health in a foaming tankard of joy-water – 'Snuff! it's enough to make a feller break down and blubber. Good luck to 2/Lt HM – skin off his nose – here goes my rum ration for the toast."[27] In April 1918 Dewi reports getting two letters from him. "He is down at Cairo and having quite a decent time but working much harder than he expected to do. Seems as if you are all expecting him home any time now but he doesn't think that at all possible. Have no doubt that he'll finish his training down in Egypt and that one day I shall have him calling in at my old bivvy in his posh uniform to see how I am at all. Wish I could have gone down on leave same time as he was there – that would have been great, eh? – we would have had a time, you bet."[28]

Dewi and Hugh were able not just to cheer each other up but also to provide further confirmation for family and friends at home of the other's welfare, particularly Hugh as the elder of the two. His next mention reports that Hugh is going strong but working hard withal. "Received a small parcel from him t'other day with fags, writing pad and envelopes and (observe the thoughtfulness) wrapped up in a ration bag and tied round with a pair of laces! A real brick, eh? You can easily tell he's been up here in the same fix – not half.[29] He complained in his letter of the scarcity of letters from home and I gave him what news I could." Hugh evidently took his duties looking after Dewi seriously, as the next mention suggests. "I have heard again from old Hugh, together with another cargo of whiffs – Jove! he's a sport. He hasn't heard from Beat since Xmas, so he tells me. Jolly hard cheese on a feller, especially when he's doomed, booked, snaffled or whatever you like to call it.[30] They all must have gone to his old Batt[alion] and he's counting on a mail bag all on his own one of these days. I don't half envy him, tho', 'cos he says he's practically wooed the old civvy looks and manners back by now – lucky dog. Guess he'll look some toff when he comes up here again. He won't know this ruffian and certainly wouldn't believe that he looked like it once upon a time. Swotting hard so he tells me and keeping cheerful – Gee Whiz! I should think so, too, look at his surroundings – Heliopolis, clean and white and sunny. Think I'd better follow his example and try for one in the old Welsh Regt. eh? You see, I can't aspire for a similar job in the Sigs. 'cos I haven't troubled to find out which opposite cable wagons attract or similar heliographs repel yet. I've had all my work cut out to keep my seat, leave alone prying into the depths of alchemy and science."[31]

There were more meetings with Cardiff friends and relatives early in 1918, including cousin Selwyn, in one of those chance encounters that seem to have characterised life in camp, when men were posted to faraway places, only to turn up again possibly months later after new orders. "I [...] met Selwyn again very unexpectedly the other day. We happened to be having a kick about with the ball one afternoon and he passed by on the road without noticing me. Luckily, I spotted him and yelled out. You can bet we had a lengthy pow-wow then and there, as we had not seen each other since last August and naturally were both anxious to know how each one had got on all

27) January 29th 1918. Winds up, finishes his letter. Joywater, beer.
28) April 29th 1918.
29) May 28th 1918. Dewi was in the hills north of Jerusalem.
30) June 8th 1918. Dewi's synonyms for engaged.
31) These references are ironic. The principles of magnetism and electricity, of course, involve poles attracting or repelling.

through the 'stunt'.[32] Jolly pleased, too, to find ourselves in the pink and none the worse for things in general lately. Very funny, too, you know, to think that I had missed him time and again on the way up 'cos on enquiring I found out that his battery had been supporting the brigade I was in in several places. Of course, if I'd known I could have had at least a few minutes with him." He was in Ramallah in billets and Selwyn appears to have been his salvation. "This meeting was before the parcel arrived for me and I may say I was jolly thankful to see him 'cos he saved my life with some fags from No. 10. Thank 'em from me – I never enjoyed a better smoke, say. The next day I visited him up at his gun position and spent the whole afternoon there being introduced to his fiancée, a very charming young lady camouflaged in the approved style and whose kisses Johnny Turk doesn't like at all at all. I helped swing her over into the required direction whilst there (nothing like making yourself useful). Anyhow, I saw Selwyn many times after. He used to pass our billet door daily and always called. Auntie and uncle will be glad to know he is in the veriest pink."

He has another piece of news in the same letter about home that he thinks they will be glad to hear. "They all knew at our place I was from Pentyrch, you bet.[33] (Don't call me a fraud, Dad, will you?) Anyhow, there were chaps there who knew Pentyrch well, having played football against them – 'nuff sed, so, passing by the cookhouse the other morning, I noticed one of our chaps talking to a gunner and he shouted, 'Dewi, here, a feller from Pentyrch – know him?' Strolled up and it was Conway Lewis – didn't know him before but he knew me. Had a long chat with him, of course, and saw more Pentyrch groups and photos of my aunts, uncles, cousins and Gia than I saw before. I'm blessed – it's jolly funny when you come to think of it – not in a Welsh village but in a miserable, typically Eastern, native village, noted as the place where Joseph and Mary first discovered the loss of Jesus.[34] 'That's a cousin of yours and that, and him and her,' – he was saying, pointing them out in a group, and, well, – blessed if I knew 'em. I tried fooling him into believing I knew 'em off by heart in alphabetical order but that game wouldn't work, 'cos when I'd say 'O! Yes, of course, that's so-and-so', it turned out to be 'O! No here's so-and-so, that's somebody else – bachgen [boy], someone else.' I shut up then, you bet, while he ran 'em thro' on his own without further interruption – and there was Gia annwyl [dear Grandma] sitting in the middle, looking as ever in the pink, and bachgen Tom having a dekko. Conway knew me alright – asked him how – 'O!' says he, 'you're one of the Davids alright, know 'em anywhere'." Dewi is also given news of another cousin, Arthur, whom he would have liked to see but, he reports, he was "back with the nags in Jerusalem", unfortunately. "I sent word down there and, sure enough, one of their drivers came up one day and called to say that Arthur wished to be remembered to me. I have every hope of seeing him, tho', in the near future when he comes up here, now that I know what mob he is in. When you go to Pentyrch you won't forget to tell Con's father about my seeing him, will you? – you might say that he is also absolutely fit as a fiddle."[35]

32) January 29th 1918. The march through the Judaean Hills.

33) Pentyrch, mentioned several times in the letters as his father's home, developed in the nineteenth century as an industrial centre based on the locally available reserves of iron, coal, and stone. Other industries included brick-making.

34) 'Now his parents went to Jerusalem every year at the feast of the Passover. And when he was twelve years old, they went up to Jerusalem after the custom of the feast. And when they had fulfilled the days, as they returned, the child Jesus tarried behind in Jerusalem; and Joseph and his mother knew not of it. But they, supposing him to have been in the company, went a day's journey; and they sought him among their kinsfolk and acquaintance. And when they found him not, they turned back again to Jerusalem, seeking him.' Luke 2:41-45. Dewi was in Ramallah at the time.

35) January 29th 1918.

Casualties of War

Events at home could, of course, have an impact on serving men, and in one letter he expresses his annoyance that the military had not made it possible for another friend to get home to see his mother, who had presumably died before he could reach her. "Glad to hear Bert Price got home alright but awfully sorry he was too late, it was a shame, you know, all the fault of the bosses, they could have easily allowed him to go earlier and see his mother."[36] Deaths in combat of friends also get noted. "Fancy Billy London transferring and in France. He's satisfied now, I know. And Alfred [Dewi's cousin] in the Northants, eh? He might be sent out here. Stanley James another addition to our Roll of Honour.[37] Dear, dear, developments, what?" The condolences keep coming to the end. "Very sorry, indeed, to hear of little Wally Shipton and your cousin, Dad – it is indeed a terrible time for Mrs Shipton. Other men he knew from home were captured, including it would seem Eddie's brother. He writes in early 1918 to say how awfully sorry he was to read about Wyndham Richards' recapture again after getting so far. "Hard luck that indeed. I can quite imagine they must be terribly disappointed at Marion Street."[38] In an earlier letter he had commented on another death. "Awfully sorry to hear poor old George Butcher has died in action with so many gallant lads. There must be a deal of sorrow in Blighty just now."[39] News of losses, mainly in France, were still filtering through towards the end of his service and give rise to emotional responses. "I was shocked to hear of the deaths of George Daniel and Horatio in action and cannot find words to express my deep sorrow. It is all so terribly sad and Walter [his cousin] at home an invalid.[40] Please extend my condolences to Mr Daniel in his great loss and thank him for his kind regards. I can scarcely credit it – it seems so cruel and the sad news hit me hard. It will be a great consolation to think that they fell like Welsh gentlemen."[41]

Other more fortunate friends from Cardiff had received less sympathy. "Surprised to hear about the departure of Ralph Roberts and Thos. John. They have gone very much abroad, haven't they? I expect Thos. John was glad to get away after such a long time in training. The linemen in E. Africa get a busy time, I hear, with the giraffes chewing up the air lines."[42] What this means is not clear but it perhaps suggests he thought men sent out to East Africa were having a particularly cushy time of it. In a largely forgotten sideshow to the Great War a total of at least 130,000 British Empire troops plus Portuguese and Belgian forces, sent to attack German East Africa, were tied down until the end of the war by 3,500 German and 12,000 African soldiers under the leadership of the very able General Paul von Lettow-Vorbeck, a feat that has been described as the greatest single guerrilla operation in history, and the most successful.[43]

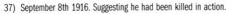

36) May 14th 1916.

37) September 8th 1916. Suggesting he had been killed in action.

38) February 3rd 1918.

39) July 31st 1916. Blighty was a widespread term used to refer to Britain and commemorated in the World War One song
Take Me Back to Dear Old Blighty.

40) His cousin, Walter, son of his father's oldest brother Enoch died in May 1918, presumably from his injuries.

41) May 28th 1918.

42) June 15th 1916.

43) Barnett, p56.

His cousin, Tom, who had been sent as a volunteer in France, suffered a number of injuries that required hospitalisation, eventually succumbing to a gas attack that left him gasping for much of the remainder of his life in his home in Carlisle Street, Cardiff, three doors away from his widowed sister, Hughie's fiancée Beat.[44] Shortly after arriving in Gallipoli, he writes to say he was grateful to learn that Tom had "pulled through" and that he had written to him. In the spring of 1916 Dewi wishes he could be in France to help him.[45] "Poor old Tom, I wish he were out here as well. I guess he's done his bit and deserves a rest now, if anyone does. I'd like to go out there and get attached to his brigade. We'd make 'em dance. He'd be able to give me heaps of tips about plugging 'em, as he used to about sparring some time ago. Remember when I hit him through the sofa?"[46] A few weeks earlier he had written to say how proud he was that Tom was making himself popular with the good work he was doing but sorry to hear he was having such a "rough time".[47] Tom was promoted in June, possibly to sergeant and possibly as a result of the heavy casualties now being recorded on the Western Front. He was wounded a month later. "I was awfully sorry to hear about Tom having been wounded in the glorious advance and was pretty anxious until I received your letter saying he was making good headway towards recovery. I'm very glad to hear that, indeed, but it's such rotten luck after being so fortunate, although I *was* surprised to hear he had been in hospital before and never said anything about it. That's the spirit and I admire his pluck and feel proud of my old pugilistic tutor...... Poor Bopa [Aunt] Mary must have been fearfully upset and I hope she has been given the strength to bear it.[48] As for me – well guarding the old Canal is quite good enough for kids, they seem to think." His cousin wrote to tell him he ought to consider himself lucky to be able to have a dip [in the Suez Canal] when he liked and to be away from such a place as France.[49]

For one of his periods of treatment Tom was returned to a hospital in the West of England, many miles from home and difficult for his family to visit. (Dewi's father wrote a personal letter to David Lloyd George asking that he be moved to Wales, which, co-incidentally or not, happened shortly afterwards. Lloyd George subsequently never had more loyal supporters, convinced he had been the main reason Britain had won the war and dismissive of any and every criticism the Liberal leader encountered.) Tom was getting better in August and regularly corresponding with Dewi – probably a decade his junior – in Egypt. "I received a letter from Tom a few days ago, and you may guess how pleased I was to get one from him. My letter and photo evidently pleased him, too, and he thanked me very much for them.[50] [...] He has gone through a lot, poor fellow, and certainly doesn't seem to have had good grub out there. Anyhow, it's a blessing he's improving and will soon be as right as rain once more. I must hurry up and answer him." Tom continues to be a cause of concern and much comment in the letters to the end, one of thousands of other casualties now being sent back from the Front in France

44) Hughie died shortly after returning from the war.
45) November 14th 1915.
46) April 7th 1916.
47) March 25th 1916.
48) July 31st 1916. The 'glorious advance' was possibly the battles of the Somme. Bopa (Aunt) Mary was his mother's sister.
49) July 31st 1916 and September 9th 1916.
50) September 9th 1916.

to hospitals or on leave in Britain. He has, we learn from one letter, been "under X-rays", a relatively recent medical procedure, and Dewi hopes "this agony of hospital life for him will soon end".[51] In fact, it is not until June that he is able to write home saying the news about Tom (contained in one of their letters to him) was very satisfactory. "Now that he will soon have the lead out of his arm, we shan't be long before hearing from him."[52] A couple of months later, the news seems to have got worse again, with Dewi writing to say he hopes Tom is better and trusts he will soon be admitted to hospital.[53] He writes later to say he is very glad to hear that Tom has been admitted to Splott Hospital and that he has been successfully operated upon.[54] Another Tom has also been literally in the wars – Tom Gwaelod, possibly a relative on his mother's side from her home village of Gwaelod-y-Garth. In two letters written in January 1918, Dewi first expresses the hope Tom Gwaelod is O.K. again, and the hope he won't have to go again (presumably back to the front). In his next letter he describes it as a blooming shame Tom Gwaelod has had to go back "in such an unfit state". His cousin Tom had apparently said he would be happy to move to Palestine for a change but Dewi counsels against. "You better tell him that if it's like that he might do worse than go in for a few months' course marching up and down Heol Goch and the Garth just to get a bit of practice."[55]

Some of the writing about colleagues is far more sentimental than we would expect nowadays, as, for example, his reaction to a newspaper cutting his father had sent him about an individual, Billy Arnold, who seems to have made a big impression on an impressionable young man during training in the UK – a period when the war must still have appeared like a great adventure in the making. Who Billy Arnold was and why he made such a big impression we will never know, though alcohol seems to have played a part. He is possibly the officer, perhaps a major, who was in charge of their training before they left Britain but who, forcibly or otherwise, had now left the scene. What is certain is that he was what would nowadays be called a "character". "The perusal of the cuttings sent have afforded me much pleasure and, in the case of Arnold's cutting, much mirth. Good old Billy! You see I can't forget my period of service with that band of notorious dare-devil troopers rejoicing in the name of 'Billy Arnold's Cossacks of the Guard'. Those were the days, right enough, and will ever be remembered and numbered amongst the happiest I ever spent. The thrilling anecdotes I could spin about them would fill a volume. Of how we charged the targets at Dallington Range, near Northampton, when Bill shouted "Up guards, and at 'em".[56] Of the night operations at Cambridge, where he always showed his talent as a great leader, warning us against snipers, riding at our head on his coal black charger like the Napoleon he was, engrossed in his thoughts (and flask). Taking us along roads unmarked upon the map and finding the route once more by his unrivalled generalship. He was never more than 20 miles out was our Bill. Ah! how we loved him, worshipped him, our idol, our little father, our one and only Willyum. I remember the touching scene at our departure from Aberystwyth

51) February 25th 1917
52) June 19th 1917.
53) August 7th 1917.
54) August 25th 1917. Howard Gardens High Schools, which Dewi and his sister had attended, were the location for the 3rd Western General Hospital during World War One, with sectional hospitals at King Edward VII Hospital (Cardiff Royal Infirmary), and at Splott Road, Ninian Park, Lansdowne Road, and Albany Road Schools.
55) January 4th 1918, Heol Goch, a street in Pentyrch, and the Garth, the mountainside to which it clung.
56) Dallington, near Northampton, where Dewi undertook some of his basic training.

to seek fresh worlds to conquer. The townsfolk reduced to bitter tears while Bill, our chief, consoled them. 'Farewell,' said he, 'Farewell, we shall meet again on the field of a vanquished foe, remember me, if I do not return,' like the brave, unselfish marshal he was. We forgave him all his faults. There's always some good in the worst of us and always some bad in the best of us. Forgave him his whiskies and sodas and bleary eyed appearance on 6 am parade. Forgave him when he sat up the long night through, poring over plans in pubs on night manoeuvres, for a kindly heart had old Bill. I could tell you of the time when he once paid for 39 men to have a good breakfast and gave the QMS at fault the choking off of his life.[57] Neither newspaper men nor anybody else knew Bill like his own Cossack rascals knew him. But Bill, you're gorn nah, who knows! Perhaps some day you'll return to us from Elba once again, and 'Billy's Cossacks of the *Old Guard*' will once more flock to your banner in answer to your magnetic personality and the mysterious call of the clatter and jingle of 'sabre touche' and spurs.[58] Be that as it may, I, for one shall always salute 'our Bill', an officer and a true gentleman. Major, remember, privates at least never forget 'one of the very best'."[59]

Dewi, and most of the men he had joined up with, remained in the Middle East for the duration of the war and even longer but some servicemen did get to return home on leave, and were able to provide first-hand information to parents and friends. "Walter Hansford returned to us a little while ago from his Blighty leave and By Jove! I never saw such a change in a feller in all my life.[60] It's done him ten worlds of good and he's just huge compared to his old self (compared with all of us poor emaciated blighters, I'm afraid) – fat as a porker, believe me. I had a long chat with him, you bet, and was much interested in his version of Cardiff in the year 1918. He assured me that once he'd had a good hot bath, a Blighty feed, and had raked up one of his old civvy suits, collar and tie etc. he felt as if he'd never worn khaki in his life and settled down to society in no time, causing him great astonishment, indeed. Well, that was good news, you bet – I quite enjoyed that but was awfully disappointed that he had not met you. You are, too, no doubt, Dad – Gee! what a parley you'd have had. He explained to me how it was and really it was jolly hard luck 'cos he did his best – rely on old Walt for that. It seems that the few times he called at the Club you were on nights, so he decided to visit you at home one night. And, what putrid luck, too. Arriving in the vicinity of Moorland Road, he made enquiries of a Mr David from the P.O. and from what I can gather those enquiries were made at one of the houses opposite us. It was dark and either the woman was careless in her information or else Walter made a mistake. Anyhow, he rapped at no. 78, Taylors next door, for about ten minutes and getting no reply concluded you were all out. Crumbs! I could have wept and, altho' intending to pay another call at the office or the house, he was recalled at short notice, as you know. Rotten, I call it – I wouldn't have had you miss him for worlds, you bet. Still, let's hope the next lucky dog to go on leave gets better luck."

57) QMS, Quartermaster Sergeant.
58) Sabretache, a leather case worn by cavalry officers at the left side and suspended from the sword belt on long straps. Napoleon was exiled to Elba off the coast of Tuscany after his forced abdication in 1814. The Old Guard were the elite veterans of Napoleon's Imperial Guard.
59) September 8th 1916.
60) May 28th 1918.

He had previously tipped his parents off that Hansford, someone who seems to have had a world-weary take on the war, was due back. "Regarding that drily humorous cutting from the paper you sent me, describing the Holy City, well, I guess I can enlighten you a bit easy as to the author – Hansford, all the world over, Dad – it's him to the T, and just his usual style of looking at things. By the way, he's in Cardiff now, home on leave, wonder if he's called in to see you yet, as he promised me he would before leaving us."[61] By the middle of 1918, with the Turks clearly now heading for defeat the Army seems to have begun to allow more soldiers from the Middle East theatre to make the long journey home. Other callers later the same year were able to tell his parents how he was getting on. "I was very pleased to hear that you had met Sergt. Pace in town and hope in the few moments he had to spare you derived sufficient information to go on with till someone else turns up."[62] He had also told them a month earlier to look out for another colleague from the Egyptian Expeditionary Force "where leave is almost extinct as a rest". "There's a chap gone from us today on leave who lives in Cardiff, and he promised me he'd look you up. Davie Roberts, by name, and one of the very best. I know you'll be delighted to see him – don't absolutely exhaust him with questions, or try not to, won't you?"[63]

Of Reluctant Warriors

The views of people back home and what they were saying about soldiers in the various theatres would have been well known to the ordinary soldier from the newspapers and magazines regularly sent from home. In this environment there was little sympathy for men who, for one reason or another, had failed to come forward or had waited until the war was nearly over to join the Colours. Early in the war, in response, it would seem, to a question his father must have asked him in a letter from home, he writes: "Conscientious objectors and all that rot don't worry us, Oh! No. But when we see items in the news about them, well, – I shouldn't like to tell you how eloquent the b'hoys [sic] wax about them. However, we'll let those silly asses drop and get to biz."[64] There is only contempt, too, later on for those joining the Colours right at the end of the war, particularly those who would then be posted to France. "Your remarks re the scores of young men rolling up to the Colours stirred me, too – I thought they were all out. It is very gratifying news, indeed, but tell me – I'm dead serious – why the hell couldn't they have come before? Never gave it a thought, I s'pose – never dreamt in '15 of poor, brave blighters on Gallipoli holding the line with brigades only 200-300 strong, dwindling, dwindling and never a reinforcement with Turks like flies in front – and the sea a daily dreaded emergency backdoor. The state of affairs which K of K after his visit there confessed to a friend kept him awake at night 'thinking of those brave fellows and the pitiful line they held', O! yes *I* can tell you why the narrows [the Dardanelles] weren't taken.[65] Still I'm glad 'cos I'll never forget what old Mr Lloyd told me when I left, 'Boy, you're going out to a lot of heroes', and Heavens! he was right."[66]

61) April 14th 1918.
62) July 27th 1918.
63) June 28th 1918
64) May 14th 1916.
65) Lord Kitchener of Khartoum.
66) May 28th 1918. Mr Lloyd, possibly a chapel elder or neighbour.

He mocks "those young fellows who haven't lost any time but enlisted straightaway in *1918*" who, he speculates, will be fussed over – "gallant this and gallant that, go to France in time for the coup de grace, come back and get crowned with laurels etc." He contrasts this with what the men in the East reading the newspapers must have felt was the calumny of attacks on their heroism, serving in a theatre other than France. "What a difference to the way I can see the 53rd and their comrades here being treated when they go back. 'O! yes, you skulked and shirked for 3 years on Suvla, Egypt, Palestine and Salonica – hid in petty side-shows like that' – Skulked? Shirked? Hid? – my Heaven! 'the gratitude (?) of a very grateful (?) country'. And, also news filters thro', even to this benighted, accursed hole, of the rapturous applause bawled out from gallery to stalls in our London music halls in nightly hate and contempt for the victims of Miss Marie Lloyd's very popular ballad, 'If you don't want to fight, go to Palestine.' Is this not so? Bah! I'm too disgusted to be even slightly annoyed. And isn't Mrs Pankhurst suggesting that we all be exiled on some remote island in quarantine for a few years before being allowed to set foot on that dearly beloved land? – which, after all, doesn't seem to be so blamed beloved as I once imagined. How excruciatingly amusing – really! Guess Abdul Hamid, Enver Pasha and their countrymen would treat us better and certainly with more respect.[67] I've often smiled at some chaps when they express their views that 'England will be too small for 'em after this' but I don't, now, 'cos I realise what they really mean is that its loathsome attitude towards them will cause them to shake its dust from their feet for all time in highly justified disgust. We are, you see, well versed in passing events – too well versed for any hopes of an attempt at [avoiding] disillusionment meeting with success. Certainly, I do not credit to the full such exaggerated instances as I have here cited – rumours are rumours but there is a strong undercurrent, which gets my goat."[68]

Soldiers serving in less well-known campaigns have throughout the ages seen themselves as unfairly overlooked. Men in Italy in World War Two felt similarly slighted after the term D-Day Dodgers was coined to describe their service away from the Normandy landings. It gave rise to a popular sog, by Lance Sergeant Harry Pynn, sung to the tune Lili Marlene, 'We're the D-Day Dogers, out in Italy, always on the vino, alway on the spree'. Britain's Lt. Gen. Sir William Slim's Fourteenth Army was referred to as the Forgotten Army because its operations in the Burma Campaign were not well reported by the contemporary press, remaining more obscure than those in Europe for long after the war. British forces also fought in the Middle East in World War Two in forgotten campaigns in Iraq, and Palestine, and against the Vichy French in Lebanon and Syria. A further aggravation for men in the Middle East was the way in which practical support for the troops, from the public and business, was directed mainly to France. Dewi reflects bitterly in early 1918 on the Christmas puddings sent to men in France but not to them.[69]

67) Sultan Abdülhamid II, Emperor of the Ottomans, Caliph of the Faithful (also known as Abdul Hamid II or Abd Al-Hamid II Khan Ghazi) 1842–1918) was the 34th sultan of the Ottoman Empire. He oversaw a period of decline in the power and extent of the Empire, ruling from 31 August 1876 until he was deposed on 27 April 1909. Abdülhamid II was the last Ottoman Sultan to rule with absolute power, and was succeeded by Mehmed V.

68) Whether or not the reports of Marie Lloyd's songs were correct, men of the EEF felt strongly their efforts were under-appreciated in comparison with soldiers on the Western Front.

69) February 6th 1918.

Particularly wounding as far as the men in the Middle East were concerned were the comments of fellow-servicemen, catching it would seem a public mood that all soldiers serving in the war should suffer the same horrors as the men on the Western Front. Billy London, whom he seems to have looked down on for joining up as a bandsman, receives withering fire in 1918 for reporting rumours the 53rd might be transferred to France and as a result would soon experience real war. He writes: "Thanks awfully for disillusioning me as regards public opinion towards our humble lowly host. I will now quote you the very latest extract from the letter I have received upon the self-same subject. It is the opinion (the all-important, reliable, influencing one, may it be said) of a blood-stained hero of a thousand battle-marches and national anthems – one Bandsman W.F. London by name (to note his rank is to realise that he must have snatched the few moments to express this opinion when the overture waged hottest, when the trombone artillery crashed loudest, nothing could be heard except the whine and squeak of the 'shell-os' [cellos]).[70] These are the words which have fallen out of the mouth of a babe and suckling.... 'Rumour hath it that you will soon be with us here and we were saying 'Poor old – rd they'll know what a *strafe* is *now.*'[71] (Pardon me while I imbibe from the contents of my bottle for the double purpose of recovering from faintness and also to cleanse any lingering traces of the lurid epithets you have been spared here.) Note the kind, considerate, condescending, overwhelming air of sincere sympathy expressed thus by those noble breeze up windjammers – "For Tchaiskowsky [sic] my lungs, my wind, my all I give" – (with apologies to Richard and the Crusaders for which blasphemy may Heaven and them forgive me, writing it, as I am, in their own ancient arena. Note also the worlds of meaning in that aftermath of sympathy, my brethren, the calm confidence with which those knights of the clarion and triangle make use of the dread word 'strafe'." The previous month he had pointedly asked for shoulder titles to be sent out. Writing to his sister with a list of requests he says: "I should like very much to have 2 handkerchiefs, one or two indelibles, Health Salts (pretty warm you see – refresher like), Sunlight Soap (non-scented please (!), plenty of chewing gum, a pair of *thick* socks, one of Dickens' funniest and also a pair of metal shoulder titles if you can get 'em – I doubt if you can, but have a try. This sort – "T R.E. WELSH" – not forgetting the T stands for Territorial. Tall order, Doll, I'm afraid, but do what you can, please." The significance of this may be that Territorials were men who had joined up before conscription had obliged them to do so and he was keen to make this point on his return.[72]

They were being compared unfavourably with the men in France but at least the latter could get back home from time to time to rest and recuperate and had not been stuck thousands of miles away from family and friends for years at a time. He continues: "One can realise, is, in fact, given to understand, that they have forgotten more about 'strafe-horrors' than the poor, ignorant, uninitiated persons to whom they extend their doggone sympathy will ever know. The men, my friends – the men who braved a thousand bars, the baton and the breeze. (For 'bars' please substitute 'estaminets' as being a more vivid local colour.)[73]

70) July 29th 1918.

71) Dewi omits the number 53, writing 'Poor old –rd' perhaps to avoid the censor's blue pencil.

72) June 8th 1918.

73) Estaminet, French bar, contrasted with the bars in musical scores. He goes on to compare the length of tours of duty in France and the Near East.

These are they, I presume, who proceed in shining raiment across Channel onceevery 6 years – er – sorry that's E.E.F. establishment – 6 months, I should say, to extol the terrors of Flanders to horrified admiring listeners, forgetting to mention, of course, that the only horrors they have probably experienced are those of their own production in the mutilation not of that country but of the strains of *La Brabanconne*, which is after all first cousin to it and sufficient to clear any remnant of conscience.[74] O! these gallant, modest, heroes – it has caused me more mirth than a Mark Twain masterpiece, you may be sure. And, it's not so bad for Billy [London] considering that he was patrolling a Scarboro promenade in company with Betty, Amaryllis, Dorothy or whatever her name was, at the same time as I was patrolling an Ottoman promenade with Lizzie – just plain Lizzie and her sisters." Dewi reports thanking him heartily for his sympathy, and telling him how excruciatingly, murderously, funny he was getting in his senile decay. "Rich? – By hokey![75] it's enuff to make a crocodile weep champagne. I had a blamed good mind to advise him that when he comes down so low in the world as to suck odoriferous marshes and drink his own water like the – rd has done during intervals, instead of bierre [sic] and seen men go mad not from the effects of cognac but from real thirst he'll be fully qualified then to exchange notes and opinions about strafes. 'Know what a "strafe" is *now*.' Heavens above! and they [the 53rd] were practically annihilated before he got out of the range of his mother's apron strings."[76]

Somewhat unfairly he is scathing, too, about munitions workers, whose job was both unpleasant and dangerous. Commenting in April 1918 on the possibility of home leave, he writes; "Nunno, Dad, I can't possibly imagine it somehow, and when I read the picture just described – well, I feel quite frightened. Besides, I'm indispensable and I shouldn't like to see the old division going to the beastly bow-wows, which would assuredly occur if all the stickers were exchanged for sleek, comfortable, nervous greenhorns of munition workers who haven't taken the risk. It would soon lose its fame as the maddest, reckless, invincible and finest old div. as ever was. Old Johnny'd soon spot the difference first stunt, and he wouldn't half take advantage of it, and we, as we are – well, we just about got the blighter weighed up and know all his delightful little tricks. Moreover, you won't have to wait long now – it's soon going to fizzle out and so I feel sure you're quite agreeable to let me stop and see this out. It'd be more satisfying, like, and then I wouldn't care a brass farthing."[77] That the realities of war affected him is clear from a request he sent his sister to do him the favour of treasuring "that Cross snap, until my return home. Money couldn't buy that one – nor even aur Peru [the gold of Peru] or trysorau'r India Fawr [all the treasures of mighty India]." The Cross, he writes, stands in an alcove of the wall adjoining a little church in a remote Palestinian village – "one single, solitary, roughly-hewn stone cross carved by the REs – the only diminutive cemetery for the bravest of the brave – 'The Soldiers of the 53rd who fell in action in this district.' 'This district and what a district it embraced in spite of its insignificance – Suvla, Sinai, and Palestine'."

---

74) The Belgian national anthem.
75) Hokey, deception, jugglery.
76) July 29th 1918.
77) April 14th 1918.

Jokes and Japes

Inevitably, a group of men stuck out in the desert together developed a strong sense of camaraderie and, as a comparatively young member of the company, Dewi may well have been on the end of a lot of affectionate joshing as when he stops being a cook (or more probably canteen assistant) and returns to duty on a circuit in the Signal Office after the move to Serapeum on the Canal in June 1916. "The chaps are all pulling my leg a bit, saying I'm getting thin since chucking up that job [...] and they say they get twice as much of a helping now as when I dished it up, but I retaliate by saying they were living too high (?) [sic] and I was only training them, after which I have got to scoot, dodging such missiles as boots and mess tins."[78] Several letters in the first half of 1916 make joking references to his attempts to grow a moustache, perhaps to make himself look older.[79]

Long periods of familiarity had by 1918 evidently resulted in some breaking down of discipline and respect for rank, accompanied by a longing to get home. The semi-organised games of football and rugby that they had been able to play in the desert earlier in the campaign will have continued as far as possible in the Judaean hills, together with milder pastimes, such as card games. The men, however, seem to have relieved their boredom and frustrations with ever more elaborate pranks. At Ramallah, where they were getting a welcome break after the march on Jerusalem in the previous month, he writes of his companions as "some of the jolliest, rowdiest and altogether too irresistible boys you could wish for pals – a merry crew, By Jove! not half." He continues: "I roared from morning till night and if you'd seen us in our new revue, 'Hullo Tommy Atkins', at night in the billet, when we all line up and do the revue girls' stunts in the approved manner, you'd have roared, too. We had it off pat. Then there were those glorious scuffles and 'rough-houses' in the dark after lights out at night when the blankets and kits used to get in a hopeless muddle and you could no more find your socks next morning than fly. Then, again, there was the night when I and young 'Corker' stole in stealthily to the office intent on scruffing the sergeant (a proper trump) but, sad to say, payed [sic] heavily for spoiling his parting – (he played for Penarth and Cardiff) – Phew! Gee Whiz! talk about Rugger. I was sewing buttons on all day next day. That's the kind of Army for me – where they carry those chevrons lightly and a man's a – well, a man, where not only could you have a shot at scruffing him but call him 'Nut' instead of 'Sergeant' without fear of toeing the line next morning. By Jove! – if I could only march thro' St. Mary St with that desperate band – that's the height of my ambition – every man jack of us every inch anything but a 'soldier', and never intend to be and – what's more – proud of it."[80]

His next letter carries on in the same vein.[81] "Isn't all hard work in this billet of ours, tho' – nunno, these fellows – bless 'em are as mischievous as a couple of wagonloads of monkeys. Always out for killing ennui, you might say, and by Jove! they succeed exceedingly well. You see, we're up in the gallery, as you might say – up the stairs, that's where we live, and our house is our castle. Naturally, we don't allow any

78) May 31st 1916.
79) February 29th, March 25th, April 13th, June 30th 1916.
80) January 29th 1918. St. Mary Street, one of the main shopping thoroughfares in Cardiff.
81) February 6th 1918.

N.C.O.s to come in giving old buck, you bet, 'cos you see those corporals in the 'pit' downstairs have been giving a deuce of a lot of trouble lately – you wouldn't believe. They've been spoiling for a blooming rumpus for about a week now and there's been trouble in the air as you might say. In fact, it got so bad that the orderly corporal had to have an escort to take care of him when he came into our room to read the orders for next day." There follows a long description of a mock fight in which he gets sent out as a scout, is seized by the corporals and tried before one of the 'courts' soldiers used to organise informally to hold each other to their self-appointed rules. In the battle that follows the corporals, it would seem, are routed, but Dewi writes, "we're ready for 'em again whenever they feel fit enough to chance their arms, – not 'arf. O! aren't we a ragtime lot – fancy staid old warriors like us acting like a lot of schoolboys on a half holiday – 'sridiculous, isn't it?"

More escapades follow in April, suggesting the men were being left largely to their own devices now the Turks had retreated, and were subject to the lightest of discipline. "We also take a half limber wagon and tank down for our own drinking water, which rattles and bangs and jingles along 'cos we move *some* – so that's how we came to christen it 'The Fire Engine' and ourselves the 'Palestine Fire Brigade'.[82] Thus, every morn and afternoon there's a fire out here and directly we get over the ridge, it's a straight plain right across, and the Fire Brigade warms to its work, I assure you. Fun? – Lummy! it's gorgeous – pell-mell, helter-skelter we go across there at a stretch gallop – the old 'Engine' bumping and banging away – round the corner of those houses and up the long avenue of trees at a headlong pace till I fear we must frighten those Jewesses from the farm colony out of their wits. A few mornings ago a feller's saddle broke or something, and flying he went right over the mules' ears – Gosh! you never saw such a scrumptious stampede in all your born days – mules bucking and jumping and horses going stoney hatch causing us to do the strangest Broncho [sic] Bill feats imaginable."[83]

There was further mayhem some days later. "Another morning, something similar happened – all was going on smoothly and we'd have got to that fire in record time, if the old Engine hadn't met with an unfortunate accident. You see 'it' happened just near those houses – we were going to the rescue at a rattling pace as per usual, carrying all before us when Biff! – the off wheel of the 'Engine' struck a rather large pebble lying in the track and, running along for ten yards on the other wheel, turned completely turtle – wagon and tank, mules and harness all in as glorious a mix-up as you ever saw and as for poor old Supt. Gun – you couldn't see that poor blighter."[84] Dewi according to his report saved the situation, crying out 'Halt'! "It was a ridiculous order to give seeing as he'd already halted very forcibly indeed. 'Halt! the Engine', I shouted in a stentorian tone of voice, and, calmly turning on my haunches towards one of those Hebrew young ladies, who was standing near, dumbfounded and aghast at the scene, I doffed, and, smiling sweetly, said in polite tones, 'Excuse me mademoiselle Rebecca – er – but could you please inform me as to the whereabouts of the – er – conflagration?', and those rude fellows actually

---

82) April 14th 1918. Limber, the detachable front of a gun-carriage, consisting of two wheels, axle, pole and ammunition box, or in this case cable-drum.

83) Hatch, brought low. Stoney meaning utterly, cf. Stoney broke. Bronco, a wild or untrained horse, inclined to throw its rider. William Walters (Bronco Bill), 1869-1933, an outlaw in the days of the Old West in the U.S.

84) Meaning of Supt. Gun unclear.

showed their ignorance in front of a lady by rolling off their saddles in convulsions, which probably accounts for the fact that she vouchsafed no reply to my earnest query, or it may have been that she didn't compree the King's English." These Jewish girls, dressed in traditional Middle Eastern costume, were evidently as much a cause of fascination as the Arab 'belles' he had previously encountered on the Canal and in Gaza. "She was much too startled to utter a word but I fancy I can gauge the full purport of her thoughts – 'The English – mais oui – they are indeed mad.' Presently, Supt. Gun crawled gingerly from beneath the debris and chaos, and, feeling himself tenderly all over every square inch of his massive frame, inquired in a plaintive voice if it wasn't 'gross negligence on the part of the Palestine Urban District Council in not providing scavengers for the removal of banana-skins from the King's Highway'? and hurled vituperous epithets down on the head of the careless personage responsible for his beloved chargers narrowly averting serious injury."[85]

After nearly four years away from home, the units Dewi served with had developed their own rituals, and, no doubt, their own favourites and dislikes. Some may even have been members of the various lodges the Victorians had established and had brought a version of their rules and regulations for membership with them. After re-joining the company in January 1918 – "away from Frank Somers and the brigade b'hoys", he reports that his old philosophy was sustaining him and a warm welcome was awaiting him. "There's good fellers everywhere – I'm with the old clique again – the well – you knows – they're here, too, don't you worry and were blooming glad to see me – same here B'Jove! Being somewhat of a 'stranger' tho', I was welcomed to this home in the usual style and with the usual awe-inspiring pomp and ceremony. I had to pay my footing by order of the 'most worshipful Master' and most worshipful Brothers of the Lodge, you bet, my sentence being to render the first verse of that sentimental ballad 'Alice! Where art thou?'[86] Well, the Court sat around with solemn dignity, and I arose. It had to be done and the least sign of a grin would mean so many strokes of the 'Dido' (buckle end). However, I did my best and got well away but had only just got up to that pathetic part, you know, where it says 'Life's dream is o'er' – and I wasn't half letting it rip, I can tell you – full blast when the 'Grand President' silenced me with one wave of his mitt – 'Enough!' says he – 'You'll do', and so to cut a long story short, Behold me one of the 'Most Worshipful Brothers' of the Most Noble Order of Lead Swingers."[87]

The general cheeriness of men in the Division is remarked on in the divisional history. "The 53rd was a happy family; intercourse between infantry and artillery, train and medical services was free, and friendships were wide. The effort of the campaign, the hardships of resisting extremes of heat and cold, the discomfort, even the misery all were recompensed by the joviality and good cheer of fraternal meetings where troubles took flight."[88] The young man who had joined up in 1915 had now come full circle, however. Away from family, the job he had started only

85) April 14th 1918.
86) *Alice, Where Art Thou?* An American Song from 1861 by Wellington Guernsey and Joseph Ascher. 'The birds sleeping gently, Sweet Lyra gleameth bright; Her rays tinge the forest, And all seems glad tonight. The wind's sighing by me, Cooling my fever'd brow; The stream flows as ever, Yet Alice where art thou!'
87) January 29th 1918.
88) Dudley Ward, p245.

years previously, and from the places he knew and loved at home, he was now keen, no doubt like many soldiers to keep his head down and survive until the end, despite the bonding and the good times. His return would not come, however, until he disembarked at Southampton on March 21st 1919, four months after the Armistice. He passed through the huge demobilisation camp at Fovant in Hampshire the same day, reaching Splott at last on March 22nd.

(left) "Our office shift" on the Suez Canal. Dewi is in the middle of the back row.

(below) 158th Infantry Brigade Signals.
Dewi is front row, first left.

(bottom) Unknown group, probably taken in Egypt.

"The Huttites", Dewi's joking reference to the ancient Hittite people of the Middle East.

Canal Zone Signals. Men were distributed to bases at intervals along the Canal.

His friend Frank Somers, "a Subador [Indian commissioned officer] and a camel."

Hughie Mowbray, the fiancé of his older cousin Beat, who took a lively interest in Dewi's welfare.

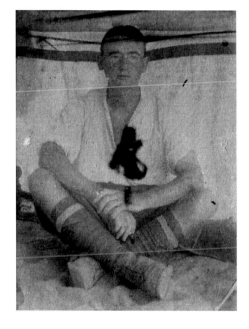

"Frank Somers and his Office."

Dewi (second left), on holiday in the 1920s with
wartime colleagues Frank Somers (left), Aubrey Mills,
(second right) and Sam Milner.

CHAPTER ELEVEN

THE FOLKS BACK HOME

Spare Not the Ink or Paper

Today, when soldiers serving abroad can text, e-mail, call up by mobile, or even Skype their families, and see and talk to their parents, siblings and children via satellite technology, it is hard to imagine how cut off from home men posted to distant lands must have felt. In Dewi's case separation from family and the only surroundings he had known for his first 17 years lasted for four years, an eventuality he could scarcely have imagined when he signed on enthusiastically in 1915 to share the experiences of his friends. Mail in World War One had to be carried by sea and in distant parts of the conflict, such as the Middle East, could take weeks to arrive or even end up at the bottom of the ocean, if the ship was attacked by enemy vessels, including the comparatively new addition to warfare, submarines. First used in warfare as far back as the American Civil War, submarines formed part of all the major navies' fleets by the start of the World War One but the biggest and deadliest were those of the Germans.[1]

Apart from his stay on the Canal for five months in 1916, Dewi was often on the move so that parcels and letters could end up in the wrong place and take weeks to be redirected, having already taken weeks to arrive from Britain. Much of his correspondence is taken up with acknowledging letters and parcels and confirming receipt or otherwise, with sympathising with his parents for the long delays in hearing from him, or consoling himself for the long gaps between deliveries from home. These delays were, of course, all the harder to bear inasmuch as troops in the Middle East theatre seem to have depended very heavily on the home front for supplies of food and even basic essentials, such as pencil leads, toothpaste and flea powder. There was also the censor to avoid, though, as noted elsewhere, their vigilance was probably never very strict. In one of his first letters he closes his letter with a Welsh phrase – Yr eiddot yn gariadus – but then translates it, Yours Lovingly, in case the censor strikes it out because he could not understand it.[2] The censor's attention and the soldiers' fears of being hauled up for divulging information evidently drops over time, however, and there is no evidence anything he ever wrote was stopped or even read.

Dewi David was lucky in that he had many correspondents, not just his father and mother, and sister, but relatives and other family, friends and neighbours, and colleagues from the Post Office. Some of these, too, sent parcels, including his Sunday School. Like many soldiers, what he wanted more than anything else, however, was a letter from Mum, and this is what he missed most of all. More than two years into his service he is still urging all three correspondents at home "to spare not – the ink or the paper", and this must surely have been the attitude of most servicemen of the era.[3] In the lower middle class Edwardian household of the sort he came from the serious business of writing letters was a task that devolved on the man, sometimes on the daughters, but probably not on the wife and mother. Her domain, as is clear from Dewi's letters, was the kitchen, where the products of her labours over the stove, sent out in regular parcels, were appreciated and lavishly

1) Germany used submarines principally to attack merchant ships bringing food and other supplies to Britain. Suspended after American pressure, the Germans resumed unlimited attacks in January 1917, precipitating US participation in the war.
2) October 18th 1915.
3) September 23rd 1917.

– some might say fulsomely – praised. Cakes from home are what seem to have kept many servicemen going, emotionally as well as physically. Yet, sometimes he admits he would have traded all her culinary efforts for a letter. He was devoted to his mother, and his correspondence, certainly when he first went abroad, is clearly that of someone still heavily under parental influence. She was, it seems, a strong moral force in his life, offering him some advice as a 17 year-old on the temptations he might now encounter in Army life, to judge by some comments he made shortly after arriving in Egypt. "Your words, Mum, will not be forgotten. I am sure the thoughts of you dear three would make me always act as you would wish me to."[4] As noted previously, it was to her that he asked that part of his Army pay of 10/- a week be allotted during his service. "Glad to hear you are getting my allotment alright. Fancy Mum trotting up for the cash every Tuesday. Payable to Hannah David. From Sapper David, B.M.E.F."[5] He received instead postal orders from home for his incidental expenditure, a procedure he stopped in August 1916 – by which time his pay had risen to 10/6 – after he found he was constantly short of funds.[6]

Even at the age of 18 and after more than a year in the military he could write describing the pleasure he took from looking at a photo and imagining her feelings.[7] "Don't I wish I were with you? Never mind, keep smiling, for when I see you like that, Mummy, in the photo, I think you are a very brave little woman." In the same letter he had made clear his homesickness on opening the letter and taking out the photo of all three of them. "I can't count the number of times I pull out the case and look at you daily and it makes me smile hugely every time but the first long look I took when it arrived brought a funny little lump in my throat. And the chaps I didn't show it to. You bet, it went all round, and they thought it a fine photo. Couldn't be selfish and keep it to myself, you see, and, of course, they all had their opinions as to who I looked like and said what lovely hair my sister had and all that. By Jove! Dad, you don't half look a toff with that waxed moustache, and Mum + Doll with their Engineers badges." He was referring to a practice that had become common in earlier campaigns from Victorian times onwards and continued into World War One. Women would wear the badges of regiments in which their loved ones were serving as a mark of support. His mother and sister were clearly proud enough of him to want to display this symbol. Photography was well-established by then, as the group photos of the era demonstrate, but the necessity of turning up at a photographic studio for a posed picture was perhaps not welcome, given the time and attention the photographer would take to getting the portrait right. "I know what an ordeal it is facing the camera," he writes, "and you've come out with flying colours. You couldn't have sent a better photo, nor I have wished for one, and now it is my most treasured possession, as you can imagine. When I come home, we'll have our photos taken together and won't it be a group, eh? Hope it'll come out half as well as this one, although I doubt it when Jim's phisog is added." This was the heyday of the professional photographer. Not a single town of any size in Britain lacked one or more studios where families could go and pose for formal group or individual photos.

4) February 6th 1916.
6) April 5th 1916. British Mediterranean Expeditionary Force.
7) June 21st 1916. He was at Serapeum.

Please Write, Mum

His mother's failure to write as often or as lengthily as he would have liked, was a constant source of disappointment to him from the very start of his campaigning, and, during his four years away, he tried everything from cajoling to mock threats, to pressure on his sister to persuade their mother. His first slightly nervous request came after he had arrived on Gallipoli towards the end of the 53rd Division's ill-fated stay on the peninsula. "I hope you are all well and happy and a Christmas gift I should be delighted to receive would be a photo of you three taken as a group. Please try and send one out. Hope Dolly is studying hard as usual and that you, Mum, will drop me a line personally and that Dad is going strong and not losing his hair too rapidly."[8] His mother evidently responded, as he soon thanks her for a letter, by which time the division had withdrawn from Gallipoli to Egypt, but he adds the plea: "I wish, Mum, you would write oftener."[9] His mother had evidently written again twice by the time of his letter of February 20th but in further letters in March he asks "Mummie" when he is going to get another one, and in April he writes to say he wants to see her signature at the bottom of a letter. Her next letter, he complains, is too short – "try and improve next time, there's a brick". By August of the same year he is asking his sister to use her best efforts to increase the flow and later in the month he is saying there will be no excuse for her not to have written from their holidays in Porthcawl.[10]

We will never know whether his mother, a slight but determined woman, whose horizons stretched only occasionally beyond Splott, the centre of Cardiff, and holidays along the south Wales coast, lacked confidence in her writing, having left this task during her married life to her husband. There is, however, a clue in one of his repeated requests, conveyed through his sister. "Ask Mum if she could possibly postpone a Thursday afternoon inspection of David Evans' museum in order to write the long, long epistle I have been long, long expecting.[11] Tell her not to be shy, as if I should not understand better than anybody else in the world." The following year it is the same plea. "And now, Mum, when am I going to hear from *you*? You know you are neglecting me something cruelly. I feel quite cut up about it but I am afraid it's no good – shall have to give it up as a bad job. Now then, are you going to stand that, Mum? Let's see what you are made of next mail – be a sport please."[12] His disappointment does not stop his taking delight at the pleasure his own letters bring, especially where his mother gets to read one before anyone else. "So glad you received mine alright but awfully sorry it was three weeks you were kept waiting – you're a real plucked 'un [plucky one], Mum, and hope you didn't get very anxious. Still, I always turn up eventually like a bad penny – always did, always do, always shall. I can imagine your surprise and delight on getting that second letter within two days of the very, very short one – I was ashamed of that, really I was. You had it all to yourself then, Mum. Gee Whiz! Shouldn't I just have liked to have seen you reading it? I bet Dad and Doll had to wait for dinner that Sunday and you didn't play the piano with the duster that morning."[13]

8) November 8th 1915.
9) January 24th 1916.
10) August 3rd 1916.
11) David Evans, linen and millinery store, Andrews Arcade, Queen Street.
12) February 25th 1917.
13) May 17th 1917.

The absence of letters from her still clearly causes him to fret, however. In September, after a further appeal in June, he tries another tactic to elicit a letter, as well as telling his mother in August to make cakes as compensation, if she will not write. "Last mail I received one from Dolly... and one from you Mum dated the – the – (you see what it has come to, Mum, I've actually got to start telling crammers – think of the 'eroic conduct of your son, telling white lies to save you from disgrace). Shocking that's what it is 'pon my san."[14] By early 1918 Dewi's writings had become more expansive and, indeed, laden with Army vernacular and slang, as another attempt in a letter to Doll to spur or shame his mother into action demonstrates. "I'm just about panned out now and this pad's looking sick. Send another of the same sort soon as poss, will you, Doll? – Ta, you're a brick, don't forget. And, mind you, write again soon. You can just imagine how I hanker after them tophole epistles. And what about you, Mum? When are you going to break all records? 'Bout time y'know – 'sfearful the way you been neglecting this chicken lately. 'No paper?' did you say. O! come orf it – just draw on a Sunlight soap wrapper or England's Glory fake [sic], that'll do me – I am not a particular sort of cove."[15] And, a few weeks later, he asks, looking forward to a letter from Doris, or a "budget" as he calls them, "How about you, Mum, let's be hearing from you.[16] Drop the work, let it rip for a day and go out for a few, just a few, exquisite and precious pages." At other times he repeats his admonitions to her to pass up on the opportunities to go shopping. On another occasion he writes asking why there has been nothing from her for ages. "Do hurry up 'cos I'm dying for one – cut the baking, ironing, scrubbing, cut everything, cut Doll's hair off and only let's have a letter, for pity's sake."[17]

He remains keen, too, for his father to write and not to prevent any of his former office colleagues from writing. "And, Dad – O! well, he isn't too bad, considering what he must have to put up with in that office. But see, anyway, if you can't give me a double number next time you're on night duty, old sport. How's things up there now? Just exercise a little discretion, Dad y'know, 'fore you run any of them 'sports' up for the jump on the carpet. Thought I'd better tell you – you see, there's Olwen Morris, f'rinstance, if you happen to dekko her scribbling on the news, don't go and shove the kybosh on it by giving her another slip, 'cos she may be dropping a few lines to this child – savvy?"[18] Exactly what his parents must have made of the change he had undergone into a seen-it-all, Army-talking Tommy, we can never know. The pleas were still coming, however, in June 1918, nearly three years after he had last set sight on his parents and sister. "Well Dad, I hopes [sic] as how you'll enjoy your week's holiday – no night duties, eh? – Good egg. Plenty of time then to write me pages and pages about your allotment trench warfare!" His father, we must assume, had by this time acquired an allotment to grow some basic foods, something the British people had been urged to do in order to counter the losses brought about by German submarine warfare. "And, what's more, bags of time to inspire, beseech, and coax a letter from Mum for me. S'no use you talking about parcels you send, Mum, as being in place of letters, Mum – notabitofit – 'Twon't do – I'd sooner one letter than umpteen parcels." His ultimate threat is a visit from the

14) September 5th 1917. Crammers, slang for lies. San, word.
15) February 6th 1918.
16) February 27th 1918.
17) May 28th 1918
18) February 6th 1918. Slip, telegraphic covering note.

authorities. "D'you know, Mum, it's a crime, if you don't write home? And that if I didn't write, my O.C. on receiving the complaint from you'd [you would] soon have me up for the jump and personally supervise the writing of one there and then? Well, what's sauce for the goose is sauce for the gander, and one of these fine days you'll get an A.P.M knocking at the door who'd bully you into sitting down right away and writing one, even if you were in the middle of one of those thousand and one attentions to your great big babies, Doll and Dad.[19] Guess that makes you tremble a bit, and it's alright – you needn't fancy you'll be able to choke him off as having floored better managers than him – at Cross Bros, D. Evans, Oliver's and other places."[20]

His mother clearly had a reputation as something of a terror when dealing with shopkeepers as his response earlier in the war demonstrates when hearing presents for Doris, presumably from his day's leave in Ismailia on November 3rd, had arrived safely.[21] "When I heard from Dolly that my parcel had arrived safely, I thought the Fates had been exceptionally kind in allowing even one to reach its destination and dare not hope for such luck with the second, containing my birthday gift to Doll. You see, there had been so many ugly rumours floating about mails lost at sea that my hopes sank to zero. Imagine my delight and gratitude when yours of the 15th inst. arrived with the good news that the trinkets had arrived. [...] Bracelets, scarves, brooches or gloves, anything in that line, – I am *the* diplomat, *the* strategist, when it comes to choosing, which requires, as you will agree, a man with his wits on the alert. In fact, I feel so confident of the impression I am creating that I am almost inclined to think that in future my esteemed mater will allow me to confront Mr Oliver, Mr Masters and Mr Jackson without a qualm on my own initiative – the dream from my earliest boyhood.[22] Mum was never an ardent enthusiast of the W.S. & P.U but I have vivid memories, the above was one woman's right, one great clause of the union from which, try as I would, she would not deviate.[23] A rigid rule from which there was no relaxation. Sometimes, when our QMS [Quarter Master Sergeant] gets reckless and issues me a tunic or a pair of breeches I am nearly reduced to tears to think what a different complexion things would assume were Mum present – how that unfortunate being would drop speedily his air of authority and cringe and cower amidst his tunics, a sickly, nervous, Certainly!-no-trouble-at-all smile upon his face. I can picture now that poor chap in the sailor suit department whose hands used to shake so much he couldn't do the buttons up."[24]

The attempts continue to persuade his mother to write, with Dewi waxing lyrical in praise of his sister's and father's efforts, and emphasising, too, his world-weariness, perhaps in an attempt to shame her into responding.[25] In place of the vernacular speech he had been using in some of his earlier letters, he is now adopting a high-flown literary style, perhaps under the influence of the many books

19) A.P.M., Assistant Provost Marshal.
20) Cross Bros., a hardware, ironmongery, and domestic appliance store with several branches in Cardiff, also a shipping supplier. Geo Oliver & Son, a chain of shoe shops.
21) Vd. letter November 4th 1916.
22) Masters, a chain of gentlemen's outfitters.
23) The Women's Social and Political Union (WSPU) Vd. Chap. 4, p93. The right is that of the consumer.
24) January 10th 1917.
25) April 14th 1918.

he had had sent out to him. "Joy of joys, they still come rolling in and here you find me attempting to repay you, as far as my poor, small powers of expression enable me, to let you realise just how much those budgets of Feb 27th and March 6th meant to me. Yours, Dad, of the former date was irresistible, and Doll's inimitable chronicle of the latter date sent me into transports of delight. I am, of a truth, kept alive and even reminded that there is still something worth living for in this wicked old world by these incomparable tonics. My thirst is still unassuaged, however – you see, it is of the insatiable variety where such ecstasies are concerned, and I would vain[26] request you never to become slack but keep on feeding me in this wise with a regularity only to be compared with that of an infant inebriate and its milk-bottle." His mother comes in, however, for the now regular reprimand. "I am pained to observe that you leave this very necessary attention to your child to Dad and Doll's awkward but well-meant efforts, since Dad, being of the male and Doll of the care-free flapper species, cannot possibly possess even the rudiments of the mother instinct and understanding. I would venture to remind you Mum of the assiduity with which in my infancy you plied me with 'Allenbury's Food'.[27] Now, essential, no doubt, as that nourishing beverage was to me then, it is none the less imperative that you should continue to be solicitous as to my welfare even at this later stage of my life when I am, as it were, bought from you temporarily body and soul for the munificent sum of one shilling. I imagine you have neglected, dear Mum, to look at the matter from this point of view and I earnestly anticipate an early renewal of the feeding process – food for thought in the form of one of your few and far between exquisite, sweet and prized missives. The disappointment I might possibly have to endure will, I assure you, have drastic effects on the philosophy you have hitherto given me credit for and my distraction could not but prove deplorably detrimental to that faculty which has always enabled you to picture me as a 'beau esprit'. Think again, I beg of you, and have compassion before you bring about this possible catastrophe."

Towards the end of his service, he resorts to what must have seemed to her to be sometimes bewildering praise of her cooking, even deeming her efforts in this line sufficient to compensate for the lack of letters he has constantly complained about previously. By now they will have known that their campaign in the Near East was coming to an end, though they would not have known whether or not they would be needed in France. "I've heard tell before of Napoleons of finance and Napoleons of this + that + the other, signifying that they're top dogs but Gee Whiz! there ain't no blessed doubt whatsoever who's Napoleon of cuisine.[28] You are entirely forgiven for having been found wanting in the letter line 'cos in making that cake you expressed more than umpteen letters would ever contain. And Blimey! you can just about stake that new summer creation in grenadine mauve tulle that Dad's going to buy you for me that we didn't half give it Home Rule for Ireland – not half."[29]

Please Stop Worrying

Hannah worried about her son, like all mothers of soldiers in the World War One – or indeed any war. In response, Dewi's letters home constantly urge his mother

239

---

26) April 14th 1918. He meant fain, not vain.

27) Allenbury's, a popular brand of baby food.

28) July 27th 1918.

29) Dress fabric in open silk or silk and wool. His only reference to Home Rule, an important contemporary issue.

not to worry. Shortly before landing at Suvla Bay while still in Lemnos he writes: "Trusting you aren't worrying about me and making yourself miserable, Mum."[30] Two years after leaving home he is still giving re-assurances that his morale is high. "I am more glad than I can say that my letters get such a reception, and it's a better tonic to me than are all the inoculations I can tell you. You think such a lot of them, although it beats me why, 'cos I know they're rambling, disjointed, and all bunkum, as far as news goes, but it spurs me on to further efforts in order to give you full money's worth in the green 'uns you wait so patiently and bravely for.[31] You make mention of my unfailing good cheer – well, how could I be otherwise when you write me, as you do, letters I wouldn't miss for – for all the iced cakes in existence, and that's saying a lot."

The image he always tries to project of himself is someone who is coping well, though he also delights at times in seeing himself as a "bullet-headed swoddy". He is always pleased when his parents praise him for his patience in trying and often tedious circumstances. He picks up on the remark that he has become a philosopher and allows himself to laugh at the contrast between his conditions now and those he enjoyed at home where he was clearly well looked after to the point almost of being pampered by his parents.[32] "I can't help being cheerful when I'm writing you because all the time I nearly split my sides laughing and chuckling to myself. For why? – because I can't help thinking what a huge joke it all is, that not so long ago, you, Mum, used to butter my bread for me and wash my socks, and Dad used to shave me and pay my tram fare and Dolly used to do a hundred and one things. Fed like a blooming baby out of a spoon, I was, waited on hand and foot like a blinking lord, and treated like a duke for seventeen blooming years – think of it – and here I am, look at me now – 'Strewth! it's too funny. "When I think of it, it's enough to burst a trousers button laughing. Take me back again, Mum, and Honest Injun! I'll never scratch the brass fender, or kick the "cadairydd", or sit on the parlour cushions, or bring the acetylene lamp in the back-kitchen – I won't, straight.[33] What's more Dad, I'll walk every blooming inch of the way to town, if you like, and, Dolly, you can have every blessed square inch of foolscap [paper] you can find in my cupboard and I'll never murmur."

His mother clearly worried a lot about his health, which is perhaps why he finishes virtually every letter by saying he is "in the pink". Early on in his campaign he has to re-assure them that he had made a good recovery from boils, which he blames on a mosquito bite, and he makes light of other incidents, such as his one short stay in a field hospital. His mother's worries ran along in parallel with his own unhappiness at not seeing her handwriting. In January 1918 he wrote a special letter home to convince her he had not become a martyr to the "blues", a conclusion he describes as very wide of the mark. "Why, the very thought that you were labouring under that delusion would be sufficient to cause me to contract that deplorable complaint." Another of his mother's worries about a parcel on the way

---

30) October 18th 1915.

31) Green Uns. Active Service envelopes.

32) May 17th, June 30th, July 13th 1916.

33) May 17th 1917. Cadairydd means chairman (now usually spelt cadeirydd), presumably his father. Developed in the US, acetylene lamps were first used in domestic lighting in 1894. By 1915 his home in Moorland Road would have been lit by electricity so this may have been an outdoor light for visiting the toilet at the rear of the property.

had caused him to laugh. "The shirt, too, I anticipate with joy, but your remarks and evident serious concern re the size and the collar induced many chuckles of mirth. I love you all the more for your fussing but it was funny, you know, to think that I *must* have the right size collar to wear, just as if I was doing it in style in Shepheards [Hotel], say, instead of being, as I am, a kind of mole living in the cliffs of a lonely seaside spot in Palestine.[34] If you saw some of the shirts worn by us out here you would appreciate my meaning all the more. 8 out of every 10 are minus any vestige of sleeves and have most convenient slits for ventilation generally stretching at the back from the neck to tail, not designed by the shirt manufacturers, I may add. He regrets in one of his letters that he had not removed some lint bandages in a photo he had sent as that, too, causes his mother to worry. "Really, I was sorry I sent it afterwards, because it is not exactly a 'gem', as you might say. I meant to have taken that lint from my knee and hand to be photographed – I certainly should have, because you seem to think it serious, but was snapped on the spur of the moment and entirely forgot. It was nothing at all as a matter of fact – I happened to cut myself in both places, and the sand getting into it turned it slightly septic, but lint and iodine soon had 'em O.K. again. Septic is a very common thing out here and you have to look after the smallest scratch – if you don't the 'poultice-wallopers' choke you off to blazes. That was the only time I ever had any. The poor old R.E.s cop it, naturally, messing about with barbed wire continually," he writes.[35]

She was worried by the different jobs he described himself as doing, including cable laying across dangerous ravines, causing him to tell her to stop being concerned.[36] "Wish you wouldn't worry over my jobs, Mum! I'm all right, you know." He also had to re-assure her that he had made a complete recovery from the bout of saddle-soreness mentioned elsewhere, which had necessitated a fortnight's stay in a field hospital after he had rashly gone riding without breeches, as part of his regular duties in the team fetching water from a nearby wadi, an offence for which he could have been court-martialled.[37] "Your highly intelligent, careless, irresponsible lordship [...] gallivants about on his thoroughbred Iwerddon [of Ireland] charger, Patsy, clad only in those nether garments, only to know about it bye and bye [...] No sooner had we arrived back in the hills than the punishment [...] set in with a vengeance." Dr Samuel, his family doctor from Cardiff, who, as previously mentioned, treated him, kept, Dewi writes, "a small marquee in the vicinity", and he recounts in humorous detail – perhaps to avoid raising his mother's anxiety level – his one and only experience of being admitted to a field hospital for treatment while away. "On the report it said, 'Please see this man who is not feeling well after the march'. Stuff and nonsense – 'not feeling well – Bosh! my dear sir, pure bunkum'. Imagine me to be feeling anything but bored after a march – Tut – tut – never marched before – it's a – er- novel experience for me – O-h-h! Y-yes, most decidedlutely. Anyhow, I went and at the question, 'What's the matter with you, my man'?, my fingers stole hesitatingly to my belt and braces and acquainted him with full particulars of the dread malady, expecting to be anointed upon the afflicted portion of my anatomy with a little soothing balm – just an ordinary nothing as it

---

34) August 7th 1917. He was at Corps headquarters at Sheikh Shabasi.
35) August 7th 1917.
36) April 29th 1918.
37) May 28th 1918.

were – it was nothing more, except, of course, the beastly inconvenience of having to eat one's tea as the Israelites partook of the feast of the Passover – off the mantelpiece, sort of thing. But, horrors, he fairly bowled me over when he remarked casually that I'd better stay there for a few days to recuperate. I submitted with, I fear, bad grace and, lo and behold, this sapper, a most lifelike imitation of a hospital patient. Hospital – I s'pose that word conjures up in your mind visions of this inconsequent child lying in a cool, white silent ward, surrounded by stern-faced matrons, gentle-voiced sisters and sympathetic, thermometer-armed VADs?[38] Disillusion yourself, I prithee, and I will paint the true to life picture for your benefit. Just an ordinary Field Dressing Station, a bivvy and a 9 ock [sic] inspection of the injured part of my person, followed by a daily close acquaintance with zinc and paraffin ointment, living on ordinary chuck (biscuits and bully not chicken and fish). That was my unenviable lot – stay, tho', not so unenviable – for I did not a blessed stroke except help the RAMC cook chop wood one day – a patient is a patient all the world over, whether he be languorously reposing in Lady Vere de Fitzpercy's[39] private hospital or Sammy's quack pill factory with the ever open Dr Barnado's door, and, well – Bless your eyebrows! ain't I old enuff soldier to know what's what? – Eh? 'Course, I winked. Why life was one sweet song, especially after I was convalescent and able to gingerly deposit myself on the rough stony surface of Palestine and sit up and look intelligent – not a single blessed fatigue – up in the morning in time for brekker only, and breaking bounds after dark to sneak out for a gorge at a canteen we found about 3 miles away. Gosh! wharra life. Such were my happy experiences when suffering acutely (?) [sic] from saddle-soreness at a Dressing Station – a rare holiday from hard graft. Saddle-soreness, they called it, so, you see, I have the consolation of having belonged to the latter classification of the sick-parade march past, viz. 'art thou weary, art thou languid, art thou *sore distressed*'."[40]

Surprisingly, Dr Samuel does not seem to recognise him or, at least, does not let on if he does. He is said to be as much of an old woman as ever. "He's *so* careful to effect a *complete* cure! and at the end of that time I managed to convince him he could do nothing more, and escape him, so he reluctantly let me go (can't understand it – trade was slack, that's about the size of it, and he wanted to experiment and sort of ointment vivisect me, I s'pose).[41] Glad? Crumbs! I should think so – I've had enough borax, zinc, sulphur and paraffin mixtures to last a lifetime and then some more. But, I've learnt this much – breeches for me every time for riding in future – never again – shorts are alright for shanks' pony but not for the real live genuine article – no thank you.[42] Besides, I was half afraid those three separate doctors, who on three separate occasions muttered something about three separate Field General Court Martials with your humble as principal boy in 'em, charged with gross disobedience of routine orders, would quit chaffing and

---

38) VADs – Voluntary Aid Detachments, formed in 1909, with the help of the Red Cross and St. John's Ambulance, to provide field nursing services. More than 38,000 volunteers served during the war in all the main theatres, acting as nurses, ambulance drivers and cooks, the majority of them women. Famous VADs – each volunteer was called a 'detachment' – included Vera Brittain, Agatha Christie, Amelia Earhart, Hattie Jacques and Freya Stark.

39) Lady Vere de Fitzpercy, a nod to Alfred (Lord) Tennyson's poem, Lady Clara Vere de Vere, in which a gardener spurns the lady of the house, whose heart she has tried to break. The Stepney Ever Open Door for destitute children was founded by Dr. Thomas Barnardo in 1874.

40) Words of a Hymn by Stephen of Mar Saba (Judea), 8th Century. Vd. also Chap 5. Gaza, p144.

41) Dr. Samuel may be the Sammy jokingly referred to above.

42) Shanks' pony, walking.

turn serious. And look what a slur that would be upon the House of David – 'desperate military criminal, drummed out etc. etc.' – 'orrible, isn't it, when you come to think of it?"

He realises it will no doubt cause her to worry yet again and seeks to re-assure. "I guess it would have been far better if I'd said nothing at all about this ridiculous escapade, 'cos I'm sure Mum'll be fretting like blazes over it, and above those 'bobby dazzlers' [eyes] (with apologies to the author Dad), there'll be a worried frown. My advice, dear Mum, is a series of 'Don'ts' – it was nothing – only foolish of me and, naturally, all I had to expect was a little punishment, which fortunately was very mild. I'm in the pink, always have been, always hope to be, never felt better all my life, besides I can squat O.K. now – my (pardon me) – er – penol [pen ôl Welsh for rear] is now cured of saddle soreness and well – in the pink as it were – not *so* pink as it was tho'.[43] Besides my complaint was what an experienced equestrian might have contracted – had he, of course, been senseless enuff to discard breeks [sic] for a thin drill garment which won't stand rough-riding stunts, as I have proved conclusively to my cost, unfortunately. All's well, then, carry on, only don't choke me off, *please*. Yes, I promise again, Mum, I'll be Oh! so careful, you wouldn't believe. That's one of my strong points is always being *too* careful, if anything. Careful to roll up for my pay, careful to roll up for canteen stores and any grub, and O! infinitely careful about work of any kind. I'm so careful of it that I only touch it (and then delicately) when it's absolutely necessary and somebody's taking an uncalled for interest in the particular job on hand. Careful, you say? Why there's only one thing in the world I'd like to be more full of and that's one of your feeds, Mum. Wait and see." His mother, as these repeated comments make clear, is the little woman at home of contemporary popular culture, the homemaker and nurse of every Victorian and Edwardian person's childhood. The typically domestic nature of her life – shopping and cleaning as well as cooking – is made evident in the frequent references to the priority she places on these ahead of what Dewi would prefer, namely a greater dedication to letter-writing.

His devotion to his mother may now seem overly sentimental to us but cannot have been untypical of the era. Addressing his father, he speculates on how devoted he, too, must have been. "Hope they are all well up at Pentyrch, and dear old Gia Mia [his grandmother]. I wonder when you saw her, *your* mother, Dad, did you think how I should like to see mine?"[44] A few weeks later his father has replied to say all are well in the village a few miles north of Cardiff. "I can quite imagine how many times she would ask you about me," Dewi says, perhaps hinting that his grandmother was now suffering from memory loss and giving us a reminder that old age was accompanied, as now, by declining mental faculties. Two years later he asks his father, when he sees Gia again to give her his love, adding, "if she remembers me". "Poor old Dad," he goes on, "it was jolly hard that the dear little old lady failed to recognise you as her baby son. Never mind, chin up, you've got memories and that is all that matters in life, isn't it?"[45] A photo of Gia – he had just sent her a post card from Egypt on her birthday – had been one of his earlier requests.[46]

243

43) May 28th 1918.
44) May 31st 1916.
45) April 14th 1918.
46) August 27th 1916.

A Modern Dad

His relationship with his father was very different and seems like that of more modern times, joshing with him at times and on one occasion telling him off for supposed indiscretions in relating his adventures. He greatly admired his father's character, and Thomas David himself seems to have been the opposite of the caricature of the stern Victorian or Edwardian era parent we think we recognise from popular drama and fiction. Dewi treats his father, his most regular correspondent, with some amusement, always mixed with deep affection. They had the kind of relationship where he could tease without offending his father, as his comment about his father losing his hair – he would by now have been in his mid-forties – makes clear. In a later letter he could mock, too his father's attempts to grow a moustache. He congratulates his father on the poetic lines he occasionally sends him on matters arising out of his letters home – in this case the button cleaning incident on Christmas Day 1916. "You're showing signs of a promising 'young' poet – I say 'young' 'cos I'm thinking of your moustache."[47] He had followed his father into the Post Office, as we have noted, and it seems likely that they walked or caught the tram to work together at times. In one of the earliest letters he talks about racing his father to the water's edge at Porthcawl and remarks on how fit he must be, thinking of taking up running.[48] "The strain of your letter smacks of 'not too old at...' eh?" He clearly felt able to rib his father at will, knowing it would only cause amusement. "I twigged", as you say, Mum in the hairdressing act in the rushes. It is very good and quite natural. That's what I want, not artificial poses. You'll take some of yourselves about the house, won't you, for instance Mum in the middle of some ironing and you and Doll moping around waiting for tea, or better still, combing Doll's hair and you trying to look pleasant behind the "Echo". Tell you what I really would like, though, is a photo of Mum writing me a letter and one of Dad singing one of his Italian operas."[49] His father, a deacon at Jerusalem chapel in Splott, had a fine voice, and may have been familiar with opera music from the gramophone, now becoming common in many households, or from one of the many concerts regularly held in chapels and other venues at the time. The family possessed a piano, which Dewi and Doris had both learnt to play proficiently, and it may also be that they sang to the sheet music that was then readily available.

One of the main butts of his humour at his father's expense is his involvement with the 3rd Volunteer Battalion in the Boer War, a puzzling episode that runs counter to the stern opposition of his father's hero, Lloyd George, to Britain's South African war. His exact involvement is not clear, though there is mention in one of the letters of his old tunic.[50] The likelihood is that he went out to South Africa on secondment to work on telegraph communications. Sappers engaged in telegraph work in the Boer War were supported by non-enlisted men from engineer militias and volunteer companies. In this he was anticipating his son's own later war work. In a letter from Serapeum on the Canal Dewi recalls what he suggests was another

47) February 25th 1917.
48) November 14th 1915.
49) August 27th 1916.
50) September 8th 1916. Volunteer battalions provided volunteer Active Service Companies to serve in South Africa during the Second Boer War 1900-1902. Members of the 3rd Welsh Battalion were attached to the regular 2nd Battalion, South Wales Borderers.

heroic campaign by his father – the taking of a small country station in Devon manned by one porter, 99 years old, and the capture of the GWR Bristol buffet and its hasty evacuation by the Blue Ribbon brigade – the tale of some holiday expedition to the West Country that had clearly become a standing family joke.[51] The 3rd V.B. crops up again in the next letter, where he describes Lock's Common in Porthcawl as the scene of some of his father's adventures. "The details of those fierce skirmishes have long been impressed on my memory. You veterans can spin the yarn of blood and fire alright, just like the famous Captain Ginger and Bill Adams.[52] You're right, Dad, we young swaddies (sic) don't know we're born yet, in fact, we have a few times been inclined to think we were dead. [...] As for the Mtn Ash and Treorchy attachments they must have been excellent company ever desirous of advancing themselves, relieving another of a small vow (or a small watch occasionally I expect), or to risk their bodies for the exaltation of their ladyes just the same as knights of yore.[53] Methinks I can picture them returning to camp from ye jousts at P'cl [Porthcawl] bearing their honourable scars (swollen optics etc.)."[54] Later in the year, on hearing the news of the birth of a child to his cousin, Ethel Hughes (née David), who had emigrated to the US during the war, he jokingly asks his father whether it was a 3rd V.B. tie clip or brass button he had swallowed as a child and much later he refers to his father's walking pace on the way to work as being "the old 3rd Welsh V.B. pace". The 3rd V.B. was, it seems, the subject of mirth in the family, though exactly what part his father played, and how much it had simply become a part of family myth-making and holiday memories, is impossible to know.

His devotion to his father did not prevent him, however, from chiding him on more than one occasion.[55] He is particularly agitated to learn that his father has met a man named Evans who has reported news about himself. He has always, he tells his father, "looked him [Evans] plumb in the optics in a way closely allied to what is known in this glorious military institution as 'dumb insolence'. Dewi seems to be still sore over an incident when he joined up in 1915. "Married is he? Bless him, well, she needn't be jealous of us – she's got every particle of the blamed love. And to think that you saluted him, Dad, when I joined up that day at Park St – I'll never forgive you for that – no, never.[56] Still, I s'pose it's the old veteran 3rd V. B, touch – the sight of a Sam Brown (which covers a multitude of sins) and your hand wanders unconsciously aloft but, really, you should use discretion, Dad.[57] You do as I do, if I may presume to give such audacious advice to my respected pater. When I see old Lt. Hugh Mowbray looming up one of these fine days, it'll be me for a click of the heels 1 – 2 and hup 'em hartly, me boys, and proud of the opportunity, I'll be.[58] Ditto, you, Dad – three paces before and three paces after, if I'm not insulting your memory of the old campaigning days in the year of the 'Battle of the Blue Ribbon'! – He's one of the very best, you see, there's *men* and – well outsiders. Trust the rank and file to weigh 'em up."

51) June 30th 1916.
52) The heroes of a series of boys' adventures by Isabel Anderson, published in 1910 and 1911. Boston, C.M. Clark.
53) Mountain Ash in the Cynon Valley, and Treorchy in the Rhondda Valley.
54) Presumably black eyes.
55) May 28th 1918.
56) Drill Hall, Park Street.
57) The Sam Brown, a wide belt, usually leather, supported by a strap going diagonally over the right shoulder that helps to bear the weight of an officer's sword and accoutrements.
58) Hup 'em hartly, the command to salute that would have been given by the sergeant-major.

A year earlier he had been irritated when he drew the conclusion (wrongly, it seems) that his father had let it be known in the office that life in Egypt was comfortable for the troops.[59] (He later apologises on finding that someone else was responsible.) By now fatigue with the war and absence from home were clearly setting in and, as described elsewhere in the letters, there was the definite feeling that the lads in France were getting all the attention and that those troops facing and chasing 'Johnny' Turk in the Near East were being neglected. There was a degree of sensitivity that their own hardships were being under-rated and he implies that he made a deliberate point not to over-emphasise the conditions under which they were serving. "Well, Dad, [...] I s'pose, as you say, that it's no good getting ratty about it but, mind you, I don't write home for the express purpose of 'playing to the gallery', as it were, like some of these silly asses who consider themselves budding journalists and write to the newspapers. We look down with contempt on this sort of 'prize fathead'. There used to be one of 'em in our mob, such a fool, and this is how he started off in one to the papers – 'And this is war-r-r? Oh! God, when is it going to end?'. Quite dramatic wasn't it? – the – the burbling jabberwocky. Well, you can just guess what we thought about *him*. When I wrote that I was as innocent as a newly born babe – never dreamt it was going any further than 76. I'm only telling you this so that you won't do anything indiscreet. What's more I have very good reason to believe that the Inst. Room has been privileged to hear it." He explains how he has learned what he considers to be this unfortunate breach of confidence on his father's part, who, he believes, had taken at face value remarks he had offered in a spirit of bravado about their times campaigning. "It was like this. I happened to be drawing my tea the other afternoon when one of our sergeants came up and in front of the whole queue accosted me, "O! so it's you, is it, who writes home wonderful descriptions of the glorious time we're having camped under orange groves and pomegranate trees, ye blighter?" (Picture my discomfort. That queue didn't half *look*, and pull my leg, I can tell you.) He told me afterwards that his father had written him to say that Mr David had been telling them (Inst. Room) that he had received a letter from his son etc. etc. O! Dad, Chuck it – if you would spare me the cutting disdain of the elite."[60]

Admiration and affection shines through, however, in the very same letter in which he puts some of his feelings on paper. "Which reminds me of a letter which I had from old Bill London t'other day. Fanny had been speaking to you, it seems, and had told Bill about it, saying that either I was very much like you in everything, or else you were very much like me! "That so," says I to Bill per return, 'Well, you can bet your boots, there's nobody I wish to be like half as much as I do Dad.' He is forced to apologise in a subsequent letter for his previous 'rattiness'. "Dad, I'm most terribly sorry – please accept my profound apology for the manner in which I slandered and rated you over the oranges and lemon groves stunt and various other flights of fancy I suspected you guilty of.[61] I am fully enlightened once and for all as to the true state of affairs in the Cardiff P.O. You can rest assured that sergeant is going to cop it thick and heavy when he returns from hospital. He always was a bit of a leg-puller."[62]

59) June 19th 1917.
60) June 19th 1917.
61) Rated, scolded angrily, as in berate.
62) August 31st 1917.

In Spring 1918, when there was still no end in sight, his father and uncle had enlisted for possible service, should the war continue, which causes him to worry. By now the chapels had begun to turn against the war but this antipathy had presumably not yet affected many of those who had sons serving. "So, you and Uncle Elias are 'in it' now, Dad – dashing young men of 40-50 eh? Good lads – that's the spirit – I'm filled with admiration – my word! you've got a stiff upper lip, Dad.[63] You talk so determinedly, I'm thrilled – and afraid. Please God, we'll pull thro' without the old hands. I couldn't bear that. On reading that portion of your epistle I almost imagined you to be a young rooky in the early twenties – you'd have been a better soldier than I am, Dad. And a credit to the glorious old 53rd (*Welsh*)." Three years earlier, when the British public was still only beginning to realise it would not be a short, sharp and victorious war, his father had written to tell him the last of the junior members of staff had gone [on military service]. "Well it's all for the best, I suppose. The sooner it will be all over and we are all back again the better," he had commented. "I wonder if they will call up your class next, Dad?"[64] He had been shocked, however, by a letter his much younger cousin, Elvet, his uncle Enoch's youngest son, had written, displaying the enthusiasm for war that must still then have been prevalent among impressionable boys not yet in their teens. He had appreciated receiving this and other letters "except for one little phrase where he says that in about another ten years he will be out here. It's worse than a saying we have out here i.e. 'After the first seven years you get used to it'."

His grocer uncle, Elias, was clearly a go-ahead sort of chap, no doubt encouraged by his brother-in-law. There are references in the summer of 1916 to what seems to have been a new purchase, a motor cycle and sidecar, and requests for a photo of his aunt and uncle out on a speed trial. His uncle had also become a special constable. "Fancy Uncle Elias as special. It does make me smile. Tell him I should like to see him running after the small boys. P'raps he's up to date and uses his motor bike for the purpose."[65] His uncle may only have managed to acquire his new motor bike in time. By late 1917 one British manufacturer was placing advertisements in newspapers advising potential customers that its entire production had been requisitioned by the British and Allied War Offices. His father's amiable nature becomes clear in another letter, in which Dewi gently mocks him for espousing a degree of familiarity with the new superintendent at work. In those more formal times this may have been seen as rather bold. "I wasn't in the least surprised Dad to hear of your chumming up with the new postal Supt. so quickly and easily, you're right – I'd have given a lot to have been there! 'Cheero! Bill' indeed. It wouldn't have been you, if you hadn't said something equally surprising. You are, I see, acting right up to the hilt of your famous motto that 'Life is too short to make enemies'. I await with eagerness your next escapade – they are too rich to miss. Anyhow, I hope he has the good sense to realise himself extremely fortunate in being addressed more familiarly than by his rank and number in these hard times."[66]

---

63) May 28th 1918.
64) December 6th 1915. The need for conscription had become apparent from the middle of 1915.
65) July 4th 1916.
66) July 29th 1918.

Proud Welshman

Proud Welshness was a characteristic Dewi had undoubtedly learned from his father, who will no doubt have enjoyed the references Dewi makes to Welsh history and legends. Though he wrote in English, his letters are sprinkled with Welsh words and phrases. Sometimes he is recalling a Welsh phrase for inspiration, such as fentro dy ben [you can guess] or a motto, Gwell Angau na Chywilydd, Y Ddraig Goch, Ddyry Gychwyn, or Deffro, Mae'n Ddydd.[67] At other times the Welsh is being dropped naturally into what he is writing – glaswellt hyfryd [pleasant greensward], aelwyd Cymraeg [Welsh-speaking hearth], yr Hen Aipht [Old Egypt], wrth dŵr y môr, [by the water of the sea], y bechgyn dewr [the brave boys], yr un cant pum deg a naw [the 159th brigade], yr hen iaith [the old language], Gwalia Wen [Fair Wales], pen ôl [rear quarters], Iwerddon [Ireland], breuddwyd [dream] and ar y mynydd [on the mountain]. Although the census in 1911 showed there were more people speaking Welsh than ever before or since, the fear that it might succumb to the pressures put upon it by immigration into the industrial parts of Wales and emigration from its rural communities was strong even then. More than 1m people in that year spoke Welsh out of a population of 2.5m – 43.5 per cent – and 8.5 per cent of the population had no English. Twenty years earlier almost exactly half the 1.5m population spoke Welsh and there were 21,250 monoglots – 14.3 per cent. The importance of keeping his Welsh was something his father will have instilled in him. In one of his first letters he tells his father "the half dozen words in Cymraeg [Welsh] sounded very sweet to me. They were better than 20 pages written in English and conveyed to me much more meaning".[68]

In March the same year, thanking his folks for their much-appreciated letters, he credits the praise they offer for his own efforts on his Welsh background and the access he has to Welsh thoughts when needed. "You always give me reason to believe that you think me fairly handy with a pencil and not exactly 'all at sea' as it were on paper but, believe me, there are times, and this is one of those instances, when my emotional, impulsive, Celtic temperament (Thank God for it, Dad) and those 'defnyddiau bardd' [bardic usages], which I swell with pride to think you give me credit for, arise within me to set me tingling with a mysterious 'something', (a feeling every Cymro and only a Cymro can know, Dad), which makes me realise what poor ineffective mundane things mere letters are, and so hinders me rather than aids me in my purpose of striving to put my thoughts down in black and white – letters, unfortunately, my one and only channel for conveying my thoughts to you. Deprived of that golden opportunity to be tongue-tied, I am now, alas, pencil-tied as well. But no, not quite, – not while I can remember your quotations, Dad – yr hen iaith [the old language] comes to fill the breach as ever, and no matter how very much pencil-tied I was, I should make one final supreme effort to scrawl those words you once wrote, Dad, which are imprinted on my memory and which, removing all difficulties, explain everything. Chwi wyddoch beth ddywed fy nghalon. [You know what my heart says.]"[69]

---

67) July 26th 1917, January 4th 1918, March 3rd 1918. 'Better death than dishonour', motto of the Welch Regiment and now of the Royal Regiment of Wales; 'Awake it is day', Cardiff motto; 'The Red Dragon, Ever Ready', Welsh motto.
68) November 14th 1915.
69) March 23rd 1918.

In describing his attachment to the 158th from May 28th he tells his father he has been mixing with some very good Welshmen, "and, of course, you know full well that I'll never lose yr hen iaith [the old language] – leave it to me – I hope I'm a genuine Cymro – and, well, that's one of his chief duties, isn't it? – "Fy Nuw, f'anwylyd, a'm iaith" [My God, my beloved and my language]. Dewi, whose education had been through the medium of English, was concerned his written Welsh was not as good as his spoken, though this seems not to have been the case. He wrote a faultless letter to the Sunday School in Splott to thank them for a parcel and express the hope he might soon be in their midst again, but confesses he had asked a colleague to check it. "I asked one of my pals – a Bangor man – to look it over and improve upon it but after reading it he said he quite failed to see what improvement he could make. Well, I wasn't so sure, you see, and thought he was pulling my leg as I haven't implicit confidence exactly in my writing, at least, but he convinced me in the end and now your glowing tributes have scattered any remaining doubts I might have had concerning my ability, and which, I am not ashamed to admit, have made me feel very proud indeed. If I can satisfy you and Jerusalem, with my Cymraeg [Welsh] well, that's about all I care about.[70] It's what I've always been used to – not deep, perhaps but pure, honest and straight from the shoulder for all that. [...] That same fellow was in my room when I received the parcel containing your Test. Newydd [New Testament] and he was touched and full of admiration for your inscription, 'Ac i ti er yn fachgen wybod yr ysgrythur lân' [For you, although a boy, to know the Holy Scripture].[71] He told me that he should very much like to meet you, that it was obvious you were a true blue-blooded Cymro – 'the best in this old world, Jack', I said."

His fascination with the different usages of Welsh speakers from the north, compared with south Wales has been noted elsewhere.[72] He had also thought, eighteen months earlier, that his parents would be entertained by his story of hearing a hellfire preacher from Aberdaron in north Wales. "Think you will like to hear of the incident at the YMCA here last night. I went over to finish the letter and take advantage of their tables but I failed to write a word. There was a service on, conducted by a Welsh chaplain from Aberdaron, look you. I quite enjoyed it, and he captivated the hearts of his congregation, especially those who had never heard a 'pregethwr' [preacher]. He could hardly speak English properly – awful Welshy he was, mun – and the Cymraeg style he had was amusing.[73] He had the boys in fits over his anecdotes one minute and the next he would be in a serious 'hwyl' [fit of enthusiasm]. In his prayer he started off like a lamb and finished up like a lion. I tell you, it brought back memories to me of Sundays in the past when I listened to the 'old school' again. Tonight he gives a humorous lecture at the same place and I'll be there. So, you're not the only ones who are privileged with those entertainments, although I'd sooner listen to 'yr hynod [noted] Kilsby Jones' at Jerusalem any day to a lecture on the desert!"[74]

70) Though Welsh was the language of his parents and his home, his education at Moorland Road Junior School and Howard Gardens High School in Cardiff was through the medium of English and his opportunities to write in Welsh would have been limited. Most of his reading, too, would have been in English. Jerusalem, his chapel in Splott.

71) New Testament. Vd. letter February 6th 1918.

72) May 28th 1918.

73) Myn, mun, Welsh exclamation.

74) November 27th 1916. James Rhys (Kilsby) Jones, (1813-1889), was a Congregational minister who served in numerous churches in Wales and England. Regarded as one of the most notable men of his period – famous in the eyes of his admirers but odd in those of his critics. *Dictionary of Welsh Biography*, National Library of Wales.

He knew too that they would be interested to hear of St. David's Day activities while they were out in Egypt and Palestine. In 1916 he is able to report that some of the boys had been for a ride and brought leeks or something very much like a leek back with them "so I wore a leek after all, although I am so far from dear old Wales".[75] Two years later in a postscript to one of his letters he reminds them it will soon be Dydd Gwyl Dewi [St. David's Day], and "I shall be sweet 20. Hope you ain't forgotten. Please send me a photo as a present will you?"[76] Music, too, brings bouts of homesickness. "O! the irony of it all – what d'you think, Doll, the divisional band has just struck up outside and of all the tunes they've started, "You'd be far better off in a home".[77] They will have their little joke, strafe 'em, but we've just shouted out as one man, 'Blimey not 'arf', specially my own' [...] (O! Dolly, that band's struck up 'March of the Men of Harlech' – Crumbs, there's a cold shiver all down the back of my neck and a lump in me throat......; Now it's 'Y Deryn Pur' [the Pure Bird] ... .and here she comes 'Rhys ap Thomas' – 'Cymru am Byth' [Wales for Ever] – I'm nearly blubbering, s'welp me if I ain't.)"[78] One of his letters in 1918 arrived on his birthday, which must, he says, have sent his mother into ecstasies, "after hoping it would turn out like that, and then to get her fondest hope realised. Old Dame Fortune was on our side that day alright." He would have been delighted, he says, to get a programme of the St. David's Day festival they had attended. "As for the real genuine article – the singing itself, well, I envy you no end your having been there to hear it. [...] Doesn't matter – next year for a pinch, eh? As I told you in my last, I wasn't exactly left right out in the cold tho', 'cos our band gave us a treat that night with a long programme of those beautiful airs, second to none. I never fully realised before what joy it used to be to play 'em at home on the old Johanna."[79]

Give My Regards

In late Victorian and Edwardian Britain the rapid growth of industries in the North West and North East, in south Wales, the Midlands and elsewhere, had resulted in significant population movement and the rapid growth of cities such as Cardiff, from small towns at the start of the 19th century to important regional metropolises. When one member of a family had moved from the country to a prosperous new centre, others quickly followed, as happened in the case of the Davids and his mother's family, the Jenkinses. Thomas David's eldest brother, Enoch, was established in Splott, working as a coal trimmer in Cardiff Docks and serving as a deacon in Jerusalem chapel, and other Davids soon followed him there. Hannah's sisters and their families also chose this new suburb. The results were close family networks where brothers and sisters, and the cousins who were their children, were able to pop in and out of each other's houses and shared an intimate

75) February 29th 1916. The letter will have been completed after March 1st.

76) February 27th 1918.

77) 'You'd be better off in a Home' A popular Army catchphrase originating in the late 19th century and widespread in World War One. It has been described by one writer as "sympathetic in that derisively jocular manner that constituted one of the hallmarks of the soldiers' humour. It fitted almost any occasion on which the man addressed would have been far better off in a home". The song was popular also in the Royal Navy and was turned into a World War Two comic song with topical references to Mussolini and Hitler by entertainer and ukulele player, George Formby. Dictionary of Catchphrases.

78) June 10th 1917. Welsh airs. Rhys ap Thomas, a prominent Welsh knight of the 15th century and inheritor of the Dinefwr estates in west Wales, made a major contribution to Henry VII's victory at the Battle of Bosworth, including, allegedly, killing Richard III. He was later made Governor of Wales.

79) April 29th 1918.

knowledge of each others' activities and their problems. Dewi received regular letters from his older cousin, Beatrice, (Beat) engaged to Hughie, as well as parcels from his uncle Elias and aunt Janet, who is frequently praised for her cakes and "excellent damsons".[80] As we have seen, Beat's brother, Tom – because of injuries sustained in France – was a frequent source of inquiries, as to a lesser extent was Eddie, Beat's sister Janet's beau and eventual husband. He had clearly been a popular companion, remembered for his participation in Christmas festivities, and spent the war at sea on merchant ships, leading Dewi to hope he would pass through the Canal, and perhaps let them have some provisions.[81] Just a year into the war Dewi regrets not being home at the festive season to sing *Thora*, a popular ballad of the time, with Eddie.[82] In September that year Dewi had been amused that Eddie was the cause of some quarrelling between Beat and Janet, though the reasons are not apparent. "Poor old Eddie, I always feel sorry for these fellows, y'know, they can't raise a hand in self-defence. They get bullied and hit about by persons twice their size and have a pretty rough time just for daring to go home. When I hear you mention about Beat thinking to collar him and Jan probably saying "Shan't, he's mine" etc.", I begin to wonder whether the epidemic has spread and if it would be really quite safe to return when the time comes. Perhaps, after all, it would be better to stay away altogether than face the ordeal. What ship is Eddie on? Shall have to keep my weather eye open in case he should pass by our 'appy 'ome."[83]

Sometimes aunts could be difficult for a teenager to understand, and he expresses good-humoured surprise that his mother's sister – who had no children of her own – should query his reasons for apparently not putting crosses for kisses at the end of his letters. "Auntie Janet's fears as to the crosses absolutely staggered me.[84] I 'offended'? – By George! I sincerely hope I will never have cause to be accused of such caddish and unnatural feelings. I appeal to you – is such base behaviour in harmony with my nature and temperament? – for who should be better judges on that point than yourselves? I am with you there, Dad – can't think why Auntie should think me such an awful rotter, I should indeed be a rank out and outer for harbouring such mean inclinations after the way Aunty has acted towards me not only with those delicious top-hole parcels but before ever I took to be a rolling stone. Did you not tell Auntie that even Mum has never received crosses from her neglectful son and that Dolly is always chewing me up about it? You may point out that *none* of my correspondence ever does terminate that way – me being such a funny cuss that way. I am you see a man of *action* and very poor at words and signs, which I'll prove, D.V."[85] In one of the flights of fancy that characterised his letters – no doubt stemming from his reading of Walter Scott and other romantic novelists – he goes on: "I trust I am as chivalrous and courtly a Knight Templar as ever took part in operations in the Holy Land but I emphatically and totally disapprove of the ancient rule of their Order whereby they were 'prohibited from offering to, or receiving from, even our mothers and sisters the kiss of affection'. All doubts and

80) July 31st 1916.
81) July 14th 1916.
82) December 29th 1916.
83) September 9th 1916.
84) His Aunt Janet, who also lived in Moorland Road, seems to have commented on his failure to place crosses (for kisses) at the end of his letters, and had perhaps asked if she had offended him.
85) D.V., Deo Volente, God Willing.

fears that Auntie may still have on this subject of osculation will, I fervently hope, melt away like December snows in the rays of the sun when my photo reaches her, before the beaming grin depicted upon my visage."[86] "Love", now the standard salutation between relatives and very often close friends closes only a few of his letters. In this respect the stiff upper lip is well in place, with letters usually ending merely, Yrs affec. The strongest demonstrations of affection are reserved for his sister, who alone receives correspondence kisses – XXXs – though he does sometimes use more jovial phrases, such as "Olive Oil, and "Barbed Wire".

For all her son's promptings, Hannah never became a writer, leaving to her husband the task of corresponding weekly with Doris after she had migrated to the US in the 1920s. After he had retired from the Post Office, Thomas, a much-loved figure, devoted his time to chapel and bowls, and they both continued to live quiet lives among family and friends in the same house in Splott, 76 Moorland Road, to which Dewi's many letters had been sent. Elias kept his grocery shop until well after World War Two, his wife out-surviving her younger sister and brother-in-law who both died in 1963. Beat never re-married after the loss of Hughie but continued to live in Carlisle Street, Splott, close to her relations in Moorland Road.

87) September 23rd 1917.

(top) Hugh Mowbray, a much-loved family figure who died a few years after the war.

(top) Tom Jenkins, his older cousin badly wounded in France.

(above) Hughie and Beat's wedding, with Doris, bridesmaid and Dewi, best man.

(above) Doris, taken by Mayfair Studios in Cardiff, before she left for married life in New York.

(above left) Dewi and Prue, on honeymoon in 1939, only months before the outbreak of World War Two.

(above) Prue, 1939.

(left) The Renaissance-style GPO in Cardiff where Dewi and his father both worked after the war.

CHAPTER TWELVE

LITTLE SISTER

The Pupil Teacher Stunt

Writing back home to Moorland Road, Dewi alternated between letters to all the family and individual ones to Doris, the latter usually more jocular and teasing – as one would expect of an elder brother writing to a teenage sister nearly three years his junior. At first he is keen to support her hobbies, dispatching postcards from his points of arrival for the collection she had started. Her leisure pursuits – cycling, tennis, shows and popular songs – soon form part of the correspondence – and, as she gets older, fashion, her appearance, her hair, and boys start to be discussed. He is evidently keen, too, to hear all about the commercial world that she enters on leaving school, familiar from his days in the Post Office, about her life outside work and the characters in it. Most of all, however, he wants to give the benefit of his advice.

A closeness that we would perhaps find surprising nowadays is evident, expressed in his enthusiasm for her successes and his encouragement to go on to greater things. Doris was clearly not expected to wait around until she married but was seen as being as much entitled to a career as her brother was. She was going to be more emancipated than her mother, capable of achieving whatever she wanted in life. The advances gained by women in the first half of the 20th century have often been ascribed to the breakthrough achieved when they started to replace men at the front in munitions factories and other jobs. In fact, in some lower middle class households girls were already being encouraged to study and move into the labour force. Their menfolk, too, had a softer side than we sometimes credit, and a sentimentality that was perhaps the legacy of the Victorian era. Much thought was given by Dewi, especially during his stay in Egypt, to suitable gifts and keepsakes to send home to his sister and mother, and the same was true, we can assume, of other soldiers. Gifts, apart from being novelties, were a way of thanking the folks at home for the parcels they were sending out. All over Britain at this time wives, sisters, fiancées and girlfriends would have been receiving Egyptian silks, brooches, postcards and other mementoes of their menfolk's infrequent periods of leave in Cairo, Alexandria, and Ismailia. Not all were as confident, however, as Dewi in finding the right item, as the sending of bottles of Holy Water by one of the men to his fiancée, humorously described elsewhere, demonstrates.

Born in November 1900 Doris May had followed Dewi to a grammar school education at the sister girls' school in Howard Gardens. Like her brother she was clearly no slouch, though he liked to portray her in his letters as a fun-loving, flighty young thing, no doubt the image he wanted to hold in his mind. Her ambition in her early teens to join the Pupil Teacher Scheme is mentioned several times in Dewi's early letters, presumably in reply to news she had given him about her plans. An apprenticeship for teaching that had been started in 1846, the P.T.S. had become more important once compulsory education for all children had been introduced under the Forster Act of 1870 and the need for teachers had grown. Once they reached 13 (14 after 1877), bright pupils could work as classroom assistants and continue their own education part time. They had their own extra lessons before school started and had to do homework. The head of the school was responsible for their training and could make them take fortnightly examinations. If they wanted to continue to work as pupil teachers, they had to pass additional, formal exams. In

1902 the training of teachers became established as a form of higher education, and intending teachers had to complete a course of education in secondary schools. The scheme was supplemented in 1907 and gradually replaced by a bursary system under which would-be teachers attended school until 17 or 18 and then either proceeded to a training college or became a student teacher at a public elementary school.[1]

Dewi urges his sister in several of his letters to carry on swotting for exams and to aim for "top of the form".[2] In January 1916 he writes to congratulate her on her success and offer further encouragement. "You have done splendidly and you've only got to stick it and you'll have that P.T's Exam up your sleeve. If one of the subjects happens to be Composition, you ought to take honours in that after the practice you get at writing to me." He tells her he expects to find her teaching in Splott on his return.[3] There are more congratulations a month later on her position in Terminals, a result meaning, he guesses, that she has got the Pupil Teacher "stunt" swung.[4] He is modest about his own achievements. "I am glad you are getting on so well in school and know you will stick it to please me. I don't know about that reference you made in your last letter about my being blessed with the brains and you being left the scraps. Don't forget, I never came as high in the class as 6th in all my school life. Next exam I am sure you will do better still and head the list."[5] Dewi's encouragement and praise continues in later letters. "The Whitsun exams will be soon on your track, Dolly, and I sincerely hope, no, I know, you will do your best and come out on top. Stick it, kid. Show 'em you're not 'too proud to swot'.[6] As for me giving you instruction when I return, Lor' love us, you'll whack me all ends up. But, on the other hand if you'd like tuition in handling picks and shovels, pitching tents etc. etc., I'm your man. 'S'easy as eating my breakfast now." Doris is still apparently keen to train as a teacher and is thinking about college. "Awfully glad you are looking forward about going to college etc. By Gum, Dolly David, prefect. Don't forget to be more strict in class about stopping the children chattering."[7]

There is a further hint at her intention to carry on with her academic work a few weeks later, when he writes to express surprise that she is saying she is looking forward to returning to school. "Well, I'm blessed, fancy Doris May David saying that. I can hardly believe it. I wonder if when I come home I shall see, instead of the laughing, mischievous, non-swotting Dolly, a serious, studious, prefect.[8] The pressure is still being maintained as she approaches the end of the school year. Excusing her for not writing, he says he can quite understand how very busy she must have been swotting for the terminal. "I wonder if I'm a little too previous when I congratulate you upon the excellent position you have attained top of the form. Anyhow, you must write as soon as ever possible and let me know the result, for I'm burning with impatience, as you may well imagine. So, you wrote on Egypt for a compo [composition] at school recently. Have no doubt it was a very good one."[9]

1) This made teaching less of an option for working class students, making it more attractive to the middle classes, whose families could afford to keep sons and daughters at school (not earning a wage) for longer.
2) November 4th, November 8th, November 14th, November 22nd, December 20th 1915, January 2nd 1916.
3) January 24th 1916.
4) February 20th 1916. Terminals, end of term examinations.
5) February 29th 1916.
6) April 7th 1916.
7) April 13th 1916.
8) May 16th 1916.
9) June 15th 1916.

From School to Clark's

He recommends some books of his own she might profitably study, though it would be surprising if she shared his interest in the topics he mentions. "In your letter you say something about cramming the Geog. of the B[ritish] Isles into your head. Well, Dolly, you couldn't do better than swot up my Clark's books on the subject.[10] They're just what you want and the best Geog. book you can get. If you swot them, you'll do O.K. There's a fine description of the Rly [railway] routes in them." Just the sort of thing one imagines a 15 year old girl would be fascinated by! Within a few months, however, he was writing to endorse his sister's decision to leave school and enrol at the private Clark's College in Newport Road, where Dewi himself had spent some time in lessons while training as a telegraphist. The college was evidently headed by a man – Mr John – who was a martinet and he seeks to warn his sister lightheartedly about him, drawing on his own experiences and using military analogies to paint his picture. "As I have had a little experience at that educational establishment, I can assure you that Geo. Clark [the owner] has nothing at all to do with it. It is John's kingdom, he is the iron ruler of the domain, that little insignificant, terrible, giant who signs himself T.J.J. Active as a panther, eyes like a hawk, wily as a fox, he is the absolute master, the Colonel who arranges and plans the manoeuvres, the Captain who carries them out and, last but not least, the Provost Marshal in general who metes out the Field Punishment. Heaven help him who has gone to a cinema instead of doing homework, the vengeance and sword of Democles [sic] John hangs precariously above his unsuspecting head.[11] Ditto the person found indulging in a pipeful of tobacco, the culprit enters the grim sanctum, the condemned cell, and makes his exit an hour later to return home to a frugal repast from the mantelpiece."[12]

He goes on in similar vein, though he makes it clear that Mr. John was at heart well-intentioned. "A few words of advice on this subject [...] Never breathe a word to your neighbour when the mighty chief is taking class, never let your eyes leave his, though he looks you through and through, practise the suppression of a sneeze, school yourself at home in running up and down stairs four at a time. If you do it in less at John's, you will be subjected to an interesting lecture on wasting 46.783 seconds in which you would have been better employed in solving an algebra problem and, whatever you do, on no account take crochet work to lessons, you'll have plenty of time for that when you're a P.O. [crossed through] – pardon me, when you're a teacher (I nearly said P.O. clerk. "P'raps I've rather frightened you about that fierce little typical Welshman, the principal of your new college, but he is really a holy terror, boys or girls, he is unchangeable, ever pitiless, and unmerciful. However, pass your exam, and he'll be all fuss and benignity. You'll be the most wonderful genius that ever geniused and your name will appear on the board as large as life itself. You'll

10) June 15th 1916. Clark's College was a private college specialising in civil service and commercial training, housed in two villas at no. 49-51 Newport Road on a site now occupied by Longcross Court. It closed in 1976 and was demolished in 1981. Doris may have decided by this time to go in for commercial work rather than teaching but her brother does not seem to have picked this up. He later offers his strong support for the change.

11) Damocles was an obsequious courtier in the court of Dionysius II, 4th century BC tyrant of Syracuse, Sicily. When he exclaimed that, as a great man of power and authority surrounded by magnificence, Dionysius was fortunate, the King offered to switch places with him so that he could taste that fortune first hand. Damocles sat down in the king's throne surrounded by every luxury but Dionysius arranged that a huge sword should hang above the throne, held at the pommel only by a single hair of a horse's tail. Damocles begged the tyrant that he be allowed to depart because he no longer wanted to be so fortunate.

12) August 27th 1916.

soon understand that there's a Mr. John, and a Mr. John, two different persons altogether." He re-assures her that he is backing her change of school. "Do I approve of your leaving the M.S.S and continuing at John's, most certainly, my dear girl? I think I have you weighed up pretty well and to my mind, it'll do you more good than you ever dreamt of, and when you've obtained your degree, perhaps the presence of an uncouth, illiterate, common other ranker will be most inconvenient. Am sure later on you will never regret choosing a teaching job. Gee! Look at the holidays you'll be having, and every Saturday afternoon off to see Cardiff v Newport [rugby matches]. You'll be absolutely in clover, Doll."[13] Doris was never to go into teaching, choosing instead a commercial career, the skills in which Clark's also taught. Yet again, Dewi's reaction was positive. "They do a lot for you, and you'll feel mighty pleased with yourself when the result of your examination is announced. Am quite pleased you are going in for commercial work. Perhaps, after all's said and done, the teaching profession is terribly crowded and inadvisable, therefore, to adopt. I rather think you ought to make a good opening in the line of your choice. Girls with their wits about 'em can make some brass at that game nowadays and I do not doubt for one moment you would make an excellent business-woman. Audacity is a valuable asset in the commercial world. You will find that it is necessary to put your nose to the grindstone in working for these particular posts, and I sincerely hope you will concentrate your mind upon your studies. If you do this, I feel confident you will never have cause to regret it, so Good Luck! little girl, go in and top the bill."[14]

A Commercial Career

These, it seems hard to believe, were the words of an 18 year old who had himself left school at 14. He and his father will have been familiar with women in the workplace, however. Indeed, the Post Office had been a pioneer in the employment of female clerks, although in 1910 they were still confined to routine tasks and excluded from "male posts". Nevertheless, in 1900 they accounted for just over 20 per cent of the Post Office workforce. His own experiences at Clark's, he tells her had been very positive. "For my own part I can honestly say that I took a keen delight in studying the few elementary subjects I took at the College. They were happy hours among my books and I enjoyed every single one. The Clark's method I found to be very pleasant indeed and far from irksome. It was, in fact, recreation to me after running about for 8 hours and covering perhaps 40 miles in that time for the same number of ha'pence. Although, turning up for morning lessons among that crowd, who didn't know what it was to work for a living, in the full glory of the scarlet and blue uniform of my old regiment – 'Jeffries' Own Light Infantry' – was often very embarrassing."[15] He is glad to be told his books are proving useful, although he thinks she might need texts of a more advanced character. There is one problem, however. In this tight-knit family his father has asked him to put in a good word for Doll at the college. "I don't know what to do since Dad has asked me to write Mr. John. You see, as he seemed to be rather flabbergasted when Dad told him about these stirrin' times I've bin 'aving within this last twelvemonth, the little rajah might play me a dirty trick and read it out."[16] By the end of the year he

---

13) August 27th 1916. Municipal Secondary School, later known as Howard Gardens High School.
14) September 9th 1916.
15) As a messenger boy delivering to ships, offices and other premises from the GPO in Cardiff Docks.
16) September 9th 1916.

is again immensely pleased to hear of her "huge strides" at Clark's , and a few months later is sending his heartfelt congratulations on her passing into the "advanced theory section "Dolli, I'm indeed proud of you, because I know you have done so through sheer hard work and perseverance ... By Gum! that deserves another present, and if I was anywhere near civilisation you should have it right away, s'welp me."[17]

The strict Mr John appears in another letter where Dewi expresses some apprehension at being shown as a smoker, something the principal of Clark's may have disapproved of in the young. "I see that your [photograph] album is put up for exhibition occasionally and you certainly did risk much in showing it in the front desk with Mr John in the room and all.[18] I guess you must think a heap of that little book to do that. And he saw it, did he? Rather unfortunate I should be smoking in that picture, isn't it? I know him, see, showing him a fag is like showing a red rag to a bull – Oh! he does get wild. [...] Funny thing about it is that he smokes a blooming great stovepipe himself, which is enough to knock a horse down, – I do believe it's 'Franklin's Shag' he smokes in it, straight I do. '*Fine* fellow' was I – O! Lor', he can't half tell a good tale and is absolutely the limit at stretching it." Modestly, he advises her not to take any notice of compliments Mr John might make about "absent friends" such as himself, suggesting they may only be a way of trying to spur her on. "As if my trivial little 'do' could be compared with the National Shorthand Exam and the 'distinctions' you're sure to get in many another. He certainly doesn't do you justice in speech but it's what he *thinks* that matters, take my tip, – and he's not going to let *you* know them [these thoughts] yet, you bet. I'm different, you see, and By Gum! Doll, I guess you're just 18 carat and keep on hearing surprises that make me feel prouder and prouder all the time. That's the spirit Dolly, you just keep on giving them [sic] examination papers socks every time. You've passed from "E" into "F" by now, sure thing, so in my next there'll be more congrats again. Why you just go on from victory to victory, which is great news, every time a winner." The praise keeps coming, though whether this pleased Doris, was found patronising, or merely put her under further unwanted pressure we will never know. "My heartiest congrats once more, Dolly, you're fairly making rings around 'em. I'm waiting for the full account of your promotion into "F" section when your next epistle arrives. Stick it, Doll, you're going strong."[19] Later he writes, "You surely aren't serious tho', Doll, when you say you'll soon be in an office – I'm not sorry but at the same time I don't feel extra jolly 'cos it makes me think of how much you're growing and what I've missed. I guess I'm going to get a fair knock-out when I get home – Gee! and you were only about the size of six pennorth of coppers about two years ago. "[20]

Offices in the Docks

A few months later, when she has taken a job in one of the many offices then operating in Cardiff Docks, he greets news of her further progress in the commercial world with a playful account of how he imagines she is in the work environment.[21]

17) February 25th 1917.
18) June 10th 1917.
19) June 19th 1917.
20) August 25th 1917.
21) October 10th 1917.

"Come into my office and take down this letter, will you? I don't exactly know how to approach you now, since you are a young lady in business at the Merchant's Exchange.[22] Anyhow, don't pick too many holes, please Miss, 'cos I'm only jest [sic] one o' the rank an' file and not extry [sic] good, writing down jest wot I thinks. A thousand apologies, my dear mademoiselle, I really should have known better than to give so childish an illustration to a young lady moving in the highest commercial circles, such as yourself. Still, I am not at all enamoured with the Business Correspondence terse and abrupt style and would sooner risk your displeasure at the above illustration than express my thoughts thus: – Cargo despatched 17th ult. satisfactory. Please arrange another shipment, same strata (that's your line isn't it Doll?) 'tophole'. Of course, you smile at my fantastic imagination of the manner in which you business people acknowledge and place orders but it will serve my purpose quite well. Crumbs! You know, Doll, I can't kind of realise it – it doesn't seem real that you're now earning the princely wage of 15/- in the service of one of those merchant princes at his palatial 'mint' where all is hurry, hustle, and confusion in the mad headlong race, day after day, for wealth, whose halls resound with the clatter of typewriters, serious-voiced and -minded conferences and the buzz of telephone bells, but are total strangers to music, mirth, light-hearted chatter and sounds of revelry. Say, kiddie, don't you feel a bit lost in such a drab, bleak, unromantic hole, – nay, but that would be to underestimate your abilities. Nevertheless, I really find it impossible to picture you in that scene and role – I persist in conjuring up in my mind's eye a merry free-from-care Dolly, laughing and dancing, holding court and receiving homage to her beauty in the latter gleeful surroundings."[23] He is very familiar with the firm she has joined, Aitkin and Morcom. "Know 'em?" – why, I should say so, Doll. Many and many's the time I've nipped up those stairs for a ¹/₂d [ha'penny]. I can sympathise with you, too, on getting lost in that maze of steps and lifts and stories, for many and many a time also when I was a raw recruit at the Docks have I experienced the same thing and kept wandering about, sometimes for 10 mins. – result – ¹/₂d [ha'penny] to the bad. Corys was my only hope then to make good."[24]

Doris seems to have often confided in him the frustrations she was experiencing working for demanding bosses in busy offices, including in 1918 an incident that sounds more serious. "You must be a pretty busy person nowadays, what with the rush to and from the Docks and school afterwards. Wonder to me how you can possibly find time for writing letters. The little incident of the 9.3 train [sic] amused me very much but I can just imagine it was anything but amusing for you at the time. You're right, Dolly, it's too risky altogether is that game with a feller like Aitkin to deal with – bit of a slippery customer, as far as I can judge – ain't half cute, is he? Gee! wouldn't it have been a dreadful calamity if he'd given you the sack, tho', – Our Doll given the order of the boot – I shudder to think of it. What on earth, I wonder, would Mum and Dad do without you to bring the brass home on Saturdays? Terrible prospects, I must say."[25] Whatever the previous problems were,

22) The Merchant's Exchange was a four storey building at the Pier Head containing hundreds of small and medium-sized coal, shipping and other related industries, businesses and branch offices of big international corporations trading in Welsh coal, such as Canadian Pacific Railways.

23) June 8th 1916.

24) Telegram delivery boys may have been on piece work, receiving ¹/₂d for every telegram delivered. Hence, getting lost would slow them down and they would need an easy delivery, such as at Cory Bros., the coal and shipping company next door to the Post Office, to make up their losses.

25) January 4th 1918.

however, she is soon back on track, and he is soon offering praise once more on her success in examinations. "You tell me Dolly has won another book-keeping certificate – making her fourth – well, I must say I am not surprised at any such news of our Doll now – but, you bet, I'm highly delighted. Jove! that's jolly good – well done, Dolly fach, you don't half give 'em socks – anything from exam papers to the sweetest letters I ever read, they're all the same to you, easy as easy to that busy little head and fingers. Crumbs! It does me no end of good to read of those triumphs. I'll be waiting to hear of every one." He suggests she might like to work for him as an orderly room clerk. "Think you'd like it? – not very hard you know – no crime sheets to type – O! no, not on your life, you'd be occupied all day long making out leave passes to Blighty for the E.E.F. and canteen orders. You'd do it for the poor blighters like a shot, eh?"[26]

Having shown her merits as a secretary in the offices of her employers, Doris had clearly become a force to be reckoned with in negotiation, as her successful petition for a wage increase makes clear. "I was surprised, you bet, Doll, at the changes in your office lately. By Jove! you just about put the kybosh on the old fossil that time, and so you're getting the princely wage of one quid as a consequence. Dear me! money no object whatever now, I s'pose? I have no doubt, tho', but that you earn it, every penny, as I guess tapping a typing machine all day long isn't all honey. And, by the way, Old Aitkin seems to have gone in for the honey slopes lately – sweet as honey, eh? Well, that is a great change, to be sure. I can hardly believe it, as I can only picture him from your previous descriptions as being the grumpiest, anti-smiling, miserable old sinner that ever was. Fairly put the wind up, that threatened tendering of resignations from his chiefs of staff – that's the spirit Doll – don't stand any of his blamed all-highest nonsense. Anyhow, $1^1/_2$ hours for dinner and finish at 5 is a fine job – I really don't wonder one bit why you 'feel sort of satisfied' with it (!)."[27] Whether Doris's office militancy was part of the general dissatisfaction employees were then feeling at the cost of living and low wages is impossible to tell.

Gifts and souvenirs

Apart from very occasional leave, Dewi's opportunities to provide his parents and sister at home with souvenirs from his stay in the mysterious east were few. He did, however, spend a lot of time thinking about what he could send them, and Doris in particular. The post cards already mentioned were offered as contributions to her "collection", a popular hobby in late Victorian times when people were much less widely travelled and fascinated by images of distant places. He apologises for forgetting her birthday in November 1915 – not very surprisingly as he was in Gallipoli at the time – and tells her, in response to a request, that the Turkish Delight they can get at home is as good as he would be able to find.[28] She asks about the Mummies in Cairo after a short visit he had made in February 1916 on a day's leave from camp in Abbassia "No, Doll, I didn't see the Mummies but later on, if I get to Cairo again, I intend visiting the museum to see them. Of course, you know the British Museum in London has collared most of 'em. When I come home again we'll go up there to have a decco. No doubt you will have plenty of questions to ask

26) January 29th 1918.
27) June 8th 1918.
28) February 29th 1916.

me but p'raps you will be disappointed. You know what Dad used to say about me being such an observant chap. Especially when he'd ask me what was the latest on the placards."[29] He did, however, find time to buy her one little present, which he describes as millinery, telling her he had made the shop owner show him all his wares. He stands corrected in one of his later letters, his gift having been a scarf and not therefore millinery. As a gift, however, it seems to have gone down very well. "That scarf of Dolly's arrived OK, then. Awfully glad, indeed, was afraid a green envelope [active service issue] would not be enough protection. Anyhow, all serene, the silk experts [his mother and sister] – and I know 'em, commend me and that's suffish. [...] I hope the charms I sent you will also arrive and I'll keep my peepers open for more stuff, if I fancy it, you can fentro dy ben [you can bet] (as Mum says)."[30] Doris seems to have sent in requests for what she wants, one item she specifies being a mosaic brooch.[31] Apologising for sending a short letter, he hopes she won't pay him back in the same coin. "Now, a real long book next time, if you please, your adventures at Clarks, on the bike, with the -, O! there's pages and pages you can write easily, *if* you're really not *too* busy with maths. You shall have your mosaic brooch, never fear."

In November 1916 he and a friend visited Ismailia for a day and he was soon in the shops looking for something for Doris and his mother.[32] "Well, I bought some P.C.s [...] and I feel sure you will be very pleased with them – I got a good variation – the best that money could buy. Also, I hope my little sister of fastidious taste (I suspect) will not view the little charms with derision. I assure you, Doll, I tried to get a nice brooch for you and Mum. They had some. Oh! yes, but, as you know, I come from that good old stock which will not take *anything*. I didn't exactly tell 'em I'd go to Cross's but said I'd wait till I could get some real good ones at Alex or some big place. That's the best plan, isn't it, Dolli fach [Little Dollie]. I didn't see anything at all in that line that was suitable and you really mustn't wear any old $2^1/_2$d [tuppenny ha'penny] thing. However, in the little box you will find 1) Cleopatra's needle 2) I think the bloke said it was the Karbatoosh (?) of Rameses – whatever that is, I won't swear to the correct Arabic term." He goes on to offer a historical flight of fancy.[33] "Anyhow you remember Rameses. You know, the old blighter wot said 'up guards and at 'em' to the Israelites at the battle of Omdurman, and sulked in his tent for the rest of the day drinking neat scotch.[34] Wouldn't I just like to give you one huge bear like hug in it – not 'arf. It is, of course, my favourite colour, besides, which makes me feel doubly proud of myself."[35]

---

29) April 7th 1916. Placard, news seller's street poster advertising stories inside the newspaper.
30) May 14th 1916.
31) August 27th 1916.
32) November 4th 1916.
33) Probably the *cartouche* of Rameses. A cartouche in this context is the oval ring containing hieroglyphic names and titles of Egyptian kings. Rameses the Great (Rameses II) ruled from 1279-1213 BC.
34) In the Bible Jacob and his family migrated from Asia to Egypt, settling in the land of Rameses and owning property there. (*Genesis 47:11, 27*). Eventually, the Israelites were used as slave labourers to build the city of Rameses.
    Achilles in Homer's *Iliad* sulked in his tent after the Greek leader, Agamemnon, took the slave girl he loved, Chryseis. Muhammad Ahmad, 'the Mahdi', made his military headquarters in the village of Omdurman in 1884. The conflicts that followed over the next fifteen years have become known as the Mahdist War. After the defeat of the besieged defenders of Khartoum in 1885, the Mahdi's successor, Khalifa Abdullahi ibn Muhammad, made Omdurman his capital. In 1898 in the Battle of Omdurman Lord Kitchener defeated the Mahdis, ensuring British control over Sudan.
35) October 10th 1917.

He describes himself, by now a confident British soldier but clearly longing to be with his family, lording it over the local shopkeeper in a way that we might find embarrassing. "Picture 'Jim' sitting down as cool as a cucumber near the counter, smoking cigarettes and drinking iced lemonade (both supplied by the management). But that was really a very minor reason why I was so deliberate about the business and took plenty of time – you see, cigs or no cigs, I wanted *the genuine article* – none of your cheap gaudy substitutes and imitations for this child. Soon as we kicked off he strewed the counter with the latter, trashy worthless and horrible coloured rubbish, but he soon quit that stunt. One sentence did it, – '2^1/$_2$ [piastres] for that lot', I said. He didn't quite savvy, so I adjusted my 'elmet, stood up and gave it him straight – that 'if he didn't take those hideous nightmares off the counter, take 'em away and burn 'em, I was sorry but I'd have to go to lunch'. Course, he soon got wise to the fact that he had an old hand at the game to tackle, so he behaved quite intelligently then, and we got right down to business. Well, I should think I inspected more blouses that day than I'll ever do again in the whole of my natural. It was blouses to the right of us and blouses to the left of us, blouses in front of us and blouses all about us. [...]. P'raps you wouldn't believe me now but that feller next to me (left) in the photo also bought some fralls in that shop with me – bought, I say, he did the buying but as for the choosing – well, I guess he left that part of the contract to me.[36] He's engaged, you see, poor feller, and naturally didn't want to make an ass of himself so had to enlist the services of an expert at the game. Bit of a tricky job, too, I can tell you, especially when the young lady's 23 and the article of apparel a kimono, but I fixed it up alright for him, you bet. Why, he's just heard from her last mail and, blow me if she isn't gone pretty near loopy with delight over it. He's so grateful to me about it that – well, when the happy couple are united, (which of course is a pinch, – an absolute dead cert to come off, now) I can promise you a 'samplo' of marzipan, Doll."

His opportunities for sending further souvenirs were limited while campaigning in Palestine and the quality of the offerings in Jerusalem disappoints him, as his humorous reference quoted previously to the "miserable, paltry specimens of the Birmingham jewellers' art (overseas department)", makes clear. He does, however, soon manage to find something he thinks will be liked. "I have included a small cross and another little charm, which I made a point of purchasing and dispatching to you, Dolly, as soon as ever it was possible after our entering into Jerusalem. It would indeed be a crying shame if that one of all should be lost, as I fear some must have been. [...] I hope you will forgive and understand that there isn't exactly a large varied or dainty selection to choose from."[37] The Jerusalem charm was, it seems, well-received. "I hunted around pretty thoroughly and got the best I could. Most of the stuff in the curio line was a wash-out 'cos you see they aren't very up to date establishments in that city. [...] Now that you have assured me that they are quite the thing and perfectly satisfactory, I am convinced that the other charm I sent to Cardiff will be appreciated, too. [...] I procured a similar one at the same time for Miss Turpitt, seeing that she sort of takes a sisterly interest in me as well."[38]

36) Frill-fralls, ornamented clothing materials.
37) February 6th 1918.
38) March 23rd 1918. Grace Turpitt, a slightly older colleague in the Post Office, who wrote to him and other servicemen and is mentioned in several letters.

The Future Flapper

Doris's life in Cardiff as a teenager, like that of Dewi, seems to have been one of surprising freedom. Far from her staying at home, as one might perhaps imagine of the era, there are references in the letters to playing tennis and taking long cycle rides. "That ride up to Pentyrch must have been glorious and the country round about simply lovely at this time of year. But, as you say, it is a bit of a pull up the Heol Goch. Don't suppose you tried down the hill, did you?"[39] Then two months later: "Do you cycle as much as ever, Dolly? Expect you know every inch of the country by-roads for a pretty good radius around Cardiff. Glad to hear my old bike is sticking it so well and looking as good as ever after a cleaning. Dad, I s'pose, accompanies you very often to Pentyrch, for instance. When you go up there again, ask Gia what she thought of my Post Card congratulating her on her birthday. Should like to know, and expect she was very perplexed on receiving it."[40]

There's plenty of teasing, too, for his sister, as well as the references to romances among their contemporaries. "I can see you in college now before the prodigal returns and, my word, even the camera tells me you would be a very charming student. You mustn't think, Doll, because I write in this strain I've just written one to a 'best girl'. No! You know me better than that, I reserve all this for my own little sister, although you seem rather suspicious and saucy in a certain part of your last letter. But then what about those epistles you get from 5th form youths at Howard Gardens?"[41] And a few weeks later, "Sorry you have caught such a bad cold and hope it's better now. But are you positive it was lawn tennis, (?) quite sure it wasn't through sitting out dances?[42] He waxes lyrical in a letter to his parents about the changes in Doris now evident in the photos they were sending and hints at how much he is missing all of them. Photos were of, course, the only means he had of seeing his sister growing up, as she moved through her teens, and he clearly misses greatly not being there to enjoy fun with her. "You're a blooming trump, Dad, they are a huge success and I congratulate you.[43] Only a little Kodak and when I look at 'em I seem to be amongst you all again, you seem quite near. The photo of you, Dad, on the rocks – well, I seemed to be standing on the sands at P'cwl, 20 yards from you and it's *you* from straw hat to Oliver's boots. As for the other photo taken at the same spot, who is she, Dad? Guess I'd like to know her.[44] Tall piece, too, I should think, long white dress, she looks a proper stunner. Think she's a bit too old for me? Acquaintance of Emily's, I s'pose. Must ask her for an intro. Do you think the lonely soldier stunt would work?"[45] The following year he comments on the walks she had mentioned in one of her letters and adds a few more compliments. "I see you take some long walks now. You were seen down at St. Mary's Bay by one of my correspondents and recognised simply by your photograph.[46] Think of that Dolly –

39) July 4th 1916.

40) September 9th 1916. His grandmother, whom other letters suggest might at this stage have been suffering from dementia, or 'confused', as it would then have been described.

41) July 4th 1916.

42) July 14th 1916.

43) August 27th 1916. To his parents.

44) Ironic reference to his sister.

45) It is not clear who Emily was but she may have been a friend of Doris's.

46) August 25th 1917. St. Mary's Well Bay, Lavernock, between Penarth and Sully.

I did, anyway, and the result of my think was this. By Gum! Dolly must be growing up to be a proper stunner [...] I bet you'll fairly make 'em gasp in that little present I've sent. Don't forget to let me know the result will you (!)"

With few opportunities for leave and no prospect of returning home from as distant a destination as Egypt, men in the E.E.F. clearly missed female company, as their reaction, while at Serapeum, to seeing European girls on vessels on the Suez Canal suggested.[47] In a more innocent age pleasure was gained from looking at photos of each other's sisters and girlfriends, and deciding who was the most attractive, and, if Dewi is typical, their own sisters are often the object of elaborate compliments. "After writing my letter to Dad I had another squint at the Kodak picture and when I came to that one of the girl on the rocks, whom I said I didn't know, I just glanced casually at it, then I stared, pulled the candle nearer, fished my glasses out, and – "well, I – what th – By all that's wonderful, it's Dolly," I stammered. Well, well, I don't know what to say, I'm tongue-tied absobloominlutely. And I thought it was a young lady of about 19 or 20, instead of that, it's my schoolgirl sister, the future flapper I remember when I left Blighty. I feel very much ashamed of myself, here have I been writing nonsensical childish epistles to you, which I thought appropriate for a child of tender age for goodness knows how long, and this photograph points out to me my horrid mistake. The recipient, I perceive, is quite another person, who has blossomed forth into that feminine stage immediately preceding the adoption of the latest Parisienne coiffures and intent perusal of the newest fashion books on gowns from that city. My dear madam, a thousand apologies for the inexcusable boorish attitude I have been guilty of in my erstwhile correspondence."[48]

In 1918 he is still keen to hear about the sort of things he used to do himself at home, casting his mind back to Christmas once again. "You must have had a ripping time over Xmas in spite of the very short leave those money grabbers thought fit to allow their employees. I wasn't half wishing myself there to enjoy it with you, you bet. Would have made things hum, wouldn't we, eh, Doll? I can just imagine it. You didn't tell me what luck you had on the old Xmas tree in the Vestry.[49] Eh – what's that? – don't go in for such childish pastimes now? Well, I'm blessed – dear me – I thought as much, you're growing up too fast for me to keep count." Come Summer he is remembering outdoor pastimes. "S'pose you're heart and soul in the tennis lines these balmy evenings. [...] What wouldn't I give for a set with you. [...] And by the way how's my old jigger sticking it?[50] Hope she isn't pining away for those daredevil speed trials on the Llanishen Rd. But, there, I won't half make up for it, first chance I get. Ever visit the Lake now, Doll, of an evening for a swim? No? O! you slacker. I am surprised. D'you know one of the things I'm just dying for is to go off top table once again at the old Roath Park Lake? – Gee whizz! not 'arf. Besides, me'n old Frankie Somers haven't settled that bet yet about first one out to the buoys – nights and nights we tried it but, blow me, we always touched it at one and the same time, or else if I thought there was going to be any doubt, just barge into his ribs and put the kybosh on it. (!) But you can just betcher life it's going to be some race one day in the near future. Ah, me! for the old [Suez] Canal – how I dwell on

47) July 14th 1916. Vd. also Chap 4, p90.
48) August 27th 1916, to Doris.
49) The vestry in their chapel, Jerusalem.
50) Jigger, possibly bicycle.

those good times. Matter of fact, last time I crossed it, when I went on leave, if it hadn't been that I was in a desput [sic] hurry to catch the Cairo express I'd have had a plunge there and then."[51]

Rites of Passage

One of the rites of passage for girls as they reached womanhood in early twentieth century society was "putting their hair up", a development that clearly had a wide interest and significance for family and friends as the point at which young ladies ceased to be girls and started seriously thinking about finding a beau. In one of the letters he expresses mock surprise and puzzlement. "I don't understand one sentence in your letter, something about some person *name*: – Grace sex: – probably female, putting her hair up.[52] Now, what the diggins [Dickens] does it all mean?[53] Be precise and explain in your next letter. P'raps you mean somebody in your school, or else you've put that sentence in my letter instead of somebody else's. Quite an enigma, I assure you. Can't tumble to it at all. I don't think I'm the sort of feller to be interested in anybody's plaits. And what's this you say? Important happening? Important to me, a bullet-headed swoddy of the rank and file? However, I expect you've made a mistake and I'll forgive you." Commenting later on a photo he has been sent from home, he hopes he will not be away when Doris herself puts her hair up, something which would remind him that she was a girl when he had left home but that he had returned to find her a young woman. "I feel sure I shall scarcely know you when I come home as you seem to have grown so and all I am worrying about is that if this little shindy lasts much longer you'll have your hair up when I see you next. They tell me it's a dreadful ordeal so don't be in any hurry Doll."[54]

When she writes to tell him the time has, indeed, come to put up her hair now she has started work, he accepts with equanimity. His vision of his sister is still that of the young teenager he had left behind when he signed on shortly after her 14th birthday and he returns again to that rite of passage – putting hair up. "I had a bit of a shock Doll when you told me you were 18 next birthday. Gee Whiz! I must be getting old you see I always think about you as two long black stockings and about umpteen long ropes of hair – the schoolgirl, in fact, and can't imagine any transformation. And now you're seriously thinking of tucking those tresses out of sight for ever, eh? Ah! well – business is business, I s'pose, and you, in common with the growing army of business girls, are of the opinion, no doubt, that the most conspicuous evidence of being feminine must be sacrificed for convenience and business' sake. I wonder that you have not spoken of this proposed step before, since I am sure those golden curls must be fearfully in the way on times – getting tangled up with the typewriter keys, the ends dipping in the ink-pots, and lassooing Mr A [her boss Aitkin] by accident – say couldn't you manage to choke him by design in the same manner? However you'd look just as stunnin' with it up Dolly, of that I feel sure, so if you feel that way inclined, then I'm the very last person to stop you taking the plunge. It'll be up 'fore I'm home in any case, I shouldn't mind betting."[55]

---

51) June 8th 1918.
52) Possibly Grace Turpitt, mentioned above.
53) April 13th 1916
54) July 14th 1916. Shindy, disturbance or row.
55) July 29th 1918.

Early in 1918 his sister is clearly missing him – now away for the best part of three years – and writing regularly, and he is missing her. He writes: "Very many thanks firstly for your wire [telegram] – it was very thoughtful of you and is an excellent New Year's card. First wire I've had so you can guess I didn't exactly know what the deuce to make of it at first. Telegram for me, thought I, most remarkable. However, altho' it was absolutely imposs for me to send Xmas Cards or telegrams, Dolly, you may be sure I was most thankful for the greetings and good wishes and returned them most heartily per wireless.[56] I hope you had a good Xmas this year again, and, I tell you, I wasn't half wishing myself back at 76 on the 25th ult. By Jove! It wouldn't half have been tophole, would it? – never mind, next year – what ho, she bumps – makes things hum eh?"[57] Another of her "inimitable epistles" sent at the end of November had also "bucked him up". "I can carry on now without a murmur till the next arrives," he writes. "(By the way, Doll, hope you'll be able to read this scrawl, my fingers are a bit cold, see?) One thing I was rather sorry to see, tho', Dolly in your letter – you seem to be so terribly downy, I thought anyway, 'cos I'm so long away on this Cook's tour. Rather rotten that, you know – Lummy! You simply mustn't go chucking up the sponge like that after sticking it like a Trojan all this time. You don't want *me* to have the blues, do you? – not likely – got a puffick [perfect] horror of them, you know – won't do at all. Never mind, tho', expect you all felt pretty rotten 'cos it was Xmas time – hard luck being away for this one again but keep your peckers up – never say die."

The image of himself that he presents in the same letter may well have made his sister wonder what sort of a brother would be returning. They had now been campaigning for several months and he suggests the effects were beginning to show. He was also apparently receiving letters from a number of different people whose identity he chose not to reveal. "Had a letter from another of my correspondents same time as yours arrived, and she spoke of being introduced to you, Dolly and Mum, in the Park Hall[58] Cinema t'other evening. "Your sister is exactly like you, Dewi," says she, "I should have known her in a crowd" ! – hope you're not annoyed, Dolly – you see, she only remembers me when I wore white linen collars and shot [silk] ties and creased trous [sic] – hasn't seen me since I became a villainous, evil-looking desperado with a malevolent glint in his eyes! Doesn't matter, tho' – with a bit of luck I hope really and truly to have a shave tomorrow – I feel like doing something rash."

His sister had also expressed some concern at the escapades he had described in some of his letters home but he hastens to re-assure her. "I have taken particular heed of your severe admonishment, Miss, and, of course, to read such is to obey, therefore, I shall, as ordered, not attempt any more foolhardy tricks, an' [sic] it please you. Let me please express the hope that you are not irrevocably cross with me, as, I assure you, I should be indeed melancholy to think of you in such a state.

56) Possibly he sent her back a telegram.

57) January 4th 1918. In fact, Dewi did not get back home until another year later in April 1919

58) The Park Hotel, built in the 1880s by a group of Cardiff businessmen, including department store magnate James Howell, was unusual in incorporating a public hall, which could accommodate 2,000. Used for concerts, meetings, religious services, and exhibitions, it held a Cinematograph Licence from 1910. Regular use as a cinema did not begin until World War One, at which time the hall was still in use for other purposes. A Willis concert organ accompanied film programmes, together with an orchestra. Closed in 1971, it was subsequently demolished.

Yes, quite so, I most meekly and very docilely agree with you, Mademoiselle, the lesson, as you observe so heartlessly, is well learnt and it pains me beyond measure that so humble a person as I should be the cause of upsetting you with my trifling knocks with the world. The experience will be more than sufficient you may be sure to guarantee my doing everything in my power to give both hospitals and surgeons a very wide berth indeed."[59] Just how long Doris remained sad at his absence we don't know. Towards the end of the war, however, her photos were still giving Dewi a morale boost, as is evident in the pride he shows in their reception by his comrades. "It may interest you to know that a few of the elite had a beauty competition (nunno not with their own ugly mugs) t'other evening when time hung rather heavily on our hands. Each submitted one photograph to the pool and having shuffled 'em the judges set to work. Well, to tell the truth, I knew who was going to win before we started, 'cos hadn't I submitted that small one of you above-mentioned? And so it was, too, – I beat 'em all hands down, Frankie Somers and his most serious 'affaire' included. The President of the Court expressed his grave concern that I should be making 'a hopeless ass' of myself over such a youthful looking 'peach' and took upon himself to enquire of me as to whether or not 'her ma was aware of my intentions'. 'Quite, thank you, old cock,' says I, 'you see, she happens to be my sister'. He really couldn't apologise enough after that for besmirching my hitherto unimpeachable character and went so far as to add that 'notwithstanding the lady's tender years' he had no hesitation in pronouncing his verdict, expressing a keen desire, since she showed great promise, to see her photo again on her coming of age. All of which you may consider a great compliment, coming as it does from a chap who is reputed to have the largest collection in the section."[60]

Family small talk returns when he responds to his sister's report that a toad has made a re-appearance.[61] "I was very much surprised and pleased to hear that our old friend the toad was still very much alive and kicking. Fancy putting in an appearance like that after such a long sleep. I regret I had almost forgotten about the old fellow. Please give him my fondest regards and say I hope he won't be away on business when I pay him my next visit. If the good reports of his Distinguished Conduct in the Field (or rather the Garden) continue, I shall be pleased to bring him a few specimen [sic] of our choicest scorpions and locusts for inspection. Please give my best wishes to Mrs Samuel. I hope she is still going strong and thank her very much from me, say I was very glad to hear of the continued good health of Mr Toad. In the bath where we go swimming at night there are plenty of his cousins – frogs, knocking about, and they don't half kick up a blessed shindig, too. Wark! Wark! from sunset to sunrise you wouldn't believe the life there is around the pools at night. Just when you're going to dive he pops his head up above and opens his mouth 'wark' – as if to say 'Come on, Jonah', for all the world like a miniature croc. Then all the crickets and grasshoppers start in chorus, 'Creak! Creak!' and the fireflies go sailing by on camp parade, signalling in their own secret code. In fact, I'm that childish I'm certain that one of these nights I shall be lucky enough to see a lot of elves come out in the moonlight and join in the carnival. It's a busy world at that time – nature's night life when all humans are supposed to be in the nevah-nevah land – A Midsummer's Night."

269

---

59) July 29th 1918.
60) June 28th 1918.
61) July 29th 1918..

The times he sentimentally remembers in his letters to his sister were never to come back, as perhaps he realised as his war service dragged on. Life in future would be different for all of them and they would never again be Mum, Dad, and two kids, enjoying holidays together. He had left as a Sunday-school attending, lark-playing 17 year old, when she was a schoolgirl not yet 15. On his return he had reached his majority that very month and she was an 18 year old working in an office. The "good kid", the "stunner" and the "future flapper" of his imagination and his letters now had other interests. Cardiff's commercial life went into precipitate decline after the war, once the Royal Navy and the merchant marine had completed the transition already underway from coal-firing to oil, and the Welsh mining industry was affected, too, by the peace imposed on Germany at the Treaty of Versailles. Germany was directed to send coal to France where it displaced Welsh coal. Doris in her twenties met William (Bill) Turner, the son of a Cardiff sea captain, who had decided his fortune lay on the other side of the Atlantic. He moved to New York to work in shipping there and Doris followed him, marrying from the New Jersey home of her cousin, Ethel, an emigrant herself during the early years of the war.[62] Dewi sailed across the Atlantic in the Mauretania to visit his sister in 1931 and his parents followed in 1947 on the Queen Elizabeth, staying for three months. Doris also made visits home until her death in the 1980s but for Tom and Hannah, and Dewi, the rest of their lives were spent once again writing to an absent member of the family.

---

62) Vd. Letter November 14th 1914.

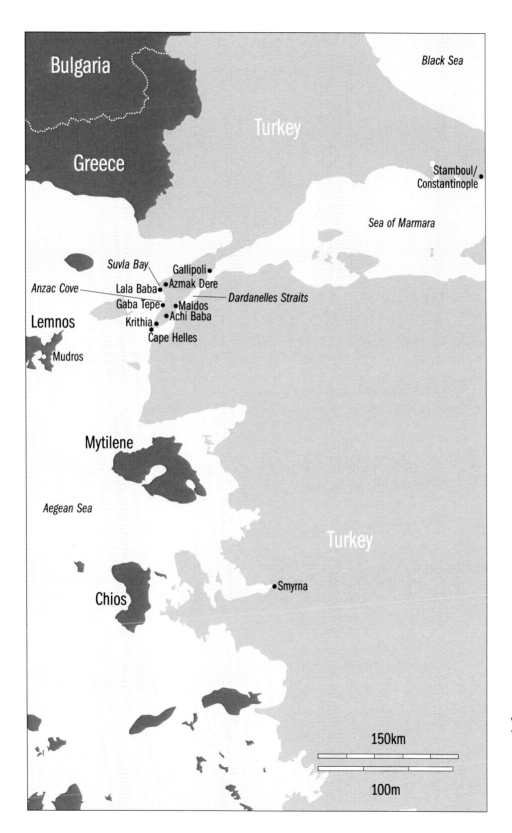

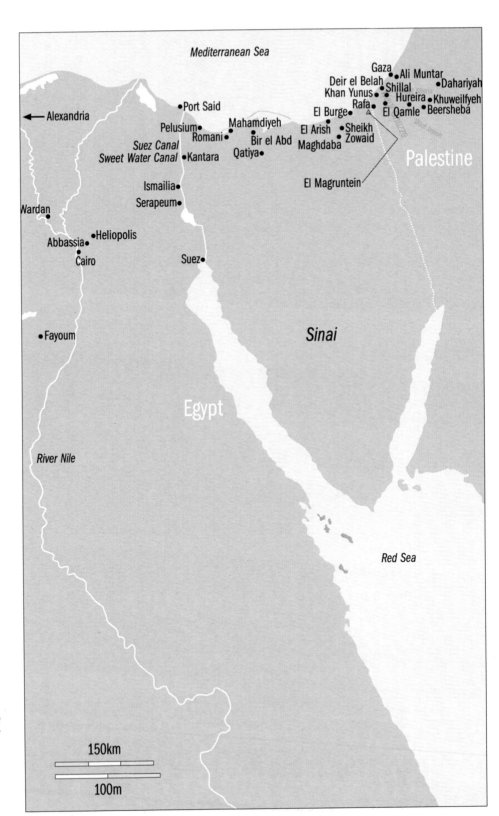

Mediterranean Sea

Gaza
Ali Muntar
Deir el Belah
Shillal
Dahariyah
Khan Yunus
Hureira
Khuweilfyeh
Rafa
El Burge
El Qamle
Beersheba
Port Said
Pelusium
Mahamdiyeh
El Arish
Sheikh
Romani
Bir el Abd
Zowaid
Suez Canal
Maghdaba
Sweet Water Canal
Kantara
Qatiya

Palestine

Alexandria

El Magruntein

Ismailia

Serapeum

Wardan

Heliopolis

Abbassia
Cairo

Suez

Sinai

Egypt

Fayoum

River Nile

Red Sea

150km

100m

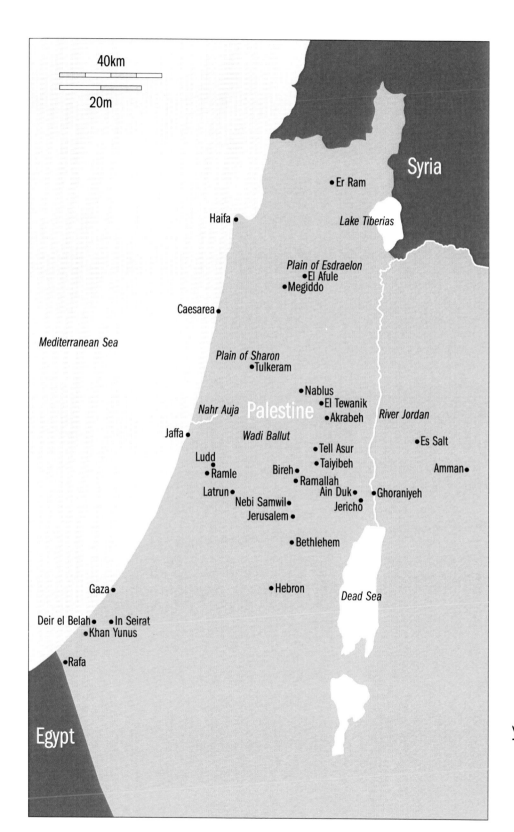

40km

20m

• Er Ram

Syria

Haifa •

Lake Tiberias

Plain of Esdraelon
• El Afule
• Megiddo

Caesarea •

Mediterranean Sea

Plain of Sharon
• Tulkeram

• Nablus
• El Tewanik
Nahr Auja   Palestine   • Akrabeh

River Jordan

Jaffa •   Wadi Ballut

• Tell Asur   • Es Salt
Ludd •   • Taiyibeh
• Ramle   Bireh •   Amman •
Latrun •   • Ramallah
Nebi Samwil •   Ain Duk •   • Ghoraniyeh
Jerusalem •   Jericho

• Bethlehem

Gaza •   • Hebron   Dead Sea

Deir el Belah •   • In Seirat
• Khan Yunus

• Rafa

Egypt

273

APPENDIX I

LOG

1915 – 1919

1915

February 28th
Yn cael fy nherbyn fel
aelod capel
[Received as member of
the chapel]

March 9th
Medically examined and
attested

March 17th
Sworn in. Uniform

March 18th
Joined 2/1 W.D.S.C[1] at
Aberystwyth

March 23rd
Cambridge

April 22nd
Northampton

June 25th
Leave Cardiff

July 2nd
Northampton

July 13th
Firing course at
Dallington.
Range 100 + 200 yds.

July 14th
Range 300, 400, 500
yds.

July 24th
Marched Bedford

September 25th
Leave Cardiff

September 29th
Bedford

October 3rd
St. Budeaux Camp,
Devonport

October 4th
Embarked *Megantic*

October 5th
Sailed

October 11th
Malta

October 15th
Lemnos

October 19th
Landed Mudros,
East Lemnos

October 21st
Embarked *Redbreast*
Arrived Suvla Bay

October 22nd
Landed C Beach.
Joined 53rd Sigs.
Lala Baba

November 26th
Washed out

December 6th
A Beach

December 13th
South Pier.
Embarked *Rowan*

December 14th
Lemnos.
Re-embarked *Karroo*

December 15th
Landed Mudros East

December 18th
Embarked
HMS *Folkestone*

December 19th
Salonica.
Wood Square Camp

December 25th
Concert

December 27th
Lembet Camp
12th Corps Signals

---

1) W.D.S.C., Welsh Divisional Signals Company

1916

January 16th
Marched Salonika
Docks. Embarked. Sailed

January 17th
Lemnos. Re-embarked
Hororata

January 19th
Sailed

January 21st
Alexandria

January 22nd
Wardan. Beni Salama
Camp

February 6th
Attached London
Brigade

February 12th
Cairo. Pyramids
Reported back HQ

February 16th
Fayoum

April 14th
Ectsa

April 15th
Reported back Fayoum

April 16th
Polygon camp, Abbassia

May 7th Cairo
Zoological Gardens

May 26th
Ismailia
Spinney [Wood] Camp

June 1st
Reported 163rd Bde Sigs
Serapeum
November 13th (D.M.)
[Doris May's birthday].
Reported Coy Ismailia

November 21st
Moascar Camp,
[Ismailia]

December 3rd
El Ferdan. Cable wagon

December 4th
Kantara. Cable wagon

December 6th
Gilban

December 7th
Pelusium

December 8th
Romani
Mahamedyr[2]

December 19th
Capture of El Arish

December 25th
Concert

---

2) Also January 3rd 1917, Mahamdiya

1917

January 3rd
First train run to
El Arish
Mahamdiya

January 22nd
Bir-el-Abd

January 31st
El Arish

February 21st
El Burg

February 22nd
Sheik Zowaiid

March 8th
El Magruntein –
Rafa, wagon

March 21st
Rafa

March 24th
Khan Yunis

March 25th
Deir-el-Belah

March 26th
158th Brigade.
Cable wagon. Mansura
Ridge. Capture of Ali-
Muntar (No1)
Gaza entered

March 27th
Retired 00.30. Div.
Reserve Mansura Ridge.
Retired El Buryabiye.
Retired Wadi-el-
Ghyuzzu[3]

March 28th
Retired Deir-el-Belah

April 11th
Sheikh Shabasi

April 17th
(No 2). Capture of
Samson's Ridge

May 8th
In-Seirat

May 23rd
Sheikh Muran

May 26th
Shillal, camels

July 31st
Deir-el-Belah

August 3rd
Sheikh Shabasi

August 16th
Proceeded on leave

August 17th
07.00 Kantara
14.30 Cairo.
Anzac Hostel

August 18th
Pyramids. Heliopolis

August 19th
Bazaars, mosques,
Heliopolis

August 20th
Matarieh

August 21st
Barrage, Nile

August 22nd
Rhoda Island

August 23rd
Proceeded Kantara

August 24th
Arrived Sheikh Shabasi

August 27th
Khan Yunus. Training

October 24th
Hiseia

October 27th
Sebil. Cable wagon.
FG & ZOH

October 28th
Reported 159th
Brigade wagon

October 30th
YEC – wagon –
Wadi Imleih

November 1st
Beersheba station –
moved out

November 3rd
159th Brigade cable
wagon. Z01 Hill Z01
Gully

November 4th
DWE

3) Wadi Ghuzza.

November 6th
Kholeh Hill

November 8th
Mott's detachment.[4]
Khuweilfyeh
Berya Well

December 3rd
Dahariya, Shilbeh

December 5th
Hebron

December 6th
Russian monastery.
Bethlehem Road[5]

December 7th and 8th
Advanced

December 9th
Bethlehem. Attack and capture of Jersualem

December 10th
Jerusalem. (Billets near Calvary)

December 17th
German Hospice
Kaiser[in] Augustine
[Augusta]Victoria
Sanatorium Mt of Olives

December 29th
Er Ram

4) Major-General S.F. Mott, G.O.C. the 53rd Division.
5) Most probably the Mar Saba monastery founded by St. Saba of Cappadocia in the 5th century.

1918

January 4th
Ram Allah (L)

January 19th
Bireh (R)
Divn. Church Ram Allah

March 2nd
Beitin

March 7th
Rummon

March 8th
Tyiber

March 9th
Dayr

March 10th
EwE

March 11th
Ad. Bde. Hq

March 13th
Beitin

March 17th
Ram Allah

March 31st
Ludd

April 2nd
159 Brigade Hadeitha
Wadi Ballut

April 19th
Rentis

April 20th
Hadeitha

April 22nd
Latrun

April 23d
Ain Duk

April 24th
2nd WTO[6]

April 25th
Home Counties Rd

May 8th
Ain Sinia

May 15th
Company

May 20th
158 Bde.

June 30th
Nablus Road

July 20th
Ain Duk

August 20th
Nablus Road

September 19th
D.K. Road N5C

September 20th
Tel Asur

September 21st
Hind Head

September 22nd
Akrabeh

September 23rd
Yanun – El Tewanik

September 27th
Hawaida

September 30th
El Tell

October 10th
Ain Duk

October 11th
Latrun

October 12th
Ramok

October 20th
Alexandria

December 30th
Metropole

6) Wireless Telegraph Office.

1919

**January 10th
and 11th**
[Alexandria. Concert
53rd Division Welsh
Male Voice Choir]

February
Cleopatra Base Signal
Depot (Draft)[7]
General Base Details
Kantara

February 19th
Haifa N.P. L. of C.[8]

March 3rd
Left Haifa

March 4th
Demob. Camp Kantara

March 8th
Malwa. Pt. Said

March 12th
Disembarked Taranto

March 13th
Entrained

March 19th
Detrained Le Havre

March 20th
Embarked Le Havre

March 21st
Southampton Fovant[9]

March 22nd
HOME

Dewi Emrys David
(details)

Regtl. No:
452339

Rank:
Sapper

Record Office:
Chatham

Service:
53rd Div Sig. Coy.
3$^1/_2$ years

North Palestine
Signal Company 28/2/19
– 3/3/19

Theatre of War:
EEF (Egyptian
Expeditionary Force)

---

7) Probably Alexandria.

8) North Palestine Line of Communication.

9) Servicemen returning to Britain through Southampton and Devonport received their discharge papers at a dispersal unit in Fovant,
near Salisbury, in Wiltshire.

Campaign Chronology

1915

April 28th
First Battle of Krithia

May 6th-8th
Second Battle of Krithia

June 4th
Third Battle of Krithia

1916

August 3rd-4th
Battle of Romani

1917

March 26th-27th
First Battle of Gaza

April 17th-19th
Second Battle of Gaza

**October 27th-
November 7th**
Third Battle of Gaza and
the capture of Beersheba

**November 3rd-
November 7th**
Capture of Tell
Khuweilfeh

December 7th-9th
Capture of Jerusalem

**December 27th-
December 30th**
Defence of Jerusalem

1918

March 8th-12th
Battle of Tell Asur

September 18th-21st
Battle of Nablus (part of
Battle of Megiddo)

APPENDIX II

PARCELS AND LETTERS SENT

1915 – 1916

Date	Letters etc.	Parcels	[Received]
1915[1]			
Oct 15th	1	Shortbread, clear gums, cigs, papers, tobacco, matches, soap, Oxo, café au lait, chocs and writing paper.	x
Oct 22nd	1		
Nov 2nd	1		
Nov 15th	2 + P.O. 10/-	Pudding, spearmint, cigs, candles, café au lait, milk writing paper.	x
Nov 22nd	1	Sardines, paper and envelopes, shortbread, cocoa, milk chocs, cigs, candles, matches, meth spirits stove, spearmint.	x
Nov 25th	1		
Nov 29th	1	Shortbread, café au lait, chocs, Pepsin, candles, 50 cigs matches, milk, Oxo	x
Dec 2nd	1	Milk tablets, chocs, pears, pineapples, socks, Helmet, newspapers and envelopes.	x
Dec 3rd	Cardiff Times, London Opinion + Echo		
Dec 8th	1 + Xmas Card		
Dec 10th	Cardiff Times + Weekly Telegraph		
Dec 13th	1		
Dec 14th		Enamel teapot full of sugar from Auntie Janet + Uncle Elias, $^1/_4$ tea, café au lait, mug, milk, spearmint, clear gums, candles, cigs.	x
Dec 16th	1		
Dec 17th	Cardiff Times + London Opinion		
Dec 22nd	1		
Dec 24th	Cardiff Times + Weekly Telegraph		
Dec 30th	1		
Dec 31st	Cardiff Times + London Opinion		

1) His father kept a log of parcels and letters sent and ticked them off when Dewi wrote back to say they had been received. Only the record of those sent until early 1917 survives.

Date	Letters etc.	Parcels	[Received]
1916			
Jan 7th	1 = Cardiff Times, Daily News and Weekly Telegraph		
Jan 10th		From 190 [relatives]	x
Jan 14th	Cardiff Times and Weekly Telegraph		
Jan 18th		Pudding, cake and socks	x
Jan 19th	1 from Mum		
Jan 22nd	1 from Doll		
Jan 24th		From 190	x
Jan 27th	1 + P.O. £1		
Feb 8th	1 + 1 from Billy		
Feb 16th	1 from Doll + birthday card	Cake, shortbread K[eating's] Powder, salmon chocs, Pepsin, clear gums. ? on Maloja[2]	
Feb 22nd	1		
Feb 24th		From 190	x
Feb 29th	1 from Doll		
Mar 2nd	1	Vermin powder, toffee, mirror. Milk tablets, quinine tablets, tea tablets, milk, saccharine, chocs, cake, Pepsin, handkerchiefs, cocoa, cake, shortbread biscuits, toothpaste, Pepsin [repeated], cigs	x
Mar 9th	1		
Mar 18th	1 + P.O. £1		
Mar 22nd	1 from Doll		
Mar 27th		Cake, shortbread, chocs, cigs, toffee, milk milk tablets, tea tablets, saccharine.	x
April 8th	London Opinion, Weekly Telegraph 1 + P.O £1 + Mum's		
April 10th		Cake, shortbread, cigs, tea tablets, saccharine, milk, clear gums, shirt.	x
April 11th	1 from Doll		
April 15th	London Opinion + Weekly Telegraph		x

2) This is one of the few parcels which is not ticked, presumably as having been acknowledged as received. His father is speculating that the parcel was being carried aboard the P & O liner, *Maloja*, which was sunk by a mine two miles off Dover on February 27th 1916.

Date	Letters etc.	Parcels	[Received]
1916 (continued)			
April 24th	London Opinion + Weekly Telegraph		
April 28th	1 + P.O. £1, 40 cigs, Handkerchiefs, Regd.		
April 28th	London Opinion + Weekly Telegraph		
April 29th		Cake, shortbread, toffee, milk, tea tablets, quinine tablets, cigs. 5.30 p.m. H.O. [Head Office]	X
April 29th	Letter from Doll 1 from Aunt Janet	+ parcel	X
May 9th	1		
May 16th	1 + London Mag, London Opinion + Weekly Telegraph		
May 20th	1 + London Opinion + Pearson's Monthly		
May 22nd		Cake, toffee, milk, chocs, cigs, salmon, sardines tea tablets. 7.30 Carlisle Street P.O.	X
May 25th	1 from Doll and Mum		
May 30th	1 letter Weekly Telegraph, London Opinion		
June 1st		Cake, pears, milk, 30 cigs, chocs, biscuits − 2.30 pm Carlisle Street	X
June 2nd		Regd. Packet. Photo, leather photo case, brush, comb knife, 160 cigs, Postal Order £1, Doll's letter + 1 from Dad + Mum − 2.30 p.m. Carlisle Street.	X
June 10th	London Opinion, Weekly Telegraph		
June 16th	Regd. Letter £1 P.O.		
June 19th	London Opinion, London Magazine (June), Weekly Telegraph.		

Date	Letters etc.	Parcels	[Received]
1916 (continued)			
June 19th	Letter from Doll		
June 20th		Cake, Pears, chocs, café au lait, Pears Soap, 2 tablets, 1 tin Players cigs, writing case	x
June 23rd	London Opinion, Weekly Telegraph + Daily Sketches		
June 24th	1 from Doll		
June 27th		Cake, Pineapple, tea tablets, milk, saccharine, quinine tablets, thirst quenchers, $^1/_2$lb acid drops, 50 Players cigs.	
June 28th	Letter containing writing paper and slip re pols etc since 22 May		
June 28th	London Opinion, Weekly Telegraph + July London Mag.		
July 3rd		Parcel from Aunt Janet and Uncle Elias	
July 7th	London Opinion + Weekly Telegraph		
July 12th	Letter from Doll		
July 13th		Registered packet, writing pad, sponge, toothpaste, pencil, £1 P.O. Letter from Dad + Mum, copy Roll Honour.	
July 14th		Parcel	
July 20th	Letter from Porthcawl		
July 29th	Letter		
Aug 1st	Letter from Doll		
Aug 1st		Parcel. Thirst quenchers, quinine tablets, tea tablets, saccharine, tin Players cigs, tin pears, tin plums, condensed milk, (acid drops $^1/_2$lb), tin Crawfords biscuits.	
Aug 1st	August London Mag, London Opinion + Weekly Telegraph		

Date	Letters etc.	Parcels	[Received]
1916 (continued)			
Aug 10th	Letter. London Opinion + Weekly Telegraph		
Aug 17th	Letter from Doll		
Aug 22nd	Registered Letter £1 P.O. + cuttings re. Major Arnold, Lloyd George at Ab.	Parcel, cake, condensed milk, Players cigs, lemon cheese, Damsons, assorted biscuits and chocolates	
Aug 29th		Parcel from Auntie Janet and Uncle Elias.	
Aug 29th	Letter from Doll, Mum and 7 snapshots		
Sept 4th	Letter from Doll and cutting re Tom		
Sept 8th	Registered letter + £1 P.O.	Parcel. Round cakes, Nectar tea, lump sugar, milk, jelly, chocs, cigs, biscuits.	
Sept 15th		Parcel 2 pkts tea, café au lait, damsons, 3 pkts. BDV cigs, tin Toffee Delight, tin Crawfords biscuits, large tin milk, $1/_2$lb caster sugar, 1 pkt chocs.	
Sept 18th	Letter		
Sept 22nd		Parcel Tin Crawfords biscuits, milk (small tin), large tin pears, tin Players cigs, beef paté, tea, sugar, toothpaste. Carlisle Street 3.30 pm.	
Sept 26th		Parcel. Khaki shirt, socks, 2 handkerchiefs, London Magazine Oct, London Opinion, + Weekly Telegraph, Rob Roy, damsons, Crawfords biscuits, small tin milk, 2d tea, $1/_2$lb sugar. (Head Office 9 am)	
Sept 28th	Letter from Doll		
Sept 29th	Letter and cuttings re Walter Hansford, Lloyd George's interview to a Yank, + Lieut. Thomas photo		
Oct 5th	Letter with 8 snapshots and letter from Mum. London Opinion + Weekly Telegraph		

Date	Letters etc.	Parcels	[Received]
1916 (continued)			
Oct 11th	Registered Packet (Camera) + Money Order £5		
Oct 11th	Letter from Doll		
Oct 17th		Parcel. Khahki shirt, handkerchief, 2 films, writing pad, lump sugar, chocs, milk, cigs, tea $^1/_4$, biscuits, ham loaf.	
Oct 20th	Registered Packet (watch).		
Oct 25th	Letter		
Oct 29th	Letter from Doll		
Nov 1st		Parcel from Auntie and Uncle	
Nov 4th	Western Mail, 28 Oct, speech Lloyd George, at unveiling statuary City Hall, London Opinion, Passing Show.		
Nov 8th	Letter		
Nov 14th		Parcel. Round cakes, jelly, custard powders, tea, sugar, milk, beef paté, damsons, cigarettes.	
Nov 28th		Parcel. Iced cakes, puddings, tin cigarettes + chocs.	
Nov 29th	Letter		
Dec 1st	Letter from Doll + Xmas card.		
Dec 11th	Letter from Doll + photo Beat, Jan + Doll		
Dec 15th	Letter		
Dec 18th	Parcel from Aunt Mary		
Dec 20th	Letter from Doll		
Dec 29th	Blighty + Daily Express with Lloyd George's speech as Prime Minister		
Dec 31st	Letter. Cuttings of [unclear] at Cory Hall.		

Date	Letters etc.	Parcels	[Received]
1917			
Jan 1st	Weekly Telegraph, Tit Bits		
Jan 3rd	Parcel from Aunt Janet		
Jan 8th	Letter from Doll		
Jan 15th	Letter		
Jan 16th		Parcel. Crawfords Quality Assorted, egg, plums, cigs, chocs, ham & chicken paste, café au lait, milk, Welsh Divn. souvenir, writing pad, cutting from Daily News.	
Jan 16th		Parcel. London Opinion, Weekly Telegraph, Gwyl Dewi Programme, Daily Chronicle 12th and 16th January.	
Jan 25th	Letter from Doll		
Feb 2nd		Parcel. Pudding, Pal's biscuits, café au lait, milk, Gold Flake cigs 50, 3 tins ham and chicken paste. 2 Echos 29th & 31st January. Chocs	

APPENDIX III

SELECTED BIBLIOGRAPHY

- 53rd (Welsh) Division), History of, C.H. Dudley Ward. Western Mail, 1927
- After the Victorians, A.N. Wilson. Arrow, 2005
- The Berlin-Baghdad Express, Sean McMeekin. Penguin, 2010
- Churchill, Roy Jenkins. Pan, 2001
- Corps of Royal Engineers, History of, Vol. VI, H.L. Pritchard. Institution of Royal Engineers, 1952
- Egypt and Palestine Campaigns, Lt.-Col. A. Kearsey. Naval & Military Press
- Farewell the Trumpets, James Morris. Penguin, 1978
- The Egyptian Expeditionary Force in World War I Michael J. Mortlock. McFarland, 2011
- The Fall of the British Empire, Colin Cross. Paladin, 1970
- First World War, John Keegan. Pimlico, 1999
- Forgotten Victory, Gary Sheffield. Review, 2001
- Gallipoli, Robert Rhodes James. B.T. Batsford, 1965
- Gallipoli, John Masefield. Heinemann, 1916
- Gallipoli, A Turning Point. Mustafa Arkin
- German Genius, Peter Watson. Simon & Schuster, 2010
- Grey Wolf, H. C. Armstrong. Penguin, 1937
- James Griffiths and his Times. Labour Party Wales
- The Great War, Correlli Barnett. Penguin, 1979
- History of Wales, John Davies. Penguin, 1990
- Life of David Lloyd George, Vol. IV, J. Hugh Edwards. Waverley
- The Mask of Merlin, Donald McCormick. Macdonald, 1963
- Millennium Cardiff, John May. Castle Publications, 1999
- Roath, Splott and Adamsdown, Jeff Childs. History Press, 2012
- Royal Mail, M.J. Daunton. Athlone, 1985
- Wales, Rebirth of a Nation, 1880-1980. Kenneth O. Morgan, OUP, 1981
- Wales in British Politics 1868-1922, Kenneth O. Morgan, University of Wales Press, 1981
- With Allenby in Palestine, Lt. Col. F.S. Brereton. Blackie & Son
- With Lawrence in Arabia. Lowell Thomas, Hutchinson

APPENDIX IV

GLOSSARY

Glossary

Abu – Father
Ain – Spring
Ali – High
Beit / Bayt / Beth – House
Bir – Well
Burj / Burge – Tower
Deir / Dayr – Monastery
Jebel – Mountain
Khan – Market
Nahr – River
Nebi – Prophet
Ram – Height
Ras – Head, cape, promontory
Sheikh – Old man, chief
Tell / Tel / Tal – Mound, mount
Wadi – Rocky watercourse

INDEX

Indexing

Page numbers in bold type refer to illustrations and maps, those in italic type refer to tables and those including an "n" e.g. 123n45 refer to footnotes.

A

Africa 218
aircraft 9, 48, 122, 203
Alexandria 39, 40, 205–6, **208**, **209**
Allenby, Field Marshal Edmund Henry 11, 40, 44, 128–9, 133, 146, 150, 167, 172, 174, 175, **190**, 203, 205
   advance towards Jerusalem 152–5
   capture of and entry into Jerusalem 156–7, 160–1, 163
   as a military commander 202
Altham, Major-General Edward 39
Amman 175–6
Arnold, Billy 220–1
art 13
Ashwell, Lena 105
Asquith, Herbert 16, 70, 71, 94
Ataturk *see* Kemal, Mustafa (Ataturk)
Australian Army 26
   Corps, Desert Mounted Corps 128, 146, 205
   Divisions
      Imperial Mounted Division 95
      Mounted Division 95, 117, 152–3, 154
   Brigades, Australian Light Horse 151, 175

B

balloons 9
Barlow, Robin 16–17
Barr, Niall 49
Beersheba 146, 147–9
Belgium 18
   Ypres 20–1
Beni Salama camp 39
Beni Salama 48–9, 55, 213
Berlin-Baghdad railway 22
Bethlehem 154, 155–6, 158, **170**
Bey, Nuri 46
bicycles 9, 265
bivouacs 52–5, 107–9, **144**, **168**, **189**
Blyth, Estelle 163–4
Boer War 244

Bouvet (ship) 24
Braithwaite, Major-General Walter 25
Breslau (ship) 23
Briand, Aristide 22
Britain
   refusal to sell battleships to Turkey 23
   strategic importance of Egypt to Britain 44–6
British Army **168**
   Cairo headquarters, size of 94–5
   censorship of letters 28–9, 132, 234
   communications 21
   conscription 17, 20
   drill 133–4
   food supplies and parcels from home 6–7, 8, 13, 30, 33–4, 35, 36, 51, 59, 76, 77–81, 109–10, 137–9, 165, 185–6, 187–8
   moving camps 73–5
   pay, lack of 36, 51–2, 59, 75–6
   postal system 102–3, 234
   punishments 53–4
   support for Welsh forces 18–19
   training 21–2, 129–30, 196–7
   volunteers 16–17
   water supplies 27, 47, 54, 55, 94, 95, 129, 147–8, 149, 193, 199
British Army Formations 184, 249
   Corps
      XX 128, 146, 147, 150, 159, 167, 192, 203, 204
      XXI 128, 146, 159, 167, 184, 192, 203, 204, 205
      Desert Mounted Corps 128
      Royal Army Medical Corps 50–1, 150
      Royal Engineers 16, 21, 25, 69, 97
   Divisions
      4th Cavalry 205
      10th 26, 146, 159
      38th 16

42nd 95
52nd 95, 121, 146, 151, 153, 159, 184
53rd (Welsh) ii, 16, 21, 25, 26, 27, 34–5, 39–40, **42**, 46, 49, 51, 61, 73, 95, 117, 118, 121, 146, 153–4, 172, 174, 177, 179, 223, 224
    cheeriness of men 228–9
    Gaza, Third Battle of 147, 148, 149
    Indian troops 192
    Jerusalem 155–7, 159, 164
    Khuweilfeh 150–1
    Megiddo, Battle of 204–5
    memorials **169**, 225–6
    Romani, Battle of 68–9
    Tell Asur 175
    Welsh Male Voice Choir 206
54th (East Anglian) 26, 39, 95, 117, 121, 123, 146, 151
60th 40, 123, 146, 156, 159, 175
74th 120, 146, 156, 159, 184
75th 146, 153, 184, 192
Brigades
    158th 97, 172, 192, 204–5, **230**, 249
    159th 57, 97, 148, 154, 172, 178, 184, 192, 204
    160th 204
    161st 117
    163rd Brigade Signals 74
    Imperial Camel Corps Brigade **92**, 95
Regiments
    5th Welch 157
    Cameronians 68–9
    Herefordshire 175
    Royal Welch Fusiliers 68, 149, 150, 175, 192
    Welsh Guards 16
Companies
    Welsh Divisional Signals Company 16, 40
Brooke, Rupert 50
Bulfin, Lieutenant General Edward 128

C
cable-laying 130–2, 137, 176–7, 178
Cairo 40, 52, 56, 61–3, **65**, **66**, 124–7
camels **66**, 84, 92, 95, 122, 155
Camp Abbassia 55–7, 63, 68
canteens 33–4, 36, 51, 101, 110
Cape Helles (Gallipoli) 25, 26
card games 199–200
Carden, Admiral Sir Sackville Hamilton 24
Cardiff
    coal exports 3–4
    development of 2
    Post Office 2, 4
    Queen Alexandra Dock 3, **14**
    sale of war bonds 161
    Splott (suburb) 2–3
casualties of war 218–22
    Gallipoli 27, **27**
    Gaza 117, 118
    Somme, Battle of the 69
    Zeppelin raids 31
censorship of letters 28–9, 132, 234
Chauvel, Major General Henry (Harry) 128, 128n44, 150
Chetwode, Sir Philip 94, 96, 117, 118, 128, 146, 147, 155, 156, 163
Christmas 35, 40, 101–3, 104–5, 165–7, 186, **209**
Churchill, Winston 22, 37, 70
cigarettes 10, 79, 110, 186–7, 260
coal exports 3–4
Collins, Acting Corporal John 149
concerts 104–5, 197–8, 206, **207**
    advertisements in programmes **207**, **208**
conscientious objectors 222
conscription 17, 20
consumer products 9, 10, 12
Cross, Colin 62

D
Daniel, George 218
Daniel, Horatio 218
Dardanelles campaign *see* Gallipoli
David, Dewi **14**, **64**, **66**, 83–6, **91**, **112**, 198–200, **230**, **232**, **253**, **254**
    campaign chronology 282
    Civil Service Commission

examinations 4–5
demobilisation 5, 40, 229
  certificates **210**
departs for Egypt 38–9
early life and education 2–3, **14**, 212
first name, choice of 2
joins the army 5, 16
letters
  attitude of people at home to soldiers in the Middle East 223
  bivouacs 52–5, 107–9, **144**, **168**, **189**
  boredom 82–3
  cable-laying 130–2, 137, 176–7, 178
  card games 199–200
  casualties of war 218–22
  Christmas 35, 40, 101–3, 104–5, 165–7, 186
  cleaning buttons 102, 103
  on comparison of life in the Middle East and on Western Front 223–5, 246
  concerts 104–5, 141–2
  conscientious objectors and late joiners 222
  devotion to his sister 8–9
  devotion to mother 234–5
  disillusionment 57
  dug-outs 31–2, **90**
  entertainment 11–12, 54–5, 56
  flies 34
  food supplies and parcels from home 6–7, 8, 13, 30, 33–4, 35, 36, 51, 76, 77–81, 109–10, 137–9, 165, 185–6, 187–8
  friends and cousins 212–17, 219–20, 250–1
  gifts and souvenirs sent home 88, 238, 256, 262–4
  hobbies and pastimes 11
  holidays 10–11
  homesickness 8, 78, 87, 201–2
  horses and riding 53, 99–100, 104, 131–2, 136, 180, 240
  Jerusalem, capture of 157–8, 160–1
  jokes and japes 226–9
  journey to, and arrival in Gallipoli 28, 29–30
  language and vocabulary 7–8, 29, 57–8, 238–9
  leave in Cairo 124–7
  on Lloyd George 72–3
  marches 98–100, 106
  medical treatment 50–1
  mess orderly 63, 226
  mock fights 226–7
  mosquitos 49–50
  mother's worries about him 239–43
  moving camps 73–5
  non-survival of letters to Dewi 7
  opinions about the enemy 179
  personal appearance 57–8
  photography 11, 83–6, 235
  promotion to Signalmaster 195–6
  reading 7, 141
  rebellious feelings and resentment 132–7, 185, 186
  relationship with father 244–7
  relationships with family and relatives 8–9, 250–2
  requests for mother to write 236–8, 239
  rituals 228
  shaving 125–6, 134–6
  training 13, 129–30, 196–7
  Welshness 248–50
  writes an essay 123
life after the war 206, 270
log 1915-1919 276–81
messenger boy for GPO 3, 4–5, 59
parcels and letters sent 284–90
service details 281
David, Doris May 3, 4, **14**, 187–8, 206, 235, **253**
  career plans 9, 256–7
  at Clark's College 103, 258–60
  Dewi's devotion to 8–9
  Dewi's failure to find Christmas present for 8, 167
  education and PTS scheme 256–7
  emigrates and marries 270
  gifts and souvenirs from Dewi 88,

238, 256, 262–4
leisure pursuits 265, 266–7
letters to 30, 50, 51, 52, 53, 57–8,
60, 61, 62, 63, 75, 78, 85, 122, 160–
1, 165–7, 174, 185–7, 194, 197, 200–
1, 224, 225–6, 237, 250, 257–70
missing Dewi 268–9
office work 131, 260–2
personal appearance and growing
up 265–6
praise from Dewi for scholastic
success 257, 258–9, 260–1
rites of passage 267–70
David, Enoch 250
David, Hannah 2, 9, **14**, 188, 252
dealing with shopkeepers 238
Dewi's devotion to 234–5
failure to write letters to Dewi
236–8, 239
worries about Dewi 239–43
David, Selwyn 193, 212, 214, 215, 216–
17
David, Thomas **14**, 201, 219, 237, 243,
252
and the 3rd Volunteer Battalion
244–5
Post Office job 2, 247
relationship with Dewi 244–7
Davies, John 17
Deir el Balah 116, 148
d'Entrecasteaux (ship) 45
Derby Scheme 17
Dobell, General Sir Charles 94, 116,
117, 118, 120
drill 133–4
dug-outs 31–2, **90**

E
Edwards, J.H. 70–1
Egypt **272**
bivouacs 52–5
bombing raids 48
British military plans 47
communications difficulties 44–5
desert conditions 48–9
expatriate population 62
harassment from the Senussi 46
logistics 47
small battles 47–8

strategic importance of 44–6
Turkish attacks on British positions
45
Egyptian Expeditionary Force (E.E.F.)
5, 8, 40, 48, 128, 146, 184, 192, 205
El Arish 94, 95, 106–7, **112**, **113**, 116
electricity 9
entertainment 11–12
see also concerts
Evans, Elias 6, 9, 247, 252
Evans, Janet 6, 35, 251–2

F
Falkenhayn, Erich von 152, 153
Fayoum 40, 46, 49, 52–5, 214
Ferdinand, Archduke 12
Ferdinand, King of Bulgaria 37
flies 34, 49, 50
Folkestone, HMS 35
food supplies and parcels from home
6–7, 8, 13, 30, 33–4, 35, 36, 51, 59, 76,
77–81, 109–10, 137–9, 165, 185–6, 187–
8
canned food 80–1
football 12, 139, 140–1
French, Field Marshal Sir John 71

G
Gallipoli 21, 28, 212–13, **271**
casualties 27, *27*
chaotic British preparations 25
consequences of failure 36–8
evacuation 27–8, 33, 34–5
Krithia 26
lack of supply base 29–30
landings 26–7
objectives 22
plans and naval attack 24
Suvla Bay 21, 26, 27, 31, 32, 33, 35,
41
Turkish preparations 24–5
water supplies 27
weather conditions 28, 31–3
gas 9–10
Gaza 96, 111, **143**
First Battle of 116–19, 128
Second Battle of 119–21
Third Battle of 142, 146–7, 151–2
Beersheba 147–9

Khuweilfeh 149–51
    plans and preparation 146–7
    topographical details 146
Geddes, Sir Auckland 17
Geddes, Sir Eric 72
George V 163
Germany 18, 19
    sends naval vessels to Turkey 23
Gia Mia (grandmother) 217, 243, 265
Gloucester, HMS 23
Goeben (ship) 23
Grainger, John D. 167
Graphic, The 163–4
Great War, The 46
Greeks 36, 62
Grey, Sir Edward 70
Griffiths, James 20
Gwaelod, Tom 220
Gwlad fy Nhadau, Rhodd Cymru i'w Byddin (Land of My Fathers, Wales's Gift to its Army) 18–19

H
Haifa 206, **208**
Haig, General Sir Douglas 44, 69–70, 70, 105, 188, 188n47
Hamilton, General Sir Ian 24, 25, 26, 27–8
Hampshire, HMS 70
Hankey, Colonel Maurice 71
Hansford, Walter 221–2
Hardcastle, Charlie 214
Hardie, Keir 20
Hardinge, HMS 45
Hart, Basil Liddell 118
Heliopolis 55–7
hobbies and pastimes 11
holidays 10–11
home front
    attitude of people at home to soldiers in the Middle East 223
    Defence of the Realm Act 1914 72
    licensing hours 72
    munitions 71–2
    rationing 13, 161–2
    strikes 12–13
    suffragettes 13, 85
    war bonds and certificates 161
honour envelopes 29

Hororata (ship) 38, **42**
horses and riding 53, 99–100, 131–2, 136, 147, 149, 180, 240
hospitals/dressing stations 240–1

I
illness 49, 50–1, 240–1
Independent Labour Party 20
Indian soldiers **113**, 192
Ireland 13
Irresistible, HMS 24
Ismailia 47, 87–9
Italy 177

J
Jenkins, Tom 57, 212, 219–20, 251, **254**
Jericho 167, 175, 181
Jerusalem 40, **189**, **273**
    advance towards 152–5, **169**
    Calvary 160
    capture of 155–9, 163–4
    Kaiser Wilhelm Augusta Victoria Sanatorium 160
    Mount of Olives 160
Joffre, General Joseph 70
Jones, Lewis 18
Jones, Sir John Morris 18, 19
Judaean Hills 146, 155

K
Karroo, HMAT 35
Kemal, Mustafa (Ataturk) 23, 38
Khan Yunus 128–30, 141–2
Khuweilfeh 149–51
Kitchener, Horatio Herbert, Field Marshall 16, 24, 33, 46, 70, 71
Kressenstein, Colonel Friedrich Freiherr Kress von 45, 47, 68, 96, 149, 154
Krithia (Gallipoli) 26

F
language and vocabulary 7–8
    ban on use of Welsh in letters 29
Law, Bonar 163
Lawrence, Colonel T.E. (of Arabia) 69
leave and rest periods 52, 103, 104, 124–7, 181–3, 184, 198–200, 221
Lemnos 28, 29, 33, 35, 38, **41**

Lewis, Conway 217
Lloyd George, David 7, 8, 16, 19–20,
70–3, 94, 118, 120, 162, 219
local people **231**
    attitudes to 59, 87–8
    Egypt 56, 60, 62, **90**, **92**, **112**
    Greeks 36, 62
    women 61, 85, 227–8
logistics 96, 155
London, Billy 213, 218, 224, 225, 246
London, Cecil 214
Lusitania (ship) 21

M
Magdhaba, Battle of 95, 96
Majestic, HMS 29
Maloja (ship) 6
Malwa (ship) 206
Manifesto of the 93 19
Marconi, Guglielmo 2
Matarieh 127, **144**
Maxwell, Lieutenant-General Sir John
39, 48
medals
    Distinguished Conduct Medal 149
    Military Cross 149
    Victoria Cross 143, 149, 150
medical treatment 50–1
Mediterranean Expeditionary Force
(M.E.F.) 5, 8, 40, 48
Megantic (ship) 21–2, 41
Megiddo, Battle of 167, 193, 202–5
Mehmet V, Sultan of Turkey 46
Meinertzhagen, Lt. Colonel Richard
148
memorials **169**, 225–6
middle classes 12
Military Service Act 1916 17
Mills, Sergt. Aubrey 40, 206, 214, **232**
Milner, Sam 206, 214, **232**
M'Mahon, Sir Henry 44
Monro, Lieutenant-General Sir
Charles 28, 39
Montgomery, General Sir Bernard 128
Moorina (ship) 46
Moorland Road 2–3, **14**
morale 165, 195, 240
Morgan, Kenneth O. 16–17
Mortlock, Michael J. 117, 202

mosquitos 49–50
Mott, Major-General S. F. 119, 137,
144, 150, 153–6, 159, 175, 204
Mowbray, Beatrice (Beat) 213, 215,
216, 251, 252, **253**
Mowbray, Hughie 97–8, **113**, 212, **213**,
214–16, 231, 245, **253**
Mrs Warren's Profession (Shaw) 85
Mudros 29–30
Municipal Secondary School **14**
munitions 71–2
munitions workers 225
Murray, General Sir Archibald 39, 48,
68, 94–5, 118, 119, 120, 128
music 11–12, 13
    see also concerts

N
Nablus Road 203–4
National Fund for Welsh Troops 18–19
National Registration Act 1915 17
New Zealand Army 175
    Corps, Desert Mounted Corps 128,
    146, 205
    Divisions, Mounted Division 95,
    117, 152–3, 154

O
Ocean, HMS 24
Ottoman Army
    Armies, Fifth Army 24
    Ottoman Suez Expeditionary Force
    45
Ottoman Empire 22, 44

P
Pace, Sergt. 202, 203, 222
Palestine **273**
Pasha, Enver 23
Pasha, Prince Hussein Kamel 44
pay, lack of 36, 51–2, 59, 75–6
Pentyrch 217
photography 11, 83–6, 235
pianos 11–12, 244
Pippen, Corpl. C.G. (Pip) 40, 206, 212
Price, Bert 218
punishments 53–4

Q

Queen Elizabeth, HMS 24

R

railways 22, 47, 69, 94, 116, 129, **143**, 148
Ramallah 172–3, 179, 217, 226
rationing 13, 161–2
Redbreast (ship) 30
refugees 37
religion 60, 249
Requin (ship) 45
Retreat from Mons 20
Richards, Wyndham 218
rituals 228
Robeck, Vice-Admiral Sir John de 24
Robertson, General Sir William 70, 95, 119
Romani 48
   battle 68–9
Roper, General A.W. 29
Rowan (ship) 35
Royal Commission on the Poor Laws and the Relief of Distress 1905-1908 4
Royal Navy 24, 70, 148, 270
rugby 12, 141
Russell, Captain Fox 150

S

Salonika 23, 35, 37, 71
Samuel, Dr 50, 240, 241
Sanders, General Otto Liman von 24, 175, **189**, 205
Schlieffen Plan 20
Senussi 46, 49
Serapeum 74–5, 82, 89, **90**, 109
Serbia 37
Sheffield, Gary 36–7
Shillal 122–3
Sinai 47, 68, **272**
smoking 10, 79, 110, 186–7, 260
social change 7–9, 12–13
Somers, Frank 5, 174, 181, 183, 184, 192, 193, 206, 212, 213, 214, **231, 232**, 266, 269
Somme, Battle of the 69–70, 72
Splott (Cardiff suburb) 2, 3
   Moorland Road 14
sport 12, 86–7, 139–41, 199

strikes 12–13
submarines 6, 21, 29, 188, 234
Suez Canal 40, 44–6, 73, 82–3, 86–7, **90, 92, 231**
suffragettes 13, 85
swimming 75, 83, 86–7, **91**, 139

T

tanks 70, 119, 161
Tara (ship) 46
technological change 9–10
telephones 137
Tell Asur 175, 178
Terry, Fred (actor) 162
Thomas, A. J. 214
'tin fish' see submarines
topographical details
   Gaza 146
   Judaean Hills 146, 155
   Khuweilfeh 150
   Nahr Auja area 172
Townshend, General Charles 48
trenches 129
Triumph, HMS 29
Turkey
   alliance with Germany 23
   Gallipoli preparations 24–5
Turkish Army 45, 68–9
   Armies
      7th Army 159
      8th Army 154, 159
   Divisions
      19th 38
   27th 151
   Beersheba 148–9
   Gaza, First Battle of 116–19
   Gaza, Second Battle of 119–21
   Gaza, Third Battle of 146–7, 151–2
   Jerusalem 155–9, 165
   Khuweilfeh 149–51
   Megiddo, Battle of 202–5
   in retreat 174–6
Turner, William (Bill) 270

U

U-boats see submarines

V

volunteers 16–17

W

Wales
    numbers serving in armed forces
    16–17
    opposition to the war 20
    role of Welsh leaders 19–20
    support for Welsh forces 18–19
    Welshness 248–50
Wales: Its Part in the War 17
Ward, Major C. H. Dudley 25, 27, 48,
118, 137
water polo 140
water supplies 27, 47, 54, 55, 94, 95,
129, 147–8, 149, 193, 199
weather conditions
    Egypt 49, 55, 56–7, 76–7, 122
    Gallipoli 28, 31–3
    Jerusalem 155–6, 164
    Ramallah 173
    sunburn 194
Western Front 48, 57, 69–70, 71, 140,
152, 161, 184, 188, 224–5, 246
Western Mail 8, 12, 25, 161, 163
Wilhelm II 22, 23
Williams, Dick 215
Williams, Prudence (Prue) 206, **253,
254**
Wilson, A. N. 22
women 13, 61, 85, 227–8

X

Xerxes 25

Y

YMCA 56–7, 124–5, 162
Ypres 20–1

Z

Zeppelins 9, 31, 72

ROGERSTONE

27/2/15